International Exchange  Locator

A Resource Directory for Educational and Cultural Exchange

2002 | Edition

ACKNOWLEDGEMENTS

For a small, four-person office with an overflowing agenda, the publication of this directory represents a significant feat that would not be possible without the help of the Department of State, Bureau of Educational and Cultural Affairs and the support of our member organizations (all of whom are indicated by an Alliance logo in the corner of their Locator listing). We believe that without this publication, we would know less about who we are and who makes the wheels of international exchange turn.

We acknowledge the steadfast, enthusiastic, and unrelenting contributions to this publication provided by Alliance trainee Liliya Dolgikh, without whom this directory would surely have drifted from its aggressive publication timetable. We also thank Alliance staff Kevin Baron for the many hours he contributed to the development of the federal agency section of this book. We are particularly grateful for the innumerable contributions by the staff of the Bureau of Educational and Cultural Affairs, contributions provided by Barry Ballow, Vanessa Relli Moreau, Leigh Sours, Caesar Jackson, and Susan Borja.

While we have attempted to be as inclusive as possible in listing organizations, some organizations involved in international exchange programs in the United States will not be listed here. Any organization which would like to be included in future editions of the Locator should contact the Alliance at the address listed below. Information for each entry was provided by the individual organiztion based on an extensive questionnaire. No judgements have been made by the editors regarding the quality of programs and services, and inclusion in no way indicates an endorsement by the Alliance or the U.S. government.

~Alliance for International Educational and Cultural Exchange, January 2002

PUBLISHERS

Alliance for International Educational and Cultural Exchange, Inc.

1776 Massachusetts Avenue NW, Suite 620
Washington, DC 20036
Tel.: 202/293-6141
Fax: 202/293-6144
Website: www.alliance-exchange.org
E-mail: info@alliance-exchange.org
Executive Director: Michael McCarry
Production Editor: Julie M. Taiber

United States Department of State, Bureau of Educational and Cultural Affairs

Office of Academic Exchange Programs
301 Fourth Street, S.W., Room 234
Washington, DC 20547
Tel.: 202/619-4360
Fax: 202/401-5914
E-mail: academic@pd.state.gov
Office Director: Barry Ballow
Project Director: Vanessa Relli-Moreau

United States Department of State

Records and Publishing Services
2201 C Street, NW, Room 1853
Washington, DC 20520
Tel.: 202/736-7470
Fax: 202/736-7472
Deputy Assistant Secretary: Frank Machak
Office Director: Gregory Liverpool
Overseas Printing Division   Mark Lundi

ISBN 0-9656459-1-6

Building on the public-private partnership that exemplifies the field of exchange in the United States, the Alliance for International Educational and Cultural Exchange and the United States Department of State, Bureau of Educational and Cultural Affairs are pleased to present to you the 2002 Edition of the International Exchange Locator: A Research Directory of Educational and Cultural Exchange.

This edition of the Locator builds on the tradition of comprehensively profiling organizations and institutions that use international exchange to further mutual understanding, acquire knowledge and skills, and develop professional expertise. In it, you will find an easy-to-use inventory of private organizations and government agencies involved in international educational and cultural exchange in the United States and the world.

We hope you find this edition of the Locator the richest and most valuable yet.

Alliance
for International Educational and
Cultural Exchange

Alliance for International Educational and Cultural Exchange

The Alliance is an association of nonprofit organizations comprising the international educational and cultural exchange community in the United States. Its mission is to formulate and promote public policies that support the growth and well-being of international exchanges between the peoples of the United States and other nations. In fulfilling this mission, the Alliance conducts government relations activities, including direct representation with policy makers and the marshaling of grassroots constituencies, to advance public policy concerns in support of the interests of the international exchange community. The Alliance and its membership are committed to building public awareness about the critical role of exchange in meeting global, national, and individual needs for international knowledge and relationships. Through publications such as the Alliance *Policy Monitor* and the expertise of the Alliance staff, the association provides comprehensive information about policy issues affecting the future of international exchanges.

MEMBER ORGANIZATIONS

Academy for Educational Development
Africa-America Institute
AFS Intercultural Programs
AIESEC, Inc.
Alliances Abroad*
American Association of Community Colleges
American Association of Intensive English Programs
American Council of Young Political Leaders
American Council on Education
American Councils for International Education:
	ACTR/ACCELS
American Institute for Foreign Study Foundation
American Intercultural Student Exchange
American-Scandinavian Foundation
American Secondary Schools for International
	Students and Teachers
AMIDEAST
Amity Institute
Association of International Education Administrators
Association for International Practical Training
Association of Professional Schools of
	International Affairs
AYUSA International
BUNAC
CDS International
CEC International Partners
Children's International Summer Villages, Inc.
The College Board
Communicating for Agriculture
Concordia Language Villages
Council of Graduate Schools
Council of International Programs USA
Council on International Educational Exchange
Council on Standards for International
	Educational Travel
Educational Testing Service
EF Foundation for Foreign Study

French – American Chamber of Commerce
The Fulbright Association
The German Marshall Fund of the United States
Girl Scouts of the USA
Institute of International Education
InterExchange
International Cultural Exchange Services
International Research and Exchanges Board
Japan-America Student Conference
LASPAU: Academic and Professional Programs
	for the Americas
The Laurasian Institution
Meridian International Center
Minnesota Agriculture Student Trainee/Practical
	Agricultural Reciprocal Training
NAFSA: Association of International Educators
National 4-H/Japanese Exchange Program
National Association of State Universities and
	Land-Grant Colleges
National Council for Eurasian and East
	European Research
National Council for International Visitors
North Carolina Center for International
	Understanding
Ohio Agricultural Intern Program
Pacific Intercultural Exchange
People to People International
Program of Academic Exchange
Sister Cities International
University and College Intensive English Program
World Education Services
World Exchange, Ltd.
World Heritage
World Learning, Inc.
YMCA International Program Services
Youth Exchange Services
Youth For Understanding

Corporate Associate Member

Alliance
MEMBER

Table of Contents

Section I – Exchange Organizations

Section II – Other Organizations with an Interest in Exchange

Section III International Organizations

Section IV – Foreign Affairs Agencies

Section V – Federal Government Exchanges

VI – U.S. Congress

Section I
Exchange Organizations

This section contains information on organizations which administer international exchange programs, provide support services, and/or have a specific interest in international exchange. "Exchange" involves the movement of people between countries for the purpose of sharing experiences, knowledge, skills, ideas, and cultures. It includes not only the reciprocal one-to-one exchange of individuals, but also all related educational, cultural, and training activities. Listed organizations are involved in all types of exchange. Some of the programs profiled are federally sponsored, such as the Fulbright program, while others are non-governmental.

Each entry contains general information about the organization, as well as information on specific programs and services. A breakdown of the types of programs, J visa categories, educational levels, and geographical areas can be viewed in the at-a-glance tables at the back of the book. Because of space limitations, information on programs, offices, publications, and services may not be exhaustive. For complete information an organization's programs and services, refer to its website or contact the organization directly.

SECTION 1

AACSB International–The Association to Advance Collegiate Schools of Business (AACSB)

600 Emerson Road
Suite 300
St. Louis, MO 63141-6762

Tel.: 314/872-8507
Fax: 314/872-8495
Website: http://www.aacsb.edu

General Inquiries:
Howard P. Hoskins,
Director of Communications
314/872-8507 x262

Chief Executive Officer:
John J. Fernandes,
President/CEO

Statement:
AACSB International–The
Association to Advance Collegiate
Schools of Business (AACSB) is a
nonprofit association of educational
institutions, corporations, and other
organizations devoted to the promotion and improvement of higher
education in business administration and management. Organized
in 1916, AACSB is the premier
accrediting agency for bachelors,
masters, and doctoral degree programs in business administration
and accounting. It also serves as
the professional organization for
management education.

Profile:
Nonprofit founded in 1916.
AACSB has 30 U.S. staff. AACSB
provides a membership program
and has 850 institutional members.

Geographic Focus:
Worldwide

Exchange Activities:
AACSB provides exchange-related
facilitative or support services.

Financial Assistance:
AACSB does not provide financial
assistance.

Publications:
Newsline, Howard Hoskins,
    Director of Communication,
    314/872-8507 x262

Funding Alert

Membership Directory

Guide to Doctoral Programs in
    Business and Management

Internationalizing the Business
    School Curriculum: A Resource
    Guide

Academic Adventures in America (AAIA)

67 Tanglewood Drive
Summit, NJ 07901

Tel.: 908/273-1756
Fax: 908/273-4913
E-mail:
AAIASANDY@worldnet.att.net

Secondary Address:
3817 Campolindo Drive
Moraga, CA 94556

Chief Executive Officer:
Rose Jackson,
Director
908/273-1756,
rosejackson@worldnet.att.net

Statement:
Academic Adventures in America
(AAIA) is a nonprofit educational
and cultural exchange program
dedicated to bringing people of all
ages closer together, resulting in a
better understanding of other cultures. Students improve their
knowledge and use of English by
living with an American family and
being immersed in the language.
The ultimate aim of the program is
to promote lifelong relationships
between students and host families.

Profile:
Nonprofit founded in 1988. AAIA
has five U.S. staff. AAIA provides
a membership program and has
two local chapters/affiliates. AAIA
employs 35 seasonal staff.

Geographic Focus:
Asia (Japan, Korea), North America
(United States, Canada), Oceania
(Australia), South America (Brazil,
Argentina), Western Europe (Spain,
France, Italy, Belgium, Scandinavia,
Germany, Finland)

Exchange Activities:
AAIA is involved in the following
exchange areas: Arts/Cultural,
Community/Citizen, Homestay,
Language Study, Short-Term
Visitors, Students/Educators. AAIA
provides exchange-related facilitative or support services. It administers exchange programs for the
following academic levels: K-12,
Teachers, Undergraduate Students.

Financial Assistance:
AAIA does not provide financial
assistance.

Exchange Programs Include:
American Students to France
Rose Jackson, Director
908/273-1756,
rosejackson@worldnet.att.net

American Students to Spain
Rose Jackson, Director
908/273-1756,
rosejackson@worldnet.att.net

Four-Day NY Orientation for
Inbound Academic Year Students
Rose Jackson, Director
908/273-1756,
rosejackson@worldnet.att.net

Host a Short-Term Foreign Visitor
Rose Jackson, Director
908/273-1756,
rosejackson@worldnet.att.net

School Exchange Program
Rose Jackson, Director
908/273-1756,
rosejackson@worldnet.att.net

Academic and Cultural Exchange (ACE)

22827 Kinross Lane
Moreno Valley, CA 92557

Tel.: 909/243-6747
Fax: 909/247-5498
Web: www.academicculturalexch.com
E-mail: ACELAF@aol.com

General Inquiries:
Laura Froehlich,
International Relations Director
909/243-6747,
ACELAF@aol.com

Chief Executive Officer:
Louise Heath,
Director

Statement:
The purpose of Academic and Cultural Exchange (ACE) is to enhance the relationship between the United States and the world by promoting international understanding. ACE addresses the need for young men and women to traverse cultural boundaries and develop a global perspective. International homestays, which give participants the opportunity to live the culture on a day-to-day basis, represent one of the best ways to promote cross-cultural understanding. ACE seeks to prepare participants for a successful and rewarding experience through careful predeparture orientations and monthly programs once students are placed with host families. Through careful attention to participants' needs, ACE provides a high quality service which promotes greater understanding among youth in today's interdependent world.

Profile:
Nonprofit founded in 1988. ACE has five U.S. staff. ACE provides a membership program. Forty-five U.S. volunteers contribute to ACE's mission.

Geographic Focus:
Asia (Japan), Eastern Europe (Yugoslavia), North America (Mexico), South America (Chile, Brazil, Columbia), Western Europe (Germany, Spain, Holland)

Exchange Activities:
ACE is involved in the following exchange areas: Homestay, Short-Term Visitors, Students/Educators. ACE provides exchange-related facilitative or support services. It administers exchange programs for the following academic levels: K-12, Teachers.

Financial Assistance:
ACE does not provide financial assistance.

Exchange Programs Include:
AYP/Semester Inbound Program
  Laura Froehlich
  acelaf@aol.com

AYP/Semester Outbound Program
  Laura Froehlich
  acelaf@aol.com

Short-Term Homestay
  Laura Froehlich
  909/243-6747, acelaf@aol.com

Short-Term Teacher Shadow Program
  Louise Heath
  800/950-4073, lheath5445@aol.com

Additional Offices:
Boseville, Livermore, CA

Overseas Offices:
Beijing, China
Arequipa, Peru
Brasilia, Brazil
Cali, Columbia
Fortaleza, Brazil
Ensinada, Mexico
Tamps, Mexico
Yucatan, Mexico
Heppenheim, Germany
Stuttgart, Germany
Bangkok, Thailand
London, United Kingdom

U.S. Department of State Designated Sponsor for the Exchange Vistor Program
Secondary school students

Academy for Educational Development (AED)

1825 Connecticut Avenue, NW
Washington, DC 20009-5721

Tel.: 202/884-8000
Fax: 202/884-8400
Website: http://www.aed.org
E-mail: admindc@aed.org

General Inquiries:
Sandra Lauffer, 202/884-8228
slauffer@aed.org
Bonnie J. Barhyte, 202/884-8257
bbarhyte@aed.org

Chief Executive Officer:
Stephen F. Moseley,
President and
Chief Executive Officer

Statement:
The Academy for Educational Development (AED), founded in 1961, is an independent, nonprofit service organization committed to solving critical social problems in the U.S. and throughout the world through education, social marketing, research, training, policy analysis and innovative program design and management. AED assists local, state, and federal government agencies; nongovernmental and private organizations; schools, colleges, and universities; and community-based organizations. Services include technical assistance, evaluation, planning, and program implementation, including the administration of major exchange, fellowships, scholarships, and training programs. Each year, AED provides services throughout the United States and over 80 countries in every region of the world. Fields of emphasis include education, democracy support, health and nutrition, family planning, energy, environment, youth development, and economic growth.

Alliance
MEMBER

Profile:
Nonprofit founded in 1961. AED has approximately 700 U.S. and overseas staff.

Geographic Focus:
Worldwide

Exchange Activities:
AED is involved in the following exchange areas: Arts/Cultural, Community/Citizen, Professional/Business, Short-Term Visitors, Students/Educators, Training. AED provides exchange-related facilitative or support services. It administers exchange programs for the following academic levels: Faculty, Graduate Students, Teachers, Undergraduate Students.

Financial Assistance:
AED does not provide financial assistance.

Publications:
Academy News

Exchange Programs Include:
Center for Leadership Development
Yvonne Williams,
Vice President and Director
202/884-8691, ywilliam@aed.org

Center for Academic Partnerships
Catherine B. Sevcenko, Director
202/884-8224, csevcenk@aed.org

Center for International Training
Mark P. Ketcham,
Vice President and Director
202/884-8147, mketcham@aed.org

National Security Education Program–
David L. Boren Graduate Fellowships
Elizabeth Veatch, Director
202/884-8281, eveatch@aed.org

Center for International Exchanges
Beverly Attallah,
Vice President and Director
202/884-8223, battallah@aed.org

Exchange Related Facilitative or Support Services Include:
Grants/Scholarships to Individuals
Center for Academic Partnerships
Catherine Sevcenko, Director
202/884-8224, csevcenk@aed.org

AED ·
Academy for Educational Development

National Security Education Program–David L. Boren Graduate Fellowships
Elizabeth Veatch, Director
202/884-8281 eveatch@aed.org

International Visitor Support
Center for International Exchanges
Beverly Attallah,
Vice President and Director
202/884-8223, battallah@aed.org

People with Disabilities
Disabilities Studies and Services Center
Carol Valdivieso,
Vice President and Director
202/884-8204, cvaldivi@aed.org

Additional Offices:
Nashville, TN
New York, NY

Overseas Offices:
Almaty, Kazakhstan
Dhaka, Bangladesh
Addis Ababa, Ethiopia
La Paz, Bolivia
Amman, Jordan
Kiev, Ukraine
Baku, Azerbaijan
Cairo, Egypt
Gaborone, Botswana
Guatemala City, Guatemala
Conakry, Guinea
Johannesburg, South Africa
Accra, Ghana
Dakar, Senegal
Tegucigalpa, Honduras
Kampala, Uganda
Moscow, Russia
Zagreb, Croatia
Port-au-Prince, Haiti
Lusaka, Zambia
Abijan, Cote D'Ivoire
New Delhi, India
Antananarivo, Madagascar
Nairobi, Kenya
Panama, Panama
Bamako, Mali
Santo Domingo, Dominican Republic
Tbilisi, Georgia
Asuncion, Paraguay
Yerevan, Armenia
Kathmandu, Nepal
Managua, Nicaragua

U.S. Department of State Designated Sponsor for the Exchange Vistor Program
College and university students

Accent on Understanding

2539 Lund Avenue, SE
Port Orchard, WA 98366

Tel.: 360/871-3805
Fax: 360/895-9393

General Inquiries:
Vicki Keller,
Treasurer
360/871-3805,
VicaRich@aol.com

Chief Executive Officer:
Jack Nelson,
Chairman
360/871-1163

Statement:
Accent on Understanding is dedicated to developing understanding between citizens of the United States and the Newly Independent States (NIS) through direct educational exchanges; sharing values, lifestyles, cultures, and customs; and establishing long-term relationships between educators, students, and communities.

Profile:
Nonprofit. Accent on Understanding provides a membership program and has 35 individual members. Thirty-five U.S. volunteers contribute to Accent on Understanding's mission.

Geographic Focus:
Newly Independent States (Russia, Belarus, Ukraine, Moldova)

Exchange Activities:
Accent on Understanding is involved in the following exchange areas: Community/Citizen, Homestay, Sister School Partnership, Students/Educators, Training. Accent on Understanding provides exchange-related facilitative or support services. It administers exchange programs for the following academic levels: K-12, Teachers.

Financial Assistance:
Scholarships may be awarded to delegates coming from the republics of the NIS to help defray transportation costs.

Publications:
Accent Brochure

Exchange Programs Include:
Sister Schools
    Vicki Keller, Treasurer
    360/871-3805, vicarich@aol.com

Teacher Delegation
    Jack Nelson, Chairman
    360/871-3654

Exchange Related Facilitative or Support Services Include:
Conference/Meetings/Workshop
    Bi-Annual Seminar
    Nancy Holmes, Chairman
    360/871-3654,
    mikeholmes@worldfront.co

Adventures in Real Communication Year Program (ARC-YP)

147 Bell Street
Chagrin Falls, OH 44022

Tel.: 800/637-5859
Fax: 440/247-9225
Website: http://www.arcyp.com

General Inquiries:
Beverly S. Wattenmaker,
President
800/637-5859,
arc@arcyp.com

Chief Executive Officer:
Beverly S. Wattenmaker,
President

Statement:
Adventures in Real Communication Year Program (ARC-YP) is committed to building international understanding through the ripple effect of one-to-one in-depth relationships that expand horizons and start the process of changing cultural perceptions, both in the United States and in partner countries. A quarter-century's experience with curriculum-based travel keeps ARC-YP focused on the educational aspects of exchange.

Profile:
Nonprofit founded in 1986. ARC-YP has ten U.S. staff. ARC-YP provides a membership program.

Geographic Focus:
Asia (Japan, South Korea), Central America (Costa Rica, Mexico), Eastern Europe (Poland), Newly Independent States (Russia), South America (Brazil, Ecuador), Western Europe (France, Germany, Italy, Spain, Switzerland)

Exchange Activities:
ARC-YP is involved in the following exchange areas: Arts/Cultural, Community/Citizen, Homestay, Language Study, Short-Term Visitors, Students/Educators. ARC-YP provides exchange-related facilitative or support services. It administers exchange programs for the following academic levels: 6-12, Undergraduate Students.

Financial Assistance:
ARC-YP does not provide financial assistance.

Publications:
Accent Brochure

Adventures in Real Communication News

Community Coordinator Handbook

Host Family Handbook

Orientation Handbook

Community Coordinator Handbook–Workshop

Exchange Programs Include:
Semester/Academic Year
Private Day School Program
    Shannon Matusicky,
    Managing Director
    800/637-5859, arc@arcyp.com

Semester/Academic Year
Public School Program
    Deidre Schrueder, Program Director
    800/637-5859, arc@arcyp.com

Short-Term Program
    Jessica Gilway,
    ARC Program Manager
    800/637-5859, arc@arcyp.com

Exchange Related Facilitative or Support Services Include:
Conference/Meetings/Workshops

Additional Offices:
Indianapolis, IN

Overseas Offices:
Braunschweig, Germany
Cartago, Costa Rica
Mexico City, Mexico

U.S. Department of State Designated Sponsor for the Exchange Vistor Program
Secondary school students

Africa-America Institute (AAI)

Chanin Building
380 Lexington Avenue
42nd Floor
New York, NY 10168-4298

Tel.: 212/949-5666
Fax: 212/682-6174
Website: www.aaionline.org
E-mail: aainy@aaionline.org

Secondary Address:
1625 Massachusetts Avenue, NW
Suite 400
Washington, DC 20036

Tel.: 202/667-5636
Fax: 202/265-6332

General Inquiries:
Lovely Mixon,
212/949-5666

Chief Executive Officer:
Mora McLean,
President

Statement:
The mission of the Africa-America Institute (AAI) is to promote enlightened engagement between Africa and America through education, training, and dialogue. Founded in 1953, AAI is a multiracial, multi-ethnic nonprofit organization with offices in New York and Washington, DC and a presence in 18 African countries. With funds provided by multilateral, U.S. Government, private foundation, and corporate donors, AAI pursues its mission through work in two program areas: 1) African Higher Education and Training, and 2) Educational Outreach and Policy.

Profile:
Nonprofit founded in 1953. AAI has 45 U.S. staff and 14 overseas staff. AAI provides a membership program.

Geographic Focus:
Africa, Caribbean

Exchange Activities:
AAI is involved in the following exchange areas: Arts/Cultural, Community/Citizen, Homestay, Professional/Business, Short-Term Visitors, Students/Educators, Training. AAI provides exchange-related facilitative or support services. It administers exchange programs for the following academic levels: Faculty, Graduate Students, Teachers, Undergraduate Students.

Publications:
AAI Annual Report

Contact Africa 2001: A Directory of U.S. Organizations Working on Africa

Exchange Programs Include:
Fulbright/Hays Seminar Abroad
 Paulette Nowden
 202/667-5636
 pnowden@aaionline.org

Global Training for Development (GTD)
 Vivian Awumey
 GTD Project Manager
 202/667-5636
 vawumey@aaionline.org

International Visitors Program (IVP)
 Paulette Nowden
 202/667-5636
 pnowden@aaionline.org

Exchange Related Facilitative or Support Services Include:
International Visitor Support
 International Visitors Program
 Paulette Nowden
 202/667-5636
 pnowden@aaionline.org

Public Policy
 Government Relations and Policy
 Director Policy Programs
 202/667-5636
 wjackson@aaionline.org

Overseas Offices:
Abidjan, Cote d'Ivore
Conakry, Guinea
Brazzaville, Congo
Bissau, Guinea Bissau
Bamako, Mali
Dar es Salaam, Tanzania
Cotonou, Benin
Accra, Ghana
Ouagadougou, Burkina Faso
Freetown, Sierra Leone
Windhoek, Namibia
Maputo, Mozambique
Lusaka, Zambia
Lagos, Nigeria
Johannesburg, South Africa
Harare, Zimbabwe
Gaborone, Botswana
Dakar, Senegal

U.S. Department of State Designated Sponsor for the Exchange Vistor Program
Trainees
College and university students
International visitors

AFS-Intercultural Programs/USA (AFS)

198 Madison Avenue, Eighth Floor
New York, NY 10016

Tel.: 800/AFS-INFO
Fax: 212/299-9090
Website: http://www.afs.org/usa

Chief Executive Officer:
Alex J. Plinio,
President

Statement:
AFS-Intercultural Programs/USA (AFS) is an international nonprofit organization that provides intercultural learning opportunities for students and adults. It operates programs in over 50 countries involving more than 30,000 students and families annually. Participants in AFS programs gain a more profound cultural understanding of other societies which is essential to the achievement of social justice and lasting peace in a diverse world.

Profile:
Nonprofit founded in 1947. AFS has 145 U.S. staff.

Geographic Focus:
Worldwide

Exchange Activities:
AFS is involved in the following exchange areas: Homestay, Language Study, Students/Educators. AFS provides exchange-related facilitative or support services. It administers exchange programs for the following academic levels: Graduate Students, K-12, Undergraduate Students, Professionals.

Financial Assistance:
AFS provides scholarships/fellowships or financial assistance to participants with demonstrated merit or need. In addition, many local AFS chapters provide financial assistance for students.

Exchange Programs Include:
Community Service and University Study Program for Ages 18+

Semester Program/Winter and Summer Departures

Summer Program/Homestay, Language Study, Homestay Plus, and Community Service

Year Program/Winter and Summer Departures

Global Educators/Intensive or Semester (Winter and Summer Departures)

Additional Offices:
Baltimore, MD
Minneapolis, MN
Portland, OR

Overseas Offices:
Cairo, Egypt
Budapest, Hungary
Brussels, Belgium
Bridgetown, Barbados
Bratislava, Slovak Republic
Beijing, China
Lima, Peru
Amsterdam, Netherlands
Frederiksberg, Denmark
Accra, Ghana
Asunsion, Paraguay
Dublin, Ireland
Zurich, Switzerland
Fontenay Sous Bois, France
Vienna, Austria
Guatemala Ciudad, Guatemala
Hamburg, Germany
Helsinki, Finland
Istanbul, Turkey
Jakarta, Indonesia
Johannesburg, South Africa
Kingston, Jamaica
Leeds, United Kingdom
Lisbon, Portugal
Madrid, Spain
San Juan, Puerto Rico
Caracas, Venezuela
Rio de Janeiro, Brazil
Riga, Latvia
Reykjavik, Iceland
Quito, Ecuador
Prague, Czech Republic
Oslo, Norway
San Jose, Costa Rica
Moscow, Russia
Santo Domingo, Dominican Republic
Wellington, New Zealand
Nonthaburi, Thailand
El Dorado, Panama
Mexico, Mexico
Santiago, Argentina
La Paz, Bolivia
Selangor, Malaysia
Siena, Italy
Stockholm, Sweden
Surry Hills, Australia
Tegucigalpa, Honduras
Tokyo, Japan
Wanchai, Hong Kong
Santa Fe de Bogota, Colombia
Montreal, Canada

**U.S. Department of State
Designated Sponsor for the
Exchange Vistor Program**
Secondary school students
Trainees

AHA International

741 SW Lincoln Street
Portland, OR 97201-3178

Tel.: 503/295-7730
Fax: 503/295-5969
Website: http://www.aha-intl.org
E-mail: mail@aha-intl.org

General Inquiries:
Isabelle Bridge
503/295-7730,
ibridge@aha.intl.org

Chief Executive Officer:
Robert L. Selby,
Executive Director

Statement:
AHA International is a nonprofit educational organization that creates, coordinates, and administers intercultural programs for both outbound American students and inbound international students. Since 1957, AHA's commitment has been to encourage an understanding of one's own cultural heritage and the cultural heritage of others.

Profile:
Nonprofit founded in 1957. AHA International has 12 U.S. staff and 14 overseas staff. AHA International provides a membership program.

Geographic Focus:
Asia (Japan, Vietnam), Western Europe (Greece, Italy, France, Spain, Austria, Germany, United Kingdom)

Exchange Activities:
AHA International is involved in the following exchange areas: Homestay, Short-Term Visitors, Students/Educators. AHA International provides exchange-related facilitative or support services. It administers exchange programs for the following academic levels: K-12, Teachers, Undergraduate Students.

Financial Assistance:
AHA International does not provide financial assistance.

Exchange Programs Include:
International Visitors
Jeff Baffaro, Director
503/295-7730,
jbaffaro@aha-intl.org

Exchange Related Facilitative or Support Services Include:
International Visitor Support
Jeff Baffaro, Director
503/295-7730,
jbaffaro@aha-intl.org

Overseas Offices:
Vienna, Austria
Granada, Spain
Oviedo, Spain
Segovia, Spain
Angers, France
Cologne, Germany
Macerata, Italy
Siena, Italy
Athens, Greece
London, United Kingdom
Morelia, Mexico
Valdivia, Chile
Rosario, Argentina

AIESEC United States, Inc. (AIESEC)

135 West 50th Street
Suite 1725
New York, NY 10020

Tel.: 212/757-3774
Fax: 212/757-4062
E-mail: aiesec@us.aiesec.org

Chief Executive Officer:
Suzanne Moyer,
President

Statement:
AIESEC is a worldwide association of students dedicated to increasing international understanding and cooperation. AIESEC's primary program is the International Traineeship Exchange Program which provides more than 5,000 students worldwide an opportunity for practical training in 85 countries.

Profile:
Nonprofit founded in 1948. AIESEC has nine U.S. staff. AIESEC provides a membership program and has 38 local chapters/affiliates. One thousand U.S. volunteers and 5,000 overseas volunteers contribute to AIESEC's mission.

Geographic Focus:
Worldwide

Exchange Activities:
AIESEC is involved in the following exchange areas: Training and internships. AIESEC provides exchange-related facilitative or support services. It administers exchange programs for the following academic levels: Graduate Students, Undergraduate Students.

Financial Assistance:
AIESEC does not provide financial assistance.

Exchange Programs Include:
International Traineeship Exchange Program (ITEP)
James Gardiner, Exchange Coordinator

Exchange Related Facilitative or Support Services Include:
Conference/Meetings/Workshops

International Visitor Support

Membership Services

Additional Offices:
Seattle, WA
Philadelphia, PA
Portland, OR
Province, RI
Raleigh, NC
St. Cloud, MN
St. Louis, MO
Tempe, AZ
New Brunswick, NJ
Washington, DC
Boulder, CO
Tuscaloosa, AL
Miami, FL
Lawrence, KS
Eau Claire, WI
Madison, WI
Milwaukee, WI
Cincinnati, OH
Columbus, OH
Oxford, OH
Buffalo, NY
New York City, NY
Bloomington, IN
West Lafayette, IN
Berkeley, CA
Pullerton, CA
Santa Barbara, CA
San Luis Obispo, CA
San Diego, CA
San Jose, CA
Athens, GA
Atlanta, GA
Arlington, TX
Austin, TX
Houston, TX
Ann Arbor, MI
East Lansing, MI
Champagne-Urbana, IL
Chicago, IL

U.S. Department of State Designated Sponsor for the Exchange Vistor Program
Trainees
Intern

Alliance for International Educational and Cultural Exchange, Inc. (Alliance)

1776 Massachusetts Avenue, NW
Suite 620
Washington, DC 20036

Tel.: 202/293-6141
Fax: 202/293-6144
Website: www.alliance-exchange.org
E-mail: info@alliance-exchange.org

General Inquiries:
info@alliance-exchange.org

Chief Executive Officer:
Michael McCarry,
Executive Director

Statement:
The Alliance for International Educational and Cultural Exchange, Inc. (Alliance) is an association of U.S.-based organizations comprising the international educational and cultural exchange community. Its mission is to formulate and promote public policies that support the efforts and programs of the international exchange community.

Profile:
Nonprofit founded in 1993. Alliance has four U.S. staff. The Alliance provides a membership program and has 65 institutional members.

Exchange Activities:
The Alliance provides exchange-related facilitative or support services.

Financial Assistance:
The Alliance does not provide financial assistance.

Publications:
Policy Monitor, Julie Taiber, Assistant Director, 202/293-6141, info@alliance-exchange.org

News News News

Action Alert

International Exchange Locator

Exchange Related Facilitative or Support Services Include:
Conference/Meetings/Workshops
Liliya Dolgikh,
Executive Assistant

Membership Services
Liliya Dolgikh,
Executive Assistant
202/293-6141
ldolgikh@alliance-exchange.org

Public Policy
Julie Taiber, Assistant Director/Sr.
Policy Specialist
202/293-6141
jmt@alliance-exchange.org

International Education and Training Coalition (IETC)
Kevin Baron,
Policy Specialist
202/293-6141
kbaron@alliance-exchange.org

Alliances Abroad

702 West Avenue
Austin, TX 78701

Tel.: 888/6-ABROAD
Fax: 512/457-8132
Website: www.alliancesabroad.com
E-mail: info@allianceabroad.com

Secondary address:
**2423 Pennsylvania Ave., NW
Washington, DC 20037**

Tel.: 866/6-ABROAD
Fax: 202/467-9460

General Inquiries:
Lauren Stone,
Vice President of
Global Business Development
202/467-9467,
lstone@alliancesabroad.com

Chief Executive Officer:
Victoria B. Lynden,
President

Statement:
Alliances Abroad is a private cultural and educational organization committed to promoting deeper understanding of other cultures. Alliances Abroad specializes in customized, full service inbound and outbound programs: work, study, intern, teach, volunteer in six continents.

Profile:
Founded in 1993. Alliances Abroad has 27 U.S. staff and 17 overseas staff. Forty U.S. local coordinators contribute to Alliances Abroad's mission.

Geographic Focus:
Africa, Asia (China, Japan, Korea, Taiwan), Central America, (Guatemala, Costa Rica), North America (United States, Canada, Mexico), Western Europe (France, Spain, Germany, Italy, Ireland, United Kingdom,) South America (Brazil, Argentina)

Exchange Activities:
Alliances Abroad is involved in the following exchange areas: Arts/Cultural, Community/Citizen, Homestay, Language Study, Professional/Business, Training, English teaching and Youth Programs provide exchange-related facilitative or support services. It administers exchange programs for all ages, particularly secondary and post secondary students.

Financial Assistance:
Alliances Abroad does not provide financial assistance.

Exchange Programs Include:
Specialty programs:
  Culinary, Arts and more

Work Abroad

Intern Abroad

Teach Abroad

Study Abroad

Volunteer Abroad

Work in the United States

Train in the United States

Exchange Related Facilitative or Support Services Include:
Admissions/Placement Service

Courses for Credit

International Visitor Support

Travel Services

Overseas Offices:
San Pedro, Costa Rica

America-Mideast Educational and Training Services (AMIDEAST)

1730 M Street, NW
Suite 1100
Washington, DC 20036-4505

Tel.: 202/776-9600
Fax: 202/776-7000
Website: http://www.amideast.org
E-mail: inquiries@amideast.org

General Inquiries:
Myriam Fizazi-Hawkins,
Senior Program Officer,
Public Relations
202/776-9613,
mfizazi@amideast.org

Chief Executive Officer:
Amb. William A. Rugh,
President & CEO

Statement:
America-Mideast Educational and Training Services' (AMIDEAST) mission is to strengthen mutual understanding and appreciation between the people of the Middle East and North Africa and the people of the United States. It provides administrative, advising, testing, training, research, recruiting, programming, and information services in support of educational and cultural exchanges.
AMIDEAST also provides technical assistance in overseas projects, produces materials, and conducts outreach to improve teaching about the Arab world in American classrooms. AMIDEAST works with other organizations to encourage and support American students and professionals participating in exchange programs to the Middle East and North Africa.

Profile:
Nonprofit founded in 1951. AMIDEAST has 46 U.S. staff and 140 overseas staff. AMIDEAST provides a membership program and has 210 institutional members. Fifteen U.S. volunteers and ten overseas volunteers contribute to AMIDEAST's mission.

Geographic Focus:
Africa (Morocco, Tunisia), Middle East (Egypt, Jordan, Lebanon, Syria, West Bank and Gaza, Kuwait, United Arab Emirates, Yemen)

Exchange Activities:
AMIDEAST is involved in the following exchange areas: Homestay, Language Study, Professional/Business, Short-Term Visitors, Students/Educators, Training. AMIDEAST provides exchange-related facilitative or support services. It administers exchange programs for the following academic levels: Faculty (post secondary), Graduate Students, Undergraduate Students.

Financial Assistance:
AMIDEAST does not provide financial assistance.

Publications:
Annual Report

The Advising Quarterly

Education in the Arab World; Vol.I

Arabic Alphabet Poster & Teacher's Handout

AMIDEAST TODAY newsletter

Exchange Programs Include:
Cyprus America Scholarship Program
Kate Archambault,
Director, Exchange Programs
202/776-9670,
karchambault@amideast.org

Fulbright Foreign Student Scholarship Program
Gail Gugel, Director,
Fulbright Program
202/776-9660,
ggugel@amideast.org

Exchange Related Facilitative or Support Services Include:
Admissions/Placement Service
Private Projects
Amy Tabash, Coordinator
202/776-9663
atasbash@amideast.org

Conference/Meetings/Workshops
Credentials Evaluation
Information Services
Leslie Nucho, Vice President
202/776-9625,
lnucho@amideast.org

Overseas Offices:
Damascus, Syria
Gaza City, Palestine
East Jerusalem, Palestine
Antelias, Lebanon
Beirut, Lebanon
Casablanca, Morocco
Rabat, Morocco
Kuwait City, Kuwait
Tunis, Tunisia
Alexandria, Egypt
Cairo, Egypt
Sana'a, Yemen
Aden, Yemen

U.S. Department of State Designated Sponsor for the Exchange Vistor Program
Short-term scholars
College and university students

Alliance
MEMBER

American Academic and Cultural Exchange (AACE)

P.O. Box 6338
Ashland, VA 23005-6338

Tel.: 804/746-8416
Fax: 804/746-5490
Web: ww.aacestudentexchange.org
E-mail: seigler@ix.netcom.com

Secondary Address:
9351 Falcon Drive
Mechanicsville, VA 23116

General Inquiries:
Irene Seigler,
President
804/746-8416,
seigler@ix.netcom.com

Chief Executive Officer:
Irene Seigler,
President

Statement:
American Academic and Cultural Exchange (AACE) was founded on the premise that positive, personal experience helps dissolve geographical, cultural, and political barriers; leads to greater human understanding; and ultimately leads to world peace. AACE provides opportunities for teenagers from all over the world to live with a host family and attend school in the United States. Conversely, high school students from the Unites States may live with a host family and attend school abroad. AACE believes that the enduring bond which develops between host family and student contributes to bringing together the many diverse cultures of the world.

Profile:
Nonprofit founded in 1993. AACE has two U.S. staff. AACE provides a membership program. Thirty U.S. volunteers and five overseas volunteers contribute to AACE's mission.

Geographic Focus:
Worldwide

Exchange Activities:
AACE is involved in the following exchange areas: Homestay, Language Study, Short-Term Visitors, Students/Educators. AACE provides exchange-related facilitative or support services. It administers exchange programs for the following academic levels: Graduate Students, K-12, Teachers, Undergraduate Students.

Financial Assistance:
AACE does not provide financial assistance.

Publications:
AACE News

Exchange Programs Include:
Full Academic Year Program
Irene Seigler, President
804/746-8416,
seigler@ix.netcom.com

Summer Cultural Program in Russia

Summer Language/Cultural Program
Irene Seigler, President
804/746-8416,
seigler@ix.netcom.com

Teacher Exchange

Teachers Outbound
Full Academic Year

Exchange Related Facilitative or Support Services Include:
Admissions/Placement Service

Additional Offices:
Charlottesville, VA

U.S. Department of State Designated Sponsor for the Exchange Vistor Program
Secondary school students

American Association of Collegiate Registrars and Admissions Officers (AACRAO)

One Dupont Circle, NW
Suite 520
Washington, DC 20036-1135

Tel.: 202/293-9161
Fax: 202/872-8857
Website: http://www.aacrao.com
E-mail: info@aacrao.com

General Inquiries:
Dale E. Gough
202/296-3359

Chief Executive Officer:
Jerry Sullivan,
Executive Director

Statement:
The American Association of Collegiate Registrars and Admissions Officers (AACRAO) serves professionals in records management, enrollment management, student services, national and international admissions, and information technology. In these areas AACRAO provides workshops and other professional development opportunities, research and recommendation on national and international education policy, guidelines and voluntary standards for best practices, and consulting services. Among its international education publications are detailed monographs on the education systems of particular countries. The AACRAO Office of International Education Services evaluates the credentials of those educated outside the U.S. and make recommendations for placement.

Profile:
Nonprofit founded in 1910.
AACRAO has 20 U.S. staff.
AACRAO is a membership association of more than 9,000 higher education officials at some 2,300 colleges and universities.

Geographic Focus:
Worldwide

Exchange Activities:
AACRAO provides exchange-related facilitative or support services.

Financial Assistance:
AACRAO does not provide financial assistance.

Publications:
Foreign Educational Credentials Required for Consideration of Admission to Universities and Colleges in the U.S.

The Guide: A Resource for International Admissions Professionals

International Academic Credentials Handbook

AACRAO Country Guide Series

Projects for International Education Research (PIER) titles

Exchange Related Facilitative or Support Services Include:
Conference/Meetings/Workshops
  Gloria Rutberg, Meetings and
  Conferences Manager
  202/293-9161 x6200

Credentials Evaluation
  Dale E. Gough, Office of
  International Education Services
  202/296-3359

Membership Services
  Martha Henebry
  202/263-0285

Federal Relations
  Jacque Gourley
  202/263-0282

Web Services
  Angela Gemza
  202/263-2091

American Association of Community Colleges (AACC)

One Dupont Circle, NW
Suite 410
Washington, DC 20036

Tel.: 202/728-0200
Fax: 202/833-2467
Website: http://www.aacc.nche.edu

General Inquiries:
Jim McKenney,
Director of Economic and
Workforce Development
202/728-0200 x233,
jmckenney@aacc.nche.edu

Chief Executive Officer:
George Boggs,
President

Statement:
The American Association of Community Colleges (AACC) represents more than 1,000 American accredited community, technical, and junior colleges. The Association provides leadership and service in the following key areas: advocacy, policy, information resources, leadership, professional development, and coordination in the promotion of community college issues and interests. The Office of International Services provides AACC member institutions with information on funding opportunities for international education; overseas exchange opportunities for faculty, administrators, and students; and legislative issues affecting international education. The international office works with the diplomatic community in Washington, D.C., briefs international educators on the two-tier college model, and responds to international requests for assistance.

Alliance
MEMBER

Profile:
Nonprofit founded in 1920. AACC has 41 U.S. staff. AACC provides a membership program and has 1,097 institutional members, 188 individual members, and 24 local chapters/affiliates.

Geographic Focus:
Worldwide

Exchange Activities:
AACC is involved in the following exchange areas: Professional/Business, Short-Term Visitors. AACC provides exchange-related facilitative or support services. It administers exchange programs for the following academic levels: Undergraduate Students.

Financial Assistance:
AACC does not provide financial assistance.

Publications:
The Community College Story (English, Spanish, French, Russian)

Global Awareness in Community Colleges: Report on a National Survey

The Community College Times

The Community College Journal

Developing the World's Best Workforce

Exchange Related Facilitative or Support Services Include:
Conference/Meetings/Workshops
Mary Ann Settlemire,
Director of Meetings and
Council Relations
202/728-0200 x229,
msettlemire@aacc.nche.edu

International Visitor Support
Jim McKenney,
Director of Economic and
Workforce Development
202/728-0200,
jmckenney@aacc.nche.edu

Membership Services
Margaret Rivera,
Director of Membership and
Information Services
202/728-0200 x234,
mrivera@aacc.nche.edu

Public Policy
David Baime, Director of
Government Relations
202/728-0200 x224,
dbaime@aacc.nche.edu

Other
Arnold Kee,
Coordinator of Minority Services
202/728-0200 x262,
akee@aacc.nche.edu

American Association of Intensive English Programs (AAIEP)

229 North 33rd Street
Philadelphia, PA 19104-2709

Tel.: 215/895-5856
Fax: 215/895-5854
Website: http://www.aaiep.org
E-mail: aaiep@drexel.edu

General Inquiries:
Jon M. Leyland,
AAIEP C.O. Manager
215/895-5856, aaiep@drexel.edu

Chief Executive Officer:
Dr. Terry Simon,
President

Statement:
AAIEP promotes ethical and professional standards for intensive English programs; encourages and facilitates evaluation of intensive English programs; acts as a liaison between intensive English programs and organizations which use their services and those whose actions affect them, including but not limited to U.S. and foreign government agencies, sponsors, admissions officers and counselors; and increases awareness abroad of opportunities for English language study in the United States.

Profile:
Nonprofit founded in 1986. AAIEP has one U.S. staff and 11 U.S. volunteers. AAIEP provides a membership program and has 293 institutional members and 24 individual members.

Geographic Focus:
Worldwide

Exchange Activities:
AAIEP is involved in the following exchange areas: Professional/Business, Language Study, Students/Educators.

Financial Assistance:
AAIEP does not provide financial assistance.

Publications:
AAIEP Member Profiles (book)
AAIEP Newsletter

Exchange Related Facilitative or Support Services Include:
Conference/Meetings/Workshops
  Jon M. Leyland,
  AAIEP C.O. Manager
  215/895-5856, aaiep@drexel.edu

Credentials Evaluation
  Jon M. Leyland,
  AAIEP C.O. Manager
  215/895-5856, aaiep@drexel.edu

Membership Services
  Jon M. Leyland,
  AAIEP C.O. Manager
  215/895-5856, aaiep@drexel.edu

Alliance MEMBER

American Association of Teachers of German (AATG)

112 Haddontowne Court
Suite 104
Cherry Hill, NJ 08034

Tel.: 856/795-5553
Fax: 856/795-9398
Website: www.aatg.org
E-mail: headquarters@aatg.org

General Inquiries:
Receptionist
856/795-5553

Chief Executive Officer:
Helene Zimmer-Loew,
Executive Director

Statement:
The American Association of Teachers of German (AATG) sends teachers and students abroad through study programs during the summer. It works in conjunction with the Goethe Institute, the German government, and various universities in Germany and Austria. Pedagogical exchange services, part of Germany's Standing Conference of Cultural Ministers, subsidizes AATG's programs.

Profile:
Nonprofit founded in 1926. AATG has eight U.S. staff. AATG provides a membership program and has 6,500 individual members and 61 local chapters/affiliates.

Geographic Focus:
Western Europe (Germany)

Exchange Activities:
AATG provides exchange-related facilitative or support services

Financial Assistance:
AATG provides some financial assistance to participants.

Publications:
Newsletter
Infoblätter
German Quarterly
Die Unterrichtsproxis

Exchange Programs Include:
German Prizewinner Program
Anita Spina, Program Coordinator
856/795-5553

German Summer-Study Program
Anita Spina, Program Coordinator
856/795-5553

Exchange Related Facilitative or Support Services Include:
Conference/Meetings/Workshops

American Council of Learned Societies (ACLS)

228 East 45th Street
New York, NY 10017-3398

Tel.: 212/697-1505
Fax: 212/949-8058
Website: http://www.acls.org
E-mail: grants@acls.org

General Inquiries:
Office of Fellowships & Grants
grants@acls.org

Chief Executive Officer:
John H. D'Arms,
President

Statement:
The American Council of Learned Societies (ACLS) is a private non-profit federation of 61 national scholarly organizations. ACLS's mission, as set forth in its constitution, is to advance humanistic studies in all fields of learning and to maintain and strengthen relations among the national societies devoted to such studies. Among its other programs, ACLS administers the Committee on Scholarly Communication with China National Program for Advanced Study and Research in China and the China Fellowship for Scholarly Development. ACLS also participates in the Vietnam Fulbright Program. At the secondary school level, ACLS offers the U.S.-China Teachers Exchange Program.

Profile:
Nonprofit founded in 1919. ACLS has 25 U.S. staff and one overseas staff. ACLS provides a membership program.

Geographic Focus:
Asia (China), Eastern Europe

Exchange Activities:
ACLS is involved in the following exchange areas:
Students/Educators. ACLS provides exchange-related facilitative or support services. It administers exchange programs for the following academic levels: Faculty, Graduate Students, Teachers.

Financial Assistance:
Programs generally provide living and travel allowances.

Exchange Programs Include:
CSCC China Programs
Fellowship Office
grants@acls.org

U.S.-China
Teachers Exchange Program
Margot Landman, Director
margot@acls.org

Exchange Related Facilitative or Support Services Include:
Admissions/Placement Service
CSCC China Programs,
Fellowship Office,
grants@acls.org

Grants/Scholarships to Individuals
CSCC China Programs
Fellowship Office,
grants@acls.org

Overseas Offices:
Beijing, China

U.S. Department of State Designated Sponsor for the Exchange Vistor Program
Professors and research scholars
Short-term scholars
College and university students
Secondary school students

American Council of Young Political Leaders (ACYPL)

1612 K Street, NW, Suite 300
Washington, DC 20006

Tel.: 202/857-0999
Fax: 202/857-0027
Website: http://acypl.org
E-mail: acypl@erols.com

General Inquiries:
Mark N. Poole,
Executive Director

Chief Executive Officer:
Mark N. Poole,
Executive Director

Statement:
The American Council of Young Political Leaders (ACYPL) was established to offer emerging political leaders an understanding and appreciation of the complexity of foreign policy formation, allow young political leaders from abroad the opportunity to directly observe the American political process, and provide an understanding of the domestic framework which guides the making of U.S. foreign policy. ACYPL also fosters relationships among emerging political leaders from diverse countries.

Profile:
Nonprofit founded in 1966. ACYPL has ten U.S. staff. ACYPL provides a membership program. Three thousand U.S. volunteers contribute to ACYPL's mission.

Geographic Focus:
Worldwide

Exchange Activities:
ACYPL is involved in the following exchange areas: Elected Officials, Short-Term Visitors. ACYPL provides exchange-related facilitative or support services.

Financial Assistance:
ACYPL does not provide financial assistance.

Publications:
Annual Alumni Directory

American Council on Education (ACE)

One Dupont Circle, NW
Suite 800
Washington, DC 20036-1193

Tel.: 202/939-9313
Fax: 202/785-8056
Website: http://www.acenet.edu
E-mail:
   barbara_turlington@ace.nche.edu

General Inquiries:
Barbara Turlington,
Director of International Education
202/939-9313,
barbara_turlington@ace.nche.edu

Chief Executive Officer:
David Ward,
President

Statement:
The American Council on
Education (ACE) is the most comprehensive of the higher education
associations, with members from
all sectors of higher education. It
serves as an advocate for a wide
range of programs and issues
affecting U.S. higher education. In
the international field, ACE, guided
by a presidential-level Commission
on International Education, works
on policy issues in the areas of
institutional and federal support for
international studies, international
collaboration and exchange, and
foreign languages. It maintains relationships with national, regional,
and international higher education
associations around the world.
Activities include research and publications on the state of internationalization of U.S. higher education,
the identification and publication of
promising practices, support for trilateral collaboration among institutions in the United States, Canada,
and Mexico and seminars for U.S.

college and university presidents
and higher education leaders in
other countries. With five other
higher education association, ACE
sponsors the Association Liaison
Office for University Cooperation
in Development.

Profile:
Nonprofit founded in 1918. ACE
has 175 U.S. staff. ACE provides a
membership program and has
1,800 member colleges, universities
and national and regional higher
education associations.

Geographic Focus:
Worldwide

Exchange Activities:
ACE provides exchange-related
facilitative or support services.

Financial Assistance:
ACE does not provide financial
assistance.

Publications:
*Guidelines for College and University
   Linkages Abroad*

*Educating Americans for a World in
   Flux: Ten Ground Rules for
   Internationalizing Higher
   Education*

*Educating for Global Competence:
   America's Passport to the Future*

*A Brief Guide to U.S. Higher
   Education*

*Preliminary Status Report 2000:
   Internationalization of U.S. Higher
   Education*

**Exchange Related Facilitative or
Support Services Include:**
Conference/Meetings/Workshops
   Barbara Turlington,
   Director of International Education
   202/939-9313

Public Policy
   Barbara Turlington,
   Director of International Education
   202/939-9313

American Councils for International Education: ACTR/ACCELS (American Councils)

AMERICAN COUNCILS
FOR INTERNATIONAL EDUCATION
A C T R ▲ A C C E L S

**1776 Massachusetts Avenue, NW
Suite 700   Washington, DC 20036**

Tel.: 202/833-7522
Fax: 202/833-7523
Website: http://www.actr.org
E-mail: general@actr.org

General Inquiries:
Heather McDonnell
Executive Assistant
202/833-7522, general@actr.org

Chief Executive Officer:
Dr. Dan E. Davidson, President

Statement:
American Councils for International Education: ACTR/ACCELS (American Councils) is a private, nonprofit educational association and exchange organization devoted to improving education, professional training, and research within and about the Russian-speaking world, including the Russian Federation and the scores of non-Russian cultures and populations inhabiting the regions of central and eastern Europe and Eurasia. American Councils provides special support for regional language research and training (including RussNet andCenAsia Net, websites for learning and teaching the languages of the NIS); textbook development for Russian and the other languages of the region; the teaching of English as a foreign language; faculty and curriculum development; and in-country immersion programs. American Councils administers more than 20 academic exchange and training programs in virtually all fields; provides educational advising and academic testing services throughout the Newly Independent States (NIS); and engages an increasingly large number of professional educators and university administrators in programs designed to improve communication among educational, research, and professional communities in the NIS and the United States.

Alliance
MEMBER

Profile:
Nonprofit founded in 1974. American Councils has 85 U.S. staff

and 265 overseas staff. American Councils provides a membership program and has 750 institutional members, and 1,285 individual members.

Geographic Focus:
Eastern Europe (Czech Republic, Hungary, Slovak Republic), Newly Independent States (Armenia, Azerbaijan, Belarus, Georgia, Kazakhstan, Kyrgyzstan, Moldova, Russian Federation, Tajikistan, Turkmenistan, Ukraine, Uzbekistan)

Exchange Activities:
American Councils is involved in the following exchange areas: Homestay, Language Study, Professional/Business, Students/Educators, Training. American Councils provides exchange-related facilitative or support services. It administers exchange programs for the following academic levels: Faculty, Graduate Students, K-12, Teachers, Undergraduate Students.

Financial Assistance:
American Councils provides scholarship support for U.S. exchangees with demonstrable financial need. It also provides substantial assistance, including a monthly stipend, for participants from the NIS to cover transportation, insurance, and partial room/board.

Publications:
ACTR Letter, George Morris,
    314/946-8780
Rovesniki/Peers (1995)
*Russian Language for Business
    Communication* (1997)
*Breakthrough! American English for
    Russian Speakers* (1995)
*Chto Vy Ob Etom Dumate? What do you
    think about that?* (1994)
*Twelve Years of Dialogue on Teaching
    Russian* (2000)

Exchange Programs Include:
Freedom Support Act Secondary
    School Program
Russian Leadership Program
Lisa Choate, Vice President
    202/833-7522, choate@actr.org
FSA Undergraduate Programs
Edmund Muskie Graduate
    Fellowship Program
Training Programs
    Jeanne-Marie Duval
    202/833-7522, duval@actr.org
Russian Language and Area Studies Program
    Graham Hettlinger
    202/833-7522, hettlinger@actr.org

Teacher Exchange Programs, Junior
    Faculty Development Program,
    Research Scholars Exchange Program
University Partnerships
    Kevin Spensley, Program Manager
    202/833-7522, spensley@actr.org

High School Academic Partnerships
    Jack Hardman, Program Manager
    202/833-7522, hardman@actr.org

**Exchange Related Facilitative or Support
Services Include:**
Conference/Meetings/Workshops
    Lisa Choate, Vice President
    202/833-7522, choate@actr.org
Courses for Credit
    Graham Hettlinger, Program Manager
    hettlinger@actr.org
Grants/Scholarships to Individuals
    Graham Hettlinger
Testing/Assessment Services
    Lisa Choate

Additional Offices:
Bryn Mawr, PA; St. Louis, MO

Overseas Offices:
Bishkek, Kyrgyzstan
Osh, Kyrgyzstan
Chisinau, Moldova
Dushanbe, Tajikistan
Almaty, Kazakhstan
Astana, Kazakhstan
Uralsk, Kazakhstan
Ust-Kamenogorsk, Kazakhstan
Ashgabat, Turkmenistan
Baku, Azerbaijan
Tashkent, Uzbekistan
Bukhara, Uzbekistan
Namangan, Uzbekistan
Nukus, Uzbekistan
Samarkand, Uzbekistan
Tbilisi, Georgia
Yerevan, Armenia
Kiev, Ukraine
Dnipropetrovsk, Ukraine
Kharkiv, Ukraine
Lviv, Ukraine
Odessa, Ukraine
Minsk, Belarus
Brest, Belarus
Gomel, Belarus
Grodno, Belarus
Mogiliev, Belarus
Vitebsk, Belarus
Samara, Russia
Volgograd, Russia
Vladivostok, Russia
Moscow, Russia
Ekaterinburg, Russia
Nizhny Novgorod, Russia
Novosibirsk, Russia
St. Petersburg, Russia

**U.S. Department of State
Designated Sponsor for the
Exchange Vistor Program**
College and university students
Professor and research scholar
Specialist
Trainees

American Cultural Exchange (ACE)

200 West Mercer Street
Suite 504
Seattle, WA 98119

Tel.: 206/217-9644
Fax: 206/217-9643
Website: www.cultural .org
E-mail: ace@cultural.org

General Inquiries:
Receptionist
206/217-9644,
ace@cultural.org

Chief Executive Officer:
David Woodward,
President
206/217-9644,
dbw@cultural.org

Statement:
American Cultural Exchange (ACE) is committed to advancing international education through a broad range of programs and services. It supports international activities through the development of communication skills, technical training, and appreciation of cultural diversity. This commitment stems from a belief that increased global understanding leads to a better world.

Profile:
Nonprofit founded in 1973. ACE has 180 U.S. staff and 16 overseas staff. ACE provides a membership program. Seventy-five overseas volunteers contribute to ACE's mission.

Geographic Focus:
Worldwide

Exchange Activities:
ACE is involved in the following exchange areas: Homestay, Language Study, Professional/Business, Short-Term Visitors, Students/Educators, Training. ACE provides exchange-related facilitative or support services. It administers exchange programs for the following academic levels: Graduate Students, K-12, Teachers, Undergraduate Students.

Financial Assistance:
A variety of scholarships may be available to qualified applicants.

Exchange Programs Include:
A.C.E. Junior Institute
    Chris McCall, Associate Director
    of Short-Term Programs
    206/217-9644

A.C.E. Language Institutes
    June Sohn,
    Enrollment Services Coordinator
    206/217-9644

International Training
    and Development
    Chris Gilman, Vice President for
    Marketing and Development
    206/217-9644

Technical Training Programs
    Chris Gilman, Vice President
    for Marketing and Development
    206/217-9644

Exchange Related Facilitative or
Support Services Include:
Admissions/Placement Service
    June Sohn,
    Enrollment Services Coordinator
    206/217-9644

Community Development/Organization
    Madeleine Pohl, Director
    206/217-9644

Additional Offices:
Bend, OR
Bozeman, MT
Chicago, IL
Mt. Vernon, WA
Seattle, WA
Tacoma, WA

Overseas Offices:
Adelaide, Australia
Tokyo, Japan

American Institute for Foreign Study

9 West Broad Street, 7th Floor
Stamford, CT 06902-3788

Tel.: 203/399-5000
Fax: 203/399-5590
Website: http://www.aifs.com
E-mail: bgertz@aifs.com

General Inquiries:
William Gertz,
Executive VP
203/399-5007,
bgertz@aifs.com

Chief Executive Officer:
Robert J. Brennan,
President & CEO

Statement:
The mission of AIFS is to provide
the highest quality educational and
cultural exchange programs to
enrich the lives of people throughout the world.

Profile:
Nonprofit founded in 1964.

Geographic Focus:
Worldwide

Exchange Activities:
AIFS is involved in the following
exchange areas: Homestay, Work
Exchanges, Au Pair. It adminis-
ters exchange programs for the
following academic levels:
Students and Teachers K-12,
Undergraduate Students.

Financial Assistance:
AIFS does not provide financial
assistance.

Exchange Programs Include:
Au Pair in America
    Ruth Ferry, Vice President
    203/399-5025
    rferry@aifs.com

Camp America/Resort America
    Dennis Regan, Sr. Vice President
    203/399-5107
    dregan@aifs.com

College Study Abroad
    Robert Cristadoro, Sr. Vice President
    203/399-5093
    bcristadoro@aifs.com

Summer Institute for the Gifted
    Dr. Philip Zipse, President
    973/334-6991
    pzipse@cgp-.com

American Council for
International Studies
    Peter Jones, President
    617/236-2051
    peter_jones@acis.com

**U.S. Department of State
Designated Sponsor for the
Exchange Vistor Program**
Au pairs
Camp counselors
Secondary school students
Summer work/travel

American Institute for Foreign Study Foundation (AIFS Foundation)

1920 N Street, NW
Suite 300
Washington, DC 20036

Tel.: 202/452-4848
Fax: 202/293-4827
Website: www.aifsfoundation.org
E-mail: aya.info@aifs.org

Secondary Address:
9 West Broad Street
Stamford, CT 06902

General Inquiries:
R.T. Curran,
Executive Director
202/452-4848

Chief Executive Officer:
R.T. Curran,
Executive Director

Statement:
The American Institute For Foreign Study Foundation helps young people from many nations and diverse cultures understand each other better. It seeks to fulfill its mission by organizing high quality educational exchange programs at affordable prices which enable young people to live and study abroad; emphasizing people to people contact through the maximum possible use of homestay programs; developing cooperative programs between organizations both public and private who share its goals; and providing grants to organizations supporting its goals.

Profile:
Nonprofit founded in 1964 with the assistance of the late Senator Robert Kennedy. AIFS Foundation provides a membership program. The AIFS Foundation and its program office, Academic Year in America (AYA) focus on high school study abroad programs for youngsters in the United States and overseas. The Foundation sponsors college study abroad programs, workshops, seminars, and special international relations programs through the *Tony Cook* Grants to U.S. institutions.

Geographic Focus:
Worldwide

Exchange Activities:
AIFS Foundation is involved in the following exchange areas: Homestay, Students/Educators. AIFS Foundation provides exchange-related facilitative or support services. It administers exchange programs for the following academic levels: K-12, Undergraduate Students.

Financial Assistance:
Grants range from $500 - $2,500 depending on the program. The foundation also provides scholarships for gifted young people from Grade 4 through Grade 11 and has special undergraduate scholarships for American students to study in St. Petersburg, Russia; Krakow, Poland; and an array of countries in other parts of the world. The *Tony Cook* awards are made annually on the basis of applications from prospective grantees.

Exchange Programs Include:
Academic Year in America
    Suzi Power-Morris, Program
    Director AYA/AIFS Foundation
    203/399-5098

Academic Year in Germany
    Michele Burnham
    203/625-0677

Exchange Related Facilitative or Support Services Include:
Conference/Meetings/Workshops

Grants/Scholarships to Individuals

Grants to Institutions/Organizations
    Tony Cook, Grants
    Kim Martin, Director of Marketing
    203/625-0677

Additional Offices:
Greenwich, CT

U.S. Department of State Designated Sponsor for the Exchange Vistor Program
Short-term scholars
College and university students
Secondary school students

Alliance
MEMBER

American Intercultural Student Exchange, Inc. (AISE)

7720 Hershel Avenue
La Jolla, CA 92037

Tel.: 858/459-9761
Fax: 858/459-5301
Website: http://www.aise.com
E-mail: mail@aise.com

General Inquiries:
Kevin Donaker-Ring,
Executive Director
619/459-9761,
mail@aise.com

Chief Executive Officer:
Anne Ring,
President

Statement:
American Intercultural Student Exchange, Inc. (AISE) was founded in the belief that international student exchange makes a vital contribution to human understanding by providing students, parents, and host families the opportunity to deepen their comprehension and respect for other cultures.

Profile:
Nonprofit founded in 1981. AISE has 26 U.S. staff. Seven hundred U.S. volunteers contribute to AISE's mission.

Geographic Focus:
Worldwide

Exchange Activities:
AISE is involved in the following exchange areas: Homestay, Short-Term Visitors, Students/Educators. AISE provides exchange-related facilitative or support services. It administers exchange programs for the following academic levels: K-12.

Financial Assistance:
AISE offers the Xernona Clayton Minority Scholarship program through the American Student Division.

Publications:
AISE American Voice

Exchange Programs Include:
School Year or Semester to Europe and Australia
    Kathy Cohrs,
    American Student Director
937/427-3858

School Year Program in America
    Kevin Donaker-Ring,
    Executive Director
    619/459-9761

Summer Abroad Program
    Kathy Cohrs,
    American Summer Student Director
    817/467-4619

U.S. Department of State Designated Sponsor for the Exchange Vistor Program
Secondary school students
Intern

American International Youth Student Exchange Program (AIYSEP)

200 Round Hill Road
Tiburon, CA 94920

Tel.: 800/347-7575
Fax: 415/499-5651
E-mail: aiysep@aol.com

Secondary Address:
4340 Redwood Highway
Suite 144
San Rafael, CA 94903

General Inquiries:
Nelda H. Forsman,
Assistant Executive Director
415/499-7669,
aiysep@aol.com

Chief Executive Officer:
Francella T. Hall,
Executive Director

Statement:
The American International Youth
Student Exchange Program (AIY-
SEP) is a nonprofit, high school
exchange program which places
foreign students in the United
States and American students in
foreign countries.

Profile:
Nonprofit founded in 1981. AIY-
SEP has five U.S. staff and five
overseas staff. Two hundred U.S.
volunteers and 100 overseas volunteers contribute to AIYSEP's mission.

Geographic Focus:
Worldwide

Exchange Activities:
AIYSEP is involved in the following
exchange areas: Arts/Cultural,
Community/Citizen, Homestay,
Language Study. AIYSEP provides
exchange-related facilitative or support services. It administers
exchange programs for the following academic levels: K-12.

Financial Assistance:
AIYSEP provides scholarships/fel-
lowships or financial assistance to
participants.

Exchange Programs Include:
AIYSEP High School Exchange

**Exchange Related Facilitative or
Support Services Include:**
Admissions/Placement Service
    Nelda Forsman,
    Assistant Executive Director

Conference/Meetings/Workshops
    Interviews, Pre-Departure,
    and Arrival Orientations

Grants/Scholarships to Individuals
    AIYSEP Grants and Scholarships
    Francella Hall, Executive Director
    aiysep@aol.com

**U.S. Department of State
Designated Sponsor for the
Exchange Vistor Program**
Secondary school students

American-Scandinavian Foundation (ASF)

58 Park Avenue
New York, NY 10016

Tel.: 212/879-9779
Fax: 212/686-2115
Website: http://www.amscan.org
E-mail: asf@amscan.org

General Inquiries:
Lynn Carter,
Executive Vice President
212/879-9779,
carter@amscan.org

Chief Executive Officer:
Edward P. Gallagher,
President

Statement:
The American-Scandinavian Foundation (ASF) is a publicly supported, nonprofit organization that promotes international understanding through educational and cultural exchange between the United States and Denmark, Finland, Iceland, Norway, and Sweden. Established in 1910, ASF carries on an extensive program of fellowships, grants, trainee placement, publishing, membership offerings, and cultural activities. More than 24,000 Scandinavians and Americans have participated in ASF exchange programs.

Profile:
Nonprofit founded in 1910. ASF has 14 U.S. staff. ASF provides a membership program and has 4,000 individual members.

Geographic Focus:
Western Europe (Denmark, Finland, Iceland, Norway, Sweden)

Exchange Activities:
ASF is involved in the following exchange areas: Arts/Cultural, Training. ASF provides exchange-related facilitative or support services.

Financial Assistance:
ASF conducts an annual award competition offering funding for post-graduate study or research from the United States to Scandinavia or Scandinavia to the United States.

Publications:
Annual Report
Scandinavian Review
Scan Newsletter
Study in Scandinavia

Exchange Programs Include:
Awards Program
 Dr. Ellen McKey,
 Program Administrator
 212/879-9779,
 mckey@amscan.org

Training Program
 Jean Prahl,
 Director of Training
 212/879-9779,
 training@amscan.org

Exchange Related Facilitative or Support Services Include:
Grants/Scholarships to Individuals
 Dr. Ellen McKey,
 Program Administrator
 212/879-9779,
 mckey@amscan.or

Grants to Institutions/Organizations
 Dr. Ellen McKey

Membership Services
 Dr. Ann Sass, Director of
 Programs and Services
 212/879-9779

Alliance MEMBER

American Secondary Schools for International Students and Teachers (ASSIST)

P.O. Box 969
Suite 2B, 133 Mountain Road
Suffield, CT 06078

Tel.: 860/668-5706
Fax: 860/668-5726
E-mail: assist@assist-inc.org

General Inquiries:
Robert A. Stanley, Jr.,
President

Chief Executive Officer:
Robert A. Stanley, Jr.,
President

Statement:
American Secondary Schools for International Students and Teachers (ASSIST) seeks to foster direct person-to-person contact between students and teachers in American schools and people of other cultures. Its mission is to provide participants with cross cultural experiences, friendships, skills, and understanding that will enable them to become effective and responsible contributors toward a more perfect world.

Profile:
Nonprofit founded in 1969. ASSIST has three U.S. staff and seven overseas staff.

Geographic Focus:
Central Asia (Azerbaijan), Eastern Europe (Albania, Bosnia-Herzegovia, Bulgaria, Croatia, Czech Republic, Hungary, Macedonia, Moldova, Romania, Slovakia), Oceania (Australia), Western Europe (Germany, Spain, Sweden)

Exchange Activities:
ASSIST provides exchange-related facilitative or support services. It administers exchange programs for the following academic levels: K-12.

Financial Assistance:
American schools participating in the ASSIST program provide scholarships, either full or partial, to ASSIST students from abroad. Overseas schools participating in the ASSIST program provide scholarships to American ASSIST students.

Publications:
A High School Year at an Independent School in the United States of America

Exchange Related Facilitative or Support Services Include:
Grants/Scholarships to Individuals
Robert A. Stanley, Jr.,
President
860/668-5706

Overseas Offices:
Cologne, Germany
Barcelona, Spain
Stockholm, Sweden
Melbourne, Australia

U.S. Department of State Designated Sponsor for the Exchange Vistor Program
Secondary school student

Alliance
MEMBER

American Youth Work Center (AYWC)

1200 17th Street, NW
Fourth Floor
Washington, DC 20036

Tel.: 202/785-0764
Fax: 202/728-0657
Website: www.youthtoday.org
E-mail: info@youthtoday.org

General Inquiries:
Melissa Kendrick,
Deputy Director

Chief Executive Officer:
William W. Treanor,
Executive Director

Statement:
American Youth Work Center (AYWC) was established to provide opportunities for practical training in the fields of counseling and social services directly related to youth in the interest of promoting international understanding.

Profile:
Nonprofit founded in 1984. AYWC has seven U.S. staff and three overseas staff. AYWC provides a membership program and has 21 institutional members.

Geographic Focus:
Caribbean (Jamaica), Western Europe (United Kingdom)

Exchange Activities:
AYWC is involved in the following exchange areas: Short-Term Visitors, Training. AYWC provides exchange-related facilitative or support services.

Publications:
Youth Today - (Newspaper)

North American Directory of Programs for Runaways

Homeless, Youths and Missing Children

Kids & Guns: A Child Safety Scandal

American Directory of Youth Work Educators & Trainers

Barriers to Developing Comprehensive & Effective Youth Services

Exchange Programs Include:
Practical Training Exchange Program for Social and Human Service Professionals
   Erica Frankel,
   International Program Officer

Exchange Related Facilitative or Support Services Include:
Conference/Meetings/Workshops

International Visitor Support

Consultations/Advisory Services

Amity Institute

10671 Roselle Street
Suite 100
San Diego, CA 92121

Tel.: 858/455-6364
Fax: 858/455-6597
Website: http://www.amity.org
E-mail: mail@amity.org

General Inquiries:
Trudy Hermann,
Assistant Director
858/455-6364,
mail@amity.org

Chief Executive Officer:
Trudy Hermann,
Interim Director

Statement:
Amity Institute, founded in 1962, is a nonprofit international teaching exchange organization at the intern and professional level. Through these exchanges, Amity Institute promotes international understanding and friendship, as well as professional and cross-cultural development opportunities for current and future educators. The programs of Amity Institute bring the world into the classroom through direct personal contact with educators from other cultures.

Profile:
Amity Institute has ten U.S. staff members and over 110 volunteer representatives in 30 countries. These representatives include members of Fulbright Commissions, Binational Centers, Overseas Advising Center, Universities and Amity alumni. Nearly 400 teachers and intern teachers participated in exchange in the 2000-2001 school year. Amity involves host schools in over 40

U.S. states and eight foreign countries. Close to 6,000 participants have been a part of Amity Institute since its inception 40 years ago.

Geographic Focus:
Africa (Cameroon, Ivory Coast, Morocco, Senegal, Togo, Tunisia), Asia (Japan), Caribbean (Martinique, Guadeloupe, Dominican Republic), Central America (Costa Rica), Newly Independent States (Russia), South America (Argentina, Brazil, Bolivia, Colombia, Chile, Mexico, Paraguay, Peru, Uruguay, Venezuela), Western Europe (Austria, Belgium, France, Germany, Spain, Switzerland)

Exchange Activities:
Amity is involved in the following exchange areas: Arts/Cultural, Homestay, Language Study, Students/Educators, Training, Work Exchanges. Amity provides exchange-related facilitative or support services. It administers exchange programs for the following academic levels: Faculty, Graduate Students, Teachers, Undergraduate Students.

Financial Assistance:
Financial assistance for program participants is provided on a limited basis according to need.

Publications:
Amity Newsletter
Amity Bulletin
Handbook for Host Schools
Handbook for Host Families
Handbook for Amity Scholars
Handbook for Exchange Teachers

Exchange Programs Include:
Amity Exchange Teacher Program

Amity Intern Teacher Program

Amity Volunteer Teachers Abroad
 Karen Sullivan, Program Counselor
 858/455-6364, avta@amity.org

U.S. Department of State Designated Sponsor for the Exchange Vistor Program
College and university students
Teachers
Specialists

Alliance MEMBER

Amizade, Ltd.

**367 South Graham Street
Pittsburgh, PA 15232**

Tel.: 888/973-4443
Fax: 412/648-1492
Website: http://amizade.org
E-mail: volunteer@amizade.org

Chief Executive Officer:
Michael Sandy,
Executive Director
888/973-4443

General Inquiries:
Michael Sandy,
Executive Director
888/973-4443

Statement:
Amizade is a nonprofit organization dedicated to promoting volunteerism, providing community service, encouraging collaboration, and improving cultural awareness in locations throughout the world. Amizade runs short-term volunteer programs which provide volunteers with the opportunity to participate firsthand in the culture in which they are working. Past projects have included building a school for street children in the Brazilian Amazon, building a health clinic in the Bolivian Andes, and renovating an environmental education center in the Greater Yellowstone region. Program locations include Brazil, Bolivia, Australia, Nepal, Thailand, the Navajo Nations (USA), and the greater Yellowstone Region.

Profile:
Nonprofit founded in 1994. Amizade has three U.S. staff and two overseas staff.

Geographic Focus:
North America (Navajo Nation, Greater Yellowstone Region, United States), South America (Brazil, Bolivia), Asia (Nepal, Thailand), Oceania (Australia)

Exchange Activities:
Amizade is involved in the following exchange areas: Alternative Break, Community/Citizen, Senior Citizens, Short-Term Visitors, Students/Educators, Homestay. Amizade provides exchange-related facilitative or support services.

Financial Assistance:
Amizade does not provide financial assistance.

Exchange Programs Include:
Volunteer in the Bolivian Andes
    volunteer@amizade.org

Volunteer in the Brazilian Amazon
    volunteer@amizade.org

Volunteer in the United States
    volunteer@amizade.org

Volunteer in Australia
    volunteer@amizade.org

Volunteer in Nepal
    volunteer@amizade.org

Greater Yellowstone Region

**Exchange Related Facilitative or
Support Services Include:**
Conference/Meetings/Workshops
    Fundraising for Short-Term
    Volunteer Programs/Organizing
    Short-Term International Programs
    Daniel Weiss

ASA International (ASAI)

7119 Church Avenue
Pittsburgh, PA 15202

Tel.: 412/761-5190
Fax: 412/734-0903
Website: www.asainternational.com
E-mail: asassc@aol.com

General Inquiries:
Penelope Cooper,
Vice President
412/761-5190,
asassc@aol.com

Chief Executive Officer:
Samuel N. Gibson,
President

Statement:
ASA International's mission is to enable high school students to attend schools in a country other than their own to improve language skills; gain a new understanding of other cultures; and enrich the life and intercultural understanding of the schools they attend and families with which they live.

Profile:
Nonprofit founded in 1996. ASAI has 11 U.S. staff. Eighty-five U.S. volunteers contribute to ASAI's mission.

Geographic Focus:
Worldwide

Exchange Activities:
ASAI is involved in the following exchange areas: Homestay, Short-Term Visitors, Students/Educators. ASAI provides exchange-related facilitative or support services. It administers exchange programs for the following academic levels: K-12.

Financial Assistance:
ASAI does not provide financial assistance.

Publications:
Bringing World Understanding To Your Door, Grant Miller, Vice-President

Exchange Programs Include:
ASA International High School Program

Exchange Related Facilitative or Support Services Include:
Admissions/Placement Service
   Penelope Cooper,
   Director of Admissions
   412/761-5190, asassc@aol.com

U.S. Department of State Designated Sponsor for the Exchange Vistor Program
Secondary school students

The Asia Foundation

465 California Street
14th Floor
San Francisco, CA 94104

Tel.: 415/982-4640
Fax: 415/392-8863
Website: www.asiafoundation.org
E-mail: info@asiafound.org

Chief Executive Officer:
William P. Fuller,
President

Statement:
The Asia Foundation is a private, nonprofit, non-governmental organization working to advance the mutual interests of the United States and the Asia-Pacific region. It is funded by contributions from corporations, foundations, individuals, governmental organizations in the United States and Asia, and an annual appropriation from the U.S. Congress. Through its programs, The Asia Foundation collaborates with partners from the public and private sectors to build leadership, improve policies and regulation, and strengthen institutions to foster greater openness and shared prosperity in the Asia-Pacific region. International exchanges serve The Asia Foundation's broader institutional and leadership development goals in the Asia-Pacific region. Professional visits abroad are part of larger foundation-funded in-country projects.

Profile:
Nonprofit founded in 1954. The Asia Foundation has 109 U.S. Staff and 194 overseas staff.

Geographic Focus:
Asia

Exchange Activities:
The Asia Foundation is involved in the following exchange areas: Professional/Business, Training. The Asia Foundation provides exchange-related facilitative or support services.

Financial Assistance:
Funding is provided to officials and staff members of Asian Pacific institutions supported by The Asia Foundation.

Publications:
Annual Report

Project Lists

Pacific Economic Outlook

Working Paper Series

Asian Perspectives Series

Exchange Programs Include:
Asian-American Exchange

Luce Scholars

Washington, DC Program

Additional Offices:
Washington, DC

Overseas Offices:
Islamabad, Pakistan
Hong Kong, China
Taipei, Taiwan
Bangkok, Thailand
Dhaka, Bangladesh
Jakarta, Indonesia
Seoul, Korea
Kathmandu, Nepal
Phnom Penh, Cambodia
Colombo, Sri Lanka
Tokyo, Japan
Ulanbaatar, Mongolia
Manila, Philippines

Asian Cultural Council (ACC)

437 Madison Avenue
37th Floor
New York, NY 10022-7001

Tel.: 212/812-4300
Fax: 212/812-4299
Web: www.asianculturalcouncil.org
E-mail: acc@accny.org

General Inquiries:
Ralph Samuelson,
Director
212/812-4300,
acc@accny.org

Chief Executive Officer:
Richard S. Lanier,
President

Statement:
The Asian Cultural Council (ACC)
awards fellowships to Asian artists
and specialists in the visual and
performing arts for research,
study, travel, and creative pursuits
in the United States, and to
American artists pursuing similar
activities in Asia.

Profile:
Nonprofit founded in 1963. ACC
has nine U.S. staff and four overseas staff.

Geographic Focus:
Asia

Exchange Activities:
ACC is involved in the following
exchange areas: Arts/Cultural.
ACC provides exchange-related
facilitative or support services. It
administers exchange programs for
the following academic levels:
Graduate Students.

Financial Assistance:
ACC provides limited financial
assistance.

Publications:
Annual Report

Exchange Programs Include:
ACC Fellowship Program

ACC Humanities Program

Asian Art and Religion Program

Japan-U.S. Arts Program

ACC Residency Program in Asia

Overseas Offices:
Hong Kong, China
Taipei, Taiwan
Tokyo, Japan

U.S. Department of State
Designated Sponsor for the
Exchange Vistor Program
Professors and research scholars
Short-term scholars

ASPECT Foundation

350 Sansome Street
Suite 740
San Francisco, CA 94104

Tel.: 415/228-8050
Fax: 415/228-8051
Website: www.aspectfoundation.org
E-mail: exchange@aspectworld.com

General Inquiries:
Vivian Fearen,
Director of Operations and
Public Relations
415/228-8050,
vivian.fearen@aspectworld.com

Chief Executive Officer:
Joan Boru,
Executive Director

Statement:
ASPECT Foundation was established to promote cross-cultural understanding between nations through international educational youth exchange programs in the United States. ASPECT also offers exchange programs for American teenagers in Japan, Uruguay, England, Ireland, Spain, France, and Germany.

Profile:
Nonprofit founded in 1982. Three hundred fifty U.S. volunteers contribute to ASPECT's mission.

Geographic Focus:
Asia (Japan, Thailand, Hong Kong), Eastern Europe (Hungary, Czech Republic, Poland, Slovakia), North America (United States, Mexico), South America (Brazil, Colombia, Venezuela, Uruguay), Western Europe

Exchange Activities:
ASPECT is involved in the following exchange areas: Homestay, Students/Educators. ASPECT provides exchange-related facilitative or support services. It administers exchange programs for the following academic levels: K-12, Undergraduate Students.

Financial Assistance:
ASPECT does not provide financial assistance.

Publications:
The Melting Pot
    (student and host newsletter)

The Spectrum
    (coordinator newsletter)

Exchange Programs Include:
Community College Program
    415/228-8050,
    exchange@aspectworld.com

High School Program
    415/228-8050,
    exchange@aspectworld.com

Outbound Program
    415/228-8050,
    exchange@aspectworld.com

Overseas Offices:
The Hague, Netherlands
Tokyo, Japan
Bogota, Columbia
Oslo, Norway
Weisbaden, Germany
Zurich, Switzerland
Stockholm, Sweden
Copenhagen, Denmark

U.S. Department of State Designated Sponsor for the Exchange Vistor Program
Secondary school students
Intern

ASSE International Student Exchange Programs (ASSE)

228 North Coast Highway
Laguna Beach, CA 92651

Tel.: 949/494-4100
Fax: 949/497-8704
Website: http://www.asse.com

General Inquiries:
Susan Hayes,
Executive Director
949/494-4100

Chief Executive Officer:
William Gustafson,
President

Statement:
ASSE International Student Exchange Programs (ASSE) aims to contribute to international understanding by establishing programs to improve the knowledge of foreign students of North American culture and language and to improve the knowledge of North American students of foreign cultures and languages through participation in family, school, and community life. Through the U.S. Department of State, ASSE has participated in the Congress-Bundestag Youth Exchange program and the Freedom Support Act program.

Profile:
Nonprofit founded in 1976. ASSE has 22 U.S. staff and four overseas staff. Nine hundred fifty U.S. volunteers and 300 overseas volunteers contribute to ASSE's mission.

Geographic Focus:
Africa (South Africa), Asia (Japan, Thailand, China, Taiwan), Eastern Europe (Czech Republic, Slovak Republic, Yugoslavia, Poland), Newly Independent States, North America (United States, Canada, Mexico), Oceania (Australia, New Zealand), South America (Brazil), Western Europe (Denmark, Finland, France, Germany, Italy, Netherlands, Norway, Portugal, Spain, Sweden, Switzerland, Turkey, United Kingdom)

Exchange Activities:
ASSE is involved in the following exchange areas: Homestay, Language Study, Students/Educators. ASSE provides exchange-related facilitative or support services. It administers exchange programs for the following academic levels: K-12, Undergraduate Students.

Financial Assistance:
Full academic year scholarships available.

Publications:
ASSE International News

Exchange Programs Include:
Academic Year/Semester
Susan Hayes, Executive Director
949/494-4100

Congress-Bundestag
Youth Exchange Program
Elizabeth Cecchetti
949/494-4100

FLEX/Freedom Support Act
Jodi Kiefer, Director
404/531-4044

Year and Summer Programs Abroad
Amy Gerety,
Outbound Administrator
949/494-4100

Additional Offices:
Alexandria, VA
Atlanta, GA
Minneapolis, MN
Seattle, WA

Overseas Offices:
Auckland, New Zealand
Montreal, Canada
Stockholm, Sweden

U.S. Department of State
Designated Sponsor for the
Exchange Vistor Program
Secondary school students
Summer work/travel

Association for International Practical Training (AIPT)

10400 Little Patuxent Parkway,
Suite 250
Columbia, MD 21044-3519

Tel.: 410/997-2200
Fax: 410/992-3924
Website: http://www.aipt.org
E-mail: aipt@aipt.org

General Inquiries:
Receptionist
410/997-2200

Chief Executive Officer:
Elizabeth Chazottes,
Executive Director and CEO

Statement:
The Association for International Practical Training (AIPT) is a non-profit international educational exchange organization that sponsors and facilitates on-the-job practical training exchanges for students and professionals between the United States and more than 70 other countries. AIPT is also the U.S. affiliate of the International Association for the Exchange of Students for Technical Experience (IAESTE), which provides international training opportunities for university students. AIPT's online placement service—PINPOINT— matches individuals seeking training opportunities with appropriate training positions in their field of education or experience. In addition, AIPT offers short-term experiential learning programs for professionals and students from many fields, and countries. AIPT's mission is to be a leader in international human resource development by conducting high quality international experiential training exchanges that enhance the ability of individual participants, employers, and host organizations to meet the opportunities and challenges of the global economy.

Profile:
Nonprofit founded in 1950. AIPT has 49 U.S. staff.

Geographic Focus:
Worldwide

Exchange Activities:
AIPT is involved in the following exchange areas: Professional/Business, Short-Term Visitors, Students/Educators, Training, Work Exchanges. AIPT provides exchange-related facilitative or support services. It administers exchange programs for the following academic levels: Graduate Students, Undergraduate Students.

Financial Assistance:
AIPT/IAESTE United States offers three Robert M. Sprinkle $1,000 scholarships for students applying to the program each year.

Publications:
Practically Speaking
AIPT Annual Report
Brochures

Exchange Programs Include:
Career Development Program
Renatte English, Director
410/997-2200, renglish@aipt.org

IAESTE United States
Jeff Lange, Director
410/997-3069, jlange@aipt.org

Americans Abroad Programs
Ann Schodde, Associate Director
515/266-5885, aschodde@aipt.org

Exchange Related Facilitative or Support Services Include:
Conference/Meetings/Workshops
Versatile J-1 Visa Seminar
Dan Ewert, Associate Director
410/997-2200, dewert@aipt.org

U.S. Department of State Designated Sponsor for the Exchange Vistor Program
Trainees

Alliance MEMBER

Association of International Education Administrators (AIEA)

411 Capen Hall
Box 601604
State University at Buffalo
Buffalo, NY 14260-1604

Tel.: 716/645-2368
Fax: 716/645-2528
Website: http://www.aieaworld.org
E-mail: rutenber@acsu.buffalo.edu

Secondary Address:
AIEA President:
Dr. JoAnn McCarthy
Dean, International Affairs
University of South Florida
4202 E. Fowler Ave., CPR 107
Tampa, FL 33620

General Inquiries:
Timothy J. Rutenber,
Director, AIEA Secretariat
716/645-2368,
rutenber@acsu.buffalo.edu

Chief Executive Officer:
Dr. JoAnn McCarthy,
President

Statement:
The Association of International
Education Administrators (AIEA) is
composed of principal international
education administrators on college
and university campuses in the
United States and abroad. It is a
unique professional association
dedicated to enhancing opportunities for key campus-based international administrators to join forces,
exchange ideas, share institutional
strategies, and provide an effective
voice on matters of public policy.

Profile:
Nonprofit founded in 1982. AIEA
provides a membership program
and has 317 institutional members.
Leadership (with contact information) changes annually when a new
president is elected.

Geographic Focus:
Worldwide

Exchange Activities:
AIEA member institutions are
involved in the following exchange
areas: Student/Educators. AIEA
member institutions provide
exchange-related facilitative or support services. They administer
exchange programs for the following
academic levels: Faculty, Graduate
Students, Undergraduate Students.

Financial Assistance:
AIEA does not provide financial
assistance.

Publications:
*Journal at Studies in International
Education* (journal published
twice a year)

AIEA Membership Directory

*A Research Agenda for the
Internationalization of Higher
Education in the United States*

*Bridges to the Future: Strategies for
Internationalizing Higher
Education*

*Guidelines for International
Education at U.S. Colleges and
Universities*

**Exchange Related Facilitative or
Support Services Include:**
Membership Services

Public Policy

Conference/Meetings/Workshops
Annual conference;
regional workshops
Timothy Rutenber, Director
716/645-2368,
rutenber@acsu.buffalo.edu

Grants/Scholarships to Individuals
AIEA Research Grant Program

Association of Jesuit Colleges and Universities (AJCU)

One Dupont Circle, NW
Suite 405
Washington, DC 20036-1136

Tel.: 202/862-9893
Fax: 202/862-8523
Website: http://www.ajcunet.edu
E-mail: blkrobe@aol.com

General Inquiries:
Melissa C. DiLeonardo,
Director of Communications
202/862-9893,
mdileonardo@ajcunet.edu

Chief Executive Officer:
Rev. Charles Currie, S.J.,
President

Statement:
The Association of Jesuit Colleges and Universities was founded with a defined mission of supporting and promoting Jesuit higher education by facilitating cooperative efforts among and providing services to its 28 member institutions, providing a forum for the exchange of experience and information, and representing the work of Jesuit higher education at the national and international levels.

Profile:
Nonprofit founded in 1970. AJCU has five U.S. staff.

Geographic Focus:
Worldwide

Exchange Activities:
AJCU provides exchange-related facilitative or support services.

Financial Assistance:
AJCU does not provide financial assistance.

Publications:
AJCU Connections

Resource Book for International Education (Jesuit Colleges and Universities)

Degrees Available (Jesuit Colleges)

AJCU/JSEA Directory

Exchange Related Facilitative or Support Services Include:
Conference/Meetings/Workshops

Membership Services

Association of Professional Schools of International Affairs (APSIA)

420 W 118th Street, Suite 1415
New York, NY 10027

Tel.: 212/854-3952
Fax: 212/864-4847
Website: http://www.apsia.org
E-mail: apsia@erols.com

General Inquiries:
Receptionist
apsia@erols.com

Chief Executive Officer:
Marcus J. Grundahl,
Director

Statement:
The Association of Professional Schools of International Affairs (APSIA) is an association of 23 graduate schools of international affairs and 14 affiliated institutions based worldwide. Learning at an APSIA school involves the application of theory to practical issues and stresses public service in international careers. Education at an APSIA school prepares graduates for careers in public sector, private enterprise, and nonprofit organizations. The association serves as a source of information on professional international affairs education, represents the interest of professional international affairs education globally through admissions and career services information, sharing best practices, and promoting international affairs as a brand of education.

Profile:
Nonprofit founded in 1989. APSIA has two U.S. staff. APSIA provides a membership program and has 37 institutional members.

Geographic Focus:
Worldwide

Exchange Activities:
APSIA is involved in the following exchange areas: Students/Educators. APSIA provides exchange-related facilitative or support services. It administers exchange programs for the following academic levels: Faculty, Graduate Students.

Financial Assistance:
APSIA does not provide financial assistance.

Exchange Related Facilitative or Support Services Include:
Admissions/Placement Service

Membership Services

APSIA Secretariat

Employer Outreach

AuPair Care

2226 Bush Street
San Francisco, CA 94115

Tel.: 415/434-8788
Fax: 415/674-5211
Website: www.aupaircare.com
E-mail: info@aupaircare.com

General Inquiries:
Information Center
1-800-4AU-PAIR

Chief Executive Officer:
John F. Wilhelm,
President

Statement:
AuPairCare provides American families with dependable, affordable child care solutions by carefully recruiting, screening and placing qualified young adults who wish to work as an au pair in the United States. The program provides young women and men with the opportunity to spend a memorable year in the U.S.A. as an au pair.

Profile:
AuPairCare is designated by the U.S. Department of State to sponsor young adults who want to work with children and satisfy their curiosity about the United States while living as a member of an American family. Each year approximately 1,300 au pairs provide up to 45 hours per week of personalized child care and light housekeeping related to child care. Au pairs receive a wide range of benefits during the program, including: a 12 month J-1 visa, round-trip international air fare, a weekly stipend, two weeks paid vacation, a $500 educational allowance, medical insurance, and full room and board. Au pairs receive a three-day orientation training program in New York City prior to arrival with their host family. AuPairCare maintains an extensive staff network to help au pairs and host families with adjustment.

Geographic Focus:
Worldwide

Exchange Activities:
AuPairCare is involved in the following exchange areas: Au Pair Child Care Programs. AuPairCare administers exchange programs for the following academic levels: Au Pairs ages 18-26. Other World Study Group Companies include AYUSA (Academic Year and Semester programs and Study Abroad programs for high school students), Intrax (English schools, group and individual homestay programs, and summer work/travel programs), and Passages Educational Tours (group travel).

Financial Assistance:
AuPairCare does not provide financial assistance.

Exchange Programs Include:
AuPairCare programs
   Heidi Woehl,
   Program Manager
   hwoehl@aupaircare.com

Additional Offices:
San Jose, CA
Grand Junction, MI
Chaska, MN

Overseas Offices:
Berlin, Germany
Budapest, Hungary
Tokyo, Japan

U.S. Department of State Designated Sponsor for the Exchange Vistor Program
Au pairs

AYUSA International (AYUSA)

2226 Bush Street
San Francisco, CA 94115

Tel.: 415/434-1212
Fax: 415/674-5223
Website: http://www.ayusa.org
E-mail: info@ayusa.org

General Inquiries:
Craig H. Brown,
Vice President
415/674-6510
cbrown@ayusa.org

Chief Executive Officer:
John F. Wilhelm,
President

Statement:
AYUSA International promotes understanding and friendship through global youth exchange. Exchange offers a unique, richly personal experience for students, volunteer families, and members of host high schools and local communities. Collectively, the AYUSA family reaches across interpersonal and international borders and celebrates worldwide community through the spirit, character and promise of youth.

Profile:
AYUSA International is a nonprofit high school exchange program which serves almost 1,900 students from over 50 countries. Host family placements are made throughout the U.S. through an extensive network of 650-strong field support staff. Over 100 students this year will study on the outbound Study Abroad Program.

Geographic Focus:
Worldwide

Exchange Activities:
AYUSA is involved in the following exchange areas: Academic Year and Semester Programs, Short-Term Homestays and Cultural Study Programs, Language Study, and Group Travel. AYUSA administers exchange programs for the following academic levels: High School Students and Educators. AYUSA is a World Study Group company. Other World Study Group Companies include AuPairCare (au pair childcare), Intrax (English schools, group and individual homestay programs, and summer work/travel programs), and Passages Educational Tours (group travel).

Financial Assistance:
AYUSA is a program sponsor for the following scholarship programs funded by the U.S. Department of State, Bureau of Educational and Cultural Affairs: Congress-Bundestag Youth Exchange (CB/YX), Future Leaders Exchange Program (FLEX); Serbian Youth Leadership Program (SYLP); and Brcko Academic Semester Program. Key Club and Kiwanis participants on AYUSA programs are eligible for special scholarships. AYUSA also has a growing scholarship fund for Study Abroad applicants made available through donations from corporations and foundations.

Publications:
AYUSA World Staff Newsletter
AYUSA Star Student Newsletter

Exchange Programs Include:
AYUSA Academic Year and
Semester in the USA
    Shelley Whelpton,
    Vice President Program Operations
    swhelpton@ayusa.org

AYUSA Study Abroad
    Mari Lockhard,
    Directory of Study Abroad,
    mlockhard@ayusa.org

AYUSA Youth Exchange in Alliance
with Kiwanis International
    Martin Vogt,
    Director of Development
    mvogt@ayusa.org

Additional Offices:
Glendale, AZ
Santa Rosa, CA
Elkhart, IN
Louisville, KY
Reeds Spring, MO
Lewisville, TX
Richland, WA

Overseas Offices:
Berlin, Germany
Budapest, Hungary
Tokyo, Japan

**U.S. Department of State
Designated Sponsor for the
Exchange Vistor Program**
Trainees
College and university students
Secondary school students
Au pairs
Intern

Better Exchange for Student Teenagers (BEST)

302 Imperial Drive
P.O. Box 689
Cloverdale, CA 95425

Tel.: 707/894-4949
Fax: 707/894-9098
E-mail: bestexchange@juno.com

General Inquiries:
Sandra Jo Decker
707/894-4949

Chief Executive Officer
Sandra Jo Decker

Statement:
Better Exchange for Student Teenagers (BEST) is a nonprofit, educational organization designated by the U.S. Department of State and dedicated to contributing to worldwide understanding and peace through a better knowledge of the culture, politics, and economics of different countries. BEST promotes student exchange to further friendship and understanding among the people of the world through exchange between families.

Profile:
Nonprofit founded in 1998. BEST provides a membership program and has one local chapter/affiliate. Six U.S. volunteers and two overseas volunteers contribute to BEST's mission.

Geographic Focus:
Asia (Japan, Vietnam), Eastern Europe (Poland), North America, South America (Brazil), Western Europe (Germany, Spain, France, Finland)

Exchange Activities:
BEST is involved in the following exchange areas: Community/Citizen, Language Study, Students/Educators. BEST provides exchange-related facilitative or support services. It administers exchange programs for the following academic levels: 9-12.

Financial Assistance:
Scholarships in the amount of $100 to $200 are available for groups.

Publications:
Semester Program (brochure)

Summer Language (ESL) Programs

Exchange Programs Include:
Semester Program

Summer ESL Program

Overseas Offices:
Düsseldorf, Germany
Helsinki, Finland
Madrid, Spain
Victoria, Brazil

British Universities
North American Club (BUNAC)

BUNAC USA, Inc.
P.O. Box 430
Southbury, CT 06488

Tel.: 800/462-8622
Fax: 203/264-0251
Website: http://www.bunac.org
E-mail: info@bunacusa.org

Chief Executive Officer:
Jim Buck,
General Manager

Statement:
BUNAC aims to provide the best
possible opportunities in international work and travel programs for
students and young people around
the world.

Profile:
Nonprofit founded in 1962.
BUNAC has ten U.S. staff and 70
overseas staff.

Geographic Focus:
Africa (South Africa, Ghana),
Western Europe (United Kingdom,
Ireland, Sweden, France), North
America (United States, Canada),
Oceania (Australia, New Zealand)

Exchange Activities:
BUNAC is involved in the following exchange areas: Training, Work
Exchanges. BUNAC administers
exchange programs for the following academic levels: Graduate
Students, Undergraduate Students.

Financial Assistance:
BUNAC offers United Kingdom to
United States Academic Top-Up
Awards.

Exchange Programs Include:
Summer Camp USA

Work America

Work in Britain

Work New Zealand

Work Australia

Overseas Offices:
London, United Kingdom
Edinburgh, United Kingdom
Auckland, New Zealand
Sydney, Australia
Melbourne, Australia
Warsaw, Poland

Camp Counselors USA-
Work Experience USA (CCUSA)

CCUSA

2330 Marinship Way, Suite 250
Sausalito, CA 94965

Tel.: 415/339-2728
Fax: 415/339-2744
Website: http://www.ccusa.com
E-mail: info@ccusa.com

General Inquiries:
415/339-2728,
info@ccusa.com

Chief Executive Officer:
William C. Harwood,
President

Statement:
CCUSA enables young people from around the globe to truly experience the world not as a tourist but as someone willing to share their culture while working, and living in the USA, Australia, New Zealand or Russia. We provide thorough screening of applicants, placement in jobs which match the personality, skills and interests of our applicants, and comprehensive training and supervision. Programs are designed to allow the participant to return home with skills and knowledge that can be shared to promote international exchange.

Profile:
Founded in 1986. CCUSA has 25 U.S. staff and 18 affiliates. Fifty overseas staff and more than 200 overseas volunteers contribute to CCUSA's mission.

Geographic Focus:
Africa (South Africa, Zambia, Botswana, Japan, Korea), Caribbean (Dominican Republic, Jamaica), Eastern Europe (Belarus, Croatia, Czech Republic, Hungary, Poland, Romania, Slovakia, Slovenia), Western Europe (Belgium, Denmark, Ireland, Spain, Finland, France, England, Scotland, Wales, Germany, Italy, Northern Ireland, Netherlands, Portugal, Sweden), Newly Independent States (Russia), North America (United States, Canada), Oceania (Australia, New Zealand, Fiji), South America (Argentina, Brazil, Peru, Colombia, Ecuador)

Exchange Activities:
CCUSA is involved in the following exchange areas: Professional/Business, Students/Educators, Training, Camp Counselors, Work Exchanges.

Financial Assistance:
Each of CCUSA's country directors recommends participants in need, who are then evaluated for full or partial scholarships.

Exchange Programs Include:
Camp Counselors USA

Work Experience USA

Work Experience Outbound

Work Experience Down Under

Practical Training USA

Exchange Related Facilitative or Support Services Include:
Admission/Placement Services
  Work Experience USA and
  Camp Counselors USA

Travel Services
  Work Experience Down Under

Practical Training USA

Overseas Offices:
Buenos Aires, Argentina
Sydney, Australia
Melbourne, Australia
Minsk, Belarus
Victoria, Brazil
Florianoplic, Brazil
Bogota, Colombia
Prague, Czech Republic
London, United Kingdom
Bad Driburg, Germany
Dublin, Ireland
Den Haag, Netherlands
Auckland, New Zealand
Warsaw, Poland
Poznan, Poland
Cluj, Romania
Moscow, Russia
Musselburgh, United Kingdom
Bratislava, Slovak Republic
Johannesburg, South Africa
Capetown, South Africa
Gotenburg, Sweden

U.S. Department of State Designated Sponsor for the Exchange Vistor Program
Trainees
Camp counselors
Summer work/travel
Intern

CDS International (CDS)

871 United Nations Plaza
15th Floor
New York, NY 10017-1814

Tel.: 212/497-3500
Fax: 212/497-3535
Website: http://www.cdsintl.org
E-mail: info@cdsintl.org

Chief Executive Officer:
Wolfgang Linz,
Executive Director

Statement:
CDS International's (CDS) mission is the advancement of international practical training opportunities that stimulate the exchange of knowledge and technological skills and contribute to the development of a highly-trained and interculturally-competent workforce. These experiences help strengthen global cooperation and understanding amongst individuals, businesses, organizations and communities. Each year, CDS serves over 2,000 young professionals and students from over 50 countries in a variety of work/study, internship and study tour programs.

Profile:
Nonprofit founded in 1968. CDS has over 20 U.S. staff.

Geographic Focus:
Asia (Japan, Singapore, Korea), North America (Canada, United States), South America (Argentina, Chile), Western Europe (Germany, Switzerland, Austria, France)

Exchange Activities:
CDS is involved in the following exchange areas: Work/study, practical training, language training, work exchange and internships. CDS provides exchange-related facilitative or support services.

Financial Assistance:
Financial assistance is offered through the Congress-Bundestag Youth Exchange for Young Professionals and the Robert Bosch Foundation Fellowship Program.

Publications:
CDSsense- (Tri-Annual Newsletter)

Exchange Programs Include:
Career Training Program-Incoming
Scott Curry,
Sr. Program Manager
212/497-3506,
scurry@cdsintl.org

Congress-Bundestag Youth
Exchange for Young Professionals
Rebecca Reagan-Delfino,
Program Director
212/497-3513,
rdelfino@cdsintl.org

Internships/Outgoing
Isabel Kowalk,
Program Officer
212/497-3520,
ikowalk@cdsintl.org

Robert Bosch Foundation Fellowship
Martin Black,
Program Director
212/497-3509,
mblack@cdsintl.org

Professional Development Program
Ute Schott,
Senior Program Manager
212/497-3514,
uschott@cdsintl.org

Programs for Canadian Co-op Students
Margaret Shonat,
Program Officer
212/497-3503,
mshonat@cdsintl.org

Additional Offices:
Los Angeles, CA

**U.S. Department of State
Designated Sponsor for the
Exchange Vistor Program**
Trainees
Intern

Alliance
MEMBER

CEC International Partners (CEC)

12 West 31st Street, Suite 400
New York, NY 10001

Tel.: 212/643-1985
Fax: 212/643-1996
Website: http://www.cecip.org
E-mail: cecny@cecip.org

General Inquiries:
Eugenia Stadnik,
Development Associate
212/643-1985 x26

Chief Executive Officer:
Dr. Michael C. Brainerd,
President

Statement:
CEC International Partners (CEC) believes that the arts are any community's most deliberate and complex means of communication. The arts can help nations overcome long histories of reciprocal distrust, insularity and conflict. CEC's collaborative international projects promote communication and cooperation, linking artists in the United States with partners in Central/Eastern Europe, Russia, and Eurasia. Affirming artistic freedom, CEC seeks out excellence in artist and arts organizations. CEC began facilitating exchanges between the United States and the Soviet Union in 1962. During the Cold War, we enabled citizens of both countries to accomplish what their governments would not do—open doors, share ideas and build mutual trust. In today's transformed and even more complex world, such ideals are no less relevant. With solid expertise and lasting partnerships in Russia, Eurasia and Central/Eastern Europe, CEC continues to be in the forefront of American organizations supporting mutually beneficial East/West projects.

Profile:
Nonprofit founded in 1962 as Peace Hostage Foundation. CEC has seven U.S. staff and one overseas staff, 15 U.S. volunteers contribute to CEC's mission.

Geographic Focus:
Newly Independent States, Central/Eastern Europe and Eurasia: Albania, Armenia, Azerbaijan, Belarus, Bosnia-Herzegovina, Bulgaria, Croatia, Czech Republic, Estonia, Georgia, Hungary, Kazakhstan, Kyrgyzstan, Latvia, Lithuania, Macedonia, Moldova, Mongolia, Poland, Romania, Russia, Slovak Republic, Slovenia, Tajikistan, Ukraine, Uzbekistan, Yugoslavia (includes Serbia, Kosovo, and Montenegro), Mongolia

Exchange Activities:
CEC is involved in the following exchange areas: Arts/Cultural, Professional/Business, Short-Term Visitors. CEC provides exchange-related facilitative or support services.

Financial Assistance:
ArtsLink has made over two million dollars in funding available to U.S. artists and arts organizations for partnerships with colleagues in Central/Eastern Europe, Russia and Eurasia. *St. Petersburg 2003* has committed over one million to cultural projects focused on St. Petersburg, Russia, which celebrates its 300th anniversary in the year 2003.

Publications:
ArtsLink Application Forms

ArtsLink Application Guidelines

Exchange Programs Include:

St. Petersburg 2003
Barbara A. Niemczyk,
Director
bniemczyk@cecip.org

ArtsLink
Fritzie Brown,
Director
212/643-1985,
fbrown@cecip.org

Russian Arts and Cultural Projects
Allison Pultz
212/643-1985,
apultz@cecip.org

Overseas Offices:
St. Petersburg, Russia

U.S. Department of State Designated Sponsor for the Exchange Vistor Program
Specialist

Alliance
MEMBER

Center for Citizen Initiatives (CCI)

Presidio of San Francisco
P.O. Box 29912
San Francisco, CA 94129-0912

Tel.: 415/561-7777
Fax: 415/561-7778
Website: http://www.ccisf.org
E-mail: info@ccisf.org

Secondary Address:
General Kennedy Avenue
Building 1008
San Francisco, CA 94129

General Inquiries:
Sara Potter,
Executive Assistant
415/561-7777

Chief Executive Officer:
Sharon Tennison,
President
415/561-7777 x212

Statement:
The Center for Citizen Initiatives
(CCI) is a San Francisco-based nonprofit organization dedicated to
empowering Russian citizens to
take responsibility for their personal futures and assisting Russia in its
transition to a market-based economy and civil society. CCI's current
programs focus on U.S.-based management training for Russian entre-
preneurs, microenterprise development in St. Petersburg, volunteer
small-business consultants working
in Russia, and sustainable agriculture projects in Russia's rural areas.

Profile:
Nonprofit founded in 1983. CCI
has 28 U.S. staff and two overseas
staff. CCI provides a membership
program and has seven local chap-
ters/affiliates. Eleven thousand
U.S. volunteers contribute to
CCI's mission.

Geographic Focus:
Newly Independent States (Russia)

Exchange Activities:
CCI is involved in the following
exchange areas:
Community/Citizen,
Professional/Business, Short-Term
Visitors, Training. CCI provides
exchange-related facilitative or sup-
port services.

Financial Assistance:
Partial scholarships are awarded
on a case-by-case basis to Russian
participants.

Exchange Programs Include:
Productivity Enhancement Program
  Lisa Susan,
  Program Officer-Outreach
  415/561-7777

Overseas Offices:
Dubna, Russia
Ekaterinburg, Russia
Rostov-on-Don, Russia
St. Petersburg, Russia
Vladivostok, Russia
Volgograd, Russia
Voronezh, Russia

Center for Cultural Interchange (CCI)

17 North Second Avenue
St. Charles, IL 60174

Tel.: 630/377-2272
Fax: 630/377-2307
Website: www.cci-exchange.org
E-mail: info@cci-exchange.org

General Inquiries:
Kathleen Baader,
Director of Development
630/377-2272,
kathleen@cci-exchange.org

Chief Executive Officer:
Emanuel Kuntzelman,
President

Statement:
The Center for Cultural Interchange (CCI) is a nonprofit student exchange organization, whose mission is to promote cultural understanding, academic development, and world peace through international exchange. CCI programs focus on the homestay experience, one of the best ways for participants to achieve a true understanding of cultures different than their own.

Profile:
Nonprofit founded in 1985. CCI has 31 U.S. staff. Two hundred fifty U.S. volunteers contribute to CCI's mission.

Geographic Focus:
Asia (Japan, Thailand, Mongolia), Eastern Europe (Poland, Czech Republic, Bulgaria, Hungary), Newly Independent States (Russia), North America (United States, Mexico), South America (Brazil, Argentina, Chile, Ecuador), Western Europe (Germany, France, Spain, Italy, Switzerland)

Exchange Activities:
CCI is involved in the following exchange areas: Community/Citizen, Homestay, Language Study, Persons with Disabilities, Short-Term Visitors, Work Exchanges. CCI provides exchange-related facilitative or support services. It administers exchange programs for the following academic levels: K-12, Undergraduate Students.

Financial Assistance:
CCI facilitates a variety of scholarship programs, including scholarships for CCI American host family members to study abroad. CCI also participates in cost-sharing scholarships in cooperation with the Soros Foundation and the federally funded Freedom Support Act.

Publications:
Cultural Programs in the United States

Discovery Abroad Programs for Teens

Discovery Abroad Programs for College Students and Adult Travelers

Discovery Abroad Programs for Groups

The Center for Cultural Interchange

Exchange Programs Include:
Academic Year in the United States (High School or College)
Stephen Foust,
U.S. Programs Director
630/377-2272,
ayp@cci-exchange.com

Discovery Abroad Programs for Americans
Jacqui Metcalf,
Outbound Programs Director
630/377-2272,
jacqui@cci-exchange.com

Group and Multi-National Group Programs in the United States

Individual Homestay Programs in the United States
Ruth Whisler,
Short-Term Program Coordinator
630/377-2272,
ruth@cci-exchange.com

Internship and Summer Work Programs in the United States
Daniel Ebert,
Director of Development
630/377-2272,
daniel@cci-exchange.com

Exchange Related Facilitative or Support Services Include:
Grants/Scholarships to Individuals
Host Family Circle Program
Kathleen Baader,
Director of Development
630/377-2272

People with Disabilities
Stephen Foust,
U.S. Programs Director
630/377-2272,
ayp@cci-exchange.com

Additional Offices:
Newark, CA
Wichita, KS
Wheeling, IL
Westmoreland, NH
Renton, WA
Orlando, FL
Moss Point, MS
Fort Collins, CO
Denver, CO
Dallas, TX
Choctaw, OK
Broken Arrow, OK
Provo, UT

Overseas Office:
Madrid, Spain

Center for Global Partnership (CGP)

152 W 57th Street
39th Floor
New York, NY 10019

Tel.:   212/489-1255
Fax: 212/489-1344
Website: www.cgp.org/cgplink
Email: info@cgp.org

General Inquiries:
Takashi Ishida,
Director

Chief Executive Officer:
Takashi Ishida,
Director

Statement: The Japan Foundation Center for Global Partnership was established to pursue the following objectives: collaboration between Japan and the United States with the goal of fulfilling shared global responsibilities and contributing to improvements in the world welfare; and to enhance dialogue and interchange between Japanese and U.S. citizens on a wide range of issues, thereby improving bilateral relations.

Profile: Nonprofit, founded in 1991. Center for Global Partnership has seven U.S. staff and four overseas staff.

Geographic Focus: Asia (Japan), North America (United States)

Exchange Activities: Center for Global Partnership is involved in the following exchange areas: Community/Citizen, Students/Educators, Training. It administers exchange programs for the following academic levels: Faculty, K-12, Teachers, Undergraduate Students. CGP provides exchange-related facilitative and support services.

Publications:
CGP Newsletter
CGP Grantee Selected Publications
Annual Report
Program Guidelines for Applicants
Program Announcements on Priority Areas of Funding

Exchange Programs Include:
Abe Fellowship Program
    212/489-1255
    info@cgp.org

PO Fellowship Program
    212/489-1255
    info@cgp.org

Exchange-Related Facilitative or Support Services Include:
Grants/Scholarships to Individuals
Grants to Institutions/Organizations
Intellectual Exchange Program,
Grassroot Exchange Program,
Education Program

Overseas Office:
Tokyo, Japan

Children's International Summer Villages, Inc. (CISV)

1375 Kemper Meadow Drive
Suite 9H
Cincinnati, OH 45240

Tel.: 888/247-8872
Fax: 513/674-9249
Website: http://www.cisvusa.org
E-mail: cisvusa@aol.com

General Inquiries:

Susan Y. Brogden,
Administrative Director
513/674-9242,
cisvusa@aol.com

Chief Executive Officer:

Jan Nymann,
President

Statement:

Children's International Summer Villages (CISV), founded by University of Cincinnati psychologist Doris Twitchell Allen, is a non-political, volunteer organization. CISV in the United States is one of 60 National Associations around the world, administered by the parent organization in England. Its programs in the United States, conducted by 20 local chapters, provide international experiences for young people based on the premise that peace is possible when individuals and groups learn to live together as friends.

Profile:

Nonprofit founded in 1951. CISV has one U.S. staff and eight overseas staff. CISV provides a membership program and has 2,300 individual members and 20 local chapters/affiliates.

Geographic Focus:

Worldwide

Exchange Activities:

CISV is involved in the following exchange areas: Community/Citizen, Homestay, Short-Term Visitors, Short-Term Youth Exchanges, Students/Educators. CISV provides exchange-related facilitative or support services. It administers exchange programs for the following academic levels: K-12.

Financial Assistance:

Each chapter has the option of providing financial assistance to children selected to participate in its programs as that chapter's individual budget permits.

Publications:

Informational Brochure

Annual Report

National Newsletter

Exchange Programs Include:
Interchange
(for young teens and their families)

Junior Counselors (for 16-17 year-olds)

Seminar Camp (for 17-18 year-olds)

Summer Camp (for 13-15 year-olds)

Village (for 11 year-olds)

Exchange Related Facilitative or Support Services Include:
Admissions/Placement Service
    All Programs

Conference/Meetings/Workshops

Leadership Training Workshops for Adult Leaders and Staff of all Youth Exchange Activities

Overseas Offices:
Newcastle-Upon-Tyne, United Kingdom

College Board-International Education (CBIE)

1233 20th Street
Suite 600
Washington, DC 20036-2304

Tel.: 202/822-5900
Fax: 202/822-5234
Website: www.collegeboard.com
E-mail: internatl@collegeboard.com

General Inquiries:
Theresa Carroll Schweser,
Director,
International Education Office
202/822-5900,
internatl@collegeboard.org

Chief Executive Officer:
Gaston Caperton,
President

Statement:
The College Board is a national, nonprofit membership association dedicated to preparing, inspiring, and connecting students to college and opportunity. Founded in 1900, the association is composed of more than 3,800 schools, colleges, universities, and other educational organizations. Each year, the College Board serves over three million students and their parents, 22,000 high schools and 3,500 colleges, through major programs and services in college admission, guidance, assessment, financial aid, enrollment, and teaching and learning. Among its best-known programs are the SAT, the PSAT/NMSQT, the Advanced Placement Program (AP), and Pacesetter. The College Board is committed to the principles of equity and excellence, and that commitment is embodied in all of its programs, services, activities, and concerns.

Profile:
Nonprofit founded in 1965. CBIE provides a membership program and has 3,900 individual members.

Geographic Focus:
Worldwide

Exchange Activities:
CBIE provides exchange-related facilitative or support services.

Financial Assistance:
CBIE does not provide financial assistance.

Publications:
International Recruitment Kit

1998 Directory of Overseas Educational Advising Centers

The International Student Handbook of U.S. Colleges

Ambassadors of U.S. Higher Education: Quality Credit-Bearing Programs Abroad

Advising for Study in the United States: A Manual for Educational Advising Professionals

Exchange Related Facilitative or Support Services Include:
Admissions/Placement Service
    Theresa Schweser,
    Director
    202/822-5900

Conference/Meetings/Workshops
    Theresa Schweser,
    Director
    202/822-5900

Membership Services
    Theresa Schweser,
    Director
    202/822-5900

Testing/Assessment Services
    Theresa Schweser,
    Director
    202/822-5900

Public Policy
    Theresa Schweser,
    Director
    202/822-5900

Additional Offices:
New York, NY
Albany, NY
Philadelphia, PA
Reston, VA
Atlanta, GA
Tallahassee, FL
Evanston, IL
Austin, TX
San Jose, CA
Sacramento, CA

College Consortium for International Studies (CCIS)

2000 P Street, NW
Suite 503
Washington, DC 20036

Tel.: 202/223-0330
Fax: 202/223-0999
Web: www.studyabroad.com/ccis
E-mail: info@ccisabroad.org

General Inquiries:
202/223-0330,
info@ccisabroad.org

Chief Executive Officer:
Harlan N. Henson,
Executive Director

Statement:
The College Consortium for International Studies (CCIS), a partnership of colleges and universities (two and four-year; large and small; public and private; domestic and foreign) encompasses the broad spectrum of international higher education. CCIS members sponsor a variety of programs, notably study abroad programs and professional development seminars for faculty and administrators, which are designed to enhance international/intercultural perspectives within the academic community. Recognizing the value of such experiences in fostering global understanding and peaceful cooperation among nations in an increasingly interdependent and rapidly changing world, CCIS is committed to developing international dimensions as an integral part of collegiate education. CCIS works to build collaborative

arrangements among institutions who share this commitment, and to facilitate linkages between member institutions and international partners. In all of its programs and activities, CCIS strives for a high level of academic excellence.

Profile:
Nonprofit founded in 1975. CCIS has five U.S. staff. CCIS provides a membership program and has 170 institutional members.

Geographic Focus:
Worldwide

Exchange Activities:
CCIS is involved in the following exchange areas: Homestay, Language Study, Professional/Business, Students/Educators. CCIS provides exchange-related facilitative or support services. It administers exchange programs for the following academic levels: Faculty, Undergraduate Students.

Financial Assistance:
CCIS does not provide financial assistance.

Publications:
CCIS Newsletter: Update,
    CCIS General Brochure

Exchange Programs Include:
Study Abroad Programs
    Program Coordinator
    info@ccisabroad.org

Exchange Related Facilitative or Support Services Include:
Conference/Meetings/Workshops
    Harlan Henson,
    Executive Director
    harlan@ccisabroad.org

Membership Services
    Harlan Henson,
    Executive Director
    harlan@ccisabroad.org

Communicating for Agriculture (CA)

112 East Lincoln Avenue
Fergus Falls, MN 56538

Tel.: 218/739-3241
Fax: 218/739-3832
Website: http://ca.cainc.org
E-mail: caep@cainc.org

General Inquiries:
Kathy Belka,
218/739-3241 x3515,
kbelka@cainc.org

Chief Executive Officer:
Milt Smedsrud,
Chairman

Statement:
Communicating for Agriculture
(CA) is a nonpartisan, nonprofit
organization dedicated to improving the quality of life and economic
opportunity for people in agriculture and small businesses in rural
America. The organization represents over 80,000 farmers, ranch-
ers, growers and self-employed
business persons in all 50 states.
Activities include public policy
issues, member benefit programs,
research, scholarship/grant programs and international exchange.

Profile:
Nonprofit founded in 1972. CA has
28 U.S. staff.

Geographic Focus:
Worldwide

Exchange Activities:
CA is involved in the following
exchange areas: Agricultural
Training. CA provides exchange-
related facilitative or support services.

Financial Assistance:
Scholarships ($500-$2,000) are
available to American participants
going overseas.

Publications:
Self Employed Country

**Exchange Related Facilitative or
Support Services Include:**
Admissions/Placement Service

Conference/Meetings/Workshops

Grants/Scholarships to Individuals

International Visitor Support

Membership Services

Travel Services

Concordia Language Villages (CLV)

901 South Eighth Street
Moorhead, MN 56562

Tel.: 800/222-4750
Fax: 218/299-3807
Web: www.ConcordiaLanguageVillages.org
E-mail: clv@cord.edu

General Inquiries:
Brenda Warren,
Public Relations Coordinator
800/222-4750 x6,
warren@cord.edu

Chief Executive Officer:
Christine Schulze,
Executive Director

Statement:
The mission of Concordia Language Villages is to prepare young people for responsible citizenship in the global community. This is accomplished by encouraging young people's enthusiasm for and interest in other languages and cultures through various hands-on activities involving the target language and culture. Concordia Language Villages offers one, two, and four-week sessions for young people of all levels of language experience. Sessions in 12 world languages are offered: Chinese, Danish, English, Finnish, French, German, Japanese, Korean, Norwegian, Russian, Spanish, and Swedish.

Profile:
Nonprofit founded in 1961. CLV has 600 U.S. staff and 400 overseas staff.

Geographic Focus:
Worldwide

Exchange Activities:
CLV is involved in the following exchange areas: Arts/Cultural, Community/Citizen, Language Study, Students/Educators. CLV provides exchange-related facilitative or support services. It administers exchange programs for the following academic levels: K-12.

Financial Assistance:
Financial assistance is based on need. The deadline to apply for assistance is March 1.

Publications:
Catalog

Parent Handbook

Staff Handbook

Exchange Programs Include:
French Credit Abroad
  800/222-4750,
  sdixon@cord.edu

German Credit Abroad
  800/222-4750,
  sdixon@cord.edu

Japanese Credit Abroad
  800/222-4750,
  sdixon@cord.edu

Spanish Credit Abroad
  800/222-4750,
  sdixon@cord.edu

Exchange Related Facilitative or Support Services Include:
Courses for Credit
  Four week language sessions offer one year of high school foreign language credit
  Grants/Scholarships to Individuals
  Concordia Language Villages Scholarships
  Finance Director
  800/222-4750

Travel Services
  Abroad Programs to Spain, Germany, France, and Japan

People with Disabilities
  Portia Danielson,
  Assistant to Director
  800/222-4750,
  danielso@cord.edu

Connect/US-Russia

430 Oak Grove Street
Suite 109
Minneapolis, MN 55403

Tel.: 612/871-5722
Fax: 612/871-5903
E-mail: 73051.2543@compuserve.com

General Inquiries:
Susan Hartman,
Executive Director
612/871-5722,
73051.2543@compuserve.com

Chief Executive Officer:
Susan Hartman,
Executive Director

Statement:
Connect/US-Russia's mission is to promote a more humane and peaceful world by creating collaborative relationships between the United States and countries of the former Soviet Union to discuss critical issues.

Profile:
Nonprofit founded in 1984. Connect/US-Russia has four U.S. staff. One hundred U.S. volunteers contribute to Connect/US-Russia's mission.

Geographic Focus:
Newly Independent States (Russia, Ukraine, Belarus, Moldova)

Exchange Activities:
Connect/US-Russia is involved in the following exchange areas: Community/Citizen, Professional/Business, Training. Connect/US-Russia provides exchange-related facilitative or support services.

Financial Assistance:
Connect/US-Russia does not provide financial assistance.

Publications:
Connections (newsletter)

Exchange Programs Include:
Community Connections
    Susan Hartman

Multidisciplinary Training to Prevent and Intervene in Domestic Violence
    Susan Hartman

Exchange Related Facilitative or Support Services Include:
People with Disabilities

Public Policy

Cooperative Extension 4-H Youth Development

3864 South Building
AG Box 0925
Washington, DC 20250-0900

Tel.: 202/720-2297
Fax: 202/720-9366
Website: http://www.4h-usa.org
E-mail:
4H-EXCHANGE@worldwise.org

Secondary Address:
1260 Mercer Street
Seattle, WA 98109

General Inquiries:
Yoko Kawaguchi,
Manager Exchange Services
800/407-3314,
4h-exchange@worldwise.org

Chief Executive Officer:
Dr. Virginia Gobeli,
National 4-H Program Leader

Statement:
Cooperative Extension 4-H Youth Development (4-H) is a youth education program of the Cooperative Extension System of the state land-grant universities and the U.S. Department of Agriculture. The mission of the 4-H and the Youth Development Program is to create supportive environments in which culturally diverse youth and adults can reach their fullest potential. The mission of 4-H international programs is to further cross-cultural understanding and international development through study and exchange of human and technical resources.

Profile:
Nonprofit founded in 1914. Cooperative Extension 4-H Youth Development has 4,300 U.S. staff and 3,150 local chapters/affiliates. Six hundred eighty thousand U.S. volunteers contribute to Cooperative Extension 4-H Youth Development's mission.

Geographic Focus:
Asia (Japan, Korea), North America (Canada, Mexico, United States)

Exchange Activities:
Cooperative Extension 4-H Youth Development is involved in the following exchange areas: Family, Homestay, Students/Educators, Training. It provides exchange-related facilitative or support services and administers exchange programs for the following academic levels: K-12.

Financial Assistance:
Limited scholarships are available for some programs.

Publications:
Windows to Our World
(quarterly newsletter)

Exchange Programs Include:
National 4-H
Japanese Exchange Program

U.S. Department of State Designated Sponsor for the Exchange Vistor Program
College and university students
Secondary school students

Alliance MEMBER

Cordell Hull Foundation for International Education (CHF)

116 West 23rd Street
5th Floor
New York, NY 10011

Tel.: 646/375-2023
Fax: 212/851-8405
Website: www.cordellhull.net
E-mail: chfny@aol.com

General Inquiries:
Marianne Mason Morrison,
President
646/375-2023,
CHFNY@aol.com

Chief Executive Officer:
Marianne Mason Morrison,
President

Statement:
The Cordell Hull Foundation for International Education is a nonprofit organization dedicated to continuing the work of one of America's greatest statesmen, the late Cordell Hull, winner of the Nobel Peace Prize as "Father of the United Nations." Embracing his goal of continually improving relations between the United States and other countries of the world, the Foundation has, for 50 years, actively promoted international peace and understanding, primarily through educational and cultural exchange.

Profile:
Nonprofit founded in 1951. Twenty U.S. volunteers contribute to CHF's mission.

Geographic Focus:
Africa (Central African Republic, Kenya, Senegal), Central America (Guatemala, Panama, Honduras, Venezuela, El Salvador, Costa Rica), North America (United States, Canada, Mexico), South America (Ecuador, Peru, Colombia, Chile, Argentina, Bolivia, Guyana), Western Europe (France, Belgium, Italy, Germany, United Kingdom, Spain), Asia (Japan, Korea), Oceania (Australia), Newly Independent States (Ukraine)

Exchange Activities:
CHF is involved in the following exchange areas: Arts/Cultural, Language Study, Short-Term Visitors, Students/Educators, Training, Work Exchanges. CHF provides exchange-related facilitative or support services. It administers exchange programs for the following academic levels: Continuing Education, K-12.

Financial Assistance:
CHF does not provide financial assistance.

Exchange Programs Include:
Exchange Teacher Program
  Marianne Morrison

Exchange Teacher Program
with Australia
  Brian Hall

Exchange Related Facilitative or Support Services Include:
Admissions/Placement Service
  Exchange Teacher Program

International Visitor Support
  Exchange Visitor Program

Additional Offices:
New Orleans, LA

Overseas Offices:
Antigua, Guatemala

U.S. Department of State Designated Sponsor for the Exchange Vistor Program
Trainees
Teachers
Secondary school students
Intern

Council for Educational Travel USA (CETUSA)

1403 View Avenue
Centralia, WA 98531

Tel.: 360/736-6472
Fax: 360/736-6525
Website: http://www.cetusa.org
E-mail: terry@cetusa.org

Secondary Address:
7365 Carnelian, Suite 225
Rancho Cucamonga, CA 91730

General Inquiries:
Terry Watson,
President
360/736-6472,
terry@cetusa.org

Chief Executive Officer:
Terry Watson,
President

Statement:
Council for Educational Travel USA (CETUSA) is a nonprofit educational and cultural exchange organization dedicated to providing youth from around the world the opportunity to exchange ideas, arts, philosophies, and ways of life with host families in the United States and abroad. Through its network of overseas representatives and American-based managers and community coordinators, CETUSA provides both inbound and outbound programs to high school-aged students including the academic year abroad program, programs for groups and individuals, and inbound community college placement. CETUSA is founded on friendship and dedicated to its mission: "Reaching out to encourage a lifelong journey of global peace and understanding."

Profile:
Nonprofit founded in 1995. CETUSA has 40 U.S. staff and eight overseas staff. Four hundred U.S. volunteers contribute to CETUSA's mission.

Geographic Focus:
Worldwide

Exchange Activities:
CETUSA is involved in the following exchange areas: Homestay, Language Study, Short-Term Visitors, Students/Educators. CETUSA provides exchange-related facilitative or support services. It administers exchange programs for the following academic levels: K-12, Undergraduate Students.

Financial Assistance:
Children of American host families may receive scholarships for programs abroad, up to 20 percent of the outbound program fee, excluding airfare.

Exchange Programs Include:
Academic Year Program and Semester High School in the United States
  Terry Watson, President
  360/736-6472,
  terry@cetusa.org

Community College Program in the United States
  Rick Anoya, Founder
  909/987-5724,
  rick@cetusa.org

Outbound Programs
  Kevin Watson, Director
  360/736-6472,
  kevin@cetusa.org

Private High School Programs in the United States
  Kevin Watson, Director
  360/736-6472, kevin@cetusa.org

Short-term Group Programs in the United States
  Rick Anoya, Founder
  909/987-5724,
  rick@cetusa.org

Exchange Related Facilitative or Support Services Include:
Admissions/Placement Service

Additional Offices:
Grand Rapids, MI

Overseas Offices:
Fukuoka, Japan
London, United Kingdom
Sofia, Bulgaria
Tirana, Albania
Moscow, Russia
Heppenshein, Germany

Council of American Overseas Research Centers (CAORC)

Smithsonian Institution
10th St. & Constitution Avenue, NW
NHB, MRC 178, CE-123
Washington, DC 20560-0178

Tel.: 202/842-8636
Fax: 202/786-2430
Website: http://www.caorc.org
E-mail: caorc@caorc.si.edu

General Inquiries:
Heidi Massaro,
Program and Finance Manager
202/842-8636,
hmassaro@caorc.si.edu

Chief Executive Officer:
Mary Ellen Lane,
Executive Director

Statement:
The Council of American Overseas
Research Centers (CAORC) supports existing overseas research
centers and assists in the development of new mechanisms for
research exchange.

Profile:
Nonprofit founded in 1981.
CAORC has four U.S. staff and
overseas staff. CAORC provides a
membership program and has 14
institutional members.

Geographic Focus:
Africa (West Regional), Asia
(Bangladesh, India, Pakistan),
Middle East (North Africa Regional,
Cyprus, Egypt, Israel, Jordan,
Turkey, Yemen, Iran), Western
Europe (Greece, Italy)

Exchange Activities:
CAORC is involved in the following
exchange areas: Arts/Cultural,
Language Study. CAORC provides
exchange-related facilitative or support services. It administers
exchange programs for the following academic levels: Faculty.

Financial Assistance:
CAORC provides financial assistance for advanced scholarly multi-
country research.

Exchange Programs Include:
Multi-Country Fellowship Program
Heidi Massaro,
Program and Finance Manager
202/842-8636,
hmassaro@caorc.si.edu

**Exchange Related Facilitative or
Support Services Include:**
Conference/Meetings/Workshops
Annual Workshop

Grants/Scholarships to Individuals
Multi-Country Fellowship Program

Overseas Offices:
Jerusalem, Israel
New Delhi, India
Amman, Jordan
Ankara, Turkey
Istanbul, Turkey
Athens, Greece
Cairo, Egypt
Dhaka, Bangladesh
Nicosia, Cyprus
Rome, Italy
Sana'a, Yemen
Tangier, Morocco
Tunis, Tunisia
Islamabad, Pakistan
Dakar, Senegal

Council of Chief State School Officers (CCSSO)

One Massachusetts Avenue, NW
Suite 700
Washington, DC 20001-1431

Tel.: 202/408-5505
Fax: 202/408-8072
Website: http://www.ccsso.org
E-mail: info@ccsso.org

General Inquiries:
Fred Czarra,
Director of International Education
202/408-5505

Chief Executive Officer:
G. Thomas Houlihan,
Executive Director

Statement:
Educational practitioners in the United States need access to information on programs, projects, and individual efforts in other countries that suggest successful methods for addressing issues or programs at the local, regional, or national level. International networks should be established to exchange compatible educational practices and materials that can bring new life and quality to existing school programs and provide innovative approaches to educational problems. By joint sponsorship of international conferences and exchange of strategies on topics such as youth transition from school to work, urban education, early childhood education, and second language study, CCSSO assists educators throughout the world in learning and adapting accomplishments from countries around the world.

Profile:
Nonprofit. CCSSO has 60 U.S. staff. CCSSO provides a membership program and has 57 institutional members.

Geographic Focus:
Worldwide

Exchange Activities:
CCSSO is involved in the following exchange areas: Arts/Cultural, Professional/Business, Short-Term Visitors, Students/Educators, Training. CCSSO provides exchange-related facilitative or support services.

Financial Assistance:
CCSSO does not provide financial assistance.

Publications:
International Education Newsletter (three issues per year)

International Dimension of Education

International Education Documents in State Education Agencies

Exchange Programs Include:
Japanese Prefectural Superintendents of Schools

Society of Education Officers of England, Wales, and Northern Ireland

Exchange Related Facilitative or Support Services Include:
Conference/Meetings/Workshops

Grants to Institutions/Organizations

Intercultural Communications

Consultations/Advisory Services

Council of Graduate Schools (CGS)

One Dupont Circle, NW
Suite 430
Washington, DC 20036

Tel.: 202/223-3791
Fax: 202/331-7157
Website: http://www.cgsnet.org
E-mail: webmaster@cgsnet.org

General Inquiries:
Marta Pérez Drake,
202/223-3791,
mdrake@cgs.nche.edu

Chief Executive Officer:
Dr. Debra W. Stewart,
President

Statement:
The Council of Graduate Schools (CGS) is dedicated to the improvement and advancement of graduate education. Its members are colleges and universities engaged in research, scholarship, and the preparation of candidates for advanced degrees. As the largest national association organized specifically to represent the interests of graduate education, CGS offers many opportunities for deans and graduate school personnel to exchange ideas and share information on major issues in graduate education. Over 450 U.S., Canadian, and international institutions are represented in the CGS membership.

Profile:
Nonprofit founded in 1961. CGS has 13 U.S. staff. CGS provides a membership program and has 450 institutional members, and four local chapters/affiliates.

Geographic Focus:
Africa, North America (United States, Canada)

Exchange Activities:
CGS provides exchange-related facilitative or support services.

Financial Assistance:
CGS does not provide financial assistance.

Publications:
Graduate School and You, Preparing Future Faculty (series)

Distance Graduate Education: Opportunities and Challenges for the 21st Century

International Graduate Students: A Guide for Graduate Deans, Faculty, and Administrators

Role and Nature of the Doctoral Dissertation

Exchange Related Facilitative or Support Services Include:
Conference/Meetings/Workshops

Grants/Scholarships to Individuals
Distinguished Dissertation Awards

Membership Services

Consultation Services

Council of International Programs USA (CIP USA)

1700 East 13th Street
Suite 4 ME
Cleveland, OH 44114-3213

Tel.: 216/566-1088
Fax: 216/566-1490
Website: www.cipusa.org
E-mail: cipusa@compuserve.com

General Inquiries:
Dorothy A. Faller,
Secretary General and CEO
216/566-1908,
cipusa@compuserve.com

Chief Executive Officer:
Dorothy A. Faller,
Secretary General and CEO

Statement:
Council of International Programs USA (CIP USA) was established to provide cross-cultural experiences and professional development training opportunities for individuals and groups in social services, businesses and nonprofit, nongovernmental and public organizations as well as educational institutions. For over 46 years, CIP USA has brought nearly 10,000 international professionals to the United States for training from 147 countries. CIP USA provides practical training internships for either four, 12 or 18 months in 15 various fields. Training programs include an orientation, program evaluation, training internship, cultural programs, academic courses, and a pre-departure program. CIP USA has three unique programs: 1) locate the international professional a training program, 2) assist international professionals with pre-arranged training programs, and 3) work with higher education students abroad with practical training programs in the United States.

Alliance MEMBER

CIP USA, in connection with its alumni association council of international fellowship, promotes observational training exchanges abroad for U.S. citizens in the human services field. These programs are in 17 different countries and provide U.S. citizens the opportunity to study on an international level.

Profile:
Nonprofit founded in 1956. CIP USA has three U.S. staff. CIP USA provides a membership program and has nine affiliates. Two hundred U.S. volunteers and 20 overseas volunteers contribute to CIP USA's mission.

Geographic Focus:
Worldwide

Exchange Activities:
CIP USA is involved in the following exchange areas: Persons with Disabilities, Professional/Business, Students/Educators, Training. CIP USA provides exchange-related facilitative or support services. It administers exchange programs for the following academic levels: Graduate Students.

Financial Assistance:
CIP USA provides room and board for its exchange visitors through host family and apartment living and provides a transportation stipend within city limits. Some affiliate offices are able to provide monthly stipends.

Publications:
What a Collection (brochure)
What is CIP? (brochure)
University Partners Program (brochure)
Global Partners Program (brochure)
The Bridge (newsletter)
1999 Annual Report

Exchange Programs Include:
Core Program

Global Partners Program

Higher Education Program

Exchange Related Facilitative or Support Services Include:
Admissions/Placement Service
    Professional Internship Placements through Affiliate Cities
    Lisa Purdy,
    International Programs Director

International Visitor Support
    Dorothy Faller,
    Secretary General and CEO

Additional Offices:
Cleveland, OH
Columbus, OH
Denver, CO
Chicago, IL
Kalamazoo, MI
Morgantown, WV
San Diego, CA
San Francisco, CA
Scranton, PA

Overseas Offices:
Vienna, Austria
Lyon, France
Athens, Greece
Berlin, Germany
Bombay, India
Dunkeid, United Kingdom
Ljubljana, Slovenia
Oslo, Norway
Prague, Czech Republic
Rome, Italy
Stockholm, Sweden
The Hague, Netherlands
Istanbul, Turkey
Helsinki, Finland
Old Jaffa, Israel
Nairobi, Kenya
Dar es Salaam, Tanzania

U.S. Department of State Designated Sponsor for the Exchange Vistor Program
Trainees

Council on International Educational Exchanges, Inc. (CIEE)

633 Third Avenue
New York, NY 10017-6706

Tel.: 212/822-2600
Fax: 212/822-2699
Website: http://www.ciee.org
E-mail: info@ciee.org

General Inquiries:
Information Center
888/268-6845,
info@ciee.org

Chief Executive Officer:
Dr. Steven Trooboff,
President and CEO

Statement:
The Council on International Educational Exchanges's (CIEE) mission is to help people gain understanding, acquire knowledge, and develop skills for living in a globally interdependent and culturally diverse world. Since 1947, CIEE has fulfilled this mission through the conduct of a wide variety of programs including study, work, internship, volunteer and travel. Today, CIEE conducts programs in more than 30 countries with administrative centers in ten locations worldwide. CIEE employs more than 400 professionals serving students at the secondary and tertiary levels of education; young professionals; and faculty and staff as well as their institutions.

Profile:
Nonprofit founded in 1947. Council has 150 U.S. staff and 300 overseas staff. Council provides a membership program and has 350 institutional members.

Geographic Focus:
Worldwide

Exchange Activities:
Council is involved in the following exchange areas: Homestay, High School Programs, Internship, Language Study, Students/ Educators, Study Abroad, Work Exchanges. Council provides exchange-related facilitative or support services. It administers exchange programs for the following academic levels: Faculty, Graduate Students, K-12, Teachers, Undergraduate and High School Students. For more information on any Council program or service, please call 1-800-COUNCIL.

Financial Assistance:
Council offers a small number of traveling scholarships and grants. For more information, call 1-800-COUNCIL.

Publications:
Journal of Studies in International Education

Exchange Programs Include:
Annual Year High School Program
info@councilexchanges.org

CIEE Study Abroad
info@ciee.org

Work in Australia
info@councilexchanges.org

Internship USA
info@councilexchanges.org

Summer Homestay Program
info@councilexchanges.org

Work and Travel USA
info@councilexchanges.org

Work, Volunteer Internship Program
info@councilexchanges.org

Faculty Development
info@ciee.org

Exchange Related Facilitative or Support Services Include:
Admissions/Placement Service
info@ciee.org

Conference/Meetings/Workshops
info@ciee.org

Courses for Credit
info@ciee.org

Membership Services
info@ciee.org

Testing/Assessment Services
info@councilexchanges.org

Work, Volunteer Internship Program
info@councilexchanges.org

Additional Offices:
68 U.S. college campuses
Boston, MA

Overseas Offices:
Berlin, Germany
Madrid, Spain
Tokyo, Japan
London, United Kingdom
Rome, Italy
Sydney, Australia
Taipei, Taiwan
Paris, France
Hong Kong, China

U.S. Department of State Designated Sponsor for the Exchange Vistor Program
Trainees
Summer work/travel

Council on Standards for International Educational Travel (CSIET)

212 South Henry Street
Alexandria, VA 22314

Tel.: 703/739-9050
Fax: 703/739-9035
Website: http://www.csiet.org
E-mail: mailbox@csiet.org

General Inquiries:
John Hishmeh,
Executive Director
703/739-9050,
jhishmeh@csiet.org

Chief Executive Officer:
John Hishmeh,
Executive Director

Statement:
The Council on Standards for International Educational Travel (CSIET) is a nonprofit organization committed to quality international educational travel and exchange for youth at the high school level. CSIET operates through a network of national and state educational associations, educational and travel exchange organizations, and community/volunteer groups. CSIET establishes standards for international educational travel, provides a system of evaluating programs in terms of those standards, monitors compliance with the standards, and shares information about organizations operating international educational travel and exchange programs at the high school level on behalf of schools, communities, and educational groups in the United States.

Profile:
Nonprofit founded in 1984. CSIET has three U.S. staff. CSIET provides a membership program and has 300 institutional members and six individual members.

Geographic Focus:
Worldwide

Exchange Activities:
CSIET provides exchange-related facilitative or support services.

Financial Assistance:
CSIET does not provide financial assistance.

Publications:
The Advisory List of International Educational Travel and Exchange Programs (updated annually)

Administering Youth Exchange: The U.S. High Schools' Guide on International Student Exchange

Exchange Related Facilitative or Support Services Include:
Conference/Meetings/Workshops
    CSIET Annual Meeting

Membership Services

Evaluation of High School
    Exchange Organizations

Publications

Alliance
MEMBER

Cross-Cultural Solutions

47 Potter Avenue
New Rochelle, NY 10801

Tel.: 800/380-4777
Fax: 914/632-8494
Web: www.crossculturalsolutions.org
E-mail:
info@crossculturalsolutions.org

General Inquiries:
Marge Rubin,
Volunteer Coordinator
914/632-0022,
marge@crossculturalsolutions.org

Chief Executive Officer:
Steven C. Rosenthal,
Executive Director

Statement:
Cross-Cultural Solutions is a non-profit organization that employs humanitarian volunteer action to empower local communities, foster cultural sensitivity and understanding, and contribute grassroots solutions to the global challenges of providing health care, education and social development. Cross-Cultural Solutions also offers insight cultural tours with a focus on people-to-people exchange.

Profile:
Nonprofit founded in 1995. Cross-Cultural Solutions has 12 U.S. staff. Eight overseas staff and more than 2,000 overseas volunteers contribute to the organization's mission.

Geographic Focus:
Africa (Ghana), Asia (China, India), Caribbean (Cuba), Newly Independent States (Russia), South America (Peru)

Exchange Activities:
Cross-Cultural Solutions is involved in the following exchange areas: Arts/Cultural, Community/Citizen, Senior Citizen, Students/Educators, Training, International Volunteering, Insight Cultural Tours to several international locations. Cross-Cultural Solutions provides exchange-related facilitative or support services. It administers exchange programs for the following academic levels: Undergraduate Students, Graduate Students, Teachers.

Financial Assistance:
Scholarships are available to help with program fees.

Exchange Programs Include:
Volunteer in Peru
    Jodie Emmett,
    Program Coordinator for Peru
    914/632-0022
    jodie@crossculturalsolutions.org

Volunteer in India
    Jodie Emmett,
    Program Coordinator for India
    914/632-0022
    jodie@crossculturalsolutions.org

Volunteer in Ghana
    Carleen Kunkel,
    Program Coordinator Manager
    914/632-0022
    carleen@crossculturalsolutions.org

Volunteer in Russia
    Carleen Kunkel,
    Program Coordinator Manager
    914/632-0022
    carleen@crossculturalsolutions.org

Volunteer in China
    Carleen Kunkel,
    Program Coordinator Manager
    914/632-0022
    carleen@crossculturalsolutions.org

Exchange Related Facilitative or Support Services Include:
Admissions/Placement Service
    International Volunteer Programs
    Marge Rubin,
    Volunteer Coordinator
    914/632-0022
    marge@crossculturalsolutions.org

Courses for Credit
    Jodie Emmett,
    Program Coordinator
    914/632-0022
    jodie@crossculturalsolutions.org

Grants/Scholarships to Individuals
    International Volunteer Programs
    Heather Melton,
    Office Manager
    914/632-0022
    heather@crossculturalsolutions.org

Travel Services
    International Volunteer Programs and
    "Visit the Field" Insight Programs
    Marge Rubin,
    Volunteer Coordinator
    914/632-0022
    marge@crossculturalsolutions.org

People with Disabilities
    Marge Rubin,
    Volunteer Coordinator
    914/632-0022
    marge@crossculturalsolutions.org

Overseas Offices:
Delhi, India
Rajgarh, India
Ho, Ghana
Shanghai, China
Yaroslavl, Russia
Lima, Peru
Havana, Cuba

Cultural Academic Student Exchange (CASE)

**19 Charmer Court
Middletown, NJ 07748**

Tel.: 732/671-6448
Fax: 732/615-9183
Website: www.exchangestudents.org
E-mail: casenj@home.com

General Inquiries:
Ellen Battaglia,
President
732/671-6448
casenj@home.com

Chief Executive Officer:
Ellen Battaglia,
President

Statement:
Cultural Academic Student Exchange (CASE) brings foreign teenage students to the United States for an academic school year. They live with approved host families and attend American high schools. The program helps improve their English, promotes cultural exchange, and international goodwill through total immersion into American life.

Profile:
Nonprofit founded in 1988. CASE has five U.S. staff. Fifty U.S. volunteers contribute to CASE's mission.

Geographic Focus:
Worldwide

Exchange Activities:
CASE is involved in the following exchange areas: Homestay, Language Study, Students/Educators. CASE provides exchange-related facilitative or support services. It administers exchange programs for the following academic levels: K-12.

Financial Assistance:
CASE does not provide financial assistance.

Publications:
CASE News and Views

Exchange Programs Include:
Academic Year Program

One Semester Program

Outbound Program

Reciprocal Outbound Program

Cultural Homestay International (CHI)

104 Butterfield Road
San Anselmo, CA 94960

Tel.: 415/459-5397
Fax: 415/459-2182
Website: http://www.chinet.org
E-mail: chimain@msn.com

General Inquiries:
Jerrine Rowley,
Office Manager
415/459-5397,
chijerrine@msn.com

Chief Executive Officer:
Thomas Areton,
Executive Director

Statement:
Cultural Homestay International
(CHI) was founded to promote
international understanding,
friendship, and goodwill through
homestay experience. It believes
that the best way to eliminate fear
and prejudice is to experience the
cultures, languages, and customs of
other countries firsthand. The
emphasis of the program is on the
education of the participating student, host family, and local community through communication
and interaction in the home, classroom, and neighborhood. It is
CHI's hope that a more informed
citizenry will ultimately contribute
to a more prosperous, democratic,
and peaceful world.

Profile:
Nonprofit founded in 1980. CHI has
46 U.S. staff and six overseas staff.

Geographic Focus:
Worldwide

Exchange Activities:
CHI is involved in the following
exchange areas: Homestay,
Language Study, Short-Term
Visitors, Sports, Students/Educators,
Work Exchanges. CHI provides
exchange-related facilitative or support services. It administers
exchange programs for the following academic levels: K-12, Teachers,
Undergraduate Students.

Financial Assistance:
CHI does not provide financial
assistance.

Publications:
Inside CHI

Exchange Programs Include:
Academic Year Program, Inbound
  Joan King, Director
  415/459-5397,
  chijoan@msn.com

Academic Year Program, Outbound
  Mary Davidson,
  Outbound Manager
  800/395-2726,
  chimaryd@msn.com

Career Exploration Program,
Work and Travel
  Gayle Empson,
  Director,
  415/459-5397,
  chigayle@msn.com

Group Homestay, Inbound
  Jackie Sant-Myerhoff,
  Director
  415/459-5397,
  chijackie@msn.com

Work and Travel, Outbound
  Brenda Solheim,
  800/395-2726,
  chibrenda@msn.com

**Exchange Related Facilitative or
Support Services Include:**
People with Disabilities
  Gayle Empson

Overseas Offices:
Vancouver, Canada
Bratislava, Slovak Republic
Seoul, Korea
Tokyo, Japan

Culturelink International Educational Programs

8201 Peters Road, Suite 1000
Plantation, FL 33324

Tel.: 954/432-2355
Fax: 954/916-2601
Website: www.culturelinkinc.com
E-mail: culture@interpoint.net

General Inquiries:
Beatriz Guzman,
President
954/432-2355,
culture@interpoint.net

Chief Executive Officer:
Dr. Jose Domingo Mujica,
Executive Director and CEO

Statement:
Culturelink is an organization engaged in the interdisciplinary study of international educational relations, culture and communication. It promotes educational opportunities across national boundaries and its activities emphasize high quality interdisciplinary linkages of crucial social and policy issues of international scope and global importance.

Profile:
Nonprofit founded in 1995. Culturelink has three U.S. staff and five overseas staff. Two overseas volunteers contribute to Culturelink's mission.

Geographic Focus:
Worldwide

Exchange Activities:
Culturelink is involved in the following exchange areas: Students/Educators, Training, Internships.

Financial Assistance:
Culturelink does not provide financial assistance.

Publications:
A Taste of Venezuela
(handbook for students going abroad)
954/432-2355
Beatriz Guzman,
President
culture@interpoint.net

Exchange Programs Include:
Study Abroad in Venezuela
Beatriz Guzman,
President
954/432-2355
culture@interpoint.net

Internships in Venezuela
Beatriz Guzman,
President
954/432-2355
culture@interpoint.net

Internships in Argentina
Beatriz Guzman,
President
954/432-2355
culture@interpoint.net

Internships in the United States
Beatriz Guzman,
President
954/432-2355
culture@interpoint.net

Internships & Study Abroad in Chile
Beatriz Guzman,
President
954/432-2355
culture@interpoint.net

Exchange Related Facilitative or Support Services Include:
Admission/Placement Services
Internships in the United States
Beatriz Guzman,
President
954/432-2355
culture@interpoint.net

Conferences/Meetings/Workshops
International Conferences, Seminars and workshops in all fields
Beatriz Guzman,
President
954/432-2355
culture@interpoint.net

Courses for Credit
Study Abroad & Internships in Venezuela, Argentina and Chile
Beatriz Guzman,
President
954/432-2355
culture@interpoint.net

Accreditation to non-U.S. institutions of higher education
Beatriz Guzman,
President
954/432-2355
culture@interpoint.net

Overseas Offices:
Caracas, Venezuela
Santiago, Chile
Buenos Aires, Argentina
Quito, Ecuador

DM Discoveries (DMDISC)

11000 Stonebrook Drive
Manassas, VA 20112

Tel.: 703/670-6664
Fax: 703/670-7973

Secondary Address:
22 Howell Avenue
Patchogue, NY 11772

Tel.: 631/475-2468
Fax: 631/475-2462

Website: members.aol.com/rmdisc/
welcome.htm
E-mail: dmdisc@aol.com

General Inquiries:
Dominique McPhail,
CEO
703/670-6664,
dmdisc@aol.com

Chief Executive Officer:
Dominique McPhail

Statement:
DM Discoveries' (DMDISC) mission is to promote world peace and better understanding of different cultures through direct exposure in the United States and abroad. DMDISC promotes the belief that by giving young people the opportunity to improve their language skills, their cross-cultural communication skills will also improve to benefit future generations in a fast growing world.

Profile:
Nonprofit founded in 1996. ERDT has two U.S. staff. Twenty-two coordinators contribute to DMDISC's mission.

Geographic Focus:
Africa (Kenya, Tanzania), Asia (Mongolia, Japan), Central America (Mexico), Western Europe (France, Germany, Albania), South America (Brazil, Peru)

Exchange Activities:
DMDISC is involved in the following exchange areas: Homestay, Community/Citizen, Short-Term Visitors. DMDISC provides exchange-related facilitative or support services. It administers exchange programs for the following academic levels: Students K-12.

Financial Assistance:
DMDISC offers a reduction of program fees to needy students upon request in a limited amount.

Exchange Programs Include:
High School Exchange Program
School Year/Semester
Dominique McPhail,
CEO
703/670-6664
dmdisc@aol.com

Total Immersion Program/Short Term
Stephanie McPhail,
CEO
631/475-2468

Exchange Related Facilitative or Support Services Include:
Admissions/Placement Service
Dominique McPhail,
CEO
703/670-6664
dmdisc@aol.com

Conferences/Meetings/Workshops
Stephanie McPhail
631/475-2468
stephdmdiscny@aol.com

Credentials Evaluation
Dominique McPhail,
CEO
703/670-6664
dmdisc@aol.com

Grants/Scholarships to Individuals
Dominique McPhail,
CEO
703/670-6664
dmdisc@aol.com

International Visitor Support
Stephanie McPhail,
Regional Advisor/Manager
631/475-2468
stephdmdiscny@aol.com

Testing/Assessment Services S.L.E.P.
Dominique McPhail,
CEO
703/670-6664
dmdisc@aol.com

Additional Offices:
Lancaster, PA
Chalmette, LA
Shawnee, OK

U.S. Department of State Designated Sponsor for the Exchange Vistor Program
Secondary school students

East-West Center (EWC)

**1601 East-West Road
Honolulu, HI 96848-1601**

Tel.: 808/944-7111
Fax: 808/944-7376
Website: www.eastwestcenter.org

General Inquiries:
Karen Knudsen,
Director, Office of External Affairs
808/944-7195,
knudsenk@eastwestcenter.org

Chief Executive Officer:
Dr. Charles E. Morrison

Statement:
The East-West Center was established by the U.S. Congress in 1960 to promote cooperation and understanding between the peoples and nations of the Asia-Pacific region, and the United States, through education, training, and dialogue. It brings together students from the Asia-Pacific region to work and study together in Honolulu. Center activities focus on the promotion of shared regional values and the building of regional agencies and arrangements; the promotion of economic growth with equity, stability, and sustainability; and the management and resolution of critical regional as well as common national political, economic, and social problems.

Profile:
Nonprofit founded in 1960. EWC has 155 staff.

Geographic Focus:
Asia, Oceania

Exchange Activities:
EWC is involved in the following exchange areas: Arts/Cultural, Professional/Business, Students/Educators, Training. EWC provides exchange-related facilitative or support services.

Financial Assistance:
EWC does not provide financial assistance.

Publications:
Asia Pacific Issues Papers

East-West Center Special Reports

Quarterly newsletter *"Observer"*

Various books and special
   publications

**Exchange Related Facilitative or
Support Services Include:**
Conference/Meetings/Workshops

Visiting Fellows

Educational Resource Development Trust (ERDT)

475 Washington Boulevard
Suite 220
Marina del Ray, CA 90292

Tel.: 310/821-9977
Fax: 310/821-9282
Website: http://www.erdtshare.org
E-mail: erdtshare@aol.com

General Inquiries:
Roger A. Riske,
President
310/821-9977

Chief Executive Officer:
Roger A. Riske,
President

Statement:
Educational Resource Development Trust's (ERDT) mission is to increase understanding and tolerance of other cultures; increase exchange students' knowledge of American culture and values; increase Americans' knowledge of other cultures and values; develop an enduring interest in other cultures; and improve students' language proficiency.

Profile:
Nonprofit founded in 1974. ERDT has 15 U.S. staff. Two hundred U.S. volunteers contribute to ERDT's mission.

Geographic Focus:
Worldwide

Exchange Activities:
ERDT is involved in the following exchange areas: Homestay, Language Study, Short-Term Visitors, Students/Educators. ERDT provides exchange-related facilitative or support services. It administers exchange programs for the following academic levels: Graduate Students, K-12, Undergraduate Students.

Financial Assistance:
ERDT provides a discount on homestay or homestay/study abroad for U.S. families who host J-1 high school exchange students.

Exchange Programs Include:
ERDT/SHARE!
High School Exchange Program
    Colin Churchill,
    Director of Academic Programs
    cchurchill@erdtshare.org

Farmstays/Ranchstays
    Karen Smith
    Director of Special Programs
    erdtspclprogdiv@aol.com

Short-Term Homestays
    Karen Smith,
    Director of Special Programs
    erdtspclprogdiv@aol.com

Study Abroad
    Karen Smith
    Director of Special Programs
    erdtspclprogdiv@aol.com

Exchange Related Facilitative or Support Services Include:
Admissions/Placement Service
    College/University/Secondary
    Boarding School Placement
    Roger Riske
    rriske@erdtshare.org

Additional Office:
Pacific, MO

U.S. Department of State Designated Sponsor for the Exchange Vistor Program
Secondary school students

Educational Testing Service (ETS)

Rosedale and Carter Roads
Princeton, NJ 08541-0001

Tel.: 609/921-9000
Fax: 609/734-5117
Website: http://www.ets.org

Secondary Address:
1800 K Street NW
Suite 900
Washington, DC 20006

Tel.: 202/659-0616
Fax: 202/659-8075

General Inquiries:
Rod Ballard,
Director,
International Development
609/683-2484,
rballard@ets.org

Chief Executive Officer:
Kurt M. Landgraf,
President

Statement:
Educational Testing Service (ETS)
is the world's premier educational
measurement institution and a
leader in educational research.
ETS, which is a nonprofit organization, develops and administers
achievement, occupational and
admissions tests, such as the
College Board's SAT, for clients in
education, government, and business. ETS annually administers
almost 11 million tests in the
United States and 180 countries.
ETS was founded to assume the
testing activities of the American

Council on Education, the
Carnegie Foundation for the
Advancement of International
Peace, and the College Entrance
Examination Board.

Profile:
Nonprofit founded in 1947. ETS
has 2,000 U.S. staff.

Geographic Focus:
Worldwide

Exchange Activities:
ETS is involved in the following
exchange areas: Assessment. ETS
provides exchange-related facilitative or support services. It administers exchange programs for the
following academic levels: Faculty.

Financial Assistance:
ETS does not provide financial
assistance.

Exchange Programs Include:
ETS Global Institute
    Debbie Stout,
    Staff Associate
    609/683-2346,

Exchange Related Facilitative or
Support Services Include:
International Visitor Support
    Jeannette File-Lamb,
    Executive Director,
    International Development
    609/734-1708

Testing/Assessment Services
    Jeannette File-Lamb,
    Executive Director,
    International Development
    609/734-1708

Education Travel & Culture, Inc. (ETC)

600 SW 10th Avenue, Suite 520
P.O. Box 4632
Portland, OR 97208

Tel.: 503/222-9803
Fax: 503/227-7224
Website: http://www.edutrav.org
E-mail: edutrav@aol.com

General Inquiries:
Sara G. Cogan,
President/CEO
Shane Sturtz,
503/222-9803

Chief Executive Officer:
Sara G. Cogan,
President/CEO

Statement:
Education Travel & Culture (ETC) is a nonprofit educational exchange organization. Its purpose is to promote international under- standing and goodwill by provid- ing high quality educational and cultural exchange opportunities in the United States and abroad. ETC provides opportunities for high school students throughout the world to study in an American high school and live with an American family. Host families provide room and board, a quiet place to study, and an American family experience for guest stu- dents during their semester or aca- demic year in the United States.

Profile:
Nonprofit founded in 1998. ETC has 15 U.S. staff. More than 50 U.S. volunteers contribute to ETC's mission.

Geographic Focus:
Worldwide

Exchange Activities:
ETC is involved in the following exchange areas: Homestay. It administers exchange programs for the following academic levels: K-12.

Financial Assistance:
ETC does not provide financial assistance.

Publications:
Program Brochure

Exchange Programs Include:
Inbound J-1 Secondary
School Exchange
    Sara Cogan or Shane Sturtz
    503/222-9803

Outbound Short-Term,
AYP & Semester Abroad
    Sara Cogan or Shane Sturtz
    503/222-9803

**U.S. Department of State
Designated Sponsor for the
Exchange Vistor Program**
Secondary school students

EF Foundation for Foreign Study (EF)

EF Center Boston
One Education Street
Cambridge, MA 02141-1883

Tel.: 617/619-1000
Fax: 617/619-1001
Website: www.effoundation.org
E-mail: foundation@ef.com

General Inquiries:
Kim Weyl Belfort,
Director of Government and
Media Relations
617/619-1000,
kim.weyl.belfort@ef.com

Chief Executive Officer:
Goran Rannefors,
President

Statement:
EF Foundation is a worldwide, non-profit organization dedicated to international student exchange and education with the aim of encouraging cultural awareness and mutual respect between nations.

Profile:
Nonprofit founded in 1979. EF has 50 U.S. staff and 50 overseas staff. Eight hundred U.S. volunteers contribute to EF's mission.

Geographic Focus:
Worldwide

Exchange Activities:
EF is involved in the following exchange areas:
Students/Educators. EF provides exchange-related facilitative or support services. It administers exchange programs for the following academic levels: K-12.

Financial Assistance:
EF Foundation offers low-cost financing to all U.S. students who wish to spend a school year abroad. In addition, ten partial scholarships are provided to U.S. students and are based on academic merit, citizenship, and teacher recommendations. The children of host families also receive scholarship funding to study abroad.

Publications:
The Exchange (written for and by exchange students and host families)

Exchange Programs Include:
Discovery Tours
Nancy Halter,
Program Director
617/619-1000,
nancy.halter@ef.com

High School Abroad
Micah Parker,
Program Director
617/619-1000,
micah.parker@ef.com

High School Year in America
Asa Finelli,
President
617/619-1000

Language and Culture Camp
Nancy Halter,
Program Director
617/619-1000,
nancy.halter@ef.com

EF Au Pair
800/333-6056,
aupair@ef.com

Overseas Offices:
Moscow, Russia
Mexico City, Mexico
Jakarta, Indonesia
Madrid, Spain
Helsinki, Finland
Copenhagen, Denmark
Bogota, Colombia
Berlin, Germany
Amsterdam, Netherlands
Milan, Rome, Italy
Stockholm, Sweden
Bangkok, Thailand
Quito, Ecuador
Zurich, Switzerland
Hong Kong, China
Sydney, Australia
Taipei, Taiwan
Tokyo, Japan
Toronto, Canada
Vienna, Austria
Oslo, Norway
Paris, France
Sao Paulo, Brazil

U.S. Department of State
Designated Sponsor for the
Exchange Vistor Program
Au pairs

Alliance
MEMBER

Eisenhower Fellowships

256 South 16th Street
Philadelphia, PA 19102

Tel.: 215/546-1738
Fax: 215/546-4567
Website: http://www.eef.org
E-mail: ike@eef.org

General Inquiries:
Arlene Pajic
aj@eef.org

Chief Executive Officer:
Adrian A. Basora,
President

Statement:
The Eisenhower Fellowships bring outstanding professionals who are emerging leaders in their countries to the United States and send their U.S. counterparts abroad. The Multi-Nation and Single Nation/Single Region Programs provide two months of coast-to-coast travel, with a custom-designed program for each participant. Introductions, observations, consultations, and conferences are tailored to his or her professional interests. To complement the professional focus, Eisenhower encourages social and cultural exchange so that fellows are exposed to diversity and vibrancy of life in the United States.

Profile:
Nonprofit founded in 1953. Eisenhower Fellowships has 19 U.S. staff.

Geographic Focus:
Worldwide

Exchange Activities:
Eisenhower Fellowships is involved in the following exchange areas: Professional/Business, Short-Term Fellowship Programs. Eisenhower Fellowships provide professional, individual agenda planning and facilitating exchange-related facilitative, or support services.

Financial Assistance:
Eisenhower Fellowships provide support for invited fellows. Eisenhower Fellowships does not support academic research.

Publications:
Annual Report

Brochures with program descriptions

Exchange Programs Include:
Multi-Nation Program

Single Nation/Single Region Program

USA Program

Exchange Related Facilitative or Support Services Include:
Grants/Scholarships to Individuals, by invitation only

U.S. Department of State Designated Sponsor for the Exchange Vistor Program
Specialists

EurAupair Intercultural Childcare Programs (EurAupair)

250 North Coast Highway
Laguna Beach, CA 92651

Tel.: 949/494-5500
Fax: 949/497-6235
Website: www.euraupair.com
E-mail: info@euraupair.com

General Inquiries:
Receptionist
949/494-5500 x2
info@europair.com

Chief Executive Officer:
Bodil Dencker,
CEO

Statement:
EurAupair Intercultural Childcare Programs (EurAupair) is a U.S.-based, nonprofit public benefit organization founded to improve understanding among people of different countries through cultural exchange. Through its network of affiliated overseas offices, EurAupair screens young people from several European countries who want to become Au Pairs. EurAupair brings bright, responsible Au Pairs to the United States who assist in caring for a host family's children in exchange for inclusion in American family life, the opportunity to study at an American college, and exposure to a new culture.

Profile:
Nonprofit founded in 1988. EurAupair has 12 U.S. staff. Four hundred fifty U.S. volunteers contribute to EurAupair's mission.

Geographic Focus:
Worldwide

Exchange Activities:
EurAupair is involved in the following exchange areas: Au Pair. EurAupair provides exchange-related facilitative or support services.

Financial Assistance:
EurAupair does not provide financial assistance.

Exchange Programs Include:
EurAupair Intercultural Childcare Programs

Additional Offices:
Atlanta, GA
Kirkland, WA
Wayzata, MN
Alexandria, VA

Overseas Offices:
Warsaw, Poland
Aix-en-Provence, France
Almere, Netherlands
Bangkok, Thailand
Gauteng, South Africa
Kastrup, Denmark
Montreal, Canada
Lainate, Italy
Prague, Czech Republic
Lisbon, Portugal
Madrid, Spain
Barcelona, Spain
Oslo, Norway
Stockholm, Sweden
Tallinn, Estonia
Tokyo, Japan
Vantaa, Finland
Zurich, Switzerland
Heidelberg, Germany
Dresden, Germany

U.S. Department of State Designated Sponsor for the Exchange Vistor Program
Au pairs

Eurocentres

101 North Union Street
Suite 300
Alexandria, VA 22314

Tel.: 703/684-1494
Fax: 703/684-1495
Website: www.eurocentres.com
E-mail: alx-info@eurocentres.com

General Inquiries:
Diane Vespucci,
Director
703/684-1494 ,
dvespucci@eurocentres.com

Chief Executive Officer:
Michael Gerber,
CEO

Statement:
Eurocentres' mission is to contribute to international understanding through the medium of cultural exchange and language training. It offers extensive immersion language learning courses in ten countries, combined with homestay programs and cultural activities.

Profile:
Nonprofit founded in 1960. Eurocentre has 15 U.S. staff and 250 overseas staff.

Geographic Focus:
Asia (Japan), Newly Independent States (Russia), Western Europe (France, Germany, Spain, Italy, United Kingdom)

Exchange Activities:
Eurocentre is involved in the following exchange areas: Homestay, Language Study, Short-Term Visitors, Training. Eurocentre provides exchange-related facilitative or support services. It administers exchange programs for the following academic levels: Faculty, Graduate Students, K-12, Teachers, Undergraduate Students.

Financial Assistance:
A certain number of tuition-only scholarships are available. Details are available from the Switzerland headquarter.

Publications:
Annual Brochure

Holiday Courses for Young Learners

Exchange Programs Include:
Learn a Language,
Live a Language-France
   info@eurocentres.com

Learn a Language,
Live a Language-Germany,
   info@eurocentres.com

Learn a Language,
Live a Language-Italy
   info@eurocentres.com

Learn a Language,
Live a Language-Japan
   info@eurocentres.com

Learn a Language,
Live a Language-Spain
   info@eurocentres.com

Exchange Related Facilitative or Support Services Include:
Admissions/Placement Service
   Central Enrollment Services
   info@eurocentres.com

Overseas Offices:
Karazawa, Japan
London, United Kingdom
Madrid, Spain
Florence, Italy
Cologne, Germany
Moscow, Russia
Zurich, Switzerland
Paris, France

Exchange: Japan

P.O. Box 12459
Hamtramck, MI 48212

Tel.: 313/874-1222
Fax: 313/874-1228
Website: www.exchangejapan.org
E-mail: exchangejapan@juno.com

Secondary Address:
Ikeda Bldg. #702
115 Shin Ogowamachi
Shinjuku-ku, Tokyo, 162-0814
JAPAN

General Inquiries:
Bill Wiitala,
Director, U.S.

Chief Executive Officer:
Bill Wiitala,
Director, U.S.

Statement:
Exchange: Japan is committed to the promotion of mutual understanding and global exchange built on excellence in Japanese language training. It has provided services and placement for 150 colleges, universities, and high schools and nearly 1,000 individuals during the past 12 years.

Profile:
Nonprofit founded in 1987.
Exchange: Japan has one U.S. staff.

Geographic Focus:
Asia (Japan), Caribbean (Puerto Rico, Virgin Islands)

Exchange Activities:
Exchange: Japan is involved in the following exchange areas: Language Study, Teacher Training. Exchange: Japan provides exchange-related facilitative or support services. It administers exchange programs for the following academic levels: Faculty, Graduate Students, K-12, Teachers, Undergraduate Students.

Financial Assistance:
Exchange: Japan provides postsecondary study scholarships in exchange for teaching Japanese at the institution.

Publications:
Exchange: Japan Today

Exchange Programs Include:
Educational Exchange Program

Teacher Training Institute

Exchange Related Facilitative or Support Services Include:
Admissions/Placement Service

Conference/Meetings/Workshops

Courses for Credit

Grants/Scholarships to Individuals

Testing/Assessment Services

Overseas Office:
Tokyo, Japan

Experience International

P.O. Box 680
Everson, WA 98247

Tel.: 360/966-3876
Fax: 360/966-4131
Website: http://www.expint.org
E-mail: ei@expint.org

General Inquiries:
Charlie Walkinshaw,
Director
360/966-3876,
ei@expint.org

Chief Executive Officer:
Charlie Walkinshaw,
Director

Statement:
Experience International is a non-profit organization that promotes quality training and professional exchanges in production agriculture and horticulture; fisheries and aquaculture; forestry; and resource management fields. The organization is a designated J-1 Exchange Visitor Trainee Program sponsor; conducts an outbound program for Americans seeking work experience abroad; and organizes Professional Study Tours for foreign nationals to the United States, and U.S. citizens abroad. The organization is involved in a range of special projects related to the design, implementation, and evaluation of training programs, development/natural resource management projects, and Forestry Certification activities throughout the Americas.

Profile:
Nonprofit founded in 1988. Experience International has four U.S. staff.

Geographic Focus:
Worldwide

Exchange Activities:
Experience International is involved in the following exchange areas: Training, Professional/Business, Outbound Programs. It provides exchange-related facilitative and support services.

Financial Assistance:
Experience International does not provide financial assistance.

Exchange Programs Include:
J-1 Exchange Visitor Trainee Program
    Valerie Normand,
    Program Coordinator
    360/966-3876,
    ei@expint.org

Training, Study Tours, Outbound,
Special Projects
    Charlie Walkinshaw,
    Director
    360/966-3876,
    ei@expint.org

Exchange Related Facilitative or Support Services Include:
Workshop Facilitation

Program Evaluation

Professional Study Tours

Training Program Design & Evaluation

Special Programs
    Charlie Walkinshaw, Director
    360/966-3876, ei@expint.org

U.S. Department of State Designated Sponsor for the Exchange Vistor Program
Trainees
Intern

Face the World Foundation

1010 B Street, Suite 350
San Rafael, CA 94901

Tel.: 415/257-4787
Fax: 415/257-4784
Website: www.facetheworld.org
E-mail: info@facetheworld.org

General Inquiries:
Mary Kass,
President
415/257-4787,
info@facetheworld.org

Chief Executive Officer:
Mary Kass,
President

Statement:
Face the World Foundation is a
nonprofit educational and cultural
organization. For over nine years,
Face the World's mission has been
to provide all participants with a
quality experience that will
enhance their growth and encourage friendships for a lifetime.

Profile:
Nonprofit founded in 1993. Face the
World Foundation has 18 U.S. staff.

Geographic Focus:
North America (United States,
Canada)

Exchange Activities:
Face the World is involved in the
following exchange areas:
Homestay, Short-Term Visitors,
Students/Educators. It provides
exchange-related facilitative or support services. Face the World
administers exchange programs for
the following academic levels: K-12.

Financial Assistance:
Face the World provides limited
scholarships on a case-by-case basis.

Publications:
Share the World (brochure)

Exchange Programs Include:
High School Academic Program

Exchange-Related Facilitative or
Support Services:
Admission/Placement Services

U.S. Department of State
Designated Sponsor for the
Exchange Vistor Program
Secondary school students

Foreign Study Language (FSL)

**1903 Old Swede Road
Douglassville, PA 19518**

Tel.: 610/689-4401
Fax: 610/689-4477
Website: www.fsleducation.com
E-mail: info@fsleducation.com

General Inquiries:
Janice Schiffman,
Margie Griesemer
610/689-4401

Chief Executive Officer:
Sarah C. and Carter P. Reese,
Chief Executive Officers

Statement:
Foreign Study Language (FSL) provides an exceptional range of educational opportunities for students from around the world. FSL's mission is to foster global understanding through international educational exchange programs at the secondary school level, and to facilitate placement for qualified international students at selected American colleges and universities.

Profile:
Nonprofit founded in 1988. FSL has 15 U.S. staff.

Geographic Focus:
Worldwide

Exchange Activities:
FSL is involved in the following exchange areas: Homestay, Language Study, Students/Educators. FSL provides exchange-related facilitative or support services. It administers exchange programs for the following academic levels: Graduate Students, K-12, Undergraduate Students.

Financial Assistance:
FSL does not provide financial assistance.

Publications:
Universities in America Brochure

Academic Year Program Brochure

Outbound Program Brochure

Exchange Programs Include:
FSL Outbound

High Schools in America
  Todd Leyland
  tleyland@studygroupintl.com

Universities in America
  Janice Schiffman
  jschiffman@studygroupintl.com

Exchange Related Facilitative or Support Services Include:
Admissions/Placement Service

U.S. Department of State Designated Sponsor for the Exchange Vistor Program
Secondary school students

Foundation for International Cooperation (FIC)

1237 South Western Avenue
Park Ridge, IL 60068

Tel.: 800/890-3543
Fax: 847/518-8384
Website: www.ficcultureswap.org
E-mail: fic@surfmail.net

General Inquiries:
Irene B. Horst

Chief Executive Officer:
John Fopeano,
President

Statement:
The Foundation for International Cooperation (FIC) promotes and facilitates intercultural exchange in the United States and in many countries of the world with its home hospitality programs and adult study tours. FIC provides cultural exchanges through its volunteer network of 13 chapters located in New York, New Jersey, Alabama, Florida, Kentucky, Indiana, Illinois, Wisconsin, Minnesota, Arizona, Texas, California, and with cooperating organizations abroad. High school exchanges are the primary work of the Buffalo, NY chapter. Membership is open to anyone interested in furthering peace and understanding.

Profile:
Nonprofit founded in 1960. FIC has one U.S. staff. FIC provides a membership program and has 300 individual members, and 13 local chapters/affiliates. Fifty U.S. volunteers and 50 overseas volunteers contribute to FIC's mission.

Geographic Focus:
Worldwide

Exchange Activities:
FIC is involved in the following exchange areas: Arts/Cultural, Community/Citizen, Homestay, Professional/Business, Senior Citizens, Short-Term Visitors. FIC provides exchange-related facilitative or support services.

Financial Assistance:
Although FAF does not provide grants directly, the Foundation provides consultation on all development programs, provides the opportunity for Companion Tours as fund raisers and offers free travel for all group leaders. Familiarization tours are also provided free of charge to certain group coordinators in advance of specific programs. All tours are fully tax deductible for all participants as allowed by law.

Publications:
News Notes (quarterly publication),
Irene Horst, 800/890-3543

Informational Brochure

Exchange Programs Include:
Domestic Tours/Regional Homestay
Irene Horst,
800/890-3543

Study Tours/Home Stays
Mary Spradlin,
630/357-1887

Additional Offices:
Clarence, NY
South Bend, IN
San Diego, CA
Ridgewood, NJ
Pensacola, FL
Minneapolis, MN
Maumee, OH
Huntsville, AL
Tucson, AZ
Chicago, IL
Austin, TX
Louisville, KY

The Foundation for Worldwide International Student Exchange (WISE Foundation)

207 North Church Street
P.O. Box 1332
Dyersburg, TN 38024

Tel.: 731/287-9948
Fax: 731/287-9949
Website: www.wisefoundation.com
E-mail: dave@wisefoundation.com

General Inquiries:
David N. Dahl,
Executive Director
731/287-9948,
dave@wisefoundation.com

Chief Executive Officer:
David N. Dahl,
Executive Director

Statement:
The goal of The Foundation for Worldwide International Student Exchange (WISE) is to promote world peace and understanding through cultural exchanges, and establish global friendships. WISE offers USA Homestays for groups and individuals, Farm and Ranch stays, International Volunteer Homestay Programs, High School Programs (one and two semesters), Hospitality Training Programs, and Work and Travel Programs.

Profile:
Nonprofit founded in 1989. WISE has 17 U.S. staff and 10 U.S. volunteers contributing to its mission.

Geographic Focus:
Asia (Japan, Korea, Taiwan, Malaysia, China), Western Europe (United Kingdom, Germany, France, Spain), South America (Brazil, Colombia, Argentina)

Exchange Activities:
WISE is involved in the following exchange areas: Arts/Culture, Professional/Business, Training, Work Exchanges, Homestay, Short-Term Visitors, Students/Educators. It administers exchange programs for the following academic levels: Graduate Students, Teachers and Students K-12, Undergraduate Students.

Financial Assistance:
WISE does not provide financial assistance.

Exchange Programs Include:
Hospitality Training Program
Todd Buchla
678/355-1226,
todd@wisefoundation.com

Work and Travel Program
Tanya Schulze
678/290-5212,
tanya@wisefoundation.com

Academic Year Program
Sid Dye
731/287-9948,
sid@wisefoundation.com

Group Homestay Program
Karen Paschal
731/287-9948,
karen@wisefoundation.com

International Volunteer and
Farmstay/Ranchstay Programs
Karen Paschal
731/287-9948,
karen@wisefoundation.com

Additional Offices:
Davis, CA
Irvine, CA
Boston, MA
Atlanta, GA

U.S. Department of State
Designated Sponsor for the
Exchange Vistor Program
Trainees
College and university students
Secondary school students
Summer work/travel
Intern

Freedom House

1319 18th Street, NW
Washington, DC 20036

Tel.: 202/296-5101
Fax: 202/296-5078
Website: www.freedomhouse.org
E-mail: fh@freedomhouse.org

Secondary Address:
120 Wall Street
New York, NY 10005

General Inquiries:
Christina Hartman,
Assistant to the Executive Director
202/296-5101 x117
fh@freedomhouse.org

Chief Executive Officer:
Jennifer Windsor,
Executive Director

Statement:
Freedom House is a clear voice for democracy around the world. Founded in 1941 by Eleanor Roosevelt, Wendell Wilkie, and other Americans concerned with mounting threats to peace and democracy, Freedom House has been a vigorous proponent of democratic values and a steadfast opponent of dictatorship on the far left and far right. Today, Freedom House is a leading advocate of the world's young democracies, which are coping with the legacies of statism, dictatorship, and political repression. It conducts an array of U.S. and international research, advocacy, education, and training initiatives promoting human rights, democracy, free market economies, rule of law, independent media, and U.S. engagement in international affairs.

Profile:
Nonprofit founded in 1941. Freedom House has 28 U.S. staff and 25 overseas staff. Twenty overseas volunteers contribute to Freedom House's mission.

Geographic Focus:
Worldwide

Exchange Activities:
Freedom House is involved in the following exchange areas: Professional/Business, Short-Term Visitors, Training. Freedom House provides exchange-related facilitative or support services.

Financial Assistance:
For Visiting Fellows and short-term U.S. training programs, FH typically covers all costs including international airfare, domestic transportation costs, accommodations, and a modest daily living stipend. For American volunteers posted abroad, FH provides international airfare and a modest living and housing stipend.

Publications:
Freedom in the World (annual global survey of political rights and civil liberties)

Nations in Transit (annual study of civil society, democracy and markets in East Central Europe and NIS)

Press Freedom (annual survey of press freedom around the world)

NGONews (newsletter for non-governmental organizations in Central/Eastern Europe and the Newly Independent States)

Religious Freedom in the World: A Global Report on Freedom and Persecution

Exchange Programs Include:
The American Volunteers for International Development (AVID)
Jennifer Whatley,
Senior Program Officer
202/296-5101 x116,
whatley@freedomhouse.org

Visiting Fellows Program
Jennifer Whatley,
Senior Program Officer
202/296-5101 x116,
whatley@freedomhouse.org

Exchange Related Facilitative or Support Services Include:
Conference/Meetings/Workshops
Regional Networking Project
Peter Wiebler, Director of the
Regional Networking Project
wiebler@freedomhouse.hu

Partnership for Reform in Ukraine
Laryssa Tatarynova, PRU Director
tatarinova@freedomhouse.kiev.ua

Rule of Law Initiative/Global
Human Rights Training and Support
Lisa Davis, RIGHTS Director
davis@freedomhouse.org

Grants to Institutions/Organizations
Regional Networking Project
Peter Wiebler, Director of the
Regional Networking Project
wiebler@freedomhouse.hu

Partnership for Reform in Ukraine
John Kubiniec,
Director of the Kiev Office
johnk@freedomhouse.kiev.ua

Rule of Law Initiative/ Global
Human Rights Training and Support
Lisa Davis, RIGHTS Director
davis@freedomhouse.org

Polish-American-Ukrainian
Cooperative Initiative (PAUCI)
John Kubiniec, PAUCI Director
kubiniec@freedomhouse.kiev.ua

The Reintegration and Leadership
Development Project in Serbia
Peter Wiebler, RNP Director
wiebler@freedomhouse.hu

Overseas Offices:
Sarajevo, Bosnia & Herzegovina
Bucharest, Romania
Budapest, Hungary
Kiev, Ukraine
Warsaw, Poland
Belgrade, Serbia
Dili, East Timor

French-American Chamber of Commerce, New York Chapter (FACC)

1350 Avenue of the Americas
6th Floor
New York, NY 10019

Tel.: 212/765-4460
Fax: 212/765-4650
Website: http://www.faccnyc.org
E-mail: icdp@faccnyc.org

General Inquiries:
Chris Gallagher,
ICDP Department Manager
212/765-4556,
icdp@faccnyc.org

Chief Executive Officer:
Serge Bellanger,
President
Cathy Baiardi,
Managing Director

Statement:
The objectives of the French-American Chamber of Commerce (FACC) are to promote trade, finance and investment between the United States and France, to offer a platform for its members to exchange views on major economic and business issues, to support the growth and development of member companies, and to help member companies educate and train the future leaders of the French-American business community. The New York Chapter of the FACC administers the program.

Profile:
Nonprofit founded in 1896 in New York. FACC has nine U.S. staff. It provides a membership program and has 4,100 members in 20 local chapters/affiliates.

Geographic Focus:
Worldwide

Exchange Activities:
FACC is involved in the following exchange area: Training.

Financial Assistance:
FACC does not provide financial assistance.

Publications:
French-American News (published quarterly in New York)

National Membership Directory (published annually)

Exchange Programs Include:
International Career Development Programs (ICDP)
Chris Gallagher, ICDP Department Manager
212/765-4556, icdp@faccnyc.org

Exchange Related Facilitative or Support Services Include:
Membership Services
International Career Development Programs (ICDP)
Chris Gallagher, ICDP Department Manager
212/765-4556, icdp@faccnyc.org

U.S. Department of State Designated Sponsor for the Exchange Vistor Program
Trainees
Intern

Alliance
MEMBER

Friendship Ambassadors Foundation (FAF)

110 Mamaroneck Avenue
Suites 7 and 8
White Plains, NY 10601

Tel.: 914/328-8589
Fax: 914/328-8578

General Inquiries:
914/328-8589,
friendlyam@aol.com

Chief Executive Officer:
Patrick Sciarratta,
Executive Director

Statement:
Friendship Ambassadors
Foundation (FAF) is a nonprofit,
cultural services agency with international affiliations and representation. FAF prepares and promotes
all aspects of intercultural exchange
for professional and educational
groups traveling abroad. The foundation helps bring similar groups
together worldwide in order to promote peace, cooperation, and mutual understanding. FAF also
believes that cultural tourism promotes sustainable development in
communities throughout the world.

Profile:
Nonprofit

Geographic Focus:
Worldwide

Exchange Activities:
FAF is involved in the following
exchange areas: Arts/Cultural,
Homestay, Other/Volunteer,
Students/Educators. FAF provides
exchange-related facilitative or support services.

Financial Assistance:
Although not a direct grantmaker,
FAF provides the opportunity for
Companion Tours as fundraisers
and provides free travel for group
leaders. Familiarization tours are
also provided free of charge to certain group coordinators in advance
of specific programs.

Exchange Programs Include:
Cultural/Educational Exchange:
Nonperformance
    Patrick Sciarratta
    914/328-8589

Domestic Programs for
Foreign Performers
    friendlyam@aol.com

Performance Tours Abroad
    Josephine Scirocco,
    Music Coordinator
    fafjosephine@aol.com

Exchange Related Facilitative or
Support Services Include:
Conference/Meetings/Workshops

International Visitor Support

Travel Services

Overseas Office:
Budapest, Hungary

Friendship Force, Inc. (FFI)

57 Forsyth Street, NW
Suite 900
Atlanta, GA 30303

Tel.: 404/522-9490
Fax: 404/681-6148
Website: www.friendship-force.org

General Inquiries:
Chip Carter,
404/522-9490
c.carter@friendship-force.org

Chief Executive Officer:
Chip Carter,
President and Founder

Statement:
The Friendship Force annually conducts 250 to 300 short-term (two to three-week) citizen exchange programs, emphasizing family homestays. Among the 500 "ambassadors" participating each year are elementary, high school, and university-level students.

Profile:
Nonprofit founded in 1977. FFI has 25 U.S. staff and four overseas staff. FFI provides a membership program and has 10,000 individual members, and 127 local chapters/affiliates. Fifteen thousand five hundred U.S. volunteers and 16,900 overseas volunteers contribute to FFI's mission.

Geographic Focus:
Worldwide

Exchange Activities:
FFI is involved in the following exchange areas: Arts/Cultural, Community/Citizen, Professional/Business, Short-Term Visitors, Students/Educators. FFI provides exchange-related facilitative or support services. It administers exchange programs for the following academic levels: K-12, Undergraduate Students.

Financial Assistance:
Limited financial aid is available through local chapters to cover program fees. FFI provides scholarships/fellowships or financial assistance to participants.

Publications:
Friends Newsletter
Friendship
The Friendship Force
Information brochures

Exchange Programs Include:
Bridgebuilders
    Harriet Kuhr
    404/522-9490

Festivals of Friendship
    Harriet Kuhr
    404/522-9490

Homestay Exchanges
    Chip Carter
    404/522-9490

Overseas Offices:
Mainz, Germany
Moscow, Russia
Sao Paulo, Brazil
Wanganui, New Zealand

Fulbright Association (FA)

1130 17th Street, NW
Suite 310
Washington, DC 20036-4672

Tel.: 202/331-1590
Fax: 202/331-1979
Website: http://www.fulbright.org
E-mail: fulbright@fulbright.org

General Inquiries:
fulbright@fulbright.org

Chief Executive Officer:
Jane L. Anderson,
Executive Director

Statement:
The Fulbright Association is a national membership organization created by Fulbright alumni. The Fulbright Association supports and promotes the Fulbright program and other programs of international educational and cultural exchange; provides hospitality and enrichment activities for visiting Fulbright students, scholars, and teachers; and facilitates continuing relationships among, and the public service of, former Fulbright grantees.

Profile:
Nonprofit founded in 1977. FA has four U.S. staff. FA provides a membership program and has 164 institutional members, 6,100 individual members, and 39 local chapters/affiliates. Two hundred U.S. volunteers contribute to FA's mission.

Geographic Focus:
Worldwide

Exchange Activities:
FA provides exchange-related facilitative or support services.

Financial Assistance:
FA does not provide financial assistance.

Publications:
The Fulbrighters' Newsletter

Exchange Related Facilitative or Support Services Include:
Conference/Meetings/Workshops
202/331-1590
fulbright@fulbright.org

Membership Services
Lisa Chapin, Director of
Member and Chapter Services
202/331-1590,
l.chapin@fulbright.org

Public Policy
202/331-1590
fulbright@fulbright.org

GeoVisions

P.O. Box 167
Chesterfield, NH 03443

Tel.: 603/363-4187
Fax: 603/363-8446
Website: www.geovisions.org
E-mail: visions@geovisions.org

General Inquiries:
Kevin Morgan,
CEO
603/363-4187,
visions@geovisions.org

Chief Executive Officer:
Kevin Morgan

Statement:
GeoVisions is committed to providing students of all ages with opportunities to learn in classroom, field and workplace environments. GeoVisions' programs focus on language, culture and skills training that help participants gain a better understanding of peoples, businesses and governments around the world.

Profile:
Founded in 2001. GeoVisions has four U.S. staff.

Geographic Focus:
Asia (China, Vietnam, Singapore, Thailand, Japan, Korea), Central America (Costa Rica), North America (United States), Oceania (Australia, New Zealand), South America (Argentina, Brazil, Ecuador)

Exchange Activities:
GeoVisions is involved in the following exchange areas: Professional/Business, Training, Senior Citizen, Work Exchanges. It administers exchange programs for the following academic levels: Undergraduate Students.

Financial Assistance:
Does not provide financial assistance.

Exchange Programs Include:
Holiday Work/Travel to the USA
    Kevin Morgan
    visions@geovisions.org

Training & Internship Programs
(TIPS USA)
    Kevin Morgan
    visions@geovisions.org

Hospitality Training in
Singapore & Thailand
    Kevin Morgan
    visions@geovisions.org

Holiday Teach & Travel
(Thailand, Vietnam, China)
    Kevin Morgan
    visions@geovisions.org

Additional Office:
San Francisco, CA

U.S. Department of State
Designated Sponsor for the
Exchange Vistor Program
Trainees
Summer work/travel
Intern

German American Partnership Program, Inc. (GAPP)

1014 Fifth Avenue
New York, NY 10028

Tel.: 212/439-8700
Fax: 212/439-8705
Website: http://goethe.de/gapp
E-mail: gappny@aol.com

General Inquiries:
Sabina Margalit,
Executive Director
212/439-8717

Chief Executive Officer:
Werner Walbroel,
President

Statement:
The main goal of the German American Partnership Program, Inc. (GAPP) is to give high school students from the United States and the Federal Republic of Germany an opportunity to interact with one another and in doing so, to improve fluency in their target language. By opening channels of communication, students gain valuable insight into the way of life of the host country. Moreover, GAPP students experience in a foreign land what they have been learning at home. Friendships between 14 to 17-year old American and German students, developed abroad, form the basis for school-to-school, community-to-community, and country-to-country relationships.

Profile:
Nonprofit founded in 1977. GAPP has two U.S. staff and two overseas staff.

Geographic Focus:
Western Europe (Germany)

Exchange Activities:
GAPP is involved in the following exchange areas: Community/Citizen, Homestay, Language Study, Students/Educators. GAPP provides exchange-related facilitative or support services. It administers exchange programs for the following academic levels: K-12 (High School).

Financial Assistance:
GAPP offers travel grants to students and their accompanying teachers. Contact GAPP for an application.

Publications:
GAPP Newsletter
GAPP Handbook
The German School Experience
The American School Experience
GAPP Survey

Exchange Programs Include:
High School Linkage

U.S. Department of State Designated Sponsor for the Exchange Vistor Program
Secondary school students

The German Marshall Fund of the United States (GMF)

11 Dupont Circle, NW
Suite 750
Washington, DC 20036

Tel.: 202/745-3950
Fax: 202/265-1662
Website: http://www.gmfus.org
E-mail: info@gmfus.org

General Inquiries:
202/745-3950,
info@gmfus.org

Chief Executive Officer:
Craig Kennedy,
President

Statement:
The German Marshall Fund of the United States' (GMF) programmatic activities seek to create a closer understanding between partners on both sides of the Atlantic by targeting both institutions and individuals.

Profile:
Nonprofit founded in 1972. GMF has 14 U.S. staff and eight overseas staff.

Geographic Focus:
Western Europe, Eastern/Central Europe, North America

Exchange Activities:
GMF is involved in the following exchange areas: Professional/Business, Short-Term Visitors. GMF provides exchange-related facilitative or support services.

Financial Assistance:
GMF does offer financial assistance which varies by program.

Publications:
GMF Brochure

Journalism Program Brochure
Julianne Smith, Program Officer
202/745-3950, jsmith@gmfus.org

Exchange Programs Include:
Marshall Memorial Fellowship
Ellen Pope,
Program Officer
202/745-3950,
epope@gmfus.org

Community Foundation
Transatlantic Fellowship
Lea Rosenbohm,
Program Associate
202/745-3950,
lrosenbohm@gmfus.org

Manfred Wörner Seminar
Julianne Smith,
Program Officer
202/745-3950,
jsmith@gmfus.org

U.S.-Spain Young Leaders
Julianne Smith,
Program Officer
202/745-3950,
jsmith@gmfus.org

Exchange Related Facilitative or Support Services Include:
Grants to Institutions/Organizations
Steve Grand,
Director of Programs
202/745-3950,
sgrand@gmfus.org

Overseas Offices:
Berlin, Germany
Bratislava, Slovak Republic
Paris, France

U.S. Department of State Designated Sponsor for the Exchange Vistor Program
Specialists

Alliance MEMBER

Girl Scouts of the U.S.A. (GSUSA)

420 Fifth Avenue
New York, NY 10018-2702

Tel.: 212/852-8000
Fax: 212/852-6514
Website: www.girlscouts.org
E-mail: admin@bbs.gsusa

General Inquiries:
Joy Williams,
Asst. Director of Communications
212/852-8529

Chief Executive Officer:
Marsha J. Evans,
National Executive Director

Statement:
Girl Scouting is a movement that gives girls from all segments of American life a chance to develop their potential, make friends, and become a vital part of their community. Based on ethical values, Girl Scouts of the U.S.A. (GSUSA) opens up a world of opportunity for girls, working in partnership with adult volunteers. Its sole focus is to meet the special needs of girls.

Profile:
Nonprofit founded in 1912. GSUSA has 500 U.S. staff. GSUSA provides a membership program. Over 801,800 U.S. volunteers contribute to GSUSA's mission.

Geographic Focus:
Worldwide

Exchange Activities:
GSUSA is involved in the following exchange areas: Community/Citizen, Short-Term Visitors. GSUSA provides exchange-related facilitative or support services.

Financial Assistance:
Assistance is available to selected participants through the Julliet Low World Friendship Fund, named for the movement's founder.

Publications:
GSUSA News, 212/852-8000

Alliance
MEMBER

Global Outreach, Inc.

P.O. Box 25883
Alexandria, VA 22313

Tel.: 703/299-9551
Fax: 703/299-9557
E-mail: info@globaloutreach.net

General Inquiries:
Diane E. Crow,
Executive Director
703/299-9551,
info@globaloutreach.net

Chief Executive Officer:
Diane E. Crow,
Executive Director

Statement:
Global Outreach is a nonprofit organization dedicated to providing international exchange opportunities for individuals interested in agriculture. Its programs provide opportunities for participants to gain practical experience in various fields of interest. Global Outreach's organizational mission is to assist youth in developing an appreciation of global cultural diversity and an understanding of the international agricultural economy.

Profile:
Nonprofit founded in 1994. Global Outreach has two U.S. staff. Fifteen overseas volunteers contribute to Global Outreach's mission.

Geographic Focus:
Central America (Costa Rica, Honduras, Guatemala), Eastern Europe (Latvia, Lithuania, Estonia, Bulgaria, Hungary, Czech Republic, Slovak Republic), North America (United States), Oceania (Australia)

Exchange Activities:
Global Outreach is involved in the following exchange areas: Homestay, Training. Global Outreach provides exchange-related facilitative or support services.

Financial Assistance:
Global Outreach does not provide financial assistance.

Publications:
The Outreach, 703/299-9551,
info@globaloutreach.net

Exchange Programs Include:
Agricultural Internship Program
Diane Crow
703/299-9551,
info@globaloutreach.net

Premiere Agribusiness
Professional Program
Diane Crow
703/299-9551,
info@globaloutreach.net

U.S. Department of State Designated Sponsor for the Exchange Vistor Program
Trainees

Homestay Educational/Cultural Foundation

655 Eunice Avenue
Mountain View, CA 94040

Tel.: 650/964-1502
Fax: 650/964-1815

General Inquiries:
Gilda Wunderman,
President

Chief Executive Officer:
Gilda Wunderman,
President

Statement:
Homestay Educational/Cultural Foundation is a nonprofit organization providing educational and cultural opportunities for youth and adults through a homestay program. The Foundation also offers homestays for one to two semesters of high school in various California cities, and serves students and adults worldwide by direct referrals or through affiliates in Japan and China.

Profile:
Nonprofit founded in 1972. Homestay Educational/Cultural Foundation has two U.S. staff and two overseas staff. One hundred fifty U.S. volunteers and four overseas volunteers contribute to Homestay Educational/Cultural Foundation's mission. More than 10,000 students and adults have participated in the program since it was founded.

Geographic Focus:
Asia (Japan, China, Taiwan, Thailand), Western Europe

Exchange Activities:
Homestay Educational/Cultural Foundation is involved in the following exchange areas: Homestay, Language Study. Homestay Educational/Cultural Foundation provides exchange-related facilitative or support services. It administers exchange programs for the following academic levels: K-12.

Financial Assistance:
Homestay Educational/Cultural Foundation does not provide financial assistance.

Publications:
Applications, Gilda Wunderman, 650/964-1502, GDHMS@aol.com

Program Focus/Rules/Expectations

Exchange Programs Include:
English Academy (in Japan)
  Fumio Kaneko

Homestay Foundation (in Japan)
  Seizo Fukuoka

Exchange Related Facilitative or Support Services Include:
Courses for Credit,
Various California High Schools

Short-Stay Programs
  for Adults and Mothers with Children, High School and College Students

U.S. Department of State Designated Sponsor for the Exchange Vistor Program
Secondary school students

Institute for the International Education of Students (IES)

33 North LaSalle Street
Chicago, IL 60610

Tel.: 800/995-2300
Fax: 312/944-1448
Website: http://www.iesabroad.org
E-mail: info@IESabroad.org

General Inquiries:
Dr. Michael Steinberg,
Vice President for
Academic Programs
800/995-2300
msteinberg@iesabroad.org

Chief Executive Officer:
Dr. Mary Dwyer,
President

Statement:
The Institute for the International Education of Students (IES) is dedicated to providing high quality academic programs outside the United States, primarily for undergraduate students, but also for adults. A nonprofit educational institution, IES is committed to the creation of a culturally diverse America enhanced by social and intellectual awareness through the exploration of other cultures. The ultimate goal of the IES experience is to enable participants to develop a critical sensitivity to the difficult issues facing an increasingly interrelated world, and to encourage them to become responsible, independent, and involved participants in their own complex societies.

Profile:
Nonprofit founded in 1950. IES has 46 U.S. staff and 65 overseas staff. IES provides a membership program and has 125 institutional members.

Geographic Focus:
Asia (China, Japan), Oceania (Australia), South America (Argentina, Chile), Western Europe (France, Germany, Spain, Italy, England, Austria, and Ireland)

Exchange Activities:
IES is involved in the following exchange areas: Arts/Cultural, Homestay, Language Study, Persons with Disabilities, Professional/Business, Students/Educators. IES provides exchange-related facilitative or support services. It administers exchange programs for the following academic levels: Undergraduate Students.

Financial Assistance:
IES provides need-based and merit-based grants for students admitted to IES programs.

Publications:
Exchange Alumni Newsletter

"Study in...." (Catalogs)

IES Program Reviews

Exchange Programs Include:
IES Student Assistantship Program
  Greg Buchanan,
  Program Associate
  800/995-2300,
  gbuchanan@iesabroad.org

Universidad Complutense de Madrid, Spain
L'Université de Paris - Sorbonne (Paris IV)
Albert-Ludwigs Universität
  Freiburg, Germany

Kanda University, Japan
Humboldt University, Germany
Universidad de Salamanca, Spain
University of Nantes, France
Universidad Nacional
  de la Plato, Argentina
Libera Universita di Lingue
  e Comunicacione, Italy

Exchange Related Facilitative or Support Services Include:
Courses for Credit
  Michael Steinberg,
  Vice President for
  Academic Programs

Grants/Scholarships to Individuals
  P.J. Shoulders,
  AUP Enrollment Management
  Director of Admissions
  pshoulders@iesabroad.org

Students with Disabilities
  Dr. Maureen Powers,
  Dean of Students
  mpowers@iesabroad.org

Overseas Offices:
Barcelona, Spain
Madrid, Spain
Salamanca, Spain
London, United Kingdom
Adelaide, Australia
Melbourne, Australia
Beijing, China
Berlin, Germany
Freiburg, Germany
Buenos Aires, Argentina
La Plata, Argentina
Milan, Italy
Nagoya, Japan
Tokyo, Japan
Vienna, Austria
Dijon, France
Nantes, France
Paris, France
Dublin, Ireland
Santiago, Chile

Institute of International Education (IIE)

809 United Nations Plaza
New York, NY 10017

Tel.: 212/883-8200 **Fax:** 212/984-5452
Website: http://www.iie.org
E-mail: info@iie.org

General Inquiries:
Receptionist
212/883-8200, info@iie.org

Chief Executive Officer:
Dr. Allan Goodman,
President and CEO

Statement:
The Institute of International Education (IIE) is the world leader in the international exchange of people and ideas. Its mission is to foster international understanding by opening minds to the world. It does this by assisting college and university students in studying abroad, advising institutions of higher education on ways to internationalize their student body, faculty and curriculum, fostering sustainable development through training programs in energy, environment, enterprise management and leadership development, and partnering with corporations, foundations, and governments in finding and developing people able to think and work on a global basis. Nearly 4,000 men and women from the United States and 14,000 from 175 countries study, conduct research, receive practical training, or provide technical assistance through IIE's 250 programs.

Profile:
Nonprofit founded in 1919. IIE has 360 U.S. staff and 100 overseas staff. IIE provides a membership program and has 600 institutional members. Six thousand U.S. volunteers contribute to IIE's mission.

Geographic Focus:
Worldwide

Alliance
MEMBER

Exchange Activities:
IIE is involved in the following exchange areas:

Arts/Cultural, Community/Citizen, Professional/Business, Short-Term Visitors, Students/Educators, Training. IIE provides exchange-related facilitative or support services. It administers exchange programs for the following academic levels: Faculty, Graduate Students, Teachers, Undergraduate Students.

Financial Assistance:
IIE administers NSEP U.S. undergraduate awards; U.S. Department of State Fulbright predoctoral and postdoctoral awards (U.S. and non-U.S.), and Gilman International Scholarships.

Publications:
Academic Year Abroad (Annual)
Short-Term Study Abroad (Annual), 800/445-0443
Open Doors: Statistics on International Mobility (Annual), 800/445-0443
Funding for U.S. Study, 800/445-0443
Intensive English USA, 800/445-0443
Fulbright Scholar Program: Grants for Faculty and Professionals, 202/686-7877
Fulbright U.S. Student Program: Grants for Graduate Study and Research Abroad, 212/984-5330
Directory of Visiting Fulbright Scholars and Occasional Lecturers, 202/686-7877
Fulbright Scholar-in-Residence Program: Guidelines for Proposals
Financial Resources for International Study 800/445-0443

Exchange Programs Include:
Development Training and Assistance
  202/326-7706, dta@iie.org
Fulbright Postdoctoral Fellowships: U.S. and Non-U.S. citizens
  202/686-4000, scholars@cies.org
Fulbright Predoctoral Fellowships: Non-U.S. citizens
  212/984-5417, www.iie.org/fulbright
Fulbright Predoctoral Fellowships: U.S. Citizens
  212/984-5329, www.iie.org/fulbright
Fulbright Visiting Scholar Program
  202/686-7877, scholars@cies.org
Hubert H. Humphrey Fellowship Program
  202/326-7701, hhh@iie.org
National Security Education Program— Undergraduate Scholarships
  800/618-6737, nsep@iie.org

Occasional Lecturer Programs
  202/686-4004, scholars@cies.org
Professional Exchange Programs (IV)
  202/326-7695, profexchg@iie.org
Scholar-in-Residence Program
  202/686-6238, scholars@cies.org
Gilman Undergraduate Study Abroad Scholarship
  713/621-6300 x25, gilman@iie.org

Exchange Related Facilitative or Support Services Include:
University Placement Services
  212/984-5503, Ltobash@iie.org
Conference/Meetings/Workshops
  Membership Services
  212/984-5375, membership@iie.org
Grants/Scholarships to Individuals
  U.S. Student Programs
  212/984-5329
Membership Services
  Peter Kerrigan,
  Manager of Membership Services
  212/984-5375, membership@iie.org
People with Disabilities
International Visitor Support
  202/326-7695, profexchg@iie.org
Peer Review Committees
  Christine Morfit,
  Deputy Director, CIES
  202/686-4007

Additional Offices:
Chicago, IL
Denver, CO
Houston, TX
San Francisco, CA
Washington, DC

Overseas Offices:
Hanoi, Vietnam
Cairo, Egypt
Jakarta, Indonesia
Bangkok, Thailand
Budapest, Hungary
New Delhi, India
Manila, Philippines
Moscow, Russia
Mexico City, Mexico
Kiev, Ukraine
Beijing, China
Pretoria, South Africa
Hong Kong, China

U.S. Department of State Designated Sponsor for the Exchange Vistor Program
Professors and research scholars
Short-term scholars
Trainees
College and university students
Teachers
Specialists

Institute of Public Administration (IPA)

411 Lafayette Street
Suite 303
New York, NY 10003

Tel.: 212/992-9898
Fax: 212/995-4876
Website: http://www.theipa.org

General Inquiries:
Lizabeth Kingsley,
Senior Staff
212/992-9895,
lizabeth.kingsley@nyu.edu

Chief Executive Officer:
David Mammen,
President

Statement:
The Institute of Public Administration (IPA) has a long-standing concern with education in the public service, dating back to the early 20th century. Today, IPA actively participates in public management training by organizing internships and study tours, providing technical assistance to public service training programs, and supervising the work of participant trainees from foreign countries. IPA's work with training arises out of projects focused on public management, policy, and performance in specific countries where long-term cooperation is sustained.

Profile:
Nonprofit founded in 1906. IPA has ten U.S. staff and five overseas staff.

Geographic Focus:
Worldwide

Exchange Activities:
IPA is involved in the following exchange areas: Community/Citizen, Other, Professional/Business, Short-Term Visitors, Students/Educators, Training. IPA provides exchange-related facilitative or support services. It administers exchange programs for the following academic levels: Graduate Students.

Financial Assistance:
IPA does not provide financial assistance.

Publications:
The IPA Report (newsletter), Lizabeth Kingsley

Exchange Programs Include:
Professional Human Resources Development Program for Indonesia
    Lizabeth Kingsley

USAID NET and GTD study tours
    Tailored Study Tours
    for Public Officials

Exchange Related Facilitative or Support Services Include:
Admissions/Placement Service
    Lizabeth Kingsley
    lizabeth.kingsley@nyu.edu

Conference/Meetings/Workshops

International Visitor Support

Public Policy

Intercambio Internacional de Estudiantes

16 Broadway
Suite 107
Fargo, ND 58102

Tel.: 701/232-1176
Fax: 701/232-1670

General Inquiries:
Cathy Taxis, Office Coordinator
800/437-4170

Chief Executive Officer:
Josefina Reyes,
Executive Director

Statement:
Intercambio Internacional de Estudiantes was originally founded in Mexico City, Mexico by Right Reverend Placid Reitmeier, O.S.B., in 1959 and was later incorporated in the state of North Dakota. It is a short-term cultural exchange program. Students 11 to 16 years of age are placed with volunteer host families who have a same gender child similar in age and with similar interests. Students become a part of a home abroad and participate in all activities of the family.

Profile:
Nonprofit founded in 1959. Intercambio Internacional de Estudiantes has three U.S. staff and three overseas staff. One hundred U.S. volunteers and 30 overseas volunteers contribute to Intercambio Internacional de Estudiantes's mission.

Geographic Focus:
Central America (Costa Rica, Panama), North America (Canada, Mexico, United States)

Exchange Activities:
Intercambio Internacional de Estudiantes is involved in the following exchange areas: Arts/Cultural, Short-Term Visitors. Intercambio Internacional de Estudiantes provides exchange-related facilitative or support services. The students audit classes with the host for six to eight weeks in winter.

Financial Assistance:
Partial scholarships are available to host families whose children want to participate through Intercambio.

Exchange Programs Include:
Short-Term Summer
Outbound Program

Short-Term Winter and
Summer Inbound Programs

Overseas Offices:
Edo De Mexico, Mexico

Intercultural Dimensions (ID)

P.O. Box 391437
Cambridge, MA 02139

Tel.: 617/864-8442
Fax: 617/868-1273
Website: www.geocities.com/
TheTropics/Coast/2323/
idhome.html
E-mail: janetid@aol.com

General Inquiries:
Janet L. Ghattas,
General Director
janetid@aol.com

Chief Executive Officer:
Janet L. Ghattas,
General Director

Statement:
Intercultural Dimensions (ID) is a
nonprofit educational organization.
It offers cross-cultural awareness
programs to Americans and multi-
nationals through travel, community service, workshop, and seminars.
ID programs are designed to stimulate interest and participation in a
different culture. ID programs have
taken groups to Burkina Faso, the
Gambia, and Senegal.

Profile:
Nonprofit founded in 1993. Two
U.S. volunteers contribute to
ID's mission.

Geographic Focus:
Africa (Senegal, Mali, Burkina Faso)

Exchange Activities:
ID is involved in the following
exchange areas: Arts/Cultural,
Homestay, Language Study, Public
Health and Women's Groups,
Students/Educators. ID provides
exchange-related facilitative or sup-
port services. It administers
exchange programs for the follow-
ing academic levels: Faculty,
Graduate Students, K-12, Teachers,
Undergraduate Students.

Financial Assistance:
ID does not provide financial
assistance.

Exchange Programs Include:
Crossing Cultures Senegal
Janet Ghattas

**Exchange Related Facilitative or
Support Services Include:**
Conference/Meetings/Workshops
Cross Cultural Sessions
Janet Ghattas

Courses for Credit
Crossing Cultures Senegal
Janet Ghattas

**U.S. Department of State
Designated Sponsor for the
Exchange Vistor Program**
Short-term scholars
College and university students
Teachers

InterExchange

161 Sixth Street
New York, NY 10013-1205

Tel.: 212/924-0446
Fax: 212/924-0575
Website: www.interexchange.org
E-mail: info@interexchange.org

General Inquiries:
Receptionist
212/924-0446

Chief Executive Officer:
Uta Christianson,
President

Statement:
InterExchange is a private, nonprofit organization involved in international, educational and cultural exchange for more than 30 years. InterExchange is dedicated to promoting international understanding through the development and implementation of affordable intercultural and educational work/training opportunities. Thousands of young people have participated in programs both here and abroad. Programs offer young adults a chance to gain insights into another culture as well as valuable experiences overseas.
InterExchange continues its dedication to international exchange through the development of programs promoting mutual understanding between nations. Its steady increase in program participants is clear testimony to the value and reputation of InterExchange's programs.

Profile:
Originally founded in 1968. Nonprofit corporation established in 1987. InterExchange has 37 U.S. staff. Seventy-two U.S. volunteers contribute to InterExchange's mission.

Geographic Focus:
Worldwide

Exchange Activities:
InterExchange is designated for the following J-1 programs: Work & Travel, Camp Counselors, Au Pairs, Trainees. In addition to these exchange programs, InterExchange provides exchange-related facilitative or support services.

Financial Assistance:
InterExchange does not provide financial assistance.

Exchange Programs Include:
Au Pair USA
    Paul Christianson
    212/924-0446

Camp USA
    Claude Joseph
    212/924-0446

Interns & Trainees
    Kim Wetzel
    212/924-0446

Work and Travel USA
    Casey Slamin
    212/924-0446

Working Abroad
    Patsy Kng
    212/924-0446

U.S. Department of State Designated Sponsor for the Exchange Vistor Program
Summer work/travel
Camp counselors
Au pairs
Trainees

Alliance
MEMBER

International Agricultural Exchange Association (IAEA)

**1000 First Avenue South
Great Falls, MT 59401**

Tel.: 800/272-4996
Fax: 406/727-1997
E-mail: usa@agriventure.com

General Inquiries:
Monica Heisler,
Exchange Consultant
800/272-4996

Chief Executive Officer:
Aksel Ostergaard,
CEO

Statement:
The International Agricultural Exchange Association's (IAEA) mission is to provide young adults with the opportunity to work abroad to experience a different culture and learn new agriculture/horticulture practices. Participants live/work with appointed host families for six-13 months. Participants must be 18-30 years of age, hold a valid drivers license, and possess some agriculture or horticulture experience. IAEA promotes a greater tolerance and understanding of foreign countries, provides a chance to gain lasting international friendships, and gives each participant the opportunity to further their agriculture/horticulture knowledge and skills for a better tomorrow. IAEA can develop special programs which fit into a participant's school or employment schedule.

Profile:
Nonprofit founded in 1963. IAEA has three U.S. staff and 11 overseas staff. One hundred U.S. volunteers and 200 overseas volunteers contribute to IAEA's mission.

Geographic Focus:
Asia (Japan), Oceania (New Zealand, Australia), Western Europe (Denmark, Sweden, Norway, Germany, Holland)

Exchange Activities:
IAEA is involved in the following exchange areas: Agriculture exchanges, Horticulture exchanges, Training, Work Exchanges. IAEA provides exchange-related facilitative or support services.

Financial Assistance:
Financial assistance may be available after completion of the scholarship application form and essay.

Exchange Programs Include:
Australia
(five, seven, eight, nine months)
Monica Heisler
800/272-4996

Japan (four, eight, 12 months)
Monica Heisler
800/272-4996

New Zealand & Australia (13 months)
Monica Heisler
800/272-4996

New Zealand
(seven, eight, nine, 12 months)
Monica Heisler
800/272-4996

Western Europe
(six, seven, nine months)
Monica Heisler

Exchange Related Facilitative or Support Services Include:
Admissions/Placement Service
Exchange Programs to Europe, Australia and New Zealand
Monica Heisler
800/272-4996

Grants/Scholarships to Individuals
IAEA USA Host
Family Scholarship Association
Monica Heisler
800/272-4996

Agricultural or Horticultural
Exchange Programs Abroad
Monica Heisler
800/272-4996

Overseas Offices:
Whakatane, New Zealand
Sydney, Australia
Kenilworth, United Kingdom
Copenhagen, Denmark
Calgary, Canada

U.S. Department of State Designated Sponsor for the Exchange Vistor Program
Trainees

International Cultural Exchange Services (ICES)

1000 South Caraway Road
Suite 202
Jonesboro, AR 72401

Tel.: 870/930-9334
Fax: 870/930-1470
Website: www.ices-services.org
E-mail: icesnatloff@hotmail.com

General Inquiries:
Cathy Johnson,
Vice President
800/344-3566

Chief Executive Officer:
John J. Crist,
President

Statement:
International Cultural Exchange Services (ICES) is a nonprofit organization dedicated to promoting a more peaceful world by increasing international awareness and understanding among the peoples of the world through experiences in cultural sharing. ICES offers both academic year and semester high school exchange programs.

Profile:
Nonprofit founded in 1991. ICES has 17 U.S. staff. ICES has 200 local chapters/affiliates. Two hundred U.S. volunteers contribute to ICES's mission.

Geographic Focus:
Asia (Japan, Mongolia, China), Eastern Europe (Albania, Armenia, Bosnia-Herzegovina, Czech Republic, Poland, Slovakia, Slovenia, Yugoslavia), Newly Independent States (Belarus, Georgia, Kazakhstan, Kyrgyzstan, Moldova, Russia, Tajikistan, Ukraine, Uzbekistan), North America (Mexico, United States), Oceania (Australia), South America (Brazil, Ecuador), Western Europe (Austria, Belgium, Denmark, Finland, France, Germany, Luxembourg, the Netherlands, Spain, Sweden, United Kingdom)

Exchange Activities:
ICES is involved in the following exchange areas: Homestay. ICES provides exchange-related facilitative or support services. It administers exchange programs for the following academic levels: K-12.

Financial Assistance:
ICES does not provide financial assistance.

Publications:
News & Notes

Exchange Programs Include:
Overall Program Operations
Inbound/Outbound
    Cathy Johnson
    800/344-3566

Exchange Related Facilitative or Support Services Include:
Admissions/Placement Service
    Cathy Johnson
    800/344-3566

Conference/Meetings/Workshops
    Cathy Johnson
    800/344-3566

Travel Services
    Cathy Johnson
    800/344-3566

Membership Services

Additional Offices:
Santa Rosa, CA
Springfield, IL
Concord, VA

U.S. Department of State Designated Sponsor for the Exchange Vistor Program
Secondary school students

Alliance
MEMBER

International Education (Inter-Ed)

7110 Lantana Terrace
Carlsbad, CA 92009

Tel.: 760/431-0793
Fax: 760/431-7098
Website: http://www.inter-ed.org
E-mail: interedorg@aol.com

General Inquiries:
Dr. T. E. Farah,
Director
intereduca@aol.com

Chief Executive Officer:
Dr. T. E. Farah,
Director

Statement:
For more than 20 years,
International Education (Inter-Ed)
has arranged academic and homestay placements for international
students. Accepting only a few
quality candidates each year, students and families alike appreciate
the extra touches provided by
Inter-Ed. High school seniors are
recruited and placed with local volunteer American families. Students
enroll in public high schools.

Profile:
Nonprofit founded in 1979. Ten
U.S. volunteers contribute to Inter-
Ed's mission.

Geographic Focus:
South America (Brazil), Western
Europe (Germany, Spain, Italy,
France)

Exchange Activities:
Inter-Ed is involved in the following exchange areas:
Students/Educators. Inter-Ed provides exchange-related facilitative
or support services. It administers
exchange programs for the following academic levels: K-12.

Financial Assistance:
Scholarships are awarded to highly
qualified students.

Exchange Programs Include:
Academic Year Program
    T. E. Farah

**Exchange Related Facilitative or
Support Services Include:**
Admissions/Placement Service
    Academic Year Program
    T. E. Farah

**U.S. Department of State
Designated Sponsor for the
Exchange Vistor Program**
Secondary school students

International Internship Programs (IIP)

One Farragut Square
1634 Eye Street, N.W., Lower Level
Washington, DC 20006

Tel.: 202/737-6980
Fax: 202/737-6976
Website: www.internprogram.org
E-mail: info@internprogram.org

General Inquiries:
Desk Officer,
202/737-6980

Chief Executive Officer:
Yoshikazu Ikeda,
Director

Statement:
The International Internship Program (IIP) was founded to promote better mutual understanding between the nations of the world through the exchange of professional and cultural ideas and business techniques. IIP provides business, educational and cultural training either through direct placement into training internships, or through the unique Model Company Program (MCP). MCP provides three to six months of coached and facilitated training at offices located two blocks from the White House in the heart of Washington, DC. As part of MCP, training internships are provided to qualified participants at sites throughout the United States. This is done at no cost to the host institution or organization. Each participant gains valuable insight into the differences in business and culture, working and living in the United States. Those legally residing in the U.S. may also participate in several of IIP's placement and training programs. Affiliates in Japan and Great Britain assist in providing

exchanges. These exchanges are designed primarily to impart a sense of world culture, language and tradition.

Profile:
IIP is a nonprofit organization founded in 1979. It is authorized by the Department of State to issue J-1 visas, by the INS to sponsor Q-1 visa placements as well as short-term programs for B visa holders, part-time internship placements for F-1 visa holders, and offers full-time internship placements for U.S. legal residents and American citizens. Ten staff members work in Washington, DC, as well as five other regional liaisons/coordinators. Over 30 recruitment, training, and placement staff work at IIP affiliates in Japan and England.

Geographic Focus:
Worldwide

Exchange Activities:
IIP is involved in nearly all areas of cultural, educational, business, and language exchange. IIP administers training placement programs for Faculty, Graduate Students, Teachers and Undergraduate Students as well as employed professionals.

Financial Assistance:
IIP may provide limited scholarships to some participants. All programs have payment installment plans.

Publications:
Japan at a Glance

*Compact Japan: Japanese Life &
    Culture at a Glance*

Teaching Japan

Training Programs:
Model Company Program (MCP)
Business Training Placements (BTP)
Reciprocal Exchanges Abroad (REA)
    U.S. Recruiting Director
    202/737-6979,
    info@internprogram.org

Overseas Offices:
Tokyo, Japan
Wigan, United Kingdom

**U.S. Department of State
Designated Sponsor for the
Exchange Vistor Program**
Trainees

International Research and Exchanges Board (IREX)

1616 H Street, NW
Sixth Floor
Washington, DC 20006

Tel.: 202/628-8188
Fax: 202/628-8189
Website: http://www.irex.org
E-mail: irex@irex.org

General Inquiries:
Information Assistant
202/628-8188

Chief Executive Officer:
Dr. Mark G. Pomar,
President

Statement:
The International Research and Exchanges Board (IREX) is an international nonprofit organization dedicated to the advancement of knowledge. Central to its mission is the empowering of individuals and institutions to participate meaningfully in civil society. IREX administers programs between the United States and the countries of Eastern Europe, the New Independent States (NIS), Asia, and the Near East.

Profile:
Nonprofit founded in 1968. IREX has 100 U.S. staff and 300 overseas staff. Seventy-one local chapters/affiliates contribute to IREX's mission.

Geographic Focus:
Asia (Armenia, Azerbaijan, Georgia, Kazakhstan, Kyrgyzstan, Mongolia, China, Tajikistan, Turkmenistan, Uzbekistan), Eastern Europe (Albania, Belarus, Bosnia and Herzegovina, Bulgaria, Croatia, Czech Republic, Estonia, Latvia, Lithuania, Macedonia, Romania, Federal Republic of Yugoslavia), Middle East (Turkey) Newly Independent States (Russia, Moldova, Ukraine)

Exchange Activities:
IREX is involved in the following exchange areas: Advanced Research, Arts/Cultural, Community/Citizen, Language Study, Training, Professional/Business, Short-Term Visitors, Students/Educators. IREX provides exchange-related facilitative or support services. It administers exchange programs for the following academic levels: Faculty, Graduate Students, Post Doctoral Research.

Financial Assistance:
IREX provides financial assistance.

Publications:
About IREX (brochure)

Policy Papers

Annual Report

Program Information Brochures

Exchange Programs Include:
Russian-US Young Leadership Fellows for Public Service
202/628-8188,
irex@irex.org

Regional Scholar Exchange Program (RSEP)

FSA Contemporary Issues Fellowship Program (CI)

Individual Advanced Research Opportunities (IARO)

Short-Term Travel Grants Program (STG)

Exchange Related Facilitative or Support Services Include:
Testing/Assessment Services

Grants to Institutions/Organizations
    Sustaining Partnerships into the Next Century Project (SPAN)

    Promoting and Strengthening Russian NGO Development Program (Pro-NGO)

    Professional Media Programs (ProMedia)

Grants/Scholarships to Individuals
    Multiple Programs

People with Disabilities

Overseas Offices:
Tirana, Albania
Minsk, Belarus
Prague, Czech Republic
Chisinau, Moldova
Bishkek, Kyrgyzstan
Yerevan, Armenia
Kiev, Ukraine
Moscow, Russia
Vladivostok, Russia
Riga, Latvia
Skopje, Macedonia
Tbilisi, Georgia
Almaty, Kazakhstan
Vilnius, Lithuania
Istanbul, Turkey
Belgrade, Serbia

U.S. Department of State Designated Sponsor for the Exchange Vistor Program
Professor and research scholar
Secondary school students
Short-term scholar

International Student Exchange (ISE)

150 Islip Avenue
Suite 7
Islip, NY 11751

Tel.: 866/367-2430 (toll free)
Fax: 576/859-3335

General Inquiries:
Mary Dye,
President
516/859-0799,
mary@iseusa.com

Chief Executive Officer:
Wayne Brewer
wayne@iseusa.com

Statement:
International Student Exchange (ISE) is dedicated to the promotion of world peace by bringing together foreign teens with volunteer American host families, and by developing programs and services which allow the students to become familiar with the American way of life through experiencing its school, homes, and communities. Regional advisors and local area representatives screen U.S. host families and provide a support system for host families, students, and schools throughout the United States. Every exchange student is assigned a local area representative whose job is to be available to the student for assistance and counseling. Regional directors are available to all program participants.

Profile:
Nonprofit founded in 1982. ISE has 12 U.S. staff. ISE has 10 local chapters/affiliates. Over a 1,000 volunteer host families contribute to ISE's mission. ISE has over 600 area representatives, 100 regional advisors, and 14 regional directors.

Geographic Focus:
Asia (China, Thailand, Japan, Taiwan, Hong Kong, Korea), Eastern Europe (Croatia, Czech Republic, Serbia, Bulgaria), Middle East (Turkey), North America (Mexico), South America (Brazil, Colombia, Venezuela, Bolivia, Argentina), Western Europe (Spain, France, Germany, Switzerland, Scandinavia)

Exchange Activities:
ISE is involved in the following exchange areas: Homestay, Short-Term Visitors. ISE provides exchange-related facilitative or support services. It administers exchange programs for the following academic levels: K-12.

Financial Assistance:
ISE does not provide financial assistance.

Publications:
ISE Family Album

ISE Corporate Brochure

ISE Positive Training Series

ISE Working With Tomorrow's Leaders

ISE Host and Student Guides

Exchange Programs Include:
Academic Year or Semester Program
    Wayne Brewer,
    CEO,
    516/859-3330,
    waynep@iesusa.com

Homestays America Short Term Visits
    Mary Dye,
    President,
    mary@iseusa.com

Individual Homestays America
    Mary Dye,
    President,
    mary@iseusa.com

Additional Offices:
Michigan Center, MI
Grand Rapids, MI
Marasaelles, IL
St. Augustine, FL
Farmington, MO
Selah, WA
Danville, VA
Lynnfield, MA
Myrtle Beach, SC
Donipham, MO

U.S. Department of State Designated Sponsor for the Exchange Vistor Program
Secondary school students

International Student Exchange Program (ISEP)

1601 Connecticut Avenue, NW
Suite 501
Washington, DC 20009-1035

Tel.: 202/667-8027
Fax: 202/667-7801
Website: http://www.isep.org
E-mail: isep@isep.org

General Inquiries:
Robert O'Quinn,
202/667-8027

Chief Executive Officer:
Mary Anne Grant,
Executive Director

Statement:
The International Student Exchange Program (ISEP) provides a cost-effective administrative and financial structure that facilitates individualized, affordable, and flexible university-level exchanges between member institutions throughout the United States and members in 38 countries. The mission of the program is to ensure that study abroad is available as an integral component of higher education at all member institutions and is accessible to all qualified participants, regardless of social and economic background. ISEP is supported by member and participant fees. Through its unique approach to educational and cultural exchange, ISEP promotes better understanding and peaceful relations between the United States and other countries of the world.

Profile:
Nonprofit founded in 1979. ISEP has 17 U.S. staff. ISEP provides a membership program and has 225 institutional members.

Geographic Focus:
Africa (Ghana, Tanzania), Asia (China, Japan, Korea, Thailand, Philippines), Central America (Costa Rica, Nicaragua), Eastern Europe (Estonia, Hungary, Latvia), Newly Independent States (Russia), North America (Canada, Mexico, United States), Oceania (Australia, Fiji), South America (Argentina, Brazil, Colombia, Uruguay), Western Europe (Austria, Finland, France, Germany, Iceland, Italy, Malta, Spain, Sweden, Switzerland, Netherlands, United Kingdom)

Exchange Activities:
ISEP is involved in the following exchange areas: Students/Educators. ISEP provides exchange-related facilitative or support services. It administers exchange programs for the following academic levels: Faculty, Graduate Students, Undergraduate Students.

Financial Assistance:
ISEP provides a limited number of scholarships.

Publications:
ISEP Membership Catalog

Exchange Related Facilitative or Support Services Include:
Admissions/Placement Service
Nana Rinehart,
Associate Director
rinehart@isep.org

Conference/Meetings/Workshops

Membership Services
Robert Schaub
schaub@isep.org

Intrax, Inc.

2226 Bush Street
San Francisco, CA 94115

Tel.: 415/434-1221
Fax: 415/674-5221
Website: http://www.intraxinc.com
E-mail: info@intraxinc.com

General Inquiries:
Philippe Kohn,
Director of Marketing
800/288-1221

Chief Executive Officer:
John F. Wilhelm,
President

Statement:
Intrax English Institute provides the highest quality English as a Second Language education and comprehensive cultural orientation to international students and professionals in a friendly, supportive environment. *Intrax Homestay* provides quality short-term academic and cultural exchange opportunities for international student groups and individuals in the United States and Canada. *Intrax Work/Travel* promotes cultural exchange and international understanding through innovative summer job, career internship, and professional training programs.

Geographic Focus:
Worldwide

Exchange Activities:
Intrax is involved in the following exchange areas: ESL programs; Homestays; Work Exchanges; and internships. Intrax administers exchange programs for the following academic levels: Students in K-12 and undergraduate students. Other World Study Group Companies include AYUSA (Academic Year and Semester programs and Study Abroad programs for high school students), AuPairCare (au pair child care programs), and Passages Educational Tours (group travel).

Financial Assistance:
Intrax does not provide financial assistance.

Exchange Programs Include:
Intrax English Institute
  James Henderson,
  Director of Operations
  jhenderson@intraxinc.com

Intrax Homestay
  Sandi Swiderski,
  Operations Manager
  sswiderski@intraxinc.com

Intrax Work/Travel
  Sean Cambern,
  Program Director
  scambern@intraxinc.com

Additional Offices:
Intrax English Institute
  IEI Chicago, IL
  IEI San Diego, CA
  IEI San Francisco, CA
  IEI Silicon Valley, CA

College and University Programs
  Simmons College, Boston
  Occidental College, Los Angeles
  Columbia University, New York
  Wagner College, New York
  Menlo College, San Francisco
  Cal State Hayward, San Francisco

Intrax Homestays
  Los Angeles, CA
  Seattle, WA

Intrax Work/Travel
  San Diego, CA
  Orlando, FL
  Chicago, IL
  New York, NY
  Portland, OR

Overseas Offices:
Berlin, Germany
Budapest, Hungary
Tokyo, Japan

Japan-America Student Conference (JASC)

606 18th Street, NW
Second Floor
Washington, DC 20006

Tel.: 202/289-4231
Fax: 202/789-8265
Website: http://www.jasc.org
E-mail: jascinc@jasc.org

General Inquiries:
Gretchen Hobbs Donaldson,
Executive Director
202/289-4231

Chief Executive Officer:
Jack Shellenberger,
President

Statement:
The Japan-America Student Conference (JASC) is an educational and cultural exchange program for university students at all levels from the United States and Japan. It was founded to promote peace through mutual understanding, friendship, and trust. JASC is student-designed and student-run. Each summer, JASC provides a student-managed 30-day forum, alternating countries, for students from the U.S. and Japan to discuss a wide variety of topics important to both nations.

Profile:
Nonprofit founded in 1934. JASC has three U.S. staff. JASC provides a membership program and has 800 individual members. Ten U.S. volunteers contribute to JASC's mission.

Geographic Focus:
Asia (Japan)

Exchange Activities:
JASC is involved in the following exchange areas: Students/Educators. JASC provides exchange-related facilitative or support services. It administers exchange programs for the following academic levels: Graduate Students, Undergraduate Students.

Financial Assistance:
Most students receive scholarships from their universities to participate. JASC provides limited scholarship support.

Publications:
Alumni Newsletter
JASC Bulletin
Executive Director's Report
Brochure
60-Year History
Application

Exchange Programs Include:
Japan-America Student Conference
   Gretchen Donaldson,
   Executive Director
   202/289-4231

Overseas Office:
Tokyo, Japan

Alliance
MEMBER

The Japan Foundation

New York Office
152 West 57th Street
39th Floor
New York, NY 10019

Tel.: 212/489-0299
Fax: 212/489-0409
Website: http://www.jfny.org/jfny
E-mail: info@jfny.org

General Inquiries:
Program Assistant
212/489-0299,
info@jfny.org

Chief Executive Officer:
Fumitomo Horiuchi,
Director General

Statement:
The Japan Foundation is a semigovernmental organization whose objective is to promote international cultural exchange and mutual understanding between Japan and other countries. Established by special legislation in the Japanese Diet in 1972, the Foundation operates on the income from an endowment and subsidies contributed by the Japanese government and private circles (approximately 16.4 billion yen in fiscal year 1997). The Japan Foundation maintains offices in North and South America, Europe, Asia and Oceania.

Profile:
Nonprofit founded in 1972. The Japan Foundation has three U.S. staff and three overseas staff.

Geographic Focus:
Asia (Japan)

Exchange Activities:
The Japan Foundation is involved in the following exchange areas: Arts/Culture, Training, Short-Term Visitors, Students/Educators. It provides exchange-related facilitative or support services. It administers exchange programs for the following academic levels: Graduate Students, Faculty (postsecondary).

Financial Assistance:
The Japan Foundation's Exchange of Persons programs include: Doctoral Fellowships, Research Fellowships, Artist Fellowships, and Cultural Properties Specialist Fellowships.

Publications:
Program Guidelines

Awards Announcement

Bridges (New York office newsletter)

Program Assistant:
212/489-0299,
info@jfny.org

Exchange Programs Include:
Doctoral Fellowship
Arts & Exchange Program Assistant
212/489-0299, info@jfny.org

Research Fellowship
Arts & Exchange Program Assistant
212/489-0299, info@jfny.org

Artist Fellowship
Arts & Exchange Program Assistant
212/489-0299, info@jfny.org

Cultural Properties Specialist Fellowship
Arts & Exchange Program Assistant
212/489-0299, info@jfny.org

Exchange Related Facilitative or Support Services Include:
Conference/Meetings/Workshops
Research/Professional
Conference Program
Program Assistant (IPS)
212/489-0299, info@jfny.org

Grants/Scholarships to Individuals
Exchange of Persons Programs
Arts & Exchange Program Assistant
212/489-0299,
info@jfny.org

Grants to Institutions/Organizations
Publication Assistance, Translation
Assistance, Staff Expansion,
Library Support
Program Assistant (IPS)
212/489-0299,
info@jfny.org

International Visitor Support
Visiting Professorship Program
Program Assistant (IPS)
212/489-0299,
info@jfny.org

Exhibitions Abroad,
Film Production Support
Arts & Exchange Program Assistant
212/489-0299,
info@jfny.org

Additional Offices:
Santa Monica, CA

Overseas Offices:
Tokyo, Japan
Sydney, Australia
São Paulo, Brazil
Toronto, Canada
Beijing, China
Cairo, Egypt
Paris, France
Köln, Germany
Budapest, Hungary
New Delhi, India
Jakarta, Indonesia
Rome, Italy
Kuala Lumpur, Malaysia
Mexico City, Mexico
Manila, Philippines
Bangkok, Thailand
London, United Kingdom
Urawa, Japan
Osaka, Japan

Japan Foundation Center for Global Partnership (CGP)

152 West 57th Street
39th Floor
New York, NY 10019

Tel.: 212/489-1255
Fax: 212/489-1344
Website: www.cgp.org/cgplink
E-mail: info@cgp.org

General Inquiries:
212/489-1255,
info@cgp.org

Chief Executive Officer:
Takashi Ishida,
Director

Statement:
The Japan Foundation Center for Global Partnership (CGP) was established to pursue the following objectives: to promote collaboration between Japan and the United States with the goal of fulfilling shared global responsibilities and contributing to improvements in the world's welfare; and to enhance dialogue and interchange between Japanese and U.S. citizens on a wide range of issues, thereby improving bilateral relations.

Profile:
Nonprofit founded in 1991. CGP has seven U.S. staff and four overseas staff.

Geographic Focus:
Asia (Japan), North America (United States)

Exchange Activities:
CGP is involved in the following exchange areas: Training, Community/Citizen, Students/Educators, Nonprofit. CGP provides exchange-related facilitative or support services. It administers exchange programs for the following academic levels: Students and Teachers K-12, Undergraduate Students, Faculty (postsecondary).

Financial Assistance:
For its Abe Fellowship Program, CGP offers financial assistance with research costs, living expenses and income compensation. For its NPO Fellowship Program, it offers assistance with stipends, travel and living expenses, and insurance.

Publications:
CGP Newsletter

CGP Grantee Selected Publications

Annual Report

Program Guidelines for Applicants

Program Announcements on Priority Areas of Funding

Exchange Programs Include:
NPO Fellowship Program
212/489-1255,
nfo@cgp.org

Abe Fellowship Program
212/489-1255,
info@cgp.org

Exchange Related Facilitative or Support Services Include:
Grants/Scholarships to Individuals
NPO and Abe Fellowship Programs
212/489-1255,
info@cgp.org

Grants to Institutions/Organizations
Intellectual Exchange Program,
Grassroots Exchange Program,
Education Program
212/489-1255,
info@cgp.org

Overseas Office:
Tokyo, Japan

Japan Society Inc.

333 East 47th Street
New York, NY 10017

Tel.: 212/832-1155
Fax: 212/755-6752
Website: www.japansociety.org
E-mail: gen@japansociety.org

General Inquiries:
Kristine Minami,
212/715-1222
kminami@japansociety.org

Chief Executive Officer:
William Clark, Jr.,
President

Statement:
The Japan Society is an American institution with individual and corporate members that promotes understanding and enlightened relations between the United States and Japan. It is a private, nonprofit, non-political organization devoted to cultural, educational, and public affairs and to exchanges and research in areas of vital interest to the people of both countries.

Profile:
Nonprofit founded in 1907. The Japan Society provides a membership program and has 350 institutional members, 2,200 individual members.

Geographic Focus:
Asia (Japan)

Exchange Activities:
The Japan Society is involved in the following exchange areas: Arts/Cultural, Community/Citizen, Language Study, Professional/ Business, Students/Educators, Training. The Japan Society provides exchange-related facilitative or support services. It administers exchange programs for the following academic levels: Teachers.

Financial Assistance:
Professional media and public policy exchange programs offer airfare, a travel grant, and stipend.

Publications:
Japan Society Calendar

Japan Society Annual Report

Other Occasional
        Proceedings/Reports

Japan Society Corporate Calendar

Exchange Programs Include:
Educators Forum on Japan
    Elaine Vukoc,
    Director, Educational Outreach
    212/715-1275

Intellectual Interchange
    Ruri Kawashima,
    Director, U.S. Japan Program
    212/715-1224

Japan Society Local Government and Public Policy Fellowship
    Ruri Kawashima,
    Director, U.S.-Japan Program
    212/715-1224

Parliamentary Exchange

United States-Japan Foundation Media Fellows Program

Exchange Related Facilitative or Support Services Include:
Conference/Meetings/Workshops
    Mark Tice, Program Officer,
    U.S.-Japan Program
    212/715-1222

Consultations/Advisory Services

Japan-U.S. Community Education and Exchange (JUCEE)

**1440 Broadway
Suite 501
Oakland, CA 94612**

Tel.: 510/267-1920
Fax: 510/267-1922
Website: http://www.jucee.org
E-mail: info-us@jucee.org

General Inquiries:
Amie Michalek,
Executive Assistant
510/267-1920,
amie@jucee.org

Chief Executive Officer:
Katsuji Imata,
Executive Director

Statement:
Japan-U.S. Community Education and Exchange (JUCEE) is an intercultural nonprofit organization dedicated to the pursuit of a global participatory society. By offering international internships and facilitating collaborative projects, JUCEE brings together individuals and community grassroots organizations to work on issues of common concern.

Profile:
Nonprofit founded in 1997. JUCEE has four U.S. staff and three overseas staff. One U.S. volunteer contributes to JUCEE's mission.

Geographic Focus:
Asia (Japan)

Exchange Activities:
JUCEE is involved in the following exchange areas:
Community/Citizen, Internships, Short-Term Visitors, Training. JUCEE provides exchange-related facilitative or support services.

Financial Assistance:
JUCEE does not provide financial assistance.

Publications:
JUCEE Newsletter

Japan-U.S. Nonprofit Internship Program Participant Essays (U.S. Program)

Japan-U.S. Nonprofit Internship Program Participant Essays (Japan Program)

Exchange Programs Include:
Fellowships Creating Partnerships Program

International Volunteers in Japan

Japan-U.S. Nonprofit Internship Program

Overseas Office:
Tokyo, Japan

Kosciuszko Foundation (KF)

15 East 65th Street
New York, NY 10021-6595

Tel.: 212/734-2130
Fax: 212/628-4552
Web: www.kosciuszkofoundation.org
E-mail: thekf@aol.com

Chief Executive Officer:
Joseph E. Gore,
President and Executive Director

Statement:
The Kosciuszko Foundation (KF) is dedicated to fostering and promoting educational and cultural relations and exchanges between the United States and Poland and to increasing knowledge and appreciation of Polish culture, history, and contributions to world civilization.

Profile:
Nonprofit founded in 1925. KF has 14 U.S. staff and one overseas staff. KF provides a membership program and has 65 institutional members and 2,460 individual members. Six U.S. volunteers contribute to KF's mission.

Geographic Focus:
Eastern Europe (Poland), North America (United States)

Exchange Activities:
KF is involved in the following exchange areas: Arts/Cultural, Language Study, Professional/Business, Students/Educators. KF provides exchange-related facilitative or support services. It administers exchange programs for the following academic levels: Faculty, Graduate Students, Teachers, Undergraduate Students.

Financial Assistance:
The Kosciuszko Foundation awards Fellowships/Grants annually to Polish scholars, professionals, or artists with doctoral degrees for advanced study, research, or teaching at universities and other institutions of higher learning in the United States. Participants receive tuition waivers (if applicable) and a stipend towards housing and other living expenses.

Publications:
The Kosciuszko Foundation Newsletter

Membership Brochure/Application

Fellowship, Scholarship and Grant Programs Brochure

Summer Study Abroad Programs Brochure/Application

Exchange Programs Include:
A Year Abroad in Poland Program
Addy Tymczyszyn, Coordinator of Programs in Poland for Americans
212/734-2130

Fellowships and Grants for Polish Citizens
Maryla Janiak,
Vice President for Educational Programs
212/734-2130

Graduate/Post Graduate Study and Research in Poland

Summer Studies Abroad

Teaching English in Poland Summer Programs
Christine Kuskowski,
Program Director
212/734-2130

Exchange Related Facilitative or Support Services Include:
Conference/Meetings/Workshops

Courses for Credit

Grants/Scholarships to Individuals

Overseas Office:
Warsaw, Poland

LASPAU: Academic and Professional Programs for the Americas (LASPAU)

25 Mount Auburn Street
Cambridge, MA 02138-6095

Tel.: 617/495-5255
Fax: 617/495-8990
Website: www.laspau.harvard.edu
E-mail: laspau@harvard.edu

General Inquiries:
Ana Maria Migliassi
617/495-0562,
ana_maria_migliassi@harvard.edu

Chief Executive Officer:
Ned D. Strong,
Executive Director

Statement:
LASPAU: Academic and Professional Programs for the Americas (LASPAU) is a nonprofit organization affiliated with Harvard University and governed by an independent inter-American board of trustees. LASPAU designs and implements academic and professional programs to meet the complex social, political, and economic challenges facing the Americas. LASPAU's expertise in Latin America and the Caribbean, and its relationships with individuals and institutions throughout the hemisphere, enable LASPAU to develop customized educational exchange programs and other learning solutions that address the evolving needs of clients and partners. LASPAU is committed to universal and equitable access to high-quality educational programs and in the continual improvement and expansion of services.

Profile:
Nonprofit founded in 1964. LASPAU has 47 U.S. staff.

Geographic Focus:
Caribbean, Central America, North America, South America

Exchange Activities:
LASPAU is involved in the following exchange areas: Arts/Cultural, Language Study, Professional/Business, Short-Term Visitors, Students/Educators, Training. LASPAU provides exchange-related facilitative or support services. It administers exchange programs for the following academic levels: Faculty, Graduate Students, Undergraduate Students.

Financial Assistance:
LASPAU administers financial aspects of sponsored programs including disbursement of scholarship tuition assistance, loan funds, and regular reports to sponsoring agencies.

Publications:
Informativo Newsletter

Annual Report

Guide for Grantees

Fulbright Programs Administered by LASPAU: A Directory of Grantees

Exchange Programs Include:
Fulbright-OAS Ecology Program
    Judith Adler,
    Senior Program Officer
    617/495-0366,
    judith_adler@harvard.edu

Distance Learning Program
    Winthrop Carty,
    Senior Development Officer
    617/495-0386,
    winthrop_carty@harvard.edu

Fulbright-LASPAU Faculty
Development Program
    Judith Adler,
    Senior Program Officer
    617/495-0366,
    judith_adler@harvard.edu

FUNDACYT
    Kim Killingsworth,
    Program Officer
    617/495-0457,
    kim_killingsworth@harvard.edu

COLCIENCIAS
    Efren Mencia,
    Program Officer
    617/495-0462
    efren_mencia@harvard.edu

Exchange Related Facilitative or Support Services Include:
Admissions/Placement Service
    Judith Adler

Conference/Meetings/Workshops
    Timothy Allen

Courses for Credit
    Judith Adler

Consulting
    Timothy Allen,
    Dir., External Relations and
    Program Development
    617/495-0565,
    tim_allen@harvard.edu

U.S. Department of State Designated Sponsor for the Exchange Vistor Program
Professors and research scholars
Short-term scholars
College and university students

Laurasian Institution

12345 Lake City Way NE
Suite 151
Seattle, WA 98125

Tel.: 425/398-1153
Fax: 425/398-8245
Website: http://www.laurasian.org

General Inquiries:
Kevin McQuade,
Director of Development

Chief Executive Officer:
Bradley Smith, President

Statement:
The Laurasian Institution's mission is to examine and seek to understand the cultural foundations of economic, political, and social policy; develop individual competency in dealing with diverse cultures; encourage realistic and mutually beneficial methodologies in dealing with cultural diversity; and to give particular attention to the cultural interaction of Asia, North America, and Europe. In pursuit of this mission, the Laurasian Institution gives special attention to communication, collaboration, and creativity.

Profile:
Nonprofit founded in 1990. The Laurasian Institution has three U.S. staff and two overseas staff.

Geographic Focus:
Asia (Asia-Pacific Economic Community Countries), Eastern Europe, North America, Western Europe

Exchange Activities:
The Laurasian Institution is involved in the following exchange areas: Homestay, Language Study. The Laurasian Institution provides exchange-related facilitative or support services. It administers exchange programs for the following academic levels: K-12.

Financial Assistance:
The Laurasian Institution does not provide financial assistance.

Exchange Programs Include:
New Perspectives: Japan (NP:J)
    Mari Maruyama
    425/398-1153

Additional Offices:
Atlanta, GA
Seattle, WA

Overseas Office:
Tokyo, Japan

LEXIA International (LEXIA)

**25 South Main Street
Hanover, NH 03755**

Tel.: 603/643-9898
Fax: 603/643-9899
Website: http://www.lexiaintl.org
E-mail: info@lexiaintl.org

Chief Executive Officer:
Edmund S. Harvey,
Executive Director

Statement:
LEXIA International is a private, independent, nonprofit educational exchange organization offering study abroad programs for undergraduate and graduate students. Academic year, semester, and summer programs are available, providing all academic, logistical, and living arrangements. Students progress from a structured to a more independent learning environment through completion of each of the six interrelated components: orientation, language study, civilization seminar, research methods seminar, field research project, and evaluation. Each component of the LEXIA program leads to a more comprehensive understanding of the host culture.

Profile:
Nonprofit founded in 1991.
LEXIA has eight U.S. staff and 37 overseas staff.

Geographic Focus:
Africa (South Africa), Asia (China, Thailand), Caribbean (Cuba), Eastern Europe (Czech Republic, Hungary, Poland), South America (Argentina), Western Europe (Germany, France, United Kingdom, Italy)

Exchange Activities:
LEXIA is involved in the following exchange areas: Arts/Cultural, Language Study, Students/Educators, Training. LEXIA provides exchange-related facilitative or support services. It administers exchange programs for the following academic levels: Graduate Students, Undergraduate Students.

Financial Assistance:
LEXIA provides partial tuition scholarships to U.S. students based on need and evidence of interest and commitment to the region of the host site.

Exchange Programs Include:
LEXIA in Berlin, Krakow, Budapest, Shanghai, Buenos Aires, Paris, Prague, Cape Town, Venice, Chiang Mai, Havana, London, Rome

Exchange Related Facilitative or Support Services Include:
Courses for Credit

Overseas Offices:
Shanghai, China
Chiang Mai, Thailand
Berlin, Germany
Budapest, Hungary
Cape Town, South Africa
Krakow, Poland
London, United Kingdom
Prague, Czech Republic
Venice, Italy
Buenos Aires, Argentina
Paris/Versailles, France
Havana, Cuba
Rome, Italy

Lisle, Inc.

900 County Road 269
Leander, TX 78641

Tel.: 800/477-1538
Fax: 512/259-0392
Website: www.lisleinternational.org
E-mail: lisle@utnet.utoledo.edu

General Inquiries:
Lisle Program Office
lisle@utnet.utoledo.edu

Chief Executive Officer:
Dr. Mark B. Kinney,
Executive Director

Statement:
Lisle, Inc. broadens global awareness and increases appreciation of cultures through programs which bring together persons of diverse religious, cultural, political, and racial backgrounds; to interact; and to reflect on their experiences. Its experiential education approach emphasizes cooperative, democratic leadership and participation. Lisle program participants enhance their communication skills, discover greater tolerance for diverse ideas, and gain greater respect for all life. Conflict resolution, community building, and increased knowledge of self are outcomes of the Lisle experience. Lisle, Inc. seeks to exemplify multicultural/multiracial decision-making, planning, and administration.

Profile:
Nonprofit founded in 1936. Lisle, Inc. has one U.S. staff. Lisle, Inc. provides a membership program and has 1,500 individual members. Twenty-six U.S. volunteers contribute to Lisle Inc.'s mission.

Geographic Focus:
Worldwide

Exchange Activities:
Lisle, Inc. is involved in the following exchange areas: Arts/Cultural, Community/ Citizen, Homestay, Short-Term Visitors, Students/Educators, Work Exchanges. Lisle, Inc. provides exchange-related facilitative or support services. It administers exchange programs for the following academic levels: Faculty, Graduate Students, Teachers, Undergraduate Students.

Financial Assistance:
Lisle, Inc. provides financial assistance to a limited number of participants per program on an as-needed basis

Publications:
Interaction

Exchange Programs Include:
Bali: Arts and Community

Costa Rica: Cultural Diversity; Cooperative Living

India: Seeking Ways to Empower

South Africa: 2000

Turkey: Ancient Land, Living Culture

USA, Pacific Northwest: Building a Sustainable Future

Exchange Related Facilitative or Support Services Include:
Conference/Meetings/Workshops
  International Conference

Courses for Credit
  University of Toledo

Professional/Volunteer Development
  Intern Program

Mansfield Center for Pacific Affairs (MCPA)

1401 New York Avenue, NW
Suite 740
Washington, DC 20005-2102

Tel.: 202/347-1994
Fax: 202/347-3941
Website: http://www.mcpa.org
E-mail: mcpadc@mcpa.org

Secondary Address:
**Maureen and
Mike Mansfield Foundation
Mansfield Library, Fourth Floor
University of Montana
Missoula, MT 59812**

General Inquiries:
Paige Cottingham-Streater
202/347-1994,
pcs@mcpa.org

Chief Executive Officer:
L. Gordon Flake,
Executive Director

Statement:
Established in 1994, the Mike Mansfield Fellowship Program provides an unprecedented opportunity for U.S. federal government officials to gain a substantial personal knowledge about the government of Japan and build a network of contacts with their counterparts in Japan's government agencies and ministries. The intensive, two-year program provides fellows with one year in Japan working in a full-time professional position in Japanese government offices, preceded by a first year of in-depth study in the United States of Japanese language and area studies.

Profile:
MCPA is the nonprofit public policy center of the Maureen and Mike Mansfield Foundation founded in 1983. MCPA has ten U.S. staff and three overseas staff.

Geographic Focus:
Asia (Japan, People's Republic of China, Korea)

Exchange Activities:
MCPA is involved in the following exchange areas: Professional/Business, Training, Work Exchanges. MCPA provides exchange-related facilitative or support services.

Financial Assistance:
The Mansfield Fellowship Program offers two year fellowship for U.S. government employees.

Publications:
Asia Perspectives (biannual magazine)

The Rule of Law: Perspectives from the Pacific Rim

The Rule of Law: A Lexicon for Policy Makers

Creating Images, American and Japanese Television News Coverage of the Other

From Abstract Learnings to Real-World Changes, Perspectives on the China-Taiwan-Hong Kong Relationship

Exchange Programs Include:
The Mike Mansfield
Fellowship Program
    Paige Cottingham-Streater
    202/347-1994

Additional Office:
Missoula, MT

Overseas Office:
Tokyo, Japan

Meridian International Center (MIC)

1630 Crescent Place, NW
Washington, DC 20009

Tel.: 202/939-5518
Fax: 202/319-1306
Website: http://www.meridian.org

General Inquiries:
Nancy Matthews,
Vice President
202/939-5518,
nmatthew@meridian.org

Chief Executive Officer:
Walter L. Cutler,
President

Statement:
Meridian International Center (MIC) is a nonprofit educational and cultural institution promoting international understanding through the exchange of people, ideas, and the arts. Meridian programs are funded by contracts with the U.S. Department of State (International Visitor and Voluntary Visitors programs) and other government agencies; grants and corporate sponsorship and contributions; and by private contributions. Meridian has an active art program which brings international exhibitions to the United States and a Traveling Exhibition Service which organizes art tours across the country. MIC also offers professional study tours, cross-cultural orientation, and programs for students and youth.

Profile:
Nonprofit founded in 1960. One thousand U.S. volunteers contribute to MIC's mission.

Geographic Focus:
Worldwide

Exchange Activities:
MIC is involved in the following exchange areas: Arts/Cultural, Homestay, Professional/Business, Short-Term Visitors, Students/Educators, Training. MIC provides exchange-related facilitative or support services.

Financial Assistance:
MIC does not provide financial assistance.

Publications:
Newsletter

Exchange Programs Include:
Arts/International
Exhibitions/Travelling Exhibition
  Nancy Matthews
  202/939-5518

Department of State
International Visitors Program
  Kenton Keith,
  Senior Vice President
  202/939-5590

U.S. Department of State
Designated Sponsor for the
Exchange Vistor Program
International visitors

Alliance
MEMBER

Metro International Program Services of New York, Inc. (Metro)

285 West Broadway
Suite 450
New York, NY 10013

Tel.: 212/431-1195
Fax: 212/941-6291
Website: http://www.metrointl.org
E-mail: info@metrointl.org

General Inquiries:
Tracy Snyder,
Assistant Executive Director
212/431-1195 x23,
tsnyder@metrointl.org

Chief Executive Officer:
Margaret Shiba,
Executive Director

Statement:
Metro International is a nonprofit membership organization dedicated to creating global learning opportunities for students, educators, and the community, in New York City and beyond. Metro serves as the officially-designated coordinator of enrichment programs for visiting Fulbright grantees in the New York area and offers programs and services to the 50,000 other international students who study at colleges and universities in the tri-state region each year. Through programs promoting interaction between international visitors and New Yorkers in diverse settings, including local neighborhoods, school classrooms, businesses, and cultural institutions, Metro works to ensure that those who study in New York today return to their home countries having made the sorts of connections that support positive international alliances tomorrow.

Profile:
Nonprofit founded in 1977. Metro has five U.S. staff. Metro provides a membership program and has 68 institutional members. One hundred fifty U.S. volunteers contribute to Metro's mission.

Geographic Focus:
Worldwide

Exchange Activities:
Metro is involved in the following exchange areas: Arts/Cultural, Community/Citizen, Homestay, Professional/Business, Short-Term Visitors, Students/Educators. Metro provides exchange-related facilitative or support services.

Financial Assistance:
Metro does not provide financial assistance.

Publications:
Inside New York: International Student Edition

Help Yourself to Housing: A Resource Guide for International Students in New York

MetroViews (newsletter)

Exchange Related Facilitative or Support Services Include:
International Visitor Support
New York Enrichment Program
Virginia Shuford,
Coordinator of
Enrichment Programs
212/431-1195 x24,
vshuford@metrointl.org

International Visitor Support
Fulbright Student/Scholar
Enrichment Program
Tracy Snyder,
Assistant Executive Director
212/431-1195 x23,
tsnyder@metrointl.org

Membership Services
Metro Membership
Tracy Snyder,
Assistant Executive Director
212/431-1195 x23,
tsnyder@metrointl.org

Public Policy
Global Classroom
Susan Hackett Noori,
Director of Global Classroom
212/431-1195 x22,
snoori@metrointl.org

Other
Fulbright Awards Dinner
Margaret Shiba,
Executive Director
212/431-1195 x25,
mshiba@metrointl.org

Minnesota Agricultural Student Trainee Program (MAST)

Room 240 Vocational Technical Education Program
University of Minnesota
1954 Buford Avenue
St. Paul, MN 55108

Tel.: 612/624-3740
Fax: 612/625-7031

General Inquiries:
Dr. Stephen P. Jones,
Director, MAST
612/624-3740
sjones@extension.umn.edu

Chief Executive Officer:
Dr. Stephen P. Jones,
Director, MAST

Statement:
The Minnesota Agricultural Student Trainee Program (MAST) improves global understanding by providing educational and cultural enrichment through international exchange. The specific objectives are to provide practical and academic experiences in agriculture and horticulture to young people from around the world. These experiences include a supervised training program on an approved practical training placement site followed by an academic experience at the University of Minnesota. The outcome of the experience provides an exchange of technology and an understanding and exchange of cultures.

Profile:
Nonprofit founded in 1949. MAST has seven U.S. staff.

Geographic Focus:
Worldwide

Exchange Activities:
MAST is involved in the following exchange areas: Agricultural, Training. MAST provides exchange-related facilitative or support services.

Financial Assistance:
MAST does not provide financial assistance.

Publications:
MAST Program Application Folder

Alumni Newsletter

In-House Newsletter

Exchange Programs Include:
MAST
Stephen Jones,
MAST Director
612/624-3740,
sjones@extension.umn.edu

Exchange Related Facilitative or Support Services Include:
Admissions/Placement Service

MAST

U.S. Department of State Designated Sponsor for the Exchange Vistor Program
Training

Mobility International USA/ National Clearinghouse on Disability and Exchange (MIUSA/NCDE)

P.O. Box 10767
Eugene, OR 97440

Tel.: 541/343-1284 (tel/tty)
Fax: 541/343-6812
Website: http://www.miusa.org
E-mail: clearinghouse@miusa.org

General Inquiries:
Intake Assistant
541/343-1284,
clearinghouse@miusa.org

Chief Executive Officer:
Susan Sygall,
Executive Director

Statement:
Mobility International USA (MIUSA) is a nonprofit organization that coordinates the National Clearinghouse on Disability and Exchange (NCDE), a project funded by the Bureau of Educational and Cultural Affairs, U.S. Department of State. The NCDE provides information and referrals to individuals with disabilities interested in participating in international programs and also advises exchange programs on how to accommodate participants with disabilities. It encourages individuals with disabilities to explore the many ways their international interests can be fulfilled through study, work, research, and community service overseas. MIUSA provides short-term international educational exchange and leadership development opportunities for people with and without disabilities. In addition, MIUSA has developed several publications and videos on international exchange, people with disabilities, and leadership development. MIUSA staff are also available for consultation and presentations at conferences.

Profile:
Nonprofit founded in 1981. MIUSA/NCDE has nine U.S. staff. MIUSA/NCDE provides a membership program and has 50 institutional members, 150 individual members, and one local chapter/affiliate. Five U.S. volunteers contribute to MIUSA/NCDE's mission.

Geographic Focus:
Worldwide

Exchange Activities:
MIUSA/NCDE is involved in the following exchange areas: Community/Citizen, Disability Rights Training, Leadership Development, Persons with Disabilities, Students/Educators, Training. MIUSA/NCDE provides exchange-related facilitative or support services.

Financial Assistance:
MIUSA/NCDE does not provide financial assistance.

Publications:
Building Bridges: A Manual on Including People with Disabilities in International Exchange Programs

Loud, Proud and Passionate: Including Women with Disabilities in International Development Programs

Equal Opportunities in the U.S. and Newly Independent States (NIS)

A World Awaits You: A Journal of Success in International Exchange for People with Disabilities

Exchange Programs Include:
Please see website for current program listings.

Exchange Related Facilitative or Support Services Include:
Conference/Meetings/Workshops Information/training on including people with disabilities in international exchange programs
Clearinghouse Manager
541/343-1284,
clearinghouse@miusa.org

People with Disabilities Exchange Coordinator
541/343-1284,
exchange@miusa.org

Other
National Clearinghouse on Disability and Exchange-Information and Referral
Clearinghouse Manager
541/343-1284,
clearinghouse@miusa.org

Mountbatten Internship Programme

50 East 42nd Street
Suite 2000
New York, NY 10017-5404

Tel.: 212/557-5380
Fax: 212/557-5383
Website: www.mountbatten.org
E-mail: info@mountbatten.org

General Inquiries:
Michael Billett,
MBE Executive Director
212/557-5380

Chief Executive Officer:
Paul Beresford-Hill, Chairman

Statement:
Mountbatten Internship Programme's mission is to organize international experiential education programs for college graduates and young professionals in the field of international business in the United States, England, and Australia. Successful completion of the program leads to a Certificate in International Business Practice, a professional qualification validated by the University of Oxford Delegacy of Local Examinations.

Profile:
Nonprofit founded in 1984. Mountbatten Internship Programme has five U.S. staff. Five U.S. volunteers contribute to Mountbatten Internship Programme's mission.

Geographic Focus:
North America (United States), Oceania (Australia), Western Europe (United Kingdom)

Exchange Activities:
Mountbatten Internship Programme provides exchange-related facilitative or support services.

Financial Assistance:
Interns receive monthly allowances, accommodations, and medical insurance for the duration of their internship.

Multinational Exchange for Sustainable Agriculture (MESA)

5337 College Avenue, Suite 508
Oakland, CA 94618

Tel.: 510/654-8858
Fax: 603/699-2459
Website: www.mesaprogram.org
E-mail: mesa@mesaprogram.org

General Inquiries:
Lauren Augusta,
Executive Director
mesa@mesaprogram.org

Chief Executive Officer:
Lauren Augusta,
Executive Director

Statement:
Multinational Exchange for Sustainable Agriculture (MESA) is dedicated to the global promotion of sustainable farming. To this end, MESA collaborates with similar organizations and universities abroad to facilitate U.S. organic, on-the-farm training programs for young foreign farmers and students. MESA also coordinates short-term organic farm and industry tours in Northern California for international groups.

Profile:
Nonprofit founded in 1994. MESA has one U.S. staff. Three U.S. volunteers and more than ten overseas volunteers contribute to MESA's mission. It provides a membership program and has more than 200 individual members.

Geographic Focus:
Worldwide

Exchange Activities:
MESA is involved in the following exchange areas: Training, Sustainable Agriculture. MESA provides exchange-related facilitative or support services.

Financial Assistance:
MESA provides all participating exchange trainees with free U.S. accommodations, stipends, medical insurance, educational seminars, domestic travel and coordinator support. MESA also awards some grants to repatriated trainees to support their own home country's farming projects.

Publications:
Bi-annual newsletter

Exchange Programs Include:
MESA Annual U.S. Organic
Training Program
Lauren Augusta,
Executive Director
mesa@mesaprogram.org

Exchange Related Facilitative or Support Services Include:
Conference/Meetings/Workshops
Organic Farm & Industry Tours
for International Groups
Lauren Augusta,
Executive Director
mesa@mesaprogram.org

Grants/Scholarships to Individuals
Agrarian Community Results
Project (ACRP)
(for MESA alumni only)
Lauren Augusta,
Executive Director
mesa@mesaprogram.org

U.S. Department of State Designated Sponsor for the Exchange Vistor Program
Trainees

Nacel Open Door

3410 Federal Drive
Suite 101
St. Paul, MN 55122

Tel.: 800/622-3553
Fax: 651/686-9601
Website: www.nacelopendoor.org
E-mail: nacel@nacelopendoor.org

General Inquiries:
Richard Banasikowski,
Vice President
800/622-3553

Chief Executive Officer:
Frank Tarsitano,
President
ftarsitano@nacelopendoor.com

Statement:
Nacel Open Door promotes international understanding and language education by offering accessible, quality exchange programs with a well-structured support network.

Profile:
Nonprofit founded in 1969. Nacel Open Door has 35 U.S. staff. Four hundred U.S. volunteers contribute to Nacel Open Door's mission.

Geographic Focus:
Africa (Ivory Coast, Morocco), Asia (Japan, Taiwan), Central America (Costa Rica), Eastern Europe (Albania, Croatia, Czech Republic, Slovak Republic, Slovenia, Yugoslavia), Middle East (Israel), Newly Independent States (Armenia, Azerbaijan, Belarus, Georgia, Kazakhstan, Kyrgyzstan, Moldova, Russia, Turkmenistan, Ukraine, Uzbekistan), North America (Canada, Mexico), South America (Argentina, Bolivia, Brazil, Chile, Colombia, Ecuador, Paraguay, Venezuela), Western Europe (France, Germany, Ireland, Italy, Spain) Turkey

Exchange Activities:
Nacel Open Door is involved in the following exchange areas: Homestay, Language Study, Students/Educators. Nacel Open Door provides exchange-related facilitative or support services. It administers exchange programs for the following academic levels: K-12.

Financial Assistance:
Nacel Open Door does not provide financial assistance.

Publications:
Poster Series with Language and Cultural Lessons for Language Teachers

Host Family Handbook

A la decouvert des Francais

Descubrio a la familia espanola

Nacel Open Door International Exchange Newsletter

Exchange Programs Include:
Educational Asian Programs
  Debra McDonough
  800/622-3553

Hosting Program
  Richard Banasikowski,
  Hosting Program Coordinator
  800/622-3553

Semester of School Year Abroad
  Carrie Little
  800/622-3553

Summer Homestays Abroad
  Carrie Little
  800/622-3553

Exchange Related Facilitative or Support Services Include:
Conference/Meetings/Workshops
  Susan Franck,
  Director of Short Term Programs
  800/622-3553

Overseas Offices:
Paris, France
Granada, Spain
Köln, Germany
Shanghai, China
Tokyo, Japan
Mexico City, Mexico
Sao Paulo, Brazil
Gdansk, Poland
Seoul, Korea
Edmonton, Canada
Rodez, France

U.S. Department of State Designated Sponsor for the Exchange Vistor Program
Secondary school students

NAFSA: Association of International Educators (NAFSA)

**1307 New York Avenue, NW
Eighth Floor
Washington, DC 20005-4701**

Tel.: 202/737-3699
Fax: 202/737-3657
Website: http://www.nafsa.org
E-mail: inbox@nafsa.org

General Inquiries:
Membership Services
202/737-3699

Chief Executive Officer:
Marlene M. Johnson,
CEO & Executive Director

Statement:
NAFSA: Association of
International Educators (NAFSA) is
an association of individuals
engaged in the field of international
education at the post secondary
level. It promotes educational
opportunities across national
boundaries, serving members,
their institutions and students, and
organizations with an interest in
international educational mobility.
The Association sets and upholds
standards of good practice, provides professional education and
training that strengthen institutional programs and services related to
international educational
exchange, and advocates for international education.

Profile:
Nonprofit founded in 1948.
NAFSA has 50 U.S. staff. NAFSA
has 8,500 individual members. One
hundred-fifty U.S. volunteers contribute to NAFSA's mission.

Geographic Focus:
Worldwide

Exchange Activities:
NAFSA provides exchange-related
facilitative or support services.

Financial Assistance:
NAFSA does not provide financial
assistance.

Publications:
International Educator

The NAFSA Newsletter

NAFSA.news

*NAFSA Adviser's Manual of Federal
  Regulations Affecting Foreign
  Students and Scholars*

NAFSA

**Exchange Related Facilitative or
Support Services Include:**
Conference/Meetings/Workshops
  NAFSA Annual Conference
  Valerie Royal, Senior Director
  for Conferences and Meetings
  202/737-3699
  conference@nafsa.org

Membership Services
  Membership Services
  Denise Jones Wold,
  Director of Membership Services
  202/737-3699
  inbox@nafsa.org

Public Policy
  Government Relations/Public Policy
  Vic Johnson,
  Associate Executive Director
  for Public Policy
  202/737-3699 x256
  govrel@nafsa.org

National Association of State Universities and Land-Grant Colleges (NASULGC)

1307 New York Avenue, NW
Suite 400
Washington, DC 20005-4701

Tel.: 202/478-6040
Fax: 202/478-6046
Website: http://www.nasulgc.org

General Inquiries:
Barbara Cummings,
Public Affairs
202/478-6042,
bcummings@nasulgc.org

Chief Executive Officer:
C. Peter Magrath,
President

Statement:
The National Association of State Universities and Land-Grant Colleges (NASULGC) strives to promote all facets of internationalization on campuses, including the facilitation of exchanges, study abroad, faculty development, international research, and language/area study and development. NASULGC does not participate in placement of graduate, professional, or undergraduate students. NASULGC's 212 individual members place students on their campuses.

Profile:
Nonprofit founded in 1887.
NASULGC has 37 U.S. staff.

Geographic Focus:
Worldwide

Exchange Activities:
NASULGC provides exchange-related facilitative or support services. It administers exchange programs for the following academic levels: Graduate Students, Professional Schools, Undergraduate Students.

Financial Assistance:
NASULGC does not provide financial assistance.

Publications:
NEWSLINE

Exchange Programs Include:
Public Policy

National Committee on United States-China Relations

71 West 23rd Street
19th Floor
New York, NY 10010-4102

Tel.: 212/645-9677
Fax: 212/645-1695
Website: http://www.ncuscr.org
E-mail: info@ncuscr.org

General Inquiries:
Rosalind Daly,
Vice-President
212/645-9677

Chief Executive Officer:
John L. Holden,
President

Statement:
The National Committee on United States-China Relations is a public, nonprofit organization which encourages understanding of China and the United States among citizens of both countries. The Committee focuses its exchange, educational, and policy activities on international relations, economic development and management, governance and legal affairs, environmental and other global issues, mass communication, and education administration, by addressing issues with respect to the People's Republic of China, the Hong Kong Special Administrative Region, and Taiwan.

Profile:
Nonprofit founded in 1966. The National Committee on United States-China Relations has 12 U.S. staff. The National Committee on United States-China Relations has 100 institutional members and 675 individual members.

Geographic Focus:
Asia (China, Taiwan), North America (United States)

Exchange Activities:
The National Committee on United States-China Relations is involved in the following exchange areas: Community/Citizen, Professional/Business. The National Committee on United States-China Relations provides exchange-related facilitative or support services. It administers exchange programs for the following academic levels: K-12.

Financial Assistance:
The National Committee on United States-China Relations does not provide financial assistance.

Publications:
Annual Report
Newsletter
China Policy Series

Exchange Programs Include:
National Committee on United States-China Relations Programs

Exchange Related Facilitative or Support Services Include:
International Visitor Support

Membership Services

Public Policy

National Council for Eurasian and East European Research (NCEEER)

910 17th Street
Suite 300
Washington, DC 20006

Tel.: 202/822-6950
Fax: 202/822-6955
Website: http://www.nceeer.org
E-mail: nceeerdc@aol.com

General Inquiries:
Jon Hutzley,
Program Assistant
202/822-6950,
nceeerdc@aol.com

Chief Executive Officer:
Robert T. Huber,
President

Statement:
The National Council for Eurasian and East European Research (NCEEER) is the largest provider of support for American scholars seeking to undertake postdoctoral research in the humanities and social sciences in the Newly Independent States (NIS) of the former Soviet Union and Central and Eastern Europe (CEE). Grants are provided for collaborative research with scholars from the NIS and CEE, field research projects for Americans in the region, and field research projects for NIS scholars in the United States. NCEEER also organizes policy forums to enable its sponsored researchers to present the results of their research to policy-making audiences, and administers the Ed A. Hewett Fellowship Program, which enables a scholar, administrator, or independent researcher with extensive background in Eurasian and East European studies to

spend a year in a federal agency working on a mutually-agreeable foreign policy project.

Profile:
Nonprofit founded in 1978. NCEEER has four U.S. staff and one overseas staff.

Geographic Focus:
Eastern Europe (Estonia, Latvia, Lithuania), Newly Independent States (Armenia, Azerbaijan, Belarus, Georgia, Kazakhstan, Kyrgyzstan, Moldova, Tajikistan, Turkmenistan, Russia, Ukraine, Uzbekistan)

Exchange Activities:
NCEEER is involved in the following exchange areas: Arts/Cultural, Public Policy, Students/Educators, Training. NCEEER provides exchange-related facilitative or support services. It administers exchange programs for the following academic levels: Faculty and post-doctoral researchers.

Financial Assistance:
All programs are for post-doctoral research.

Publications:
NCEEER Annual Report

Annotated Bibliography of NCEEER Sponsored Research

NCEEER Newsletter (quarterly)

Exchange Programs Include:
National Research Competition

Policy Research Fellowships

Regional Scholars Exchange Program
Bud Jacobs,
Vice-President
202/822-6950,
nceeerdc@aol.com

Exchange Related Facilitative or Support Services Include:
Grants/Scholarships to Individuals
Policy Research Fellowship,
America's Research Grant
Bud Jacobs,
Vice-President
202/822-6950,
nceeerdc@aol.com

Public Policy
Ed A. Hewett
Policy Fellowship Program
Robert Huber,
President
202/822-6950,
nceeerdc@aol.com

Conference/Meetings/Workshops
Policy Forums

Overseas Office:
Moscow, Russia

U.S. Department of State Designated Sponsor for the Exchange Vistor Program
Professors and research scholars

Alliance
MEMBER

National Council for International Visitors (NCIV)

1420 K Street, NW
Suite 800
Washington, DC 20005-2401

Tel.: 202/842-1414
Fax: 202/289-4625
Website: http://www.nciv.org
E-mail: wamin@nciv.org

General Inquiries:
Jill L'Heureux,
Program Associate
202/842-1414

Chief Executive Officer:
Dr. Sherry Lee Mueller,
Executive Director

Statement:
The mission of the National Council for International Visitors (NCIV), a membership network of individuals and community organizations in the United States, is to bridge cultures and build mutually beneficial relationships through person to person international exchanges. NCIV is a professional association that promotes citizen diplomacy and provides services to its members: 1) to strengthen leadership and nonprofit management skills; and 2) to build their capacity to organize professional programs, cultural activities, and home visits for participants in the State Department's International Visitor Program and other exchanges.

Profile:
Nonprofit founded in 1961. NCIV has five U.S. staff members at its national office. NCIV provides a membership program and has 120 individual members, 20 program agency members, and 97 community organization members. Each year, 80,000 volunteers are involved in NCIV member activities.

Geographic Focus:
Worldwide

Exchange Activities:
NCIV members are involved in the following exchange areas: Arts/Cultural, Community/Citizen, Homestay, Professional/Business, Short-Term Visitors, Training. The NCIV national office provides exchange-related trainings and support services.

Financial Assistance:
NCIV does not provide financial assistance.

Publications:
NCIV Network News (monthly)
The Art of Programming for International Visitors
Building an Effective Board of Directors
Nonprofit Management Resources Directory
NCIV Membership Directory
A Salute to Citizen Diplomacy

Exchange Related Facilitative or Support Services Include:
Membership Services

Conference/Meetings/Workshops

Grants to NCIV Member Organizations
   Community Support Grant
   Wendy Amin,
   Director of Programs
   202/842-1414,
   wamin@nciv.org

Orientation Programs/Internships
   Jill L'Heureux,
   Program Associate
   jlheureux@nciv.org

Public Policy
   Sherry Lee Mueller,
   Executive Director

Representation Site Visits
   Sherry Lee Mueller,
   Executive Director

Technology Projects
   Jeff Hertzog,
   Program Associate

Publications
   Jeff Hertzog,
   Program Associate

Alliance
MEMBER

National FFA (FFA)

6060 FFA Drive
P.O. Box 68960
Indianapolis, IN 46268-0960

Tel.: 317/802-6060
Fax: 317/802-6061
Website: http://www.ffa.org
E-mail: global@ffa.org

General Inquiries:
Jim Piechowski,
Global Programs
317/802-4214,
global@ffa.org

Chief Executive Officer:
Larry D. Case,
National FFA Advisor and CEO

Statement:
National FFA's international mission is to enrich the lives of young people, by developing their potential for leadership, personal growth, and career success through agricultural education. FFA believes the future productivity of America, especially the agricultural sector, will demand a global perspective of its citizens.

Profile:
Nonprofit founded in 1928. FFA provides a membership program and has 455,306 individual members, and 7,226 local chapters/affiliates.

Geographic Focus:
Worldwide

Exchange Activities:
FFA is involved in the following exchange areas: Short-Term Visitors, Students/Educators, Training. FFA provides exchange-related facilitative or support services. It administers exchange programs for the following academic levels: K-12, Undergraduate Students.

Financial Assistance:
Scholarships and financial assistance are available for qualified applicants on some programs.

Publications:
FFA Horizons

Exchange Programs Include:
Government Grant Programs

Work Experience Abroad Inbound

Work Experience Abroad Outbound and Travel Seminar

Year-Long High School Inbound

U.S. Department of State Designated Sponsor for the Exchange Visitor Program
Trainees

North Carolina Center for International Understanding (NCCIU)

**412 North Wilmington Street
Raleigh, NC 27601-2813**

Tel.: 919/733-4902
Fax: 919/733-8578
Website: www.ga.unc.edu/NCCIU

General Inquiries:
Angie Bolin,
Coordinator, Citizen Exchanges
919/733-4902,
 asb@ga.unc.edu

Chief Executive Officer:
Millie Ravenel,
State Director

Statement:
The North Carolina Center for International Understanding (NCCIU) provides international experiential education to address challenges facing North Carolina policy leaders, K-12 educators and citizens. Its programs prepare North Carolinians to live and work effectively with people of other cultures. CIU is a public service of the University of North Carolina.

Profile:
Nonprofit founded in 1979. NCCIU has nine U.S. staff. One hundred U.S. volunteers and 20 overseas volunteers contribute to NCCIU's mission.

Geographic Focus:
Worldwide

Exchange Activities:
NCCIU is involved in the following exchange areas: Community/Citizen, Homestay, Public Policy Leaders, K-12 Educators. NCCIU provides exchange-related facilitative or support services. It administers exchange programs for the following academic levels: K-12 (internet exchanges only), Teachers.

Financial Assistance:
NCIUU occasionally provides funding. Financial assistance is limited to North Carolina residents. Most funding is limited to participants recruited from specified counties.

Exchange Programs Include:
Citizens Exchange
Angie Bolin,
Citizen Exchange Coordinator
919/733-0224
asb@ga.unc.edu

International School Partnerships Through Technology
Diane Midness,
Coordinator
919/733-4902
dmidness@ga.unc.edu

Global Study Program for K-12 Policymakers
Marty Babcock,
Director of Programs
919/715-2784
martyb@ga.unc.edu

Global Study Program for K-12 Educators
Meredith Henderson,
Coordinator
919/733-0708
mlh@ga.unc.edu

Latina Initiative
Winifred Ernst,
Coordinator
919/733-5067
wwe@ga.unc.edu

North-South Center

1500 Monza Avenue
Coral Gables, FL 33146

Tel.: 305/284-6868
Fax: 305/284-6370
Website: www.miami.edu/nsc
E-mail: nscenter@miami.edu

General Inquiries:
V. Sherry Tross,
Program Director
305/284-6868,
stross@miami.edu

Chief Executive Officer:
Ambler H. Moss, Jr.,
Director

Statement:
The Dante B. Fascell North-South Center is an independent, research, and educational organization dedicated to finding practical solutions to problems facing the nations of the western hemisphere. Working in partnership with institutions in the United States and in the rest of the hemisphere, the Center develops policy relevant research and outreach projects. The Center engages and informs government and opinion leaders throughout the Americas through conferences, public affairs activities, and research publications. Through the adjunct senior research associate and the North-South Fellows program, the Center actively promotes technical and scholarly interchange and productive networks among scholars.

Profile:
Nonprofit founded in 1984. The Dante B. Fascell North-South Center has 20 U.S. staff, and numerous project partners in Latin America and the Caribbean.

Geographic Focus:
Caribbean, Central America, North America, South America

Exchange Activities:
The Dante B. Fascell North-South Center is involved in the following exchange areas: Professional/Business, Students/Educators. It provides exchange-related facilitative or support services and administers exchange programs for the following academic levels: Faculty, Graduate Students.

Financial Assistance:
A limited amount of financial assistance is available for students pursuing graduate work in international studies.

Publications:
Fault Lines of Democracy in Post-Transition Latin America

Making NAFTA Work: U.S. Firms and the New North American Business Environment

Drug Trafficking in the Americas

Women and Grass Roots Democracy in the Americas

Distant Cousins: The Caribbean-Latin American Relationship

Chile, Pinochet, and the Caravan of Death

Exchange Programs Include:
North-South Fellows
Jeffrey Stark,
Director of Research and Studies
jstark@nsc.msmail.miami.edu

Exchange Related Facilitative or Support Services Include:
Conference/Meetings/Workshops
V. Sherry Tross,
Program Director
stross@miami.edu

Grants/Scholarships to Individuals
North-South Fellows Program

International Visitor Support

Public Policy

U.S. Department of State Designated Sponsor for the Exchange Vistor Program
Short-term scholars
College and university students
Government visitors

Northwest International Study Exchange, Inc. (NISE)

600 SW Tenth Avenue
P.O. Box 4632, Suite 520
Portland, OR 97208

Tel.: 503/222-9803
Fax: 503/227-7224
E-mail: nisenw@aol.com

General Inquiries:
Sara G. Cogan,
Executive Director
503/222-9803,
nisenw@aol.com

Chief Executive Officer:
Sara G. Cogan,
Executive Director

Statement:
Northwest International Study Exchange, Inc. is a private organization devoted to promoting international understanding and goodwill by providing high quality English-language and cultural immersion programs primarily for high school students.

Profile:
Private, founded in 1983. NISE has 34 U.S. staff. Four hundred U.S. volunteers contribute to NISE's mission.

Geographic Focus:
Asia (China, Japan, Taiwan), Central America (Costa Rica, Guatemala), Eastern Europe (Bulgaria), Newly Independent States, South America (Brazil), Western Europe (France, Spain)

Exchange Activities:
NISE is involved in the following exchange areas: Homestay, Language Study, Sports, Students/Educators. NISE provides exchange-related facilitative or support services. It administers exchange programs for the following academic levels: K-12, Teachers.

Financial Assistance:
NISE does not provide financial assistance.

Publications:
Marketing Booklet
Information Brochure

NORTHWEST INTERNATIONAL STUDY EXCHANGE, INC.

Exchange Programs Include:
Individual Immersion Program
(High School and College Students)

NISE English Prep Institute
(High School and College Program)

Short Term Academic Homestay
(High School)

Summer Sports/English Language
Homestay Program (High School)

Ohio International Agricultural and Horticultural Interns Program (OIAHIP)

700 Ackerman Road
Suite 360
Columbus, OH 43202-1559

Tel.: 614/292-7720
Fax: 614/688-8611

General Inquiries:
Michael O'Keeffe,
Program Manager
614/292-7720,
mokeeffe@pop.service.ohio-state.edu

Chief Executive Officer:
Michael R. Chrisman,
Program Director

Statement:
The Ohio International Agricultural and Horticultural Interns Program is a student exchange program of the Ohio State University (OSU) which allows training of international and domestic students in the fields of horticulture and agriculture. Exchanges are individualized and offered at any time of the year at the request of the applicant. Two reciprocal programs extending one year are offered, including practical training and study at OSU. All practical training placements are fully paid positions offering opportunities for personal growth through cross-cultural experience and technical training.

Profile:
Nonprofit founded in 1979.

Geographic Focus:
Eastern Europe (Bulgaria, Czech Republic, Hungary), Western Europe (Denmark, France, Germany, Ireland, the Netherlands, Sweden, United Kingdom)

Exchange Activities:
OIAHIP is involved in the following exchange areas: Training. OIAHIP provides exchange-related facilitative or support services. It administers exchange programs for the following academic levels: Faculty, Graduate Students, Undergraduate Students.

Financial Assistance:
OIAHIP does not provide financial assistance.

U.S. Department of State Designated Sponsor for the Exchange Vistor Program
Trainees

Open Society Institute (OSI)

**400 West 59th Street
New York, NY 10019**

Tel.: 212/548-0175
Fax: 212/548-4652
Website: http://www.soros.org
E-mail: scholar@sorosny.org

General Inquiries:

Network Scholarship
Programs Department
212/548-0175,
scholar@sorosny.org

Chief Executive Officer:

Aryeh Neier,
President

Statement:

The Open Society Institute-New York (OSI-New York) was established to develop and implement programs in areas of educational, social and legal reform. OSI-New York is part of the Soros foundations network, a group of autonomous organizations created and supported by George Soros and operating in nearly 60 countries around the world, principally in Central and Eastern Europe and the former Soviet Union, but also in Guatemala, Haiti, Mongolia, West and Southern Africa and the United States. Network Scholarship Programs (NSP) fund students, scholars and professionals from Central and Eastern Europe, the former Soviet Union, Mongolia

and Burma to participate in rigorous and competitive academic programs outside their home countries. NSP support post-secondary studies and faculty development in the social sciences and humanities, professional degree programs in targeted fields, and supplemental grants to students. All network scholarships are granted via open, merit-based competitions with multi-tiered, impartial selection procedures. Students should review the website for further information on the awards available in their home country.

Profile:

Nonprofit founded in 1993. OSI has 250 U.S. staff.

Geographic Focus:

Asia (Burma, Mongolia), Eastern Europe (East Central Europe, Baltics, Balkans, Caucasus, Central Asia, Russia, Ukraine, Belarus)

Financial Assistance:

OSI offers competitive fellowships covering partial costs of academic program and living expenses in the United States. Eligibility restrictions are defined by the program. Unsolicited requests from individuals are not accepted.

Exchange Programs Include:
Undergraduate Exchange
Alex Irwin,
Program Manager
airwin@sorosny.org

Global Supplementary Grants
Vera Johnson,
Senior Program
Administrator
vjohnson@sorosny.org

Faculty Development Program
Carol Tegen,
Deputy Director
NSP/New York
ctegen@sorosny.org

Edmund S. Muskie & Freedom
Support Act Graduate Fellowship
Sonia Skindrud,
Senior Program Officer
sskindrud@sorosny.org

Mongolian Professional
Development Fellowship
Zinta Gulens-Grava,
Program Manager
zgulensgrava@sorosny.org

Organization for Cultural Exchange Among Nations (OCEAN)

2101 East Broadway Road
Suite Two
Tempe, AZ 85282-1735

Tel.: 800/28-OCEAN
Fax: 480/784-4891
Website: http://www.oceanintl.org
E-mail: ocean.intl@att.net

General Inquiries:

Laura Stahl,
Special Services Director
480/784-4671,
ocean.intl@att.net

Chief Executive Officer:

Jose DePontes,
President

Statement:

The Organization for Cultural Exchange Among Nations (OCEAN) is a nonprofit organization which sponsors international exchange students. The purpose of its program is to promote international understanding, cultural awareness, and academic excellence.

Profile:

Nonprofit founded in 1994.
OCEAN has seven U.S. staff.
OCEAN has 50 local chapters/affiliates. Ten U.S. volunteers contribute to OCEAN's mission.

Geographic Focus:

Asia (South Korea, Kyrgyzstan, Thailand, Vietnam), Western Europe (Germany, Spain, France), North America (Mexico, United States), Oceania (Philippines), South America (Brazil, Venezuela, Colombia), Eastern Europe (Yugoslavia, Bulgaria, Albania)

Exchange Activities:

OCEAN is involved in the following exchange areas: Arts/Cultural, Homestay, Language Study, Short-Term Visitors, Students/Educators. OCEAN provides exchange-related facilitative or support services. It administers exchange programs for the following academic levels: Faculty, K-12.

Financial Assistance:

OCEAN offers full and partial scholarships to qualified students that would not be financially able to participate otherwise.

Exchange Programs Include:
High School Exchange
    Laura Stahl,
    Special Services Director
    480/784-4671,
    ocean.intl@att.net

Additional Office:
Grand Junction, CO

Overseas Offices:
Tirana, Albania
Goiania, Brazil
Lages, Brazil
Curitiba, Brazil
Fortaleza, Brazil
Rio de Janeiro, Brazil
Sofia, Bulgaria
Oldenburg, Germany
Bonn, Germany
Seoul, Korea
Bishkek, Kyrgyzstan
Hermosillo, Mexico
Bangkok, Thailand
Belgrade, Yugoslavia

U.S. Department of State Designated Sponsor for the Exchange Vistor Program
Secondary school students

Pacific Intercultural Exchange (PIE)

402 West Broadway
Suite 1910
San Diego, CA 92101

Tel.: 619/238-6767
Fax: 619/238-6717
Website: http://www.pieusa.org
E-mail: info@pieusa.org

General Inquiries:
John M. Doty,
Executive Director
619/238-6767,
execdir@pieusa.org

Chief Executive Officer:
Guy V. Pacurar,
President

Statement:
Pacific Intercultural Exchange (PIE) is dedicated to fostering international understanding through the placement of foreign high school students in academic and cultural immersion programs with families throughout the United States. American students are also provided the opportunity to participate in reciprocal exchange programs in foreign schools around the world. Since its founding, PIE has provided exchange opportunities for more than 20,000 students. PIE is represented throughout the United States and in countries where American students are placed by a network of local community area representatives and regional coordinators who work cooperatively with students, high schools, and host families.

Profile:
Nonprofit founded in 1975. PIE has 30 U.S. staff. Four hundred fifty U.S. volunteers contribute to PIE's mission.

Geographic Focus:
Worldwide

Exchange Activities:
PIE is involved in the following exchange areas: Arts/Cultural, Community/Citizen, Homestay, Language Study, Short-Term Visitors, Students/Educators. PIE provides exchange-related facilitative or support services. It administers exchange programs for the following academic levels: K-12.

Financial Assistance:
PIE provides a limited amount of financial assistance through its international partners on an as-needed basis and as determined by a panel of program directors.

Publications:
Host Family Handbook

International Student Manual

Here and Abroad Newsletter

Exchange Programs Include:
Academic Semester and Year Abroad
   John Doty, Executive Director
   619/238-6767,
   execdir@pieusa.org
Short-Term Group Programs

Additional Offices:
Idaho City, ID
Washington, DC
New York, NY
Comanche, OK
Apple Valley, CA
Alvin, TX
Ionia, MI

Overseas Offices:
Beijing, China
Asuncion, Paraguay
Belgrade, Yugoslavia
Perth, Australia
La Plat, Argentina
Buenos Aires, Argentina
Hanoi, Vietnam

U.S. Department of State Designated Sponsor for the Exchange Vistor Program
Secondary school students

Partners of the Americas (PARTNERS)

1424 K Street, NW
Suite 700
Washington, DC 20005

Tel.: 202/628-3300
Fax: 202/628-3306
Website: http://www.partners.net
E-mail: info@partners.net

General Inquiries:

Richard Lamporte,
Vice President of
Development and New Projects
202/628-3300,
rl@partners.net

Chief Executive Officer:

Malcolm Butler,
President and CEO

Statement:

The mission of Partners of the
Americas (Partners) is to promote
the involvement of the United
States, Latin American, and
Caribbean citizens in community
development and local governance
activities. Partners of the Americas
links 45 U.S. states and the District
of Columbia with 31 Latin
American and Caribbean countries.
Currently, there are 60 such partnerships. Citizens on both sides of
the partnership determine communities' needs and mobilize people
and resources to carry out projects.

Profile:

Nonprofit founded in 1964.
Partners has 24 U.S. staff and four
overseas staff. Partners provides a
membership program. Six thousand U.S. volunteers and 6,000
overseas volunteers contribute to
Partners's mission.

Geographic Focus:

Caribbean, Central America, North
America (United States, Mexico),
South America

Exchange Activities:

Partners is involved in the follow-
ing exchange areas: Arts/Cultural,
Community/Citizen, Homestay,
Language Study, Persons with
Disabilities, Professional/Business,
Senior Citizens, Short-Term
Visitors, Sports, Students/Educators,
Training. Partners provides
exchange-related facilitative or sup-
port services. It administers
exchange programs for the follow-
ing academic levels: Faculty,
Graduate Students, K-12, Teachers,
Undergraduate Students.

Financial Assistance:

Partners does not provide financial
assistance.

Publications:

Partners (quarterly newsletter)

Directions (journal)

Partners Tools for Training

Partners Reach Out (media guide)

Exchange Programs Include:

InterAmerican Democracy Network
  Martha Villada,
  Director
  202/628-3300,
  mcv@partners.net

Citizen Participation Program
  Martha Villada,
  Director
  202/628-3300,
  mcv@partners.net

Cultural and Educational Programs
  Amb. William Stedman,
  Director for Cultural and
  Educational Programs
  202/628-3300,
  ws@partners.net

Farmer to Farmer
  Anabella Bruch,
  Director
  202/628-3300,
  ab@partners.net

Youth Conservation Corps
  John Chater, Director
  52-99-258-805,
  jchater@datum.com

Exchange Related Facilitative or Support Services Include:

Conference/Meetings/Workshops
  Barbara Bloch, Vice President for
  Leadership & Training
  202/628-3300,
  bb@partners.net

International Visitor Support
  Director, Education & Culture
  202/628-3300,
  ds@partners.net

Membership Services
  Claudia Calderon, Board Liaison
  202/628-3300,
  cc@partners.net

Overseas Offices:

Brasilia, Brazil
Recife, Brazil
Tegucigalpa, Honduras

PeopleLink

103 H Street
Suite A
Petaluma, CA 94952

Tel.: 707/769-5152
Fax: 707/769-0195
Website: www.peoplelink.org
E-mail: linkpeople@aol.com

General Inquiries:
Megan Beauvais,
Marketing Assistant/AYP
Administration
707/769-5152,
linkpeople@aol.com

Chief Executive Officer:
Shelley M. Hyde,
Director

Statement:
PeopleLink's mission is to provide
an educational and cultural experience for young people and adults
with citizens from other cultures to
help eliminate fear and prejudice
caused by a lack of understanding
between individuals and to help
promote peace and harmony
among all people.

Profile:
Nonprofit founded in 1991.
PeopleLink has 18 U.S. staff and
four overseas staff. Three thousand
U.S. volunteers contribute to
PeopleLink's mission.

Geographic Focus:
Worldwide

Exchange Activities:
PeopleLink is involved in the following exchange areas:
Arts/Cultural, Community/Citizen,
Homestay, Language Study, Short-
Term Visitors, Students/Educators.
PeopleLink provides exchange-
related facilitative or support services. It administers exchange programs for the following academic
levels: K-12.

Financial Assistance:
PeopleLink does not provide financial assistance.

Publications:
PeopleLink Trifold Brochure

*Creating a Global Neighborhood
Through Language* (textbook)

*Creating a Global Neighborhood
Through Language* (textbook-
Canadian version)

Teacher Guide Reference Book

Field Coordinator Manual

Exchange Programs Include:
Academic Year Program
Megan Beauvais, Academic Year
Program Administrator
707/769-5152,
linkpeople@aol.com

Outbound Program
Destiny Aman,
Outbound Program Coordinator
707/769-5152,
peoplelink@peoplelink.org

Short Range Program
Barbara La Rue,
Director
707/769-5152,
linkpeople@aol.com

Additional Offices:
Chula Vista, CA
Escalon, CA
Phelan, CA
Palmdale, CA
Pomona, CA
Lebanon, OR

Overseas Offices:
Kelowna, Canada
White Rock, Canada
Tokyo, Japan

**U.S. Department of State
Designated Sponsor for the
Exchange Vistor Program**
Secondary school students

People to People International (PTPI)

501 East Amour Boulevard
Kansas City, MO 64109-2200

Tel.: 816/531-4701
Fax: 816/561-7502
Website: http://www.ptpi.org
E-mail: ptpi@ptpi.org

General Inquiries:
Roseann Rosen,
Vice President of Operations
816/531-4701

Chief Executive Officer:
Mary Eisenhower,
CEO

Statement:
The purpose of People to People International (PTPI) is to enhance international understanding and friendship through educational, cultural and humanitarian activities involving the direct exchange of ideas and experiences among people of different countries and diverse cultures.

Profile:
Nonprofit founded in 1956. PTPI has 13 U.S. staff. PTPI provides a membership program and has 35,000 individual members, and 259 local chapters/affiliates. One thousand U.S. volunteers contribute to PTPI's mission.

Geographic Focus:
Asia, Africa, Eastern Europe, Newly Independent States, North America, Oceania (Australia, New Zealand), Western Europe

Exchange Activities:
PTPI is involved in the following exchange areas: Artistic Ambassador Program, Civics education, Community/Citizen, Homestay, International Youth Leadership Conferences, Professional Internship Training, Professional/Business, Short-Term Visitors, Students/Educators. PTPI provides exchange-related facilitative or support services. It administers exchange programs for the following academic levels: Graduate Students, K-12, Undergraduate Students.

Financial Assistance:
PTPI provides scholarships or financial assistance to participants including interest-free loans to high school students; congressional award scholarships; matching grants with U.S. chapters and partial college scholarships to alumni of student programs. PTPI also has an International Friendship Fund that enables its chapter networks to assist each other in times of need or disaster.

Publications:
People, Cindy Spake,
Managing Director of
Publications,
816/531-4701

Exchange Programs Include:
Citizen Ambassadors Professional Counterpart Exchange
Theresa Stock,
Managing Director
of Membership Services
816/531-4701

Internships/Study Abroad
Jill Sigler,
Adult Programs
816/531-4701

High School Student Ambassadors
Theresa Stock,
Managing Director
of Membership Services
816/531-4701

International Visitors Program
(Homestays)
Jewelee Stoffle,
Membership and
Homestay Coordinator
816/531-4701

Meeting the Americans & Chapter Development
Theresa Stock,
Managing Director
of Membership Services
816/531-4701

Exchange Related Facilitative or Support Services Include:
Conference/Meetings/Workshops
Karen Hoch,
Director of
Conferences and Meetings
816/531-4701

Development
Dr. Tim Barry,
Vice President of Development
816/531-4701

Alliance MEMBER

Phelps-Stokes Fund (PSF)

75 Trinity Place
Suite 1303
New York, NY 10006

Tel.: 212/619-8100
Fax: 212/619-5108
Website: http://www.psfdc.org
E-mail: phelps@admin.con2.com

Secondary Address:
1420 K Street, NW
Suite 800
Washington, DC 20005

General Inquiries:
Viola Morris-Buchanan,
Assistant to the President
212/619-8100,
phelps@admin.con2.com

Chief Executive Officer:
Dr. Badi G. Foster,
President

Statement:
Phelps-Stokes Fund's mission is to address educational needs of the urban and rural poor of Africa and the United States with particular attention to the needs of people of color. The Fund's activities are founded on the conviction that true education depends on a fundamental respect for human dignity, the development of the full capacities inherent in each human being, and the cultivation of social harmony. In Africa, the Fund develops and guides programs that aim to engender respect for human rights; support participatory democracy; foster sustainable development; and train new leaders.

Profile:
Nonprofit founded in 1911. PSF has ten U.S. staff and four overseas staff.

Geographic Focus:
Africa (Liberia, sub-Saharan Africa)

Exchange Activities:
PSF is involved in the following exchange areas:
Professional/Business, Short-Term Visitors, Students/Educators. PSF provides exchange-related facilitative or support services.

Financial Assistance:
PSF does not provide financial assistance.

Publications:
Dialogue (newsletter)

The Africa Papers

New Global Realities Program: An International Relations Curriculum

Exchange Programs Include:
International Visitor Program
Stafford Kay
202/371-9544,
exchange@psfdc.org

U.S. Department of State Designated Sponsor for the Exchange Vistor Program
International visitors
Intern

Presidential Classroom

119 Oronoco Street
Alexandria, VA 22314-2015

Tel.: 800/441-6533
Fax: 703/548-5728
Web: www.presidentialclassroom.org
E-mail:
info@presidentialclassroom.org

General Inquiries:
Sevaun Palvetzian,
International Programming Director
703/683-5400 x25,
spalvetzian@presidentialclass-
room.org

Chief Executive Officer:
Jay Wickliff,
Executive Director

Statement:
Since 1968, Presidential Classroom
has offered a unique opportunity
for cultural exchange. The Future
World Leaders Summit brings
together student leaders from
around the world to explore international relations, diplomacy, and
the changing world economy. This
program is designed for foreign
national students (aged 16-19) and
U.S. students interested in multi-
national affairs. Students spend
one week with unprecedented
access to Washington's halls of
power and the people shaping
international relations. These
international student leaders participate in the World Trade Game,
visit their country's embassy, tour
renowned sites in Washington, DC
and meet and question influential
world leaders.

Profile:
Nonprofit founded in 1968.
Presidential Classroom has 16 U.S.
staff. Two hundred fifty U.S. and 50
overseas volunteers contribute to
Presidential Classroom's mission.

Geographic Focus:
Worldwide

Exchange Activities:
Presidential Classroom is involved
in the following exchange areas:
Students/Educators, Short-Term
Visitors. Presidential Classroom
provides exchange-related facilitative or support services. It administers exchange programs for the
following academic levels: K-12.

Financial Assistance:
Partial tuition scholarships available to students from under-represented countries based on financial
need and academic standing.

Publications:
Recruiting Brochure/Application

Exchange Programs Include:
Future World Leaders Summit
    Sevaun Palvetzian
    800/441-6533,
spalvetzian@presidentialclassroom.org

ProAmerican Educational and Cultural Exchange (PEACE)

40 Water Street
New Philadelphia, PA 17959

Tel.: 800/377-2232
Fax: 570/277-0607
Website: http://www.peace-inc.org
E-mail: paz@peace-inc.org

General Inquiries:
Richard S. Page,
Executive Director
800/377-2232,
page@peace-inc.org

Chief Executive Officer:
Richard S. Page,
President and Executive Director

Statement:
"Uniting the Americas Through Our Children" is the motto of the ProAmerican Educational and Cultural Exchange (PEACE), an interdenominational faith-based program promoting an ecumenical mission of international goodwill and understanding through foreign student exchanges. PEACE is committed to the development of leaders and a spiritual union and bonding of families, schools, and communities across national borders. Specializing in exchanges within the Americas, PEACE views itself as implementing the Monroe Doctrine, the cornerstone of American foreign policy, in the most effective way—giving the coming generations the bilingual skills and bicultural understanding essential to more cooperative relations in this hemisphere.

Profile:
Nonprofit founded in 1988. PEACE has 12 U.S. staff. Compensated volunteers, including 34 in the United States and 17 overseas, contribute to PEACE's mission.

Geographic Focus:
Central America (Panama), North America (United States, Mexico), South America (Brazil, Colombia, Ecuador, Peru, Venezuela)

Exchange Activities:
PEACE is involved in the following exchange areas: Homestay, College Intensive English. PEACE provides exchange-related facilitative or support services. It administers exchange programs for the following academic levels: K-12, Intensive English ages 19 and up.

Financial Assistance:
PEACE offers two Merit Scholarships each year and limited financial aid.

Publications:
The Host Family Survival Kit
Exchange Student Survival Kit
Perspectives de Paz (bi-monthly newsletter)
Host Family Handbook
Student Handbook
Representative Manuals (U.S. and International)
School Enrollment Kit
Spanish Teacher Kit

Exchange Programs Include:
Academic Year or Semester to USA

Academic Year or Semester Abroad

Summer Homestay to USA or Abroad

Winter Quarter Study/Homestay to USA

Keystone Intensive English Program (Age 19+)

Exchange Related Facilitative or Support Services Include:
Admission/Placement Services
  Student and Host Screening

Conference/Meetings/Workshops
  Orientation for Students & Hosts

Grants/Scholarships to Individuals
  Up to 50 per cent
  Student Scholarships

Grants to Institutions/Organizations
  Donations to Religious and
  Educational Organizations

International Visitor Support
  Bilingual Counseling

Testing/Assessment Services
  Institutional TOEFL

Overseas Offices:
Caracas, Venezuela
Panama City, Panama
Santiago, Panama
Medallin, Colombia
Fortaleza, Brazil
Cheuca, Ecuador
Araquippe, Peru
Monterrey, Mexico
Chihuahua, Mexico
Monclova, Mexico
Puebla, Mexico
Altamirano, Mexico
Merida, Mexico
Agnascaliente, Mexico
Eacatecas, Mexico
San Luis Potusi, Mexico
Esquinappa, Mexico

**U.S. Department of State
Designated Sponsor for the
Exchange Vistor Program**
Secondary school students

Program of Academic Exchange (PAX)

PAX
academic exchange

71 Arch Street
Greenwich, CT 06830

Tel.: 800/555-6211
Fax: 203/629-0486
Website: http://www.pax.org
E-mail: academicexchange@pax.org

General Inquiries:
Yvonne Forman,
Executive Director
203/629-8144,
academicexchange@pax.org

Chief Executive Officer:
Libby Cryer,
President

Statement:
Program of Academic Exchange (PAX) is an educational foundation. Its mission is to increase mutual respect among the people of the world, foster an appreciation of differences and similarities, and enhance the ability to communicate with one another. The foundation believes that this mission is served by providing young people with the opportunity to study abroad and live with a host family for an extended period of time. PAX offers both inbound and outbound high school/homestay programs. The programs are built on the simple concept that students can best learn about a different culture and master its language by living as a family member in that country. For the host family, sharing everyday life with a teenager from another country provides firsthand exposure to the customs and language of that country.

Profile:
Nonprofit founded in 1990. PAX has 15 U.S. staff. Three hundred U.S. community coordinators contribute to PAX's mission.

Geographic Focus:
Worldwide

Exchange Activities:
PAX is involved in the following exchange areas: Homestay, Students/Educators. PAX provides exchange-related facilitative or support services. It administers exchange programs for the following academic levels: K-12.

Financial Assistance:
Need based scholarships offered to qualified applicants selected by sending organizations.

Exchange Programs Include:
PAX Abroad
　Libby Cryer
　800/555-6211,
　academicexchange@pax.org

PAX at Home
　Yvonne Forman
　800/555-6211,
　academicexchange@pax.org

U.S. Department of State Designated Sponsor for the Exchange Vistor Program
Secondary school students

Alliance
MEMBER

Project Harmony

**5197 Main Street
Unit 6
Waitsfield, VT 05673**

Tel.: 802/496-4545
Fax: 802/496-4548

General Inquiries:
Bonnie Smoren,
Office Manager
802/496-4545
ph@projectharmony.org

Chief Executive Officer:
Barbara Miller,
Co-Director

Statement:
Project Harmony is a nonprofit organization founded on the belief that active citizenship and community involvement strengthens and energizes the global community. Project Harmony has expanded to include constituents from other areas engaged in exploring civil society and creating new patterns of citizenship. Its programs provide opportunities for participants to develop leadership, attitude, and skills essential in an interdependent world. Dedicated to creating new models of cross-cultural educational initiatives and professional enhancement, Project Harmony combines interactive projects, hands-on training, homestays, and collaboration for individuals of diverse backgrounds to explore issues of common interest. It fosters ongoing dialogue and sustained relationships which encourage participants to examine closely their own assumptions and perspectives on the world and gain concrete knowledge and leadership skills.

Profile:
Nonprofit founded in 1985. Project Harmony has 20 U.S. staff and 100 overseas staff. One thousand U.S. volunteers and 1,000 overseas volunteers contribute to Project Harmony's mission.

Geographic Focus:
Newly Independent States (Armenia, Russia, Ukraine, Georgia, Moldova), Western Europe (Finland, Ireland)

Exchange Activities:
Project Harmony is involved in the following exchange areas: Arts/Cultural, Community/Citizen, Homestay, Language Study, Professional/Business, Training. Project Harmony provides exchange-related facilitative or support services. It administers exchange programs for the following academic levels: Faculty, Graduate Students, K-12, Teachers, Undergraduate Students.

Financial Assistance:
Project Harmony does not provide financial assistance.

Publications:
Project Harmony Newsletter

Exchange Programs Include:
Community Connections
   Jared Cadwell
   Co-Director
   802/496-4545,
   cc@projectharmony.org

Law Enforcement Exchange Programs
   Charlie Hosford
   Co-Director
   802/496-4545,
   leep@projectharmony.org

School Linkages Program
   Barbara Miller
   Program Manager
   802/496-4545,
   students@projectharmony.org

Teacher Exchange Programs
   Barbara Miller
   Co-Director
   802/496-4545,
   ph@projectharmony.org

Exchange Related Facilitative or Support Services Include:
Admissions/Placement Service
   Teacher Internship Program
   Barbara Miller
   802/496-4545,
   ph@projectharmony.org

Conference/Meetings/
Workshops & Training
   Domestic Violence Community
   Partnership Program
   Ed Cronin
   978/343-0371,
   edsue@net1plus.com

ISLP - Internet Exchange for Schools
   Colleen Haley
   Program Coordinator
   802/496-4545,
   ph@projectharmony.org

Additional Offices:
Boston, MA
Fitchburg, MA
Portland, MN

Overseas Offices:
Irkutsk, Russia
Moscow, Russia
Petrozavodsk, Russia
St. Petersburg, Russia
Kiev, Ukraine
Lviv, Ukraine
Odessa, Ukraine

Resource Euro-Asian American Cultural Homestay, Inc. (REACH)

308 Englewood
Lufkin, TX 75901

Tel.: 800/947-3224
Fax: 936/634-6731
Website: http://www.reachtx.org
E-mail: reachtx@lcc.net

General Inquiries:
Lora Whiteley,
Director
reachtx@lcc.net

Chief Executive Officer:
Mark Earwood,
CEO

Statement:
Resource Euro-Asian American Cultural Homestay, Inc. (REACH) was established to provide out-reach services to advance cultural understanding through education and to promote student exchange between the United States and other countries. REACH brings foreign teenage students to the United States who live with host families for ten months while attending high school. The exchange enables students to acquire a knowledge of life in the United States, especially with regard to education, family life, community life, and other related experiences, and to promote the general interests of international educational and cultural exchange.

Profile:
Nonprofit founded in 1991. REACH has three U.S. staff. Six U.S. volunteers contribute to REACH's mission.

Geographic Focus:
Asia (Japan, Taiwan, Thailand), South America (Brazil), Western Europe

Exchange Activities:
REACH is involved in the following exchange areas: Homestay. REACH provides exchange-related facilitative or support services. It administers exchange programs for the following academic levels: K-12.

Financial Assistance:
REACH does not provide financial assistance.

Exchange Programs Include:
Academic Year/Semester Program
Lora Whiteley,
Director
409/639-6877,
reachtx@lcc.net

U.S. Department of State Designated Sponsor for the Exchange Vistor Program
Secondary school students

Rotary International

1560 Sherman Avenue
Evanston, IL 60201

Tel.: 847/866-3000
Fax: 847/328-8554
Website: http://www.rotary.org
E-mail:
scholarshipinquiries@rotaryintl.org

Chief Executive Officer:
Ed Futa,
General Secretary

General Inquiries:
scholarshipinquiries@rotaryintl.org

Statement:
Rotary International is a world-wide organization of business and professional leaders who provide humanitarian service, encourage high ethical standards in all vocations, and help build goodwill and peace in the world. Rotary's exchange programs hold as their primary purpose the advancement of international understanding and friendly relations among people of different countries.

Profile:
Nonprofit founded in 1917. Rotary is an organization of business and professional leaders united world-wide who provide humanitarian service, encourage high ethical standards in all vocations, and help build goodwill and peace in the world. In more than 160 countries worldwide, approximately 1.2 million Rotarians belong to more than 29,000 Rotary clubs.

Geographic Focus:
Worldwide

Exchange Activities:
Rotary International is involved in the following exchange areas: Language Study, Professional/Business, Short-Term Visitors, Students/Educators. Rotary International provides exchange-related facilitative or support services. It administers exchange pro-grams for the following academic levels: Faculty, Graduate Students, Undergraduate Students.

Financial Assistance:
Academic-Year Ambassadorial Scholarships provide funding for one academic year (usually nine months) of study, specifically to cover round-trip transportation, tuition, room and board expenses, and some educational supplies, not to exceed $25,000 or its equivalent. *Multi-Year Ambassadorial Scholarships* are for two years of degree-oriented study. A grant of $12,000 or its equivalent will be provided per year to be applied toward the costs of a degree pro-gram. *Cultural Ambassadorial Scholarships* are for either three or six months of intensive language study and cultural immersion and provide funds to cover round-trip transportation, language training expenses, and homestay living arrangements, not to exceed $12,000 and $19,000 respectively. Applications are considered for candidates interested in studying Arabic, English, French, German, Hebrew, Italian, Japanese, Korean, Mandarin Chinese, Polish, Portuguese, Russian, Spanish, Swahili, and Swedish. *Grants for University Teachers* provide funds to higher education faculty to travel abroad to teach at colleges and universities in developing countries. Two types of grants are available: a $12,500 grant for three to five months of teaching service and $22,500 grant for six to ten months of teaching service. Grant funds may be used for round-trip trans-portation, living expenses, teaching and research costs, and miscellaneous ambassadorial expenses.

Publications:
The Rotarian Magazine,
    Cary Silver, 847/866-3000

Exchange Programs Include:
Rotary Foundation Ambassadorial Scholarships Program
    Matthew Welch,
    Supervisor
    847/866-3323

Rotary Foundation
Group Study Exchange Program
    Stephanie Veit,
    Supervisor
    847/866-3327

Rotary Grants for University Teachers to Serve in Developing Countries
    Matthew Welch,
    Supervisor Scholarship Program
    847/866-3310

Rotary Youth Exchange Program
    Meredith Leigh,
    Program Coordinator
    847/866-3421

Exchange Related Facilitative or Support Services Include:
Community Development/Organization

Grants/Scholarships to Individuals

Professional/Volunteer Development

Overseas Offices:
Warwickshire, United Kingdom
Paramatta, Australia
Delhi, India
Seoul, Korea
Zurich, Switzerland
Buenos Aires, Argentina
São Paulo, Brazil
Tokyo, Japan

Scandinavian Seminar, Inc.

24 Dickinson Street
Amherst, MA 01002

Tel.: 413/253-9736
Fax: 413/253-5282
Web: www.scandinavianseminar.com
E-mail:
   study@scandinavianseminar.com

Chief Executive Officer:
Jacqueline D. Waldman,
Chief Operating Officer

Statement:
Scandinavian Seminar, Inc. was
founded in 1949 as a total immersion, year-abroad study program
for young Americans, promoting
inter-cultural understanding.
Today, Scandinavian Seminar
offers short-term study programs
for people of all ages and college
semester programs.

Profile:
Nonprofit founded in 1949.
Scandinavian Seminar, Inc. has four
U.S. staff and four overseas staff.

Geographic Focus:
Eastern Europe, Western Europe
(Scandinavia)

Exchange Activities:
Scandinavian Seminar, Inc. provides exchange-related facilitative
or support services. It administers
exchange programs for the following academic levels: K-12,
Undergraduate Students.

Financial Assistance:
Scandinavian Seminar, Inc. has limited scholarships for select programs based on merit and need.

Publications:
Scandinavian Seminar Today
Ambassadors for the Environment
Elderhostel Catalogs
En Route Catalogs

Exchange Programs Include:
Ambassadors for the Environment

From Mountains to Fjord

Elderhostels

En Route

Folk School Program

Cultural Exploration

Overseas Offices:
Lahti, Finland
Fredensborg, Denmark
Trosa, Sweden
Sogndal, Norway

School Year Abroad (SYA)

Phillips Academy
Andover, MA 01810

Tel.: 978/725-6828
Fax: 978/725-6833
Website: http://www.sya.org
E-mail: mail@sya.org

General Inquiries:
Whitney Shugrue,
Director of Admissions
978/725-6828,
mail@sya.org

Chief Executive Officer:
W. W. Halsey II,
Executive Director

Statement:
School Year Abroad (SYA) is the only secondary level program that allows students to live in a foreign family while earning academic credit towards graduation and to prepare for U.S. colleges and universities. Each year, eleventh and twelfth graders travel to France, Spain, and mainland China to study at the unique schools created by SYA 34 years ago. The central elements of SYA, a homestay and an academic program in which the majority of courses are taught exclusively in Chinese, French, or Spanish, assure that students receive a challenging dose of their adopted language. At the same time, instructors from sponsoring schools guarantee that they do not lose ground in their core American courses, math and English. In China, history and science are also taught in English. Extracurricular activities and organized travel round out the year.

Profile:
Nonprofit founded in 1964. SYA has seven U.S. staff and 30 overseas staff.

Geographic Focus:
Asia (China), Western Europe (France, Italy, Spain)

Exchange Activities:
SYA is involved in the following exchange areas: Homestay, Language Study, Students/ Educators. SYA provides exchange-related facilitative or support services. It administers exchange programs for the following academic levels: K-12.

Financial Assistance:
SYA provides need-based financial assistance to participants. In 2000-01, 40 per cent of SYA students received financial aid with grants averaging $18,527.

Publications:
School Year Abroad Catalog

Questions and Answers about School Year Abroad (brochure)

School Year Abroad College Profile

The Newsletter

Exchange Programs Include:
School Year Abroad
   W. Halsey II,
     Executive Director

Overseas Offices:
Zaragoza, Spain
Beijing, China
Rennes, France
Viterbo, Italy

Sister Cities International (SCI)

1424 K Street, NW
Suite 600
Washington, DC 20005

Tel.: 202/347-8630
Fax: 202/393-6524
Website: www.sister-cities.org
E-mail: info@sister-cities.org

General Inquiries:
Tracy Green,
Office Manager
202/347-8630

Chief Executive Officer:
Tim Honey,
Executive Director

Statement:
Sister Cities International (SCI) is the world's premiere citizen diplomacy network that partners over 1,200 U.S. cities, counties, and states with similar jurisdictions in 125 countries worldwide. SCI's major goals are to create opportunities for citizens to explore other cultures through long-lasting community partnerships; build opportunities for economic and community development; and stimulate environments through which people learn, work, and solve problems together through varied municipal business, health, educational, and other professional and cultural exchange, training, and development programs.

Profile:
Nonprofit founded in 1967. SCI has 11 U.S. staff. SCI provides a membership program and has 700 institutional members. Two hundred fifty thousand U.S. volunteers contribute to SCI's mission.

Geographic Focus:
Worldwide

Exchange Activities:
SCI is involved in the following exchange areas: Arts/Cultural, Community/Citizen, Law Enforcement, Persons with Disabilities, Professional/Business, Students/Educators, Training. SCI provides exchange-related facilitative or support services.

Financial Assistance:
SCI does not provide financial assistance.

Publications:
SCI Annual Directory

Sister Cities International Newsletter

SCI Report to the Membership

Exchange Programs Include:
U.S.-N.I.S. Domestic Violence Prevention Program
    Julie Johnson
    jjohnson@sister-cities.org

Exchange Related Facilitative or Support Services Include:
Conference/Meetings/Workshop
    Deanita Holland,
    Conference Director

Membership Services
    Justine Morgan

U.S. Department of State Designated Sponsor for the Exchange Vistor Program
Secondary school students

Alliance
MEMBER

STS Foundation (STS)

110 North Royal
Suite 501
Alexandria, VA 22314

Tel.: 800/522-4678
Fax: 703/518-4347
Website: www.stsfoundation.org
E-mail: info@stsfoundation.org

General Inquiries:
Blanka Vackova,
Program Manager
703/518-4753

Chief Executive Officer:
Georgina Taddiken,
Executive Program Director

Statement:
STS Foundation (STS) believes that
intercultural student exchange promotes understanding, respect, and
goodwill among people of all
nations. Students, families, schools,
and communities have an opportunity to learn more about one another's cultures as they share the
exchange experience.

Profile:
Nonprofit founded in 1986. STS
has ten U.S. staff and ten overseas
staff. Three hundred fifty U.S. volunteers contribute to STS's mission.

Geographic Focus:
Africa (South Africa), Eastern
Europe (Hungary, Poland, Czech
Republic), Oceania (Australia, New
Zealand), South America (Brazil),
Western Europe (Sweden, Finland,
Denmark, Norway, France, Italy,
Netherlands, Germany)

Exchange Activities:
STS is involved in the following
exchange areas:
Students/Educators. STS provides
exchange-related facilitative or support services. It administers
exchange programs for the following academic levels: K-12.

Financial Assistance:
STS does not provide financial
assistance.

Exchange Programs Include:
Inbound High School
Semester Year Program
　Georgina Taddiken,
　Executive Program Director
　703/518-4753

Outbound High School Semester,
Year, Summer Homestay
　Blanka Vackova,
　Program Manager
　703/518-4753

U.S. Department of State
Designated Sponsor for the
Exchange Vistor Program
Secondary school students

United States Servas, Inc. (US Servas)

11 John Street
Suite 505
New York, NY 10038-4009

Tel.: 212/267-0252
Fax: 212/267-0292
Website: http://www.usservas.org
E-mail: info@usservas.org

Secondary Address:
Kevin Newham
P.O. Box 1086
Arlie Beach
Queensland, Australia, 4802

General Inquiries:
Carole D. Wagner,
Office Manager

Chief Executive Officer:
Lara Fisher,
Administrator

Statement:
U.S. Servas is a part of an international network which promotes peace and cross-cultural understanding by providing opportunities for personal contact between people of diverse cultures and backgrounds. By participating in homestay visits at no charge, hosts and travelers educate each other, sharing their lives, interests, and concerns about national and international issues.

Profile:
Nonprofit founded in 1948. US Servas has three U.S. staff. US Servas provides a membership program and has five institutional members, 4,500 individual members, and 50 local chapters/affiliates. Three hundred fifty U.S. volunteers and 50 overseas volunteers contribute to US Servas's mission.

Geographic Focus:
Worldwide

Exchange Activities:
US Servas is involved in the following exchange areas: Arts/Cultural, Community/Citizen, Homestay, Persons with Disabilities, Senior Citizens, Short-Term Visitors. US Servas provides exchange-related facilitative or support services.

Financial Assistance:
Small travel stipends are available for low-income travelers visiting Servas hosts in the United States.

Publications:
U.S. Host List: Northeast

U.S. Host List: Central and Southeast

U.S. Host List: West Coast and Rockies

U.S. News Open Doors (quarterly newsletter)

Servas International News (annual)

Exchange Related Facilitative or Support Services Include:
Membership Services
    Host Program

Travel Services
    International,
    Domestic Travel Program

People with Disabilities

Overseas Office:
Queensland, Australia

United Studies Student Exchange (USSE)

106 Ridgeway
Suite C
Hot Springs, AR 71901

Tel.: 501/321-2000
Fax: 501/321-2001
Website: www.unitedstudies.org
E-mail: info@unitedstudies.org

General Inquiries:
Sonia White,
Director
501/321-2000,
swhite@unitedstudies.org

Chief Executive Officer:
Greg C. White,
President

Statement:
United Studies Student Exchange (USSE) is an exchange program for secondary level students featuring academic semester and academic year exchanges both inbound to the United States and outbound from the United States. United Studies is committed to building bridges of understanding through cultural and academic exchange.

Profile:
Nonprofit founded in 1985. USSE has six U.S. staff. Forty U.S. volunteers contribute to USSE's mission.

Geographic Focus:
Asia (Japan, China), Newly Independent States (Armenia, Azerbaijan, Belarus, Georgia, Kazakhstan, Moldova, Russia, Tajikistan, Turkmenistan, Ukraine, Uzbekistan), North America (United States), South America (Brazil, Colombia), Western Europe (Spain, Germany), Eastern Europe (Yugoslavia)

Exchange Activities:
USSE is involved in the following exchange areas: Homestay, Persons with Disabilities, Students/Educators. USSE provides exchange-related facilitative or support services. It administers exchange programs for the following academic levels: K-12.

Financial Assistance:
USSE does not provide financial assistance.

Publications:
Program Brochures
USSE Host Family Handbook
USSE Student Handbook

Exchange Programs Include:
Academic Semester Abroad

Academic Semester in America

Academic Year Abroad

Academic Year in America

Future Leaders Exchange Program

Exchange Related Facilitative or Support Services Include:
People with Disabilities

University and College Intensive English Programs in the USA (UCIEP)

**English Language Institute
MSN 4C4
George Mason University
Fairfax, VA 22030-4444**

Tel.: 703/993-3660
Fax: 703/993-3664
Website: http://www.uciep.org
E-mail: info@uciep.org

General Inquiries:
Kathryn Trump,
Central Office Coordinator
703/993-3660,
ktrump@gmu.edu

Chief Executive Officer:
Scott Stevens,
President, University of Delaware
302/831-2674,
sstevens@udel.edu

Statement:
University and College Intensive English Programs (UCIEP), founded in 1967, is a consortium of intensive English programs that are governed by universities and colleges in the United States. The mission of UCIEP is to promote excellence in intensive English program administration, curriculum, and instruction by 1) establishing guidelines for member programs, 2) encouraging and sponsoring professional development as well as cooperation and communication among member programs, and 3) advocating on behalf of member programs, the organization, and the field of English as a second language.

Profile:
Nonprofit founded in 1967. UCIEP has 10 U.S. volunteers. It provides a membership program and has 67 institutional members.

Geographic Focus:
Worldwide

Exchange Activities:
UCIEP is involved in the following exchange areas: Language Study, Short-Term Visitors, Students/Educators. UCIEP provides exchange-related facilitative or support services. It administers exchange programs for the following academic levels: Undergraduate Students, Graduate Students.

Financial Assistance:
UCIEP does not provide financial assistance.

Publications:
UCIEP Member Profiles

Member Guidelines

UCIEP Governing Rules
    Kathryn Trump, Central Office
    703/993-3660, ktrump@gmu.edu

Exchange Related Facilitative or Support Services Include:

Admission/Placement Services
    Individual ESL Program Directors
    (see Profile book)

Courses for Credit
    Individual ESL Program Directors
    (see Profile book)

Testing/Assessment Services
    English Language Assessments
    Individual ESL Program Directors
    (see Profile book)

People with Disabilities
    Individual ESL Program Directors
    (see Profile book)

U.S. Department of State Designated Sponsor for the Exchange Vistor Program
Professors and research scholars
Short-term scholars
College and university students

USDA Graduate School
International Institute (USDA/GS/II)

600 Maryland Avenue, SW
Suite 320
Washington, DC 20024

Tel.: 202/314-3500
Fax: 202/479-6803
Website: http://www.grad.usda.gov
E-mail: intlinst@grad.usda.gov

General Inquiries:
Earl Mathers, Director,
International Institute
202/314-3500,
earl_mathers@grad.usda.gov

Chief Executive Officer:
Lynn Edwards,
Executive Director (acting),
Graduate School, USDA

Statement:
The primary mission of the
International Institute of the
Graduate School, USDA, is to facilitate the exchange of knowledge,
skills, and culture among nations of
the world. Since 1961, the Institute
has assisted U.S. government agencies, foreign governments, international organizations, and individuals. The Institute employs a wide
variety of delivery mechanisms
including technology enabled learning, classroom training, observational and consultation training,
exchanges, and organizational
development programs.

Profile:
Nonprofit founded in 1921. Three
hundred eight U.S. volunteers contribute to the International
Institute's mission.

Geographic Focus:
Worldwide

Exchange Activities:
USDA/GS/II is involved in the following exchange areas:
Government, Professional/Business,
Short-Term Visitors,
Students/Educators, Training.
USDA/GS/II provides exchange-
related facilitative or support services. It administers exchange programs for the following academic
levels: Faculty, Teachers.

Financial Assistance:
The International Institute does not
provide financial assistance.

Publications:
Graduate School Newsletter

Exchange Programs Include:
Fulbright Teacher Exchange Program
Jennifer Nupp,
Program Administrator
202/314-3521,
jennifer_nupp@grad.usda.gov

Island Training Program
Jack Maykoski,
Associate Director
202/314-3509,
john_maykoski@grad.usda.gov

Visitor and Exchange Program
Jack Maykoski,
Associate Director

Additional Offices:
San Francisco, CA
Atlanta, GA
Chicago, IL
Dallas, TX
Honolulu, HI
Philadelphia, PA

Wo International Center (WIC)

Punahou School
1601 Punahou Street
Honolulu, HI 96822

Tel.: 808/944-5871
Fax: 808/944-5712
Web: www.punahou.edu/wo.html
E-mail: wen@punahou.edu

General Inquiries:
Wendy Lee,
Program Coordinator
808/944-5871

Chief Executive Officer:
Hope Kuo Staab,
Director

Statement:
The Wo International Center (WIC) offers educational programs focusing on foreign languages and civilization studies in Japan, the People's Republic of China, India, France, and Spain for secondary students in public and private schools. Reciprocally, it receives students in Hawaii from countries such as Japan, China, French Polynesia, Germany, India, and Taiwan for study of the English language and American civilization. On the Punahou campus, WIC also conducts intensive immersion programs for selected Hawaiian students entitled "Focus on Japan," "Focus on China," "Focus on Europe," and "Focus on Korea."

Profile:
Nonprofit founded in 1968. WIC has four U.S. staff. Two U.S. volunteers contribute to WIC's mission.

Geographic Focus:
Asia (China, India, Japan, Taiwan), Oceania (Tahiti), Western Europe (France, Germany, Spain)

Exchange Activities:
WIC is involved in the following exchange areas: Students/Educators. WIC provides exchange-related facilitative or support services. It administers exchange programs for the following academic levels: K-12.

Financial Assistance:
Scholarships, based on financial need, are given to students who are residents of Hawaii. These partial scholarships range from one-sixth to two-thirds of the cost of the program.

Exchange Programs Include:
Pan-Pacific Program in Hawaii

Summer Trip to China

Summer Trip to France

Summer Trip to Japan

Summer Trip to Spain

Exchange Related Facilitative or Support Services Include:
Courses for Credit
Summer Trips to Japan, China, France, and Spain

World Education Services Foundation

2111 Franklin Street
Oakland, CA 94612-3003

Tel.: 800/937-6397
Fax: 510/452-9430
Website: http://www.wesusa.org
E-mail: info@wesusa.org

General Inquiries:
Manuel Cabello,
President
510/452-0200

Chief Executive Officer:
Manuel Cabello

Statement:
World Education Services Foundation conducts a program to bring foreign teenage students to the United States to live with selected American families for a period of five to ten months while attending school. World Education Services Foundation strives to enable such students to acquire a knowledge of various aspects of American life and culture to promote international exchange.

Profile:
Nonprofit founded in 1984. World Education Services Foundation has eight U.S. staff. Twenty U.S. volunteers contribute to its mission.

Geographic Focus:
Africa, Asia, Central America, Eastern Europe, South America, Western Europe

Exchange Activities:
World Education Services Foundation is involved in the following exchange areas: Homestay, Students/Educators. World Education Services Foundation provides exchange-related facilitative or support services. It administers exchange programs for the following academic levels: K-12.

Financial Assistance:
A limited number of scholarships are available, including the "Winston Dwight Cabello Memorial Scholarship."

Publications:
WES Handbook
WES High School
WES Local Coordinators
WES Small Towns
WES Host Families

Exchange Programs Include:
High School Academic Exchange

U.S. Department of State Designated Sponsor for the Exchange Vistor Program
Secondary school students

World Education Services, Inc. (WES)

P.O. Box 745
Old Chelsea Station
New York, NY 10113-0745

Tel.: 800/937-3895
Fax: 212/739-6100
Website: http://www.wes.org
E-mail: info@wes.org

General Inquiries:
212/966-6311,
info@wes.org

Chief Executive Officer:
Mariam Assefa,
Executive Director

Statement:
World Education Services, Inc.
(WES) facilitates the exchange of
students and professionals through
foreign credential evaluation.
WES's mission is to provide information on educational systems
through individual evaluations,
research, publications, and workshops. WES evaluates credentials
for more than 45,000 individuals
annually. WES evaluation reports
allow universities, licensing boards,
employers and government agencies to assess foreign applications
from foreign-educated candidates
accurately and efficiently.

Profile:
Nonprofit founded in 1974.
Ninety two staff contribute to
WES's mission.

Geographic Focus:
Worldwide

Exchange Activities:
WES is involved in the following
exchange areas: Adult Education,
Professional/Business,
Students/Educators. WES provides
exchange-related facilitative or support services.

Financial Assistance:
WES does not provide financial
assistance.

Publications:
World Education News and Reviews
(WENR)

**Exchange Related Facilitative or
Support Services Include:**
Credentials Evaluation
Margarita Sianou,
Director of Evaluations
212/966-6311,
msianou@wes.org

World Education Workshops
Topics: Foreign Credential Evaluation
and International Student Recruitment
John Lembo,
Manager, Academic Services
212/219-7330,
jlembo@wes.org

Additional Offices:
Chicago, IL
Miami, FL
Washington, DC
San Francisco, CA

Overseas Office:
Toronto, Canada

Alliance
MEMBER

World Exchange

7 White Birch Road
Putnam Valley, NY 10579

Tel.: 800/444-3924
Fax: 845/528-9187
Website: www.worldexchange.org
E-mail: info@worldexchange.org

General Inquiries:
Michael Sklaar,
President
845/526-2505

Chief Executive Officer:
Michael Sklaar,
President

Statement:
World Exchange is an international exchange organization specializing in short-term, intercultural, and linguistically-based homestays in the United States and Canada. High school students stay with volunteer host families. Linguistic stays, either with volunteer host families or with language teachers, are offered to college students and adults through World Exchange's Language Partners International program. Custom, small-group, and individual language/intercultural programs are offered to corporate clients. Programs share the common goal of creating an interesting and rewarding learning experience in a safe environment overseen by highly qualified staff. Intellectual and personal growth in turn foster better international relations on a person-to-person level.

Profile:
Nonprofit founded in 1985. World Exchange has two U.S. staff. One hundred U.S. volunteers and eight overseas volunteers contribute to World Exchange's mission.

Geographic Focus:
Worldwide

Exchange Activities:
World Exchange is involved in the following exchange areas: Arts/Cultural, Homestay, Language Study, Short-Term Visitors, Sports. World Exchange provides exchange-related facilitative or support services.

Financial Assistance:
World Exchange does not provide financial assistance.

Publications:
Invite the World Home

Welcome the World Home

Language Partners International

Language Enrichment Program

Exchange Programs Include:
Language Partners International Programs-Incoming/Outgoing

Homestay Program for High School-Age Students-Incoming

Exchange Related Facilitative or Support Services Include:
Admissions/Placement Service Admissions, Preparation and Orientation
Vera Sklaar,
Director
845/526-2299

Conference/Meetings/Workshops Staff Workshops, Host Family Orientation Meetings
Vera Sklaar,
Director
845/526-2299

Other, Peace Projects
Michael Sklaar, President
845/526-2505

Alliance
MEMBER

World Experience
Teenage Student Exchange (WE)

2440 South Hacienda Boulevard
Suite 116
Hacienda Heights, CA 91745

Tel.: 800/633-6653
Fax: 626/333-4914
Website: www.worldexperience.org
E-mail:
weworld@worldexperience.org

General Inquiries:
Virginia Thompson,
USA Staff Specialist

Chief Executive Officer:
Bobby Jean Fraker,
President

Statement:
The mission of World Experience (WE) is to forge international links of communication, friendship, support, and understanding among students, families, and communities.

Profile:
Nonprofit founded in 1977. WE has seven U.S. staff and 30 overseas staff. Eighty-five U.S. volunteers and 12 overseas volunteers contribute to WE's mission.

Geographic Focus:
Asia (China, Japan, Thailand), Central America (Panama), Eastern Europe (Bulgaria, Czech Republic, Hungary, Poland, Serbia, Slovak Republic), Middle East (Turkey), Newly Independent States (Georgia, Russia), North America (Canada, Mexico, United States), Oceania (New Zealand), South America (Brazil, Colombia, Ecuador, Uruguay, Venezuela), Western Europe (Denmark, Finland, Germany, Greece, Italy)

Exchange Activities:
WE is involved in the following exchange areas: Homestay, Short-Term Visitors. WE provides exchange-related facilitative or support services. It administers exchange programs for the following academic levels: K-12.

Financial Assistance:
World Experience provides three Ron Crookshank Scholarship Awards to Latin America for program fees. Ten per cent of student fees are awarded to individuals who can prove need.

Publications:
Overview Brochure

Student Catalog

Pangaea (Newsletter)

Exchange Programs Include:
One Semester/Homestay Study

Summer Homestay

Two Semester/Homestay Study

Additional Office:
Topsham, ME

U.S. Department of State Designated Sponsor for the Exchange Vistor Program
Secondary school students

World Families

1023 SW 316th Place
Federal Way, WA 98023

Tel.: 253/528-0220
Fax: 253/941-0927
Website: www.world-families.org
E-mail: info@world-families.org

General Inquiries:
Sheila Dolak,
Director
253/528-0220,
sheila@world-families.org

Chief Executive Officer:
Sheila Dolak,
Director

Statement:
World Families' mission is to provide international exchange experiences for youth and families. World Famillies values family-based programs that provide an unparalleled environment for intercultural learning. It believes that international exchange fosters mutual understanding and acceptance of others. World Families' focus is a successful educational experience and personal growth for its participants.

Profile:
Nonprofit founded in 2000. World Families has three U.S. staff. Ten U.S. volunteers contribute to its mission.

Geographic Focus:
Asia (Japan, Korea), North America (United States, Canada, Mexico)

Exchange Activities:
World Families is involved in the following exchange areas: Arts/Culture, Professional/Business, Homestay, Short-Term Visitors, Language Study, Sports. It administers exchange programs for the following academic levels: K-12.

Financial Assistance:
World Families does not provide financial assistance.

Exchange Programs Include:
Short Program-Inbound
    Sheila Dolak,
    Director
    253/528-0220,
    info@world-families.org

Travel Abroad/Homestay
    Damon Berbert,
    Program Manager
    253/528-0220,
    info@world-families.org

Career Observation
    Damon Berbert,
    Program Manager
    253/528-0220,
    info@world-families.org

World Heritage
International Student Exchange (WH)

3891 Jackson Way
Thornton, CO 80233

Tel.: 303/252-8215
Fax: 303/252-0629
Website: www.world-heritage.org
E-mail: whwest@aol.com

General Inquiries:
Mary Loving,
Executive Director
303/252-8215,
whwest@aol.com

Chief Executive Officer:
Michelle Garcia Hicks,
CEO

Statement:
World Heritage, originally founded
to promote the Spanish language
and culture in the United States
and the English language and culture in Spanish-speaking countries,
now works to promote the languages and cultures of several
countries. Through student
exchange, it helps create a much
better understanding among the
countries involved.

Profile:
Nonprofit founded in 1971. WH
has ten U.S. staff and 20 overseas
staff. Two hundred U.S. volunteers
and 250 overseas volunteers contribute to WH's mission.

Exchange Activities:
WH provides exchange-related
facilitative or support services.

Financial Assistance:
Overseas offices provide scholarships.

Overseas Offices:
Bangkok, Thailand
Madrid, Spain
Bergisch Gladbach, Germany
Leon, Mexico
Surrey, United Kingdom
Paris, France
São Paulo, Brazil

U.S. Department of State
Designated Sponsor for the
Exchange Vistor Program
Secondary school students

Alliance
MEMBER

World Learning, Inc.

Kipling Road
P.O. Box 676
Brattleboro, VT 05302-0676

Tel.: 802/257-7751 **Fax:** 802/258-3483
Website: www.worldlearning.org
E-mail: info@worldlearning.org

Secondary Address:
1015 15th Street, NW
Suite 750
Washington, DC 20005

Tel.: 202/408-5420 **Fax:** 202/408-5397

General Inquiries:
Jerold Goldberg,
Vice President, Communications
802/258-3121,
jerry.goldberg@worldlearning.org

Chief Executive Officer:
Dr. James A. Cramer,
President and CEO

Statement:
World Learning is an international educational services and development organization whose programs enable participants—individuals and institutions—to develop the leadership capabilities and cross-cultural competence needed to function effectively in the global arena. Through its projects division, World Learning is a private voluntary organization administering social and economic development activities under U.S. government and international contracts and grants. Its accredited institution of higher education, the School for International Training, offers masters degrees in international and intercultural management and in teaching, and study abroad programs for undergraduates from over 200 U.S. colleges and universities. World Learning also offers programs in intensive language and culture training to professionals from international corporations, as well as overseas cultural exchange experiences to high school students.

Profile:
Nonprofit founded in 1932. World Learning has 370 U.S. staff.

Geographic Focus:
Worldwide

Exchange Activities:
World Learning is involved in the following exchange areas: Arts/Cultural, Community/Citizen, Homestay, Language Study, Professional/Business, Training. World Learning provides exchange-related facilitative or support services. It administers exchange programs for the following academic levels: Graduate Students, Undergraduate Students, Teachers K-12, Faculty (postsecondary).

Financial Assistance:
World Learning offers scholarships/fellowships or financial assistance to participants in the College Semester Abroad, high school summer abroad, and graduate degree programs. Assistance includes direct student aid and loans.

Publications:
World Odyssey Magazine

World Learning Annual Report

SIT Graduate Bulletin

SIT Study Abroad Catalogue

The Experiment in International Living Catalogue

Exchange Programs Include:
Delphi Program–a core contract with the Department of State for study tours of international visitors
Peter Simpson, Program Director
202/898-0950,
peter.simpson@delphi.worldlearning.org

SIT Study Abroad Program
Rebecca Hovey, Dean,
SIT Study Abroad
802/258-3288,
rebecca.hovey@sit.edu

The Experiment in International Living
Tony Allen, Director
973/783-1965,
eiltony@bellatlantic.net

Exchange Related Facilitative or Support Services Include:
International Visitor Support
International Student and Scholar Advisor
802/258-3276

Courses for Credit
Director of Admissions
802/258-3276

Grants/Scholarships to Individuals
SIT Financial Aid
802/258-3281

Professional/Volunteer Department
Resource Center
802/258-3396

Intercultural Communications
Masters Program in International and Intercultural Management
802/258-3332

Library/Information
Library Services Department
802/258-3354

Professional/Volunteer Department
Professional Development Resource Center
802/258-3396

People with Disabilities
Program Manager for Diversity and Affirmative Action
802/258-3111

U.S. Department of State Designated Sponsor for the Exchange Vistor Program
Trainees
International visitors
College and university students
Government visitors

Alliance MEMBER

WorldTeach

**Center for International
Development
79 JFK Street
Cambridge, MA 02138**

Tel.: 800/4-TEACH-0
Fax: 617/495-1599
Website: www.worldteach.org
E-mail: info@worldteach.org

General Inquiries:
Admissions Coordinator
617/495-5527

Chief Executive Officer:
Helen Sievers,
Executive Director

Statement:
WorldTeach, a private, nonprofit organization based at the Harvard Institute for International Development, was formed in 1986 with the purpose of contributing to education in developing countries. It places volunteers as teachers of English as a Foreign and Second Language in countries which request assistance. North Americans and other speakers of English are given opportunities for cultural exchange and experience in international development.

Profile:
Nonprofit founded in 1986. WorldTeach has four U.S. staff and six overseas staff. Two hundred fifty overseas volunteers contribute to WorldTeach's mission.

Geographic Focus:
Africa (Namibia, South Africa), Asia (China), Central America (Costa Rica, Honduras), North America (Mexico), South America (Ecuador)

Exchange Activities:
WorldTeach is involved in the following exchange areas: Students/Educators. WorldTeach provides exchange-related facilitative or support services. It administers exchange programs for the following academic levels: Faculty, Graduate Students, K-12, Teachers, Undergraduate Students.

Financial Assistance:
Limited, need-based financial aid is available. WorldTeach distributes a booklet of fund-raising ideas that have been proven successful by past volunteers. Volunteers receive housing and a small stipend.

Publications:
Application

Program Profiles

Shanghai Summer Teaching
    Program Application

Brochure

The WorldTeach Dispatch

Exchange Programs Include:
Six-Month Teaching Programs
    Harriet Wong, Program Officer

Summer Programs - Eight Weeks
    Harriet Wong, Program Officer

Year-Long Teaching Programs
    Harriet Wong, Program Officer

**Exchange Related Facilitative or
Support Services Include:**
Admissions/Placement Service

Conference/Meetings/Workshops
    Orientation

Grants/Scholarships to Individuals
    Need-based Financial Aid

Travel Services
    Volunteer Travel Logistics

People with Disabilities

Overseas Offices:
Quito, Ecuador
San Jose, Costa Rica
Windhoek, Namibia
Yantai, China

YMCA International Program Services (YMCA-IPS)

71 West 23rd Street
Suite 1904
New York, NY 10010

Tel.: 888/477-9622
Fax: 212/727-8814
Web: www.ymcainternational.org
E-mail: ips@ymcanyc.org

General Inquiries:
Sharon Pollack,
Associate Executive Director
212/727-8800 x114

Chief Executive Officer:
Alice L. Mairs,
Executive Director

Statement:
YMCA International Program Services (YMCA-IPS) offers values-based programs that have positive local and global impact, enhance understanding of the world, and enable people to work together toward peace and justice. YMCA-IPS works locally helping New Yorkers to develop a sense of themselves as global citizens. Nationally, it operates exchange programs and services which develop global perspectives by integrating international activities into the ongoing life of a family, a camp, a youth program or a local organization. YMCA-IPS represents the world YMCA at the United Nations (UN), bringing information to YMCAs around the world, while utilizing the UN as a program resource for teens and adults. YMCA-IPS is part of a global network of YMCAs active in over 130 countries. It also has many collaborative relationships with like-minded organizations, both in the United States and around the world.

Profile:
Nonprofit founded in 1911. YMCA-IPS has 35 U.S. staff. YMCA-IPS is branch of the YMCA of Greater New York.

Geographic Focus:
Worldwide

Exchange Activities:
Inbound and outbound exchange of Camp Counselors, Trainees, Short-Term Visitors, and Summer Work Travel Participants. The International YMCA provides exchange-related facilitative and support services, as well as educational programs to build global awareness.

Financial Assistance:
Global Teen and YMCA Go Global participants are eligible to receive limited financial assistance awards. International Camp Counselor participants receive transportation assistance and may receive limited financial assistance awards.

Exchange Programs Include:
YMCA Global Teens

YMCA International Camp Counselor Program

YMCA Go Global

International Career Advancement Program

Multinational Leadership Training Program

Summer Work Travel

Exchange Related Facilitative or Support Services Include:
International Visitor Support Arrivals Program

Educational Programs:
Face to Face

Flying Circus

U.S. Department of State Designated Sponsor for the Exchange Vistor Program
Trainees
Secondary school students
Camp counselors
Intern
Summer work/travel

Youth Exchange Service, Inc. (YES)

1600 Dove Street
Suite 460
Newport Beach, CA 92660

Tel.: 800/848-2121
Fax: 949/955-0232
Website: http://www.yesint.com
E-mail: info@yesint.com

General Inquiries:
Maria Laguna,
Project Manager
949/955-2030

Chief Executive Officer:
Leonardo Flores, Jr.,
Executive Director

Statement:
Youth Exchange Service's (YES) mission is to immerse future leaders in American life by placing them with an American family and community. Students learn American culture, language, and educational principles. YES creates an environment for relationships to develop between family and student.

Profile:
Nonprofit founded in 1974. YES has 15 U.S. staff and 25 overseas staff. Three hundred U.S. volunteers and 100 overseas volunteers contribute to YES's mission.

Geographic Focus:
Worldwide

Exchange Activities:
YES is involved in the following exchange areas: Arts/Cultural, Community/Citizen, Homestay, Language Study, Professional/Business, Short-Term Visitors. YES provides exchange-related facilitative or support services.

Financial Assistance:
YES does not provide financial assistance.

Exchange Programs Include:
Inbound Program
Maria Laguna
949/955-2030

Outbound Program

Exchange Related Facilitative or Support Services Include:
Admissions/Placement Service
Lucy Thome

Community Development/Organization
Lucy Thome

Conference/Meetings/Workshops
Leonardo Flores

Grants/Scholarships to Individuals

International Visitor Support
Leonardo Flores

Intercultural Communications

U.S. Department of State Designated Sponsor for the Exchange Vistor Program
Secondary school students

Alliance
MEMBER

Youth for Understanding (YFU)

3501 Newark Street, NW
Washington, DC 20016-3199

Tel.: 202/966-6800
Fax: 202/895-1104
Web: www.youthforunderstanding.org
E-mail: pio@us.yfu.org

General Inquiries:
Admissions
1-800-TEENAGE

Chief Executive Officer:
Marsha Dickey,
Acting Executive Director

Statement:
Youth for Understanding
International Exchange (YFU) is a
private, nonprofit, educational
organization dedicated to international understanding and world
peace through exchange programs
primarily for high school students
in 50 countries.

Profile:
Nonprofit founded in 1951. YFU
has 140 U.S. staff and 160 overseas
staff. YFU has five local
chapters/affiliates. Two thousand
three hundred U.S. volunteers and
7,500 overseas volunteers contribute to YFU's mission.

Geographic Focus:
Worldwide

Exchange Activities:
YFU is involved in the following
exchange areas: Arts/Cultural,
Community College, Homestay,
Persons with Disabilities, Sports,
Students/Educators. YFU provides
exchange-related facilitative or support services. It administers
exchange programs for the following academic levels: 9-12,
Undergraduate Students.

Financial Assistance:
YFU offers a broad range of both
merit and need-based scholarships.
Nearly 800 students are awarded
merit-based scholarships funded
annually by the governments of the
United States, Japan, Germany,
Finland, as well as corporations
and private foundations. In addition, YFU awards partial financial
aid awards.

Publications:
Introduction to Japan: A Workbook

*Planning and Conducting Re-Entry
  Orientations*

Exchange Programs Include:
Academic Year and Semester High
School Exchange
    David Barber,
    Director, U.S. Programs
    202/895-1124,
    barber@us.yfu.org

Community College Programs
    202/895-1180

Congress Bundestag
    David Barber,
    Program Director
    202/895-1124,
    barber@us.yfu.org

Japan-America Friendship
Scholars Program
    David Barber,
    Program Director
    202/895-1124,
    barber@us.yfu.org

Summer Abroad Program
    David Barber,
    Director, U.S. Programs
    202/895-1124,
    barber@us.yfu.org

**Exchange Related Facilitative or
Support Services Include:**
Grants/Scholarships to Individuals
    David Barber,
    Director, Program Management
    202/895-1124

Additional Offices:
Edmonds, WA
Tom Bean, TX
Des Moines, IA
Bridgeport, MI
Boston, MA

Overseas Offices:
Hamburg, Germany
Thun, Switzerland
Buenos Aires, Argentina
Helsinki, Finland
Madrid, Spain
Guadalajara, Mexico
Rio de Janeiro, Brazil
Vinksveen, Netherlands
Tokyo, Japan
Pymble, Australia

Alliance
MEMBER

Section II
Other Organizations with an Interest in Exchange

The organizations listed in Section II contribute to international exchange through a variety of means, although they do not have exchange as their core mission. Some administer one or more exchange programs to further an international mission, while others engage in research and support services that broadly benefit international understanding and engagement.

Such contributions may include: administration of a professional exchange program; scholarly research; holding conferences, meetings, briefings, or workshops; developing communication networks; providing support to international exchange participants; publishing and disseminating information; and broadening understanding of global concerns.

Each profile includes the organization's address, mission statement and a description of the exchange activity, research, or support service. Readers should contact the organizations directly for more information on their exchange programs and other activities.

Africa Action

110 Maryland Ave, NE #508
Washington, DC 20002

Tel.:   202/546-7961   **Fax:** 202/546-1545
Website: http://www.africapolicy.org
E-mail: apic@igc.org

General Inquiries:
Salih Booker,
Executive Director, 202/546-7961

Mission Statement: Africa Action is a progressive American organization devoted to educating and mobilizing Americans to fight for positive U.S. and international policies toward Africa and supporting African struggles for political and economic justice, as well as combating global racism.

Exchange Research/Support Services: Africa Action focuses on U.S. and international policies towards Africa that affect economic, political and social justice issues throughout the continent including the AIDS pandemic and the larger health emergency, the cancellation of Africa's foreign debts, reparations, and the need for effective international support for Africa's peace efforts and pro-democracy struggles. Africa Action presses for greater equity for Africa in international relations while sharing information and analysis on a wide range of African affairs to shape public policy debates.

Alfred Friendly Press Fellowships

2000 L Street, NW, Suite 200
Washington, DC 20036-4997

Tel.:   202/416-1691   **Fax:** 202/416-1695
Website: http://www.pressfellowships.org
E-mail: afpf@aol.com

General Inquiries:
Susan M. Albrecht,
Program Manager, 202/416-1691

Industry Focus:
Journalism/Publishing

Mission Statement: In the conviction that a strong, free press is essential to the healthy functioning of a democracy, the late Alfred Friendly, a Pulitzer prize winning journalist and former managing editor of *The Washington Post*, conceived a program that would both impart American journalistic traditions and respond to worldwide interest in the dissemination of fair and accurate news. The Alfred Friendly Press Fellowships are the result of his vision.

Exchange Programs: Each year, the Alfred Friendly Press Fellowships bring approximately 10 professional journalists from developing countries and emerging democracies for six-month working fellowships to the United States to learn about the American free press. Roughly 45 news publications from all across the United States work with the fellows. The program has three primary objectives: 1) to provide participants with experience in reporting, writing, and editing that will enhance their future professional performance; 2) to enable participants to gain a practical understanding of the function and significance of the free press in American society; and 3) to foster continuing ties between free press institutions and journalists in the United States and their counterparts in other countries.

American Association of Colleges for Teacher Education (AACTE)

1307 New York Avenue, Suite 300
Washington, DC 20005-4701

Tel.:   202/293-2450   **Fax:** 202/457-8095
Website: http://www.aacte.org
E-mail: jyff@aacte.org

General Inquiries:
Joost Yff, 202/293-2450

Mission Statement: The American Association of Colleges for Teacher Education (AACTE) fosters the exploration of global education, cross-cultural education, and international teacher education as well as faculty development in these areas. The Association encourages member involvement in international teacher education, develops activities with a global/international focus for the AACTE Annual Meeting, encourages the network of interested members in conjunction with the Special Study Group on Global/International Education, and selects the recipient for the Best Practice Award for Global and International Teacher Education.

Exchange Research/Support Services: The Association provides access to American teacher education leaders for international study tours. The Association has collaborated with UNESCO/Paris, the Agency for International Development, and the U.S. Department of State on several projects, and participates in the Japan/U.S. Consortium on Teacher Education (JUSTEC) and the U.S.A./SINO consortium.

American Association of Museums (AAM)

1575 Eye Street, NW, Suite 400
Washington, DC 20005

Tel.:   202/289-1818   **Fax:** 202/289-6578
Website: http://www.aam-us.org

General Inquiries:
Helen Wechsler,
Director, International Programs, 202/218-7699
hwechsler@aam-us.org

Industry Focus:
Art/Humanities, Education, Science

Mission Statement: Founded in 1906, the American Association of Museums (AAM) is dedicated to promoting excellence within the museum community. Through advocacy, professional education, information exchange, accreditation, and guidance on current professional standards of performance, AAM assists museum staff, boards, and volunteers across the country to better serve the public.

Exchange Programs: The International Partnerships Among Museums (IPAM) program was created in 1980 by AAM to assist U.S. and foreign museums in establishing long-term institutional linkages through the exchange of mid-level professionals who develop and implement joint or complementary projects. IPAM receives its primary funding from the U.S. Department of State. The program operates on a two-year cycle, funding approximately 30 partnerships per cycle.

American Association of State Colleges and Universities (AASCU)

1307 New York Avenue, NW, Fifth Floor
Washington, DC 20005-4701

Tel.: 202/293-7070 **Fax:** 202/296-5819
Website: http://www.aascu.org
E-mail: worldview@aascu.org

General Inquiries:
Patricia Fesci, International Program Manager
Division of Academic Leadership and Change,
202/478-4668
fescip@aascu.org

Industry Focus:
Education

Mission Statement: The American Association of State Colleges and Universities (AASCU) is a higher education association of more than 400 public colleges, universities, and university systems across the United States and Puerto Rico, Guam, and the Virgin Islands. AASCU has four fundamental purposes: 1) to promote broad public understanding of the essential role of public higher education; 2) to monitor public policy at the national, state, and campus levels; 3) to provide policy leadership and programmatic assistance to strengthen academic quality, intellectual diversity and academic freedom; and 4) to provide professional development opportunities and support for institutional leaders, especially presidents and chancellors.

Exchange Programs: AASCU sponsors missions abroad to facilitate the continuing professional development and education of university presidents, establishes campus linkages, promotes joint research and development activities and fosters student, faculty, and administrative staff exchanges. The association also maintains a database of international activity on state college and university campuses, including extensive information about campuses' study abroad and exchange activities.

American Association of University Professors (AAUP)

1012 14th Street, NW, Suite 500
Washington, DC 20005

Tel.: 202/737-5900 **Fax:** 202/737-5526
Website: http://www.aaup.org
E-mail: aaup@aaup.org

General Inquiries:
Debra Davis,
ddavis@aaup.org
202/737-5900

Mission Statement: Founded in 1915, the American Association of University Professors' (AAUP) mission is to advance academic freedom and shared governance; to define fundamental professional values and standards for higher education; and to ensure higher education's contribution to the common good. Membership is open to college and university faculty members, administrators, graduate students and the general public.

Exchange Research/Support Services: The AAUP conducts research, holds meetings and organizes conferences to support issues in higher education such as academic freedom and tenure. It advocates collegial governance and develops policies ensuring due process.

American Association of University Women Educational Foundation (AAUW Foundation)

1111 16th Street, NW,
Washington, DC 20036-4873

Tel.: 800/326-AAUW **Fax:** 202/872-1425
Website: http://www.aauw.org
E-mail: info@aauw.org

General Inquiries:
Nancy Eynon Lark
Fellowship and Grants Program/Foundation,
202/728-7602

Industry Focus:
Education

Mission Statement: The American Association of University Women Educational Foundation (AAUW Foundation) provides funds to advance education, research, and self-development for women, and fosters equity and positive societal change.

Exchange Programs: International Fellowships are awarded for full-time study or research at accredited institutions to women who are not U.S. citizens or permanent residents. Six of the 47 awards are available to members of International Federation of University Women affiliate organizations. Recipients of these awards may study in any country other than their own. The Foundation also awards several annual Home Country Project Grants ($5,000-$7,000 each). These grants support community-based projects designed to improve the lives of women and girls in the fellow's home country.

American Bar Association/Central and East European Law Initiative (ABA/CEELI)

740 15th Street, NW, Eighth Floor
Washington, DC 20005-1022

Tel.: 202/662-1950 **Fax:** 202/662-1597
Website: http://www.abanet.org/ceeli
E-mail: ceeli@abanet.org

General Inquiries:
David Tolbert,
Director, 202/662-1960

Industry Focus:
Law

Mission Statement: The Central and East European Law Initiative (CEELI) is a public service project of the American Bar Association designed to advance the rule of law in the world by supporting legal reform in Central and Eastern Europe and the Newly Independent States of the former Soviet Union.

Exchange Programs: ABA/CEELI programs are designed to offer continuing and practical assistance to emerging democracies in reforming their judiciaries, legal profession, and legal education. These assistance efforts are carried out by U.S. attorneys, judges, law professors, and other legal professionals who serve overseas for periods ranging from one week to two years. Since 1990, over 5,000 legal professionals have participated in CEELI programs overseas and in the United States.

American Bar Association/Fund for Justice and Education

750 North Lakeshore Drive
Chicago, IL 60611

Tel.:   312/988-5404   **Fax**: 312/988-6392
Website: http://www.abanet.org/publiced
E-mail: KauperK@staff.abanet.org

General Inquiries:
Krista Kauper

Industry Focus:
Law

Mission Statement: The American Bar Association Fund for Justice and Education (ABA/FJE) is a 501(c)(3) tax-exempt public charity created in 1961 to solicit and accept gifts and grants on behalf of the public service and educational programs of the American Bar Association. The mission of the ABA/FJE is to improve the American legal system through law-related public service and educational programs that promote quality in legal service, equal access to justice, a better understanding of the law, and improvements in the justice system.

Exchange Programs: Activities include information dissemination, conferences, technical assistance (written), training workshops, research, and evaluation.

American Bar Association/International Legal Exchange (ABA/ILEX)

740 15th Street, N.W.
Washington, DC 20005-1022

Tel.:   202/662-1034   **Fax:** 202/662-1669
Website: http://www.abanet.org/intlaw
E-mail: intlaw@abanet.org

General Inquiries:
Mauricio J. Pastora
International Projects Administrator,
202/662-1034

Industry Focus:
Government, Law

Mission Statement: The objective of ILEX is to promote the exchange of ideas worldwide. Through ILEX, the ABA arranges briefing trips throughout the world, offers legal assistance and training for foreign lawyers and other professionals, and facilitates entry into the U.S. by foreign attorneys who have been offered training by U.S. law firms.

Exchange Programs: Country Briefing Trips for Legal Professionals provide participants with first-hand knowledge of the legal and judicial systems of the particular host country or region,

often focusing on trade and investment issues. The trips also provide a unique opportunity for delegation members to interact with legal, business, and governmental leaders of the countries visited and to develop personal and professional contracts throughout the world. ILEX organizes these trips in coordination with the government or bar association of the host country, specifically drawing on the expertise of section members. Each year ILEX organizes two briefing trips: an outbound trip (to a foreign country or region), and an inbound trip (to Washington, D.C. and New York). ILEX also arranges programs and meetings for prominent foreign lawyers, judges and scholars with legal professionals in the United States. This program allows foreign nationals to study a particular area of U.S. jurisprudence, to learn more about the ABA, and to become better acquainted with the U.S. legal system. While ILEX does not place foreign lawyers with U.S. firms, it assists foreign lawyers who have been offered training by a foreign law firm or legal office. It assists them by certifying their eligibility for exchange visitor status under the J-1 visa, and facilitating their entry into the United States. The application and documentation for this type of visa are provided by ILEX.

American Center for International Labor Solidarity (ACILS) Solidarity Center

International Affairs Department, AFL-CIO
888 16th Street NW, 5th Floor,
Washington, DC 20006

Tel.:   202/637-4500   **Fax:** 202/778-4525
Website: www.ned.org/grants/solidarity.html
E-mail: acils@acils.org

Industry Focus:
Civil Society/Democracy

Mission Statement:
The AFL-CIO's Solidarity Center provides struggling unions the support and technical know-how they need to grow stronger and to contribute to the development of sustainable democracies. Jointly funded by the AFL-CIO, the U.S. Agency for International Development and the National Endowment for Democracy, the Solidarity Center is committed to strong trade unions around the world.

Exchange Programs: In consultation with AFL-CIO affiliates and under direction of the Executive Council, the Solidarity Center – a consolidation of the AFL-CIO's international institute for Africa, Asia, Latin America and Europe – will provide hands-on help to workers abroad to help them build unions and challenge repression and injustice. The Solidarity Center works to promote the vital role of trade unions in countries making the transition to democracy. As demonstrated in Poland, South Africa and elsewhere, a strong trade union movement is a necessary precondition to building and maintaining a democracy. Through their unions, workers can experience democracy firsthand, fight to defend their rights and create transparent, accountable and representative processes and organizations.

The American Council on International Intercultural Education (ACIIE)

Oakton Community College
1600 East Golf Road
Des Plaines, IL 60067

Tel.:   847/635-2605   **Fax:** 847/635-1764
Website: http://www.aciie.org
E-mail: lkorbel@oakton.edu

General Inquiries:
Linda A. Korbel,
Executive Director, 847/635-2605

Mission Statement: The American Council on International Intercultural Exchange (ACIIE) is the affiliate council of the American Association of Community Colleges (AACC) with membership comprised of approximately 120 colleges involved in international and intercultural education. ACIIE shares expertise and provides

information on topics such as cultural diversity, multi-cultural relations, foreign student recruitment and exchanges, faculty exchanges, professional development programs, and funding opportunities for international and intercultural activities. ACIIE helps community colleges cultivate educational partnerships and participate in programs with organizations worldwide.

Exchange Research/Support Services: ACIIE pursues its mission through annual conferences, a bi-monthly newsletter for its membership, a listserve and website, teleconferences and other programs and activities which foster the dissemination of information and networking among members.

American Council on International Personnel (ACIP)

515 Madison Avenue
New York, NY 10022

Tel.: 212/688-2437 **Fax:** 212/593-4697
Website: http://www.acip.com
E-mail: info@acip.com

General Inquiries:
George Marshall,
Program Manager,
george_marshall@acip.com

Industry Focus:
Business/Commerce

Mission Statement: The American Council on International Personnel, Inc. (ACIP) is a not-for-profit professional association dedicated to facilitating the international movement of personnel. To this end, ACIP provides a number of comprehensive products and services to its members. ACIP works to keep its member organizations informed of the latest changes in immigration policy and procedures. Immigration Services include the United States Department of State Exchange Visitor (J-1 Visa) Program. This program is designed to allow ACIP's Members to bring foreign nationals into the U.S. for training.

Exchange Program: ACIP operates two programs designed to help bring foreign national employees to the U.S. for training: The ACIP Managerial, Professional and Specialty program is designed for member companies who wish to bring their overseas employees to the U.S. for a period of up to 18 months of training. The ACIP U.S.-Canada exchange program is designed to permit qualifiing companies the opportunity to bring Canadian students to the U.S. for a period of up to 18 months of practical training. Membership in ACIP is not a requirement to participate in program.

American Council on the Teaching of Foreign Languages (ACTFL)

6 Executive Plaza
Yonkers, NY 10701

Tel.: 914/963-8830 **Fax:** 914/963-1275
Website: http://www.actfl.org
E-mail: headquarters@actfl.org

General Inquiries:
June Hicks,
Director of Member Services,
914/963-8830 x210
jhicks@actfl.org

Mission Statement: The American Council on the Teaching of Foreign Languages (ACTFL) is dedicated to promoting the study of foreign languages and cultures as an integral component of American education and society. Launched in 1967 by the Modern Language Association, ACTFL remains the only national organization representing teachers of all levels of education.

Exchange Research/Support Services: Through its numerous programs and publications, ACTFL seeks to provide effective leadership for the improvement of teaching and learning languages within the United States. Over the past 30 years, ACTFL has become synonymous with innovation, quality, and reliability in meeting the changing needs of foreign language educators and their students. From the development of proficiency guidelines, to its leadership role in the creation of national standards, ACTFL focuses on issues critical to the growth of both the profession and the individual teacher.

American Dance Festival (ADF)

1697 Broadway, Suite 900
New York, NY 10019

Tel.:   212/586-1925   **Fax:** 212/397-1196
Website: http://www.americandancefestival.org
E-mail: adfny@AmericanDanceFestival.org

General Inquiries:
Charles and Stephanie Reinhart,
Co-Directors, 212/586-1925

Industry Focus:
Arts/Humanities

Mission Statement: Established in 1934, the American Dance Festival (ADF) is a magnet for choreographers, dancers, teachers, critics, and scholars, drawing them together to create, learn, and experiment. ADF's programs are developed based on its mission to support new modern dance work; to preserve the history of modern dance through continued presentation of classic works; to build wider national and international audiences for modern dance; to enhance public understanding and appreciation of the art form and its cultural and historical significance; to provide professional education and training of young dancers; and to disseminate information on dance education.

Exchange Programs: ADF sponsors the annual International Choreographers Residency program. ADF conducts international linkage programs with institutions in Asia, Africa, Latin America, and Central and Eastern Europe. ADF's six-week summer festival in Durham, North Carolina includes professionals from over 40 countries.

American Federation of Teachers Educational Foundation

AFT International Affairs Department
555 New Jersey Avenue, NW
Washington, DC 20001

Tel.:   202/879-4448   **Fax:** 202/879-4502
Website: http://www.aft.org/international/
E-mail: iad@aft.org

General Inquiries:
David Dorn,
Director, ddorn@aft.org

Industry Focus: Education

Mission Statement: The mission of the American Federation of Teachers, AFL-CIO, is to improve the lives of its members and families, to give voice to legitimate professional, economic and social aspirations, to strengthen institutions, to improve the quality of services, to bring together all members to assist and support one another and to promote democracy, human rights and freedom in our union, in the U.S. and throughout the world.

Exchange Activities: The International Affairs Department (IAD) provides information to AFT members and leadership on human and trade union rights and other international issues. The IAD conducts international activities in four main areas: technical and material assistance to democratic teachers' unions; materials development, consultation, and teacher training workshops on civic education abroad under the Education for Democracy/International Project; defense of human and trade union rights for teachers and others; and representation at international conferences and other programs.

American Foreign Policy Council (AFPC)

1521 16th Street, NW
Washington, DC 20036

Tel.:   202/462-6055   **Fax:** 202/462-6045
Website: http://www.afpc.org
E-mail: afpc@afpc.org

General Inquiries:
Herman Pirchner, Jr.,
202/462-6055

Industry Focus:
Civil Society/Democracy

Mission Statment: The American Foreign Policy Council's (AFPC) mission is to bring information to those who make or influence the foreign policy of the United States and to assist leaders in the former Soviet Union and other parts of the world in building democracies and market economies.

Program Exchange: AFPC organizes delegations primarily to and from Russia, Ukraine, and China. The delegations provide a forum for policy makers and analysts to meet with their counterparts and to gain first-hand knowledge of various issues.

American Friends Service Committee (AFSC)

1501 Cherry Street
Philadelphia, PA 19102

Tel.:   215/241-7000   **Fax:** 215/241-7275
Website: http://www.afsc.org
E-mail: afscinfo@afsc.org

General Inquiries:
Barbara Smith,
Regional Director, International Programs,
215/241-7148
idlac@afsc.org

Industry Focus:
Civil Society/Democracy, Development

Mission Statment: The American Friends Service Committee (AFSC) is a Quaker organization that includes people of various faiths who are committed to social justice, peace, and humanitarian service. Its work is based on the Religious Society of Friends (Quaker) belief in the worth of every person, and faith in the power of love to overcome violence and injustice.
Founded in 1917 to provide conscientious objectors with an opportunity to aid civilian victims during World War I, today the AFSC has programs in the United States, Africa, Asia, Latin America, and the Middle East that focus on issues related to economic justice, peace-building and demilitarization, social justice, and youth.

Exchange Programs: The Dialogues and Exchange Program consists of short-term events, exchanges, or meetings which bring people together, from across various divides, who would not normally be able to meet. The goal of the program is to break down barriers created by conflict, ideology, class, and culture, and to open new opportunities for mutual support among groups and individuals who are working for justice and peace. The activities are normally identified through and implemented in connection with AFSC field programs around the world. Project selection takes place in Philadelphia, where the entire set of activities is centrally monitored and audited. A recent example is a women's exchange among Korea, China, and Vietnam that explored the effects of rapid industrialization on women.

American Historical Association (AHA)

400 A Street, SE
Washington, DC 20003

Tel.:   202/544-2422   **Fax:** 202/544-8307
Website: http://www.theaha.org
E-mail: aha@theaha.org

General Inquiries:
Anastasia Tate,
Membership Assistant, 202/544-2422

Mission Statement: In 1889, the U.S. Congress chartered the American Historical Association (AHA), charging it to act "in the interest of American history, and of history in America." One hundred years later, a review committee defined the mission emerging from this charge as service to history professionals (defined as individuals with graduate degrees or some formal training in history) who practice history either in teaching or research or both.

Exchange Research/Support Services: The profession communicates with students in textbooks and classrooms; to other scholars and the general public in books, articles, exhibits, films, and historic sites and structures; and to decision-makers in memoranda and testimony.

The American Institute of Architects (AIA)

1735 New York Avenue, NW
Washington, DC 20006-5292

Tel.:   202/626-7415   **Fax:** 202/626-7426
Website: http://www.aiaonline.com
E-mail: keuner@aiamail.aia.org
             aiaonline@aiamail.aia.org

General Inquiries:
Mary Felber,
Director, Scholarship Programs, 202/626-7511

Industry Focus:
Architecture

Mission Statment: The American Institute of Architects (AIA) is the professional society of architects for over 140 years. Dedicated to the success of the profession, AIA works to advance the value of architects and architecture and increase the living standards of people by improving their built environments.

Exchange Programs: The Delano and Aldrich/Emerson Fellowship, established in 1932, is awarded annually to a French architect in support of individual professional development in the United States. One six-month fellowship ($15,000, including travel) is awarded each year. The RTKL Traveling Fellowship ($2,500) is awarded each year to encourage and support foreign travel undertaken to further education toward a professional degree. The Richard Morris Hunt Fellowship, established in 1990, is cosponsored by the American Architectural Foundation and the Friends of Vieilles Maisons Françaises, Inc. as part of a commitment to stewardship of American and French heritage. It is awarded to architects pursuing careers in historic preservation. The recipients alternate each year between the United States and France.

American Library Association (ALA)

50 E. Huron Street
Chicago, IL 60611

Tel.: 800/545-2433 **Fax:** 312/440-9374
Website: http://www.ala.org
E-mail: intl@ala.org

General Inquiries:
Alisha White,
Administrative Assistant,
awhite@ala.org

Industry Focus:
Education

Mission Statement: The American Library Association (ALA) provides leadership for the development, promotion, and improvement of library and information services and the profession of librarianship in order to enhance learning and ensure access to information for all.

Exchange Programs: The International Relations Office promotes the exchange of professional information, techniques and knowledge, as well as personnel and literature between and among libraries and individuals throughout the world; administers programs of the ALA focused on international relations (awards, recognition, exchanges); promotes program and publication activities on international relations by the Association and its divisions and committees; maintains communication, when appropriate, with other library and information service organizations concerned with international relations; represents the Association's view to organizations and agencies outside the ALA that are concerned with international relations of libraries; and encourages active participation by U.S. librarians in the work of international organizations. The International Relations Roundtable, open to all ALA members, provides hospitality and information to visitors from abroad.

American Nurses Foundation (ANF)

600 Maryland Avenue, SW, Suite 100W
Washington, DC 20024-2571

Tel.: 202/651-7000 **Fax:** 202/651-7001
Website: http://www.nursingworld.org
E-mail: anf@ana.org

General Inquiries:
International Nursing Center,
202/488-8461

Industry Focus:
Science

Mission Statement: The American Nurses Foundation (ANF) was founded in 1955 as the research, education, and charitable affiliate of the American Nurses Association (ANA). The Foundation complements the work of ANA, the largest nursing organization in America, by raising funds and developing and managing grants to support advances in research, education, and clinical practice. The mission of the American Nurses Foundation is to promote the goals of the ANA and the nursing profession through research, education, and assistance to nurses.

Exchange Programs: The ANF publishes reports relating to international issues in nursing, such as the International Classification For Nursing Practice Project; hosts occasional receptions to recognize the distinguished international careers of American nurses; and works with the International Council of Nurses.

American Political Science Association (APSA)

1527 New Hampshire Ave, NW
Washington, DC 20036-1206

Tel.:   202/483-2512   **Fax:** 202/483-2657
Website: http://www.apsanet.org
E-mail: apsa@apsanet.org

Industry Focus:
Government; Civil Society/Democracy

Mission Statement: With more than 13,500 members residing in over 70 countries worldwide, the American Political Science Association is the world's largest professional organization for the study of politics. With APSA's extraordinary range of programs and services for individuals, departments, and institutions, the Association brings together political scientists from all fields of inquiry, regions, and occupational endeavors in order to expand our awareness and understanding of political life.

Exchange Programs: APSA's *Congressional Fellowship Program* is a highly selective, nonpartisan, early to mid-career program devoted to expanding knowledge and awareness of Congress. For nine months, selected fellows serve on congressional staffs and acquire "hands on" experience while gaining insight into the legislative process, politics, and public service. Through this unique opportunity, APSA seeks to improve the quality of scholarship on and teaching of Congress and American national politics, thereby enhancing public understanding of Congress and policy-making. The *APSA-MCI WorldCom Fellowship* is intended for scholars and journalists who have an analytical interest in communications and public policy and who show promise of making a significant contribution to the public's understanding of the political process.

American Research Institute in Turkey (ARIT)

University of Pennsylvania Museum
33rd & Spruce Street
Philadelphia, PA 19014-6324

Tel.:   215/898-3474   **Fax:** 215/898-0657
Website: http://mec.sas.upenn.edu/ARIT
E-mail: leinwand@sas.upenn.edu

General Inquiries:
Linda Leinwand,
Administrator, 215/898-3474

Mission Statement: American Research Institute in Turkey (ARIT) was founded in 1963 to promote U.S. scholarly research and exchange in Turkey.

Exchange Research/Support Services: ARIT promotes U.S. scholarships in Turkey and exchange with Turkish scholars. These exchanges are facilitated through the granting of fellowships to U.S. scholars and advanced graduates for research in Turkey and through maintaining research centers in Turkey (Istanbul and Ankara) with libraries, hostels, lecture, and travel programs.

American Studies Association (ASA)

1120 19th Street, NW, Suite 301
Washington, DC 20036

Tel.:   202/467-4783   **Fax:** 202/467-4786
Website: http://www.georgetown.edu/
crossroads/asainfo
E-mail: asastaff@erols.com

General Inquiries:
Dr. John F. Stephens,
Executive Director, 202/467-4783

Mission Statement: Chartered in 1951, the American Studies Association has more than 5,000 members including persons concerned with American culture; teachers and other professionals whose interests extend beyond their specialty; faculty and students associated with American Studies programs in universities, colleges, and secondary schools; museum directors and librarians interested in all segments of American life; public officials; and educators concerned with the broadest aspects of education.

Exchange Research/Support Services: ASA organizes briefings for both U.S. and foreign scholars, teachers, and officials on American Studies. It recommends scholars who participate in a variety of exchange programs and provides technical advice and assistance in the United States and abroad. ASA sponsors American Studies Electronic Crossroads, an information resource for American Studies scholars. ASA also publishes *The American Quarterly*, the *Guide to American Studies Resources*, the *ASA Newsletter*, and the *Directory of Graduate Programs in American Studies in the United States*.

Americans for the Arts

1000 Vermont Avenue, N.W., 12th Floor
Washington, DC 20005

Tel.:   202/371-2830   **Fax:** 202/371-0424
Website: http://www.artsusa.org
E-mail: books@artsusa.org

General Inquiries:
Devin Cogswell,
Administrative Assistant,
dcogswell@artsusa.org

Industry Focus:
Arts/Humanities

Mission Statement: Americans for the Arts is a national organization for groups and individuals across the United States dedicated to advancing the arts and culture. Founded by the American Council for the Arts, representing a broad network of arts supporters, patrons and business leaders, and the National Assembly of Local Arts agencies, the country's largest alliance of community arts organizations, Americans for the Arts strives to make the arts more accessible to every adult and child in America. To this end, Americans for the Arts works with cultural organizations, arts and business leaders, and patrons to provide leadership, advocacy, visibility, professional development, research, and information that will advance support for the arts and culture in U.S. communities.

Exchange Programs: Americans for the Arts' primary exchange activity is to publish and sell *Money for International Exchange in the Arts*. The book provides information on grants, fellowships and awards for travel and work abroad; support and technical assistance for international touring and exchange; international artists' residencies; programs that support artists' professional development; and more.

Amigos de las Americas (AMIGOS)

5618 Star Lane
Houston, TX 77057

Tel.: 800/231-7796 **Fax:** 713/782-9267
Website: http://www.amigoslink.org
E-mail: info@amigoslink.org

Mission Statement: Amigos de las Americas (AMIGOS) is an international, voluntary, non-governmental, nonprofit organization which provides leadership development opportunities for young people; promotes community health; and facilitates cross-cultural understanding in the Americas.

Exchange Program:
In partnership with international development agencies, local nonprofit and government agencies, and local communities, AMIGOS volunteers conduct community health and development services in Latin America.

Archaeological Institute of America (AIA)

656 Beacon Street, 4th Floor
Boston, MA 02215-2006

Tel.: 617/353-9361 **Fax:** 617/353-6550
Website: http://www.archaeological.org
E-mail: aia@bu.edu

General Inquiries:
Allegra Valborg,
617/353-9361

Industry Focus:
Arts/Humanities

Mission Statment: The Archaeological Institute of America (AIA) is dedicated to the encouragement and support of archaeological research and publication, and to the protection of the world's cultural heritage for more than a century. A nonprofit cultural and educational organization chartered by the U.S. Congress, it is the oldest and largest archaeological organization in North America, with more than 11,000 members around the world.

Exchange Programs: AIA publishes the *Archaeological Fieldwork Opportunities Bulletin*, a listing of archaeological programs throughout the world ranging from excavations and field schools to special programs. The various projects seek volunteers and students interested in participating in archaeology.

Asia Society

**725 Park Avenue
New York, NY 10021-5088**

Tel.: 212/288-6400 **Fax:** 212/517-8315
Website: http://www.asiasociety.org

General Inquiries:
Public Relations Department, 212/288-6400

Mission Statement: The Asia Society is a leading American institution dedicated to fostering understanding of Asia and communication between Americans and the peoples of Asia and the Pacific. The Asia Society is headquartered in New York, with regional centers in Washington, DC; Houston, Texas; Los Angeles, California; Hong Kong, People's Republic of China; and Melbourne, Australia and has program coordination offices in San Francisco, California; Seattle, Washingon; Shanghai, People's Republic of China; and Manila, Philippines.

Exchange Research/Support Services: A nonprofit, nonpartisan educational institution, the Asia Society presents a wide range of programs including major art exhibitions, performances, media programs, seminars, international conferences, and lectures.

Asian Cultural Council

**437 Madison Avenue, 37th Floor
New York, New York 10022-7001**

Tel.: 212/812-4300 **Fax:** 212/812-4299
Website: http://www.asianculturalcouncil.org
E-mail: acc@accny.org

General Inquiries:
Receptionist

Mission Statement: The Asian Cultural Council supports cultural exchange between Asia and the United States in the performing and visual arts, primarily by providing individual fellowship grants to artists, scholars, students, and specialists from Asia for study, research, travel and creative work in the United States. Some grants are also awarded to Americans engaged in similar activities in Asia and to arts organizations and educational institutions for specific projects of particular significance to Asian-American cultural exchange.

Exchange Program: The Japan-United States Arts program provides grants to individuals and institutions in Japan and the United States for exchange activities which encourage the study and understanding of Japanese art and culture. Individual fellowship grants enable Japanese artists, scholars, and specialists to travel to the United States for research, observation, and creative work and allow their American counterparts to visit Japan for similar purposes.

The Aspen Institute

One Dupont Circle, NW, Suite 700
Washington, DC 20036

Tel.: 202/736-5800 Fax: 202/467-0790
Website: http://www.aspeninst.org

General Inquiries:
Switchboard, 202/736-5800

Mission Statement: The Aspen Institute is an international nonprofit educational institution dedicated to enhancing the quality of leadership through informed dialogue. It convenes men and women who represent diverse viewpoints and backgrounds from business, labor, government, the arts, and the nonprofit sector.

Exchange Research/Support Services: The Aspen Institute's Policy Programs are designed to assist leaders, both in the United States and in the international community, to deal more effectively with emerging challenges. The Institute provides neutral ground on which different points of view can be exchanged among diverse participants from the private sector, government, the academic world, the media, and elsewhere. International partners in Germany, France, Italy, and Japan conduct independently developed and supported programs, conferences, and seminars on region-specific issues, global challenges, and leadership development.

Association for Asian Studies (AAS)

1021 East Huron Street
Ann Arbor, MI 48104

Tel.: 734/665-2490 Fax: 734/665-3801
Website: http://www.aasianst.org
E-mail: members@aasianst.org

General Inquiries:
Michael Paschal,
Executive Director
mpaschal@aasianst.org

Mission Statement: The Association for Asian Studies (AAS) was founded in 1941, originally as publisher of the *Far Eastern Quarterly* (now the *Journal of Asian Studies*). The AAS —the largest society of its kind in the world—is a scholarly, non-political, non-profit professional association open to all persons interested in Asia. It seeks through publications, meetings, and seminars to facilitate contact and an exchange of information among scholars to increase their understanding of East, South, and Southeast Asia. It counts among its members scholars, business people, diplomats, journalists, and interested lay persons.

Exchange Research/Support Services: The AAS has gone through a series of reorganizations to serve better the broadening disciplinary and geographical interests of its membership. The AAS actively participates with its sister societies in a wide range of activities, including joint participation in research, computerized abstracts and informational exchanges.

Association of American Publishers (AAP)

71 Fifth Avenue
New York, NY 10003-3004

Tel.: 212/255-0200 **Fax:** 212/255-7007
Website: http://www.publishers.org

General Inquiries:
Barbara J. Meredith,
International Committee Staff,
bmeredith@aap.publishers.org

Industry Focus:
Journalism/Publishing

Mission Statment: The Association of American Publishers (AAP), with approximately 200 members located throughout the United States, is the principal trade association of the book publishing industry. AAP's mandate covers both the general and the specific—broad issues important to all publishers as well as issues of specific concern to particular segments of the industry.

Exchange Program: The Association's "core" programs deal with matters of general interest: intellectual property; new technology and telecommunications issues of concern to publishers; first amendment rights, censorship and libel; international freedom to publish; funding for education and libraries; postal rates and regulations; and tax and trade policy. The International Committee serves as a liaison with various agencies involved in promoting American books overseas (including the State and Commerce Departments, and the World Bank). The International Committee continues co-sponsorship of an internship program, which brings publishers from Central and Eastern Europe to the Frankfurt Book Fair and gives them an opportunity to work at the stands of AAP members.

The Association of American University Presses (AAUP)

71 West 23rd Street, Suite 901
New York, NY 10010

Tel.: 212/989-1010 **Fax:** 212/989-0275
Website: http://aaupnet.org
E-mail: aaupny@aol.com

General Inquiries:
Linda McCall,
Office Manager, 212/989-1010 x30

Mission Statement: The Association of American University Presses (AAUP) is a cooperative, nonprofit organization of university presses. Formally established in 1937, the AAUP promotes the work and influence of university presses, provides cooperative marketing efforts, and helps its members respond to the changing economic environment.

Exchange Research/Support Services: As the publishing arm of their parent universities, university presses have access to the best ideas and research produced by the scholarly community. By publishing these ideas in books and journals, university presses help shape the dialogue within the scholarly community, and between the scholarly community and the rest of the world. AAUP staff and personnel from its member presses have participated in a number of U.S. Department of State programs designed to help increase the level of professionalism in scholarly publishing. These programs have been held in countries from China to Azerbaijan. Many have also involved visits by publisher-delegates from the host country to AAUP members in the United States.

Atlantic Center for the Environment/ Quebec-Labrador Foundation (QLF)

55 South Main Street
Ipswich, MA 01938

Tel.:   978/356-0038   **Fax:** 978/356-7322
Website: http://www.qlf.org
E-mail: atlantic@qlf.org

General Inquiries:
Brent Mitchell,
brentmitchell@glf.org

Industry Focus:
Civil Society/Democracy, Education,
Environment

Mission Statment: The Atlantic Center for the Environment and its parent organization, the Quebec-Labrador Foundation (QLF), have over 35 years of experience in building local support for conservation in rural communities of New England and eastern Canada. QLF's mission is to improve the quality of life and environment for people living in rural northeastern North America. It conducts a broad range of programs in the areas of international exchange, wildlife and habitat protection, rural community development, river conservation, and land stewardship.

Exchange Program: For over a decade, the Atlantic Center's International Programs division has worked in partnership with local institutions in target regions which include Central and Eastern Europe, the Caribbean, Latin America, and most recently, the Middle East to conduct training and fellowship programs, exchanges, and practical workshops.

The Atlantic Council of the United States (ACUS)

910 17ᵗʰ Street, NW, Suite 1000
Washington, DC 20006

Tel.:   202/778-4964   **Fax:** 202/463-7241
Website: http://www.acus.org
E-mail: info@acus.org

General Inquiries:
Jennifer L. Chomistek,
Program Coordinator, 202/778-4945

Mission Statement: The Atlantic Council of the United States is a bipartisan network of private individuals committed to enhancing U.S. initiatives and leadership through sound and skillfully administered policies that identify and pursue national interests in a framework of global interdependence, and through the education of future leaders.

Exchange Research/Support Services: The Atlantic Council provides students, young leaders, and academics with access to its resources, networks, and program results in order to prepare future generations of international leaders and promote understanding of democratic values. The Atlantic Council maintains academic associates in almost 400 colleges and universities, holds young leaders seminars, and administers the John A. Baker Leadership Program.

Australian Studies Association of North America

Edward A. Clark Center for Australian Studies
Harry Ransom Humanities Research Center
Suite 3.362
The University of Texas at Austin
Austin, Texas 78713-7219

Tel.:   512/471-9607   **Fax:** 512/471-8869
Website: www.utexas.edu/depts/cas/asana
E-mail: ffcushing@mail.utexas.edu

General Inquiries: Frances F. Cushing

Mission Statement: The Australian Studies Association of North America (ASANA) is an organization dedicated to the study of Australia. Its members include academics teaching or studying Australian topics, government officials involved with Australia, students interested in Australian topics or study in Australia, and persons from the business and general population with an interest in Australia. ASANA is an inter-disciplinary non-profit association that promotes teaching about Australia and the scholarly investigation of Australian topics and issues throughout institutions of higher education in North America.

Exchange Research/Support Services: The services of the Association include strengthening and deepening bilateral relationships between Australia and North America; maximizing the use of existing resources through exchange of information among North American institutions of higher education; encouraging undergraduate and graduate educational exchanges and academic internships; facilitating contacts and exchanges between North American and Australian scholars and encouraging collaborative projects of mutual benefit.

The Brookings Institution

1775 Massachusetts Avenue, NW
Washington, DC 20036

Tel.:   202/797-6000   **Fax:** 202/797-6004
Website: http://www.brook.edu
E-mail: brookinfo@brook.edu

General Inquiries:
Office of Public Affairs, 202/797-6105

Mission Statemnt: The Brookings Institution is an independent, nonpartisan research organization seeking to improve the performance of American institutions, the effectiveness of government programs, and the quality of U.S. public policies. It addresses current and emerging policy challenges and offers practical recommendations for dealing with them, expressed in language that is accessible to policy makers and the general public alike.

Exchange Research/Support Services:
Brookings' Center for Public Policy Education is recognized as an international leader in providing high-quality, innovative executive education programs on timely domestic and global policy issues. Each year, these programs attract more than 2,500 decision makers from the public and private sectors to 150 seminars and conferences in the United States and abroad.

Business Council for International Understanding (BCIU)

1212 Avenue of the Americas, 10th Floor
New York, NY 10036

Tel.: 212/490-0460 **Fax:** 212/697-8526
Website: http://www.bciu.org

General Inquiries:
Charles Olbricht,
Director of External Affairs, 212/490-0460 x243
c-olbricht@bciu.org

Mission Statement: The Business Council for International Understanding's (BCIU) mission is to promote U.S. commerce in overseas markets by strengthening the relationship between American business and government.

Exchange Research/Support Services: BCIU organizes briefings (private meetings and multi-industry group discussions) for both U.S. and foreign government officials to engage in dialogue with senior-level executives from U.S. companies that are active or interested in trade and investment in the official's country of assignment. BCIU also provides commercial training programs for newly assigned U.S. commercial officers.

Center for Civic Education (CCE)

5146 Douglas Fir Road
Calabass, CA 91302

Tel.: 818/591-9321 **Fax:** 818/591-0527
Website: http://www.civiced.org
E-mail: international@civiced.org

General Inquiries:
Jack N. Hoar,
Director of International Programs,
800/350-4223

Industry Focus:
Civic Society/Democracy, Education, Government, Law

Mission Statement: The mission of the Center for Civic Education (CCE) is to promote an enlightened, competent, and responsible citizenry. The Center's goals are to promote increased understanding of constitutional democracy and its fundamental values and principles; develop the skills necessary to participate as informed, effective, and responsible citizens; and increase the willingness to use democratic procedures when making decisions and managing conflicts.

Exchange Program: CCE conducts an array of international efforts to improve civic education. CIVITAS: An International Civic Education Exchange Program is an international consortium of organizations, individuals, and governments. The CIVITAS Consortium aims at strengthening effective education for informed and responsible democratic citizenship. Consortium members, which include leading civic education organizations from the United States and Eastern Europe and countries of the Newly Independent States, are dedicated to strengthening civic education and constitutional democracy throughout the world. Civitas@Bosnia and Herzegovina is a special initiative designed to promote the study of civics and democracy in the schools of Bosnia and Herzegovina.

The Center for Quality Assurance in International Education

One Dupont Circle, NW, Suite 515
Washington, DC 20036

Tel.:   202/293-6104   **Fax:** 202/293-9177
Website: http://www.cqaie.org
E-mail: cqaie@aacrao.edu

General Inquiries:
Marjorie Peace Lenn,
Executive Director, 202/293-6104

Mission Statement: Founded in 1991, the Center for Quality Assurance in International Education is a policy organization serving as a focal point for discussion and collaboration within the United States and between the United States and other country associations concerned with issues of quality, access and fairness in the international mobility of students, scholars, and professionals; the credentialing and recognition of programs; and sustaining quality-assured international education linkages.

Exchange Research/Support Services: The services, programs, and activities of the Center for Quality Assurance in International Education fall into six major categories: 1) assisting countries in the development of quality assurance systems for higher education; 2) convening international conferences and workshops on the globalization of the profession; 3) monitoring quality issues relative to the globalizing of U.S. higher education; 4) providing international trade and educational consultation services; 5) providing access to timely, policy-oriented publications, databases, and other information on global educational systems, institutions, and distance/transnational education programs; and 6) providing opportunities for global networking.

Center for Russian & East European Studies (CREES)

Stanford University
Building 40, Main Quad
Stanford, CA 94305-2006

Tel.:   650/723-3562   **Fax:** 650/725-6119
Website: www.stanford.edu/dept/CREES
E-mail: kollmann@leland.stanford.edu

General Inquiries:
Nancy Kollman,
Director, 650/723-9475

Mission Statement: The Center for Russian and East European Studies (CREES) at Stanford was established in 1966. Its mission is to promote and support the interdisciplinary study of the area. The center has been designated one of 16 Russia and Eastern European *National Resource Centers* by the U.S. Department of Education. The purpose of the NRC program is to train specialists in modern foreign languages and area studies. CREES sponsors special seminars, lectures, conferences, distinguished visitors and visiting scholars, and coordinates teaching and research relating to this area.

Exchange Research/Support Services: The Center organizes and sponsors public lectures, round-table discussions, conferences and occasionally other events, such as concerts, slide-lectures, theatrical productions, and special film showings which are free and open to the public. In cooperation with the *World Affairs Council of Northern California* and the Bay Area Global Education Program of the Stanford School of Education, CREES conducts a series of annual workshops for high school teachers and community college instructors, focused on a topical issue confronting the former Soviet Union.

Center for Strategic and International Studies (CSIS)

1800 K Street, NW, Suite 400
Washington, DC 20006

Tel.: 202/887-0200 **Fax:** 202/466-5141
Website: http://www.csis.org
E-mail: csis@csis.org

General Inquiries:
Receptionist, 202/887-0200

Mission Statement: The Center for Strategic and International Studies (CSIS) is a public policy research institution dedicated to analysis and policy impact. CSIS is the only institution of its kind that maintains resident experts on all the world's major geographical regions. It also covers key functional areas, such as international finance, U.S. domestic and economic policy, and U.S. foreign policy and national security issues.

Exchange Research/Support Services: CSIS provides, on a reciprocal basis, research opportunities in various fields of study including political-military studies; domestic policy and economic issues; global communication; global organized crime; Asian, African, Middle East, and European studies; and international finance. Additionally, CSIS promotes the broad field of international education and cultural exchange. CSIS convenes 700-800 meetings, seminars, and conferences in Washington and throughout the world each year.

Center for West European Studies (CWES)

Jackson School of International Studies
University of Washington
120 Thompson Hall
Box 353650
Seattle, WA 98195-3650

Tel.: 206/543-1675 **Fax:** 206/616-2462
Website: http://jsis.artsci.washington.edu/
programs/cwesuw
E-mail: cwes@u.washington.edu

General Inquiries:
John Keeler, Director
keeler@u.washington.edu

Mission Statement: The University of Washinton's Center for West European Studies (CWES), founded in 1994, is one of five federally funded National Resource Centers for West European Studies in the United States. Its mission is to enhance the quality of teaching and research on West European politics, society, and culture through outreach to universities, business, the general public, and the K-12 community.

Exchange Research/Support Services: One of the major functions of CWES is to bring experts on Western Europe to the Northwest for the presentation of research or the discussion of current public policy. Each year, the CWES Politics and Society Colloquium Committee and the Culture Colloquium Committee organize individual talks, thematic speakers' series, and small conferences. The Center also provides funding for at least one major international conference per year and organizes several teacher training workshops on topics relevant to the 9th-12th grade curriculum, often in conjunction with the larger conferences noted above. CWES also offers International Updates, a dinner/lecture series for the general public, International Business Briefs, downtown Seattle lectures for the business and media communities, and other teaching training events around the region.

Chamber of Commerce of the United States of America

1615 H Street, NW
Washington, DC 20062-2000

Tel.: 202/659-2000 **Fax:** 202/463-3114
Website: http://www.uschamber.org
E-mail: intl@uschamber.com

General Inquiries:
Willard Workman,
Vice President International, 202/463-5460

Mission Statement: The Chamber of Commerce of the United States of America is a national federation of business organizations, including local chambers of commerce, trade, professional associations, and companies. It studies national issues affecting the economy of the United States, and makes recommendations to the government; works to advance human progress through an economic, political and social system based on individual freedom and initiative; and informs and trains members to participate in policymaking at the federal, state, and local levels. The Chamber is the world's largest business federation representing an underlying membership of more than three million businesses and organizations of every size, sector, and region.

Exchange Research/Support Services: The International Division is concerned with foreign governments' policies as they affect the U.S. business community. Chamber affiliates in 74 countries promote bilateral trade, conduct seminars, compile statistics, and maintain databases for local, international and American businesses in those countries.

The Commonwealth Fund

One East 75th Street
New York, NY 10021

Tel.: 212/606-3800 **Fax:** 212/606-3500
Website: http://www.cmwf.org
E-mail: cmwf@cmwf.org

General Inquiries:
Ned Butikofer
212/606-3874

Industry Focus:
Health, Government

Mission Statement: The Commonwealth Fund is a philanthropic foundation established in 1918 by Anna M. Harkness with the broad charge to enhance the common good. The Fund carries out this mandate through its efforts to help Americans live healthy and productive lives and to assist specific groups with serious and neglected problems.

Exchange Program: Access to health care and concern over the quality of care delivered are issues near the top of the national agenda in other industrialized countries as well as in the United States. Recognizing this, the International Program in Health Care Policy and Practice works to build an international network of policy-oriented health care researchers, spark innovative health policy thinking and high level exchanges that benefit the United States and other countries, and encourage cross-national comparative research and collaboration.

Community Colleges for International Development (CCID)

6301 Kirkwood Boulevard, SW
Cedar Rapids, IA 52406

Tel.: 319/398-5653 **Fax:** 319/398-1255
Website: http://www.ccid.kirkwood.cc.ia.us
E-mail: jhalder@kirkwood.cc.ia.us

General Inquiries:
Theresa Mikulas,
319/398-1257

Industry Focus:
Business/Commerce, Civil Society/Democracy,
Development, Education, Environment,
Government

Mission Statement: Community Colleges for
International Development, Inc. (CCID) is a
consortium of more than 90 member and affiliate colleges from the United States, Canada,
and six other countries. The expertise of the
Consortium, of specific interest to overseas
clients, is predominantly vocational/technical
education and training. Through contracts and
grants, CCID provides training and technical
assistance in occupational, vocational, and
technical education; opportunities for international study, exchange, and professional development for the students and faculty of U.S.,
Canadian, and CCID cooperating institutions
abroad; and leadership and educational services in relevant disciplines and technologies.

Exchange Program: CCID sponsors student and
scholar exchanges on behalf of the colleges
within the consortium. CCID colleges market
student study abroad activities through the consortium. The CCID Faculty Exchange Program
has enabled hundreds of scholars the opportunity to work overseas for periods of one semester
to one academic year. CCID exchange agreements are in place with cooperating institutions
in Hungary, the Czech Republic, Romania,
Russia, and Australia. Individual colleges within the organization have hundreds of relationships with colleges and universities around the
world, providing an unparalleled resource.
CCID hosts delegations and individuals from
around the world. Of specific interest to visitors is the ability of CCID to offer visitors multiple opportunities to visit colleges in every part
of the country, covering every possible academic and vocational discipline.

The Conference Board

845 Third Avenue
New York, NY 10022-6679

Tel.: 212/759-0900 **Fax:** 212/980-7014
Website: http://www.conference-board.org
E-mail: info@conference-board.org

General Inquiries:
Clayton Shedd,
Sr. Program Manager, International Division,
212/339-0253

Mission Statement: The Conference Board,
founded in 1916, is the premier business membership and research network worldwide, linking executives from different companies, indus-
tries and countries. The Conference Board has
become the leader in helping executives build
strong professional relationships, expand their
business knowledge, and find solutions to a
wide range of business problems. The Board's
twofold purpose is to improve the business
enterprise system and to enhance the contribution of business to society. A non-profit, non-
advocacy organization, The Conference Board's
membership includes more than 3,000 companies and other organizations in 67 countries.

Exchange Research/Support Services: The
Conference Board identifies global best business
practices helping companies improve performance and increase corporate competitiveness. It
is relied upon worldwide for its objective and
pragmatic applications. Within the management research area, the majority of Conference
Board reports focus on global corporate experiences, including U.S., European, and Asian perspectives. Sponsorship of research projects and
participation in working research groups are
available to members.

Consortium for North American Higher Education Collaboration (CONAHEC)

University of Arizona
888 N. Euclid
University Services Building, Room 414
P.O. Box 210158
Tucson, AZ 85721-0158

Tel.: 520/621-7761 **Fax:** 520/621-6011
Website: http://www.conahec.org
E-mail: fmarmole@u.arizona.edu

General Inquiries:
Margo Stephenson,
Associate Project Director, 303/541-0270
mstephenson@wiche.edu

Mission Statement: The Consortium for North American Higher Education Collaboration (CONAHEC) was formed in 1993 in response to public debate about the North American Free Trade Agreement and the critical need for higher education to better prepare students for a global economy. Currently, the Consortium has over 90 member institutions spanning more than 200 campuses enrolling 1.9 million students. CONAHEC's three primary goals are to enable higher education leaders and practitioners to examine and act upon significant educational policy issues; develop new binational and tri-national academic exchanges in North America; and to broaden understanding of the educational systems and the role of higher education in response to global economic and social change.

Exchange Research/Support Services: The Consortium brings the most current information about higher education in North America to the attention of its members. It advises institutions interested in establishing or strengthening academic collaboration programs in the region; represents the efforts of North American higher education collaboration to institutions and agencies internationally; provides a forum where diverse entities come together; and shares institutions' resources and strengths as they seek to maximize opportunities for higher education collaboration in North America. Furthermore, the Institute for North American Higher Education provides opportunities for campus administrators to be involved in exchanges and international training in Mexico, Canada, and the United States.

The Council for European Studies (CES)

Columbia University
1203A Int'l Affairs Building
MC 330
420 West 118th Street
New York, NY 10027

Tel.: 212/854-4172 **Fax:** 212/854-8808
Website: http://www.europanet.org
E-mail: ces@columbia.edu

General Inquiries:
Victoria de Grazia,
Executive Chair, 212/854-4172

Mission Statement: The Council for European Studies is the leading American professional association for the study of Europe in the social sciences and humanities. The Council's 1,200 individual members come from the United States, Canada, and 39 countries across the globe. Its 80 institutional members comprise a network of universities and colleges throughout North America. In light of momentous changes in Europe at the end of the twentieth century, the Council has undertaken many initiatives to act as a leader in encouraging research and interdisciplinary debate. The Council is hosted at Columbia University, the Institute for the Study of Europe, and the Harriman Institute.

Exchange Research/Support Services: The Council for European Studies offers three types of summer pre-dissertation fellowships for research in Europe, all of which are restricted to doctoral candidates at member universities. CES provides travel subsidies to European scholars who have been invited to lecture at member institutions and holds a biennial Conference of Europeanists. Publications such as archival guides and reports on European Studies are produced by the organization. The Council maintains a series of pages for easy access to web-based resources, including the *European Press* on the web, special pages on current events, archives in Europe, and a series of thematic links for scholars.

Council on Foreign Relations, Inc.

The Harold Pratt House
58 East 68th Street
New York, NY 10021

Tel.:   212/434-9400   **Fax:** 212/434-9800
Website: http://www.foreignrelations.org
E-mail: communications@cfr.org

General Inquiries:
Lisa Shields
Acting Director of Communications,
212/434-9888

Mission Statement: The Council on Foreign Relations is one of the leading nonprofit organizations dedicated to improving the understanding of international relations and U.S. foreign policy. Its 3,600 members include nearly all past and present U.S. Presidents, secretaries of state, defense, and treasury, other senior U.S. government officials, renowned scholars, and major leaders of business, media, human rights, and other non-governmental organizations.

Exchange Research/Support Services: Each year, the Council sponsors several hundred meetings including televised debates and other media events, and publishes *Foreign Affairs*, the preeminent journal in the field, as well as dozens of other reports and books by noted experts.

Doctors Without Borders

6 East 39th Street, 8th floor
New York, NY 10016

Tel.:   212/679-6800   **Fax:** 212/679-7016
Website: www.doctorswithoutborders.org
E-mail: doctors@newyork.msf.org

General Inquiries:
Ann Saunders,
Field Volunteer Coordinator, 212/679-7016

Industry Focus: Science

Mission Statement: Doctors Without Borders was founded in 1971 by a small group of French doctors who believed that all people have the right to medical care and that the needs of these people supersede respect for national borders. It was the first non-governmental organization to both provide emergency medical assistance and publicly bear witness to the plight of the populations they served. Doctors Without Borders delivers emergency aid to victims of armed conflict, epidemics, and natural and man-made disasters, and to others who lack health care due to social or geographical isolation.

Exchange Programs: A private, nonprofit organization, Doctors Without Borders is at the forefront of emergency health care as well as care for populations suffering from endemic diseases and neglect. Each year, more than 2,000 volunteer doctors, nurses, other medical professionals, logistics experts, water/sanitation engineers, and administrators join 15,000 locally hired staff to provide medical aid in more than 80 countries. Doctors Without Borders provides primary health care, performs surgery, rehabilitates hospitals and clinics, runs nutrition and sanitation programs, trains local medical personnel, and provides mental health care. Through longer-term programs, Doctors Without Borders treats chronic diseases such as tuberculosis, malaria, sleeping sickness, and AIDS; assists with the medical and psychological problems of marginalized populations including street children and ethnic minorities; and brings health care to remote, isolated areas where resources and training are limited. It is an international network with sections in 18 countries.

Earthwatch Institute

SECTION 2

3 Clocktower Place, Suite 100
Box 75
Maynard, MA 01754

Tel.:   978/461-0081   **Fax:** 978/461-2332
Website: http://www.earthwatch.org
E-mail: cfr@earthwatch.org

Industry Focus:
Development, Environment, Science

Mission Statement: Earthwatch is an international organization which supports scientific field research worldwide through its volunteers and scientists working together to improve our understanding of the planet. Earthwatch's mission is to build a sustainable world through an active partnership between scientist and citizen. Through public participation in field research, Earthwatch helps scientists gather data and communicate information that will empower people and governments to act wisely as global citizens.

Exchange Program: Earthwatch offers the public the opportunity to work side by side with distinguished field scientists in their work in seven focused areas of sponsored research: world oceans, world forests, biodiversity, cultural diversity, learning from the past, monitoring global change, and world health. Projects are divided into roughly one to three-week long programs to enable members of the public to participate with successive teams of scientists over the research duration. Earthwatch Institute provides fully funded field placements for those who will benefit personally and professionally from joining an Earthwatch field project. Each year Earthwatch Europe supports between 350 - 500 Fellowships for teachers, students, and conservationists.

Ecologists Linked for Organizing Grassroots Initiatives and Action (ECOLOGIA)

P.O. Box 268, 4 Mill Street
Middlebury, VT 05753

Tel.:   802/388-8075   **Fax:** 802/388-8069
Website: http://www.ecologia.org
E-mail: ecologia@ecologia.org

General Inquiries:
Kimberly Wolf,
Administrative Director

Industry Focus:
Civil Society/Democracy, Environment

Mission Statment: Founded in 1989, ECOLOGIA now operates in nearly a dozen countries in transition in Central America, Eastern Europe, the Newly Independent States, the Baltics, and China, enabling ordinary citizens to exercise better control over decisions which affect their lives. ECOLOGIA's flagship programs include a global pioneering online philanthropy effort (the

Virtual Foundation), encouraging industry-community dialogue in Russia, providing mini-grants to Baltic environmental NGOs, and supporting grassroots initiatives in China.

Exchange Program: ECOLOGIA has developed numerous exchange programs, which lay the foundation for long-term partnerships, focusing on the environment, democracy building, social services, and NGO management. ECOLOGIA develops workshops, site visits, and field experiences which allow participants to share their insights with trainers, staff, and each other. ECOLOGIA has hosted exchanges in the U.S. and Russia covering the following topics: NGO management training, internet training, public participation, environmental journalism, forested land management, wetlands management, water quality management, social services for the elderly, and ISO 14000 standards training.

Educational Commission for Foreign Medical Graduates (ECFMG)

2401 Pennsylvania Avenue, NW, Suite 475
Washington, DC 20037

Tel.: 202/293-9320 **Fax:** 202/457-0751
Website: http://www.ecfmg.org/ifme/index.html

General Inquiries:
William R. Ayers, M.D.,
Vice President, Administration and
Program Development

Industry Focus:
Educational (Medical)

Mission Statement: The Educational Commission for Foreign Medical Graduates (ECFMG) has the responsibility of evaluating qualifications of graduates of foreign medical schools who seek entry into postgraduate medical education positions in the United States, and has an organizational commitment to promote excellence in international medical education.

Exchange Program: In keeping with one of its missions, that of promoting excellence in international medical education, the Educational Commission for Foreign Medical Graduates (ECFMG) administers the International Fellowships in Medical Education. This program allows faculty from schools of medicine abroad to gain access to educational opportunities in the United States that are tailored toward specific home country needs. Fellows study aspects of medical education that have the potential to improve and expand medical education programs in their home country institutions and departments. The ECFMG is authorized by the U.S. Department of State (DOS) to sponsor foreign national physicians as Exchange Visitors in accredited programs of graduate medical education or training or advanced research programs (involving primarily observation, consultation, teaching or reasearch). Approximately 20 fellowships are awarded annually.

Education Development Center

Education Development Center, Inc.
55 Chapel Street
Newton, Massachusetts 02458-1060

Tel.: 617/969-7100 **Fax:** 617/969-5979
Website: http://www.edc.org
E-mail: http://www@edc.org

Industry Focus:
Education

Mission Statement: EDC is committed to education that builds knowledge and skill, makes possible a deeper understanding of the world, and engages learners as active, problem-solving participants. Over the decades, the best of EDC's projects have helped people raise and explore questions of importance in their lives. Today, fundamental questions of equity, diversity, and social justice take on special significance in all of our work. As our society becomes more plu-

ralistic and the world more interconnected, we need to find new ways to learn from each other and use both our differences and our commonalities to improve the quality of life for all. EDC programs are designed to enhance learning opportunities for people of all ages, backgrounds, and abilities.

Exchange Activities: In collaboration with international agencies and governments, EDC promotes sustainable economic and social development around the world. We ease the transfer of learning and technology by assisting other countries in the identification and adaptation of solutions that best fit their settings, as we work to develop comprehensive systems for health, nutrition, and education in diverse communities. Underlying all of our international efforts is a dedication to sharing knowledge and building human capacity.

The Ford Foundation

320 East 43rd Street
New York, NY 10017

Tel.:   212/573-5000   **Fax:** 212/351-3677
Website: http://www.fordfound.org
E-mail: office-communications@fordfound.org

General Inquiries:
Carmen D. DaCosta,
Executive Assistant, 212/573-5000

Mission Statement: The Ford Foundation goals are to strengthen democratic values; reduce poverty and injustice; promote international cooperation; and advance human achievement. The Foundation makes loans or grants that build knowledge and strengthen organizations and networks.

Exchange Research/Support Services: The Ford Foundation holds conferences and seminars, provides matching funds for specific programs and individual grants, produces a range of publications and research, and provides technical assistance. The International Fellowships Program (IFP) provides opportunities for advanced study to exceptional individuals who will use this education to become leaders in their respective fields, furthering development in their own countries and greater economic and social justice worldwide. To ensure that Fellows are drawn from diverse backgrounds, IFP will actively recruit candidates from social groups and communities that lack systematic access to higher education.

Foreign Policy Association (FPA)

470 Park Avenue South
New York, NY 10016-6819

Tel.:   212/481-8100   **Fax:** 212/481-9275
Website: http://www.fpa.org
E-mail: info@fpa.org

General Inquiries:
Receptionist,
212/481-8100

Mission Statement: The Foreign Policy Association's (FPA) mission is to serve as a catalyst for developing awareness, understanding, and informed opinions on U.S. foreign policy and global issues.

Exchange Research/Support Services: FPA's flagship publication, *Great Decisions*, is an annual briefing book on eight key foreign policy issues which serves as a foreign policy resource for discussion groups, lecture series, students and teachers. FPA offers a wide range of membership categories with benefits including publications, invitations to special events featuring international policymakers, leading experts in global affairs, and lecture series addressing major current issues.

Frank Foundation Child Assistance International (FFCAI)

1030 15th Street, NW, Suite 1020
Washington, DC 20005

Tel.:	202/452-8279 **Fax:** 202/452-0719
Website:	http://www.frankfoundationcai.org
E-mail:	ffcai1991@aol.com

Industry Focus:
Civil Society/Democracy, Education

Mission Statement: Frank Foundation Child Assistance International (FFCAI) was founded in 1992 in response to the tremendous need of Russian orphans. FFCAI's mission is to provide assistance to children in need throughout the Newly Independent States (NIS) of the former Soviet Union through an extensive orphanage assistance and adoption program. This mandate quickly expanded to include numerous cultural, humanitarian and educational programs that have benefited hundreds of children and youth throughout *Russia, Kazakstan* and *Georgia*.

Exchange Program: With the support of grant awards from the U.S. Department of State, FFCAI designs and facilitates exchange programs for secondary school students and educators from the Republic of Georgia and the United States. These exchanges provide unique opportunities for participation in thematic academic and cultural exchange experiences. Project REACH (Raising Educational Achievement through Community Service and Hope) gives school students the chance to travel to another country and interact with their peers with the goal of raising civic responsibility awareness and promoting diversity. REACH is specifically designed to reach out to students from both economically depressed Georgia and working class families in the United States who would not have otherwise been able to afford to take part in the program and experience the world beyond their own backyard.

The Global Alliance for Transnational Education (GATE)

9697 East Mineral Avenue
Englewood, CO 80112

Tel.:	303/784-8212 **Fax:** 303/784-8547
Website:	http://www.edugate.org
E-mail:	gate@edugate.org

General Inquiries:
Ana Mostaccero,
Director of Operations,
amostaccero@edugate.org

Mission Statement: The global marketplace and new technology are contributing to the rapid globalization of higher education worldwide. Today's business environment draws its professional workforce from all corners of the globe. Available through both the higher education and corporate sectors, transnational education can be found in multiple forms, including electronically and through traditional on-site instruction and training programs. Issues of quality, purpose, and responsibility abound in this new borderless educational arena. To this end, The Global Alliance for Transnational Education (GATE) is an alliance of business, higher education, and government dedicated to principled advocacy for transnational educational programs.

Exchange Research/Support Services: The GATE database is a source of information for corporate human resource professionals, international admissions officers, immigration/labor authorities, and professional societies to search by educational program or institution to show the program characteristics, course comparisons, and the program and institution recognition.

Global Ventures LC

1214 Iron Street
Kellogg, IA 50135

Tel.:   515/526-3378   **Fax:** 515/526-3379
Website: www.iris-center.org/global-ventures
E-mail: iris@iris-center.org

General Inquiries:
Dean K. Vera,
Vice President, Training and Programming,
dean@iris-center.org

Industry Focus:
Business/Commerce, Education, Government

Mission Statement: Global Ventures develops and implements specialized training programs in the United States for the international business and academic communities. Focusing primarily on language and culture programs, Global Ventures draws upon Iowa's unique resources to provide community-based language and cultural immersion experiences that include a homestay. Global Ventures also designs and implements highly tailored training projects in the United States, such as benchmarking, visiting scholars, study tours, and company visits.

Exchange Program: Global Ventures develops and implements professional, student, and educator exchange programs relating to the fields of language and cross-cultural training.

Global Volunteers

375 East Little Canada Road
St. Paul, MN 55117

Tel.:   800/487-1074   **Fax:** 651/482-0915
Website: http//:www.globalvolunteers.com
E-mail: email@globalvolunteers.org

General Inquiries:
651/407-6100

Industry Focus:
Science, Education/Development

Mission Statement: Global Volunteers, a private non-profit, non-sectarian development organization, was founded in 1984 with the goal of helping to establish a foundation for peace through mutual international understanding. As a non-governmental organization (NGO) in special consultative status with the United Nations, Global Volunteers is uniquely positioned to represent local leaders in a national and international arena, and to engage short-term volunteers in local development efforts with long-lasting results.

Exchange Programs: At the request of local community leaders and/or host country partner organizations, Global Volunteers sends teams of eight to 20 volunteers for two to three weeks, four to 12 times each year to assist with local work projects. Teams work primarily in rural communities in Africa, Asia, Europe, Latin America, North America and the Pacific. The volunteers put their labor, energy, skills and education at the service of local people. Each team is led by a Global Volunteers team leader and the groups live and work in the community, learning first-hand about the culture, lifestyle, economy, and structure of the community. The teams also meet with business, government, education, and religious leaders in the cities and countryside to better understand the issues and various approaches to development. The program is designed to send up to four teams a year to the same community with the understanding that each team will devote at least ten working days to community projects.

Healing the Children

PO Box 9065
Spokane, WA 99209-9065

Tel.:   800/347-3340   **Fax:** 425/252-4306
Website: http://www.healingthechildren.org
E-mail: respond@healingthechildren.org

General Inquiries:
Norm Colon,
Executive Director, 800/347-3340

Industry Focus:
Science

Mission Statement: Founded in 1981 as a non-profit organization, Healing the Children is comprised of 15 chapters operating in 23 states. Healing the Children envisions a world where every child has access to medical care.

Exchange Programs: Each year, Healing the Children chapters organize medical trips and travel to host countries to treat children and young adults free of charge. Volunteer medical and surgical health professionals travel at their own expense. They treat patients and share their expertise with host country health professionals during procedures and in-service sessions. Other volunteers unpack and prepare medical equipment and medicines, provide transportation, organize patients, and document activities. Most trips last 8 to 10 days, and often the doctors treat as many as 100 children and screen scores more for possible treatment in the United States. Specialties most often perform plastic and maxillofacial surgery, dental services, ear, nose and throat services, and ophthalmologic, neurosurgical, general surgical, and orthopedic procedures. Many doctors report feeling renewed commitment to their profession and new certainty that what they do is worthwhile.

Health Volunteers Overseas

PO Box 65157
Washington, DC 20035

Tel.:   202/296-0928   **Fax:** 202/296-8018
Website: http://www.hvousa.org
E-mail: info@hvousa.org

General Inquiries:
Barbara Edwards,
Program Assistant, 202/296-0928

Industry Focus:
Science

Mission Statement: Health Volunteers Overseas (HVO) is dedicated to improving the quality and availability of health care in developing countries through education. The cornerstone of the organization is a core of talented, innovative volunteers. Since 1986, more than 3,100 volunteers have served overseas with HVO and more than $13 million of educational materials have been donated to over 45 sites.

Exchange Programs: Health Volunteers Overseas (HVO) sends qualified professionals overseas to train local health care providers in the following specialties: anesthesia and nurse anesthesia, dentistry, internal medicine, oral and maxillofacial surgery, orthopedics, pediatrics, hand surgeons, nurses, and physical therapy. These highly skilled and experienced volunteers come from both private practice and university settings. HVO has projects in Africa, Asia, Latin America, Eastern Europe, and the Caribbean. Currently HVO supports over 50 projects in more than 20 countries. Each project is different depending on the educational needs and technological capacity of the country.

Heartland International

226 S. Wabash, Suite 500
Chicago, IL 60604

Tel.:   312/583-9430   **Fax:** 312/583-9434
Website: http://www2.uic.edu/orgs/heartland

General Inquiries:
Karen A. Egerer,
President, 312/413-8591

Industry Focus:
Business/Commerce, Civil Society/Democracy,
Education, Government

Mission Statement: Heartland International is a
women-managed, nonprofit organization based
in Chicago, Illinois. Established in 1989, the
organization designs, implements, and manages
political, economic, and social development
projects, as well as international educational
exchange programs. Through its programs,

Heartland International seeks to bring to bear
the traditionally underutilized resources of the
Midwest on international programs; act as a catalyst in strengthening emerging democratic
institutions; provide training and technical assistance to encourage microenterprise development; support the role of women in economic,
political, and social affairs in emerging democracies; provide a forum for the exchange of
ideas between U.S. and foreign policymakers;
and promote mutual understanding between
various segments of U.S. society and their international counterparts.

Exchange Program: Heartland International
conducts training programs for nongovernmental organization leaders, government officials,
and other professionals who are involved in
strengthening democratic institutions.

Helping Hands

948 Pearl Street
Boulder, CO 80302

Tel.:   303/449-4279   **Fax:** 303/440-7328
Website: http://nepal.cudenver.edu/helpinghands
E-mail: tdpeden@carbon.cudenver.edu

General Inquiries:
Narayan Shrestha,
President, 303/448-1811

Industry Focus:
Science

Mission Statement: Helping Hands has provided free-of-charge health care in Nepal since
1988. The organization brings doctors, nurses
and non-medical volunteers to Nepal to participate in year-round relief clinics in an effort to
combat the serious health problems from which
the rural people of Nepal suffer.

Exchange Programs: Volunteers live for two
weeks in the same manner in which the Nepali
people live. In the past, volunteers have
remained in Nepal for up to one year, and many
are repeat volunteers. As high quality health-
care is limited in Nepal, there is a need for
health care specialists such as pediatricians,
dentists, OB/GYN, ophthalmologists, nurses,
public health specialists, general practitioners,
and water sanitation specialists. Helping Hands
also has positions for many non-medical volunteers in triage, administration and other general
assistance positions.

The Heritage Foundation

214 Massachusetts Avenue, NE
Washington, DC 20002-4999

Tel.:   202/546-4400   **Fax:** 202/546-8328
Website: http://www.heritage.org
E-mail: info@heritage.org

General Inquiries:
staff@heritage.org

Mission Statement: Founded in 1973, The Heritage Foundation is a research and educational institute whose mission is to formulate and promote conservative public policies based on the principles of free enterprise, limited government, individual freedom, traditional American values, and a strong national defense.

Exchange Research/Support Services: The Kathryn and Shelby Cullom Davis International Studies Center conducts research and publishes papers annually on a wide variety of international political, economic, and security issues. Recent major projects include the Index of Economic Freedom and Restoring American Leadership. Heritage's operating units include The United Nations Assessment Project, the Asian Studies Center, the Russian Reform project, the Institute for Hemispheric Development and the America Trader Initiative.

Institute for Democratic Strategies (IDS)

909 Duke Street
Alexandria, VA 22314

Tel.:   703/739-4224   **Fax:** 703/739-4232
E-mail: demstrat@clark.net

General Inquiries:
Joe Balcer,
Vice President, 703/739-4224

Industry Focus:
Business/Commerce, Civil Society/Democracy, Development, Government, Journalism/Publishing

Mission Statement: The Institute for Democratic Studies (IDS) is a nonprofit organization devoted to fostering an integrated approach to democratic development and economic reform, by strengthening democratic institutions, and encouraging the sustainable development of nongovernmental organizations (NGO) in emerging democracies. IDS integrates policy guidance with practical program design incorporating technical assistance, leadership training, and civic education.

Exchange Program: IDS exchange programs are individually designed to serve the specific requirements of clients, rather than generic programs conducted on an ongoing basis. IDS works with its clients to identify individual needs among the exchange program participants and then designs an agenda which not only addresses those needs but also expands participants' knowledge base beyond those expressed needs. Participants in IDS programs tend to be senior government officials, business executives, and NGO leaders.

The Institute for International Cooperation and Development (IICD)

PO Box 520
Williamstown, MA 01267

Tel.:   413/458-9828   **Fax:** 413/458-3323
Website: http://berkshire.net/ ~ iicd1
E-mail: iicd@Berkshire.net

General Inquiries:
Zo Skinner
413/458-9828

Industry Focus:
Education, Development

Mission Statement: The IICD is a private non-profit organization, founded in 1987. By the year 2000, more than 600 students participated in 60 programs with IICD, working with development projects in Zambia, Mozambique, Angola, Zimbabwe and Nicaragua and traveling in Central and South America, the Caribbean, North Africa and Europe.

Exchange Programs: IICD trains volunteers to participate in development work in Africa, India, and Latin America, and runs educational travel study programs to Brazil. IICD prepares the participants, who then work three months to a year with development organizations in the third world. IICD and its volunteers also educate Americans about the developing world, giving presentations about the countries that its volunteers travel in and producing educational resources. Students and teachers of the Institute have traveled in over 50 countries. They have planted trees, vegetables and flowers, taught children and agricultural workers, and built schools, workshops, latrines, childcare centers and friendships.

Institute for Representative Government

1755 Massachusetts Avenue, NW, Suite 416
Washington, DC 20036

Tel.:   202/745-0002   **Fax:** 202/797-1355
E-mail: ifrg@aol.com

General Inquiries:
Melissa Ford,
Assistant Director, 202/745-0002

Industry Focus:
Government

Mission Statement: The Institute for Representative Government's mission is to provide professionally focused programs for parliamentarians of developing countries.

Exchange Program: The Institute for Representative Government brings delegations to the United States from foreign legislatures for two weeks of intensive study of the Congress and the American political system. Participants are selected in consultation with the U.S.

Department of State, which provides funding support for the Institute, and the relevant American embassies. Throughout, special attention is given to the effects of the U.S. constitutional structure, including federalism, the separation of powers, the timing of elections, etc. There is also a focus on the role of interest groups and lobbying, and American geographic, economic, ethnic, and other diversity. In general, the programs include examination of Congress in the U.S. political system; congressional structure, party organization and leadership; the lawmaking process; the role of Congress in budgeting and finance; how Members of Congress are chosen, financed and staffed, and how they function within Congress; the role of the General Accounting Office, the Congressional Budget Office, and the Congressional Research Service, and of Member and Committee staffs in providing Congress with its own source of information.

Institute for the Study and Development of Legal Systems (ISDLS)

The Presidio of San Francisco
Building 1004
O'Reilly Avenue, PO Box 29921
San Francisco, CA 94129-0921

Tel.:   415/561-2191   **Fax:** 415/561-2194
Website: http://www.isdls.org
E-mail: webmaster@isdls.org

Industry Focus:
Law; Civil Society/Democracy

Mission Statement: Institute for the Study and Development of Legal Systems (ISDLS), a non-profit corporation, is a leader in the assessment and reform of legal processes. The collective experience of the ISDLS Board of Directors, International Board of Advisers, and sixty-four delegates offer an incomparable concentration of expertise and innovation in process assessment and reform. ISDLS legal studies projects have produced remarkable civil and criminal justice reform throughout Africa, Asia, Latin America, and the Middle East.

Exchange Programs: ISDLS has the expertise to identify the significant problems and needs of civil and criminal justice processes and the ability to restore, reform and modernize those legal processes in order to guarantee a fair and efficient administration of justice. ISDLS projects guarantee modernization of studied legal systems because the reforms are carefully tailored to be integrated into the existing processes through a joint effort of the host-country, legal opinion leaders (represented by a designated "Legal Study Group") and the legal delegation of ISDLS. ISDLS assists in the implementation of the selected legal reforms through practical legal training seminars at judicial institutes, law schools and bar associations in the various legal communities. In this area, ISDLS has introduced and established clinical legal education in seven countries in Asia, seven countries in Latin America and two countries in the Middle East.

International Center for Foreign Journalists (ICFJ)

1616 H Street NW, Third Floor
Washington, DC 20006

Tel.:   202/737-3700   **Fax:** 202/737-0530
Website: http://www.icfj.org
E-mail: editor@icfj.org

General Inquiries:
Patrick Butler, Program Director,
patrick@icfj.org

Industry Focus:
Journalism/Publishing

Mission Statement: The International Center for Foreign Journalists (ICFJ) was established in 1984 to improve the quality of journalism in nations where there is little or no tradition of independent journalism. ICFJ believes that a vigorous, independent press is one of the most powerful weapons available in the struggle for freedom and civil rights. Working with overseas colleagues—providing journalistic, media management, and technical expertise as well as information and support services—is critical to the development of an effective, independent press that is ethically grounded and financially stable.

Exchange Program: The International Center for Journalists provides professional development programs that promote excellence in news coverage of critical community and global issues. The Center offers many fellowships and exchanges, conducts a variety of training seminars, workshops and conferences, and provides a range of consulting services. Since 1984, the Center has worked with over 8,000 journalists and other media professionals from 170 countries. The Center administers many fellowship programs for U.S. and overseas journalists. Its annual programs include the Knight International Press Fellowship Program, the largest private sector media assistance program in the United States; the Freedom Forum/American Society of Newspaper Editors International Journalism Exchange, a study program for foreign editors; the Arthur F. Burns Fellowship; a German-American exchange for young journalists; the ICFJ-KKC Journalism Fellowships in Japan; and the Senator John Heinz Fellowship in Environmental Reporting.

International Education Research Foundation (IERF)

P.O. Box 66940
Los Angeles, CA 90066

Tel.: 310/390-6276 **Fax:** 310/397-7686
Website: http://www.ierf.org
E-mail: info@ierf.org

General Inquiries:
Receptionist,
info@ierf.org

Mission Statement: The International Education Research Foundation (IERF) is a nonprofit foundation whose mission is to research and disseminate information on world educational systems, and to facilitate the integration of people educated outside the United States into the U.S. educational system and workforce. IERF carries out its mission primarily through its Credential Evaluation Service, publications and grants.

Exchange Research/Support Services: IERF's Credentials Evaluation Service provides reports evaluating foreign academic credentials in terms of the U.S. educational system. Evaluation reports are used by U.S. admissions professionals, employers, immigration, and state licensing boards. An annual grant competition encourages and promotes research on world educational systems supporting applied comparative education, specifically, the evaluation of foreign educational credentials. The grants are also intended to aid in the publication and distribution of the results of such research.

International Executive Service Corps (IESC)

333 Ludlow Street
P.O. Box 10005
Stamford, CT 06904-2005

Tel.: 203/967-6000 **Fax:** 203/324-2531
Website: http://www.iesc.org
E-mail: SBrown@mail.iesc.org

General Inquiries:
Marsha Thaler-Smith
Assistant Vice President, Program Development
msmith@iesc.org

Industry Focus:
Business/Commerce, Civil Society/Democracy, Development, Environment, Government

Mission Statement: The mission of the International Executive Service Corps (IESC) is to assist in the development of sound, free-market economies and democratic civil societies in developing countries and emerging democracies by transferring the proven expertise of volunteer American business professionals to beneficiaries in both the private and public sectors. During the past 30 years, IESC has sent more than 20,000 experts to share their business experience in more than 120 countries in the areas of agriculture, education, health care administration, public administration, transportation, construction and industrial equipment, and textile and apparel manufacturing.

Exchange Program: Short-term assignments are made to firms that request managerial or technical assistance. IESC administers the following programs: Technical and Managerial Assistance and Training; Business Development; American Business Linkage Enterprise; Public Administration; and Quality Assurance Management.

International Farmers Aid Association (IFAA)

91 Gregory Lane, Unit 4
Pleasant Hill, CA 94523-4914

Tel.:   925/682-4804   **Fax:** 925/682-2931
Website: http:/homepages.go.com/
             ~ifaa/index1.html
E-mail: ifaa@value.net

General Inquiries:
Akida Fukuda, President
Chris McNulty, Alternate Responsible Officer,
925/682-4804

Industry Focus:
Agriculture

Mission Statement: International Farmers Aid Association's (IFAA) primary concern is to alleviate world hunger by promoting the dissemination of modern agricultural techniques among farmers of different nations and fostering the development of a new generation of agricultural leaders. In addition, IFAA is committed to furthering international goodwill and friendships through its exchange activities with farmers and farm organizations around the world.

Exchange Program: Within the context of structured training, IFAA's program emphasizes the practical application of modern theories of farming through learning-by-doing. Placed on American farms for six to 18 months, participants work and learn under the direction and supervision of qualified farmer-trainers. Hosts are encouraged to expose trainees to the American culture and way of life by including them in professional and family social activities and community events. During the program, trainees are exposed to seasonal changes in farm activities. While on the farm, they also attend IFAA educational seminars and field trips organized in cooperation with agricultural universities and leading American agribusinesses. IFAA also administers a reciprocal program for young American agriculturalists who wish to participate in a similar program in Japan.

International Foundation for Art Research (IFAR)

500 Fifth Avenue, Suite 1234
New York, NY 10110

Tel.:   212/391-6234   **Fax:** 212/391-8794
Website: http://www.ifar.org
E-mail: kferg@ifar.org

General Inquiries:
Kathleen Ferguson, 212/391-6234

Industry Focus:
Arts/Humanities

Mission Statement: The International Foundation for Art Research (IFAR) is a nonprofit organization dedicated to educating the public about and providing a forum for debate on issues related to art authentication, connoisseurship, and art and cultural property law and ownership. IFAR works to prevent the circulation of forged, misattributed, or misappropriated art.

Exchange Program: IFAR plays a leadership role in the art world by participating worldwide in discussions and symposia concerning the repatriation of looted art, the restitution of holocaust era art, the protection of cultural property, the trafficking in stolen art, and the problems encountered in authenticating works of art. In addition, IFAR publishes a quarterly magazine, IFAR Journal, which features articles about these and other related topics and which reaches an international audience of art scholars, dealers, and collectors; art lawyers; museums; law enforcement personnel; and insurance companies.

International Law Institute (ILI)

1615 New Hampshire Avenue,
Washington, DC 20009

Tel.:   202/483-3036   **Fax:** 202/483-3029
Website: http://www.ili.org
E-mail: training@ili.org

General Inquiries:
training@ili.org

Mission Statement: The International Law Institute (ILI) trains public and private sector officials from developing countries and new market economies to manage their organizations more effectively and to negotiate on an equal footing with foreign investors, multilateral organizations, contractors, and suppliers.

Exchange Research/Support Services: The ILI offers a schedule of 20-25 seminars annually on management, law, and international finance at its Washington, DC office, and develops tailored seminars by contract for such funding agencies as The World Bank, Asian Development Bank, and the Agency for International Development.

International Management and Development Institute (IMDI)

1615 L Street, NW, Suite 900
Washington, DC 20036

Tel.:   202/337-1022   **Fax:** 202/337-6678
Website: http://members.aol.com/imdiweb
E-mail: imdimail@aol.com

General Inquiries:
Brent Crane,
Vice President, 202/337-1022
www.imdi.gspia.pitt.edu

Mission Statement: The International Management and Development Institute (IMDI) is a nonprofit educational institute promoting government-business dialogue and cooperation covering international trade, finance, economic, and foreign policy issues.

Exchange Research/Support Services: Throughout its 30-year history, IMDI has achieved renown for its ability to bring together the top leaders in the legislative and executive branches of government with business to address the issues of the day. Independent research is undertaken and published in IMDI *News and Issue Briefs.* The assessments and recommendations of IMDI members have been used by decision-makers to formulate sound international economic and investment policies.

International Student Placements

4966 El Camino Road, Suite 225
Los Altos, CAQ 94022

Tel.: 650/940-1560 **Fax:** 650/969-9857
Website: http://www.isphomestays.com
E-mail: info@isphomestays.com

General Inquiries:
Jean Ikeda,
CEO/Director, 650/940-1560

Mission Statement:. For the past ten years, International Student Placements (ISP) has successfully placed hundreds of international students with local host families. ISP provides students the opportunity to live with local hosts and improve their English language skills as well as experience local customs.

Exchange Research/Support Services:
International Student Placements (ISP) offers college students in the northern California area the opportunity to live with local host families while studying. Students experience American culture, gain exposure to the English language, and immerse themselves in the lives of their host families. ISP staff is dedicated to assisting the student with his or her adjustment to American life.

The International Tax and Investment Center (ITIC)

1250 H Street, NW, Suite 750
Washington, DC 20007

Tel.: 202/530-9799 **Fax:** 202/530-7987
Website: http://iticnet.org
E-mail: iticwdc@compuserve.com

General Inquiries:
Marie Hasson, Office Assistant, 202/530-9799

Mission Statement: The International Tax and Investment Center (ITIC) is an independent nonprofit research and education foundation with offices in Russia, Kazakhstan, the United Kingdom, and the United States. Organized in 1993, the ITIC serves as a clearinghouse for tax and investment policy information, transferring Western taxation and investment know-how to improve the investment climate of transition countries, thereby spurring business formation and economic prosperity. ITIC also serves as a training institute for key policy makers in the former Soviet Union and other transition economies to provide a better understanding of market economy business practices.

Exchange Research/Support Services: ITIC's Education and Outreach programs educate senior and mid-level government and parliamentary officials on the objectives of tax and economic reform and help build political support. Long after the programs are over, ITIC continues to work with these officials to apply their experience to Russian and Kazakhstani issues.

The International Theater Institute of the United States (ITI/US)

47 Great Jones Street, Fifth Floor
New York, NY 10012

Tel.:   212/254-4141   **Fax:** 212/254-6814
Website: http://www.iti-usa.org
E-mail: info@iti-usa.org

General Inquiries:
Martha W. Coigney,
Director, 212/254-4141

Industry Focus:
Arts/Humanities

Mission Statement: The International Theater Institute (ITI/US) was founded by UNESCO in 1948 "to promote the exchange of knowledge and practice in the theater arts." The mandate of its 92 centers throughout the world is to tighten the bonds between theaters of all nations, improve their understanding of one another, and reinforce their artistic and spiritual alliances.

Exchange Program: The role of the ITI/US is to initiate and promote special projects and programs, including services to foreign visitors, research, publications, information exchange, and representation at international meetings and congresses. Its reference library documents theatrical activities in 146 countries. Building upon its commitment to theater professionals, ITI/US has also established University and Theatre Partner Programs in order to work more closely with institutions interested in international exchange.

Interplast, Inc.

300-B Pioneer Way
Mountain View, CA 94041-1506

Tel.:   650/962-0123   **Fax:** 650/962-1619
Website: http://www.interplast.org
E-mail: IPnews@Interplast.org

General Inquiries:
Beverly Kent,
Professional Services Coordinator, 650/934-3312,
PrfSvcsCoord@Interplast.org

Industry Focus:
Science

Mission Statement: Interplast's mission is to provide free reconstructive surgery for people in developing nations, and to help improve health care worldwide. The organization's goals are to establish, develop, and maintain host-country, domestic-patient, and educational programs in the areas of patient care for reconstructive sur-gery, medical independence in host-country medical colleagues, and enabling recipients of care to become care providers in new sites.

Exchange Programs: Interplast schedules up to 40 surgical trips each year, sending volunteer medical teams to sites in Bolivia, Brazil, Ecuador, Honduras, Laos, Myanmar (Burma), Nepal, Nicaragua, Peru, the Philippines, Tibet, Vietnam, and Zambia. The medical teams typically spend two weeks at each site, and generally provide 75 to 100 surgeries per trip. Interplast thus provides nearly 3,000 surgeries annually with 500 volunteers participating in the trips each year. The medical teams include plastic surgeons, anesthesiologists, pediatricians, nurses, and secretaries/translators. Volunteers work side-by-side with host colleagues screening patients, performing surgery, and providing related care.

Iowa Resource for International Service, Inc. (IRIS)

1214 Iron Street
Kellogg, IA 50135

Tel.:   515/526-3378   **Fax:** 515/526-3379
Website: http://www.iris-center.org
E-mail: iris@iris-center.org

General Inquiries:
Robert Anderson,
President, 515/526-3378

Industry Focus:
Business/Commerce, Civil Society/Democracy,
Education, Government, Journalism/Publishing,

Mission Statement: The Iowa Resource for International Service (IRIS) utilizes rural Iowa as an education resource for international professionals and helps Iowans increase their global awareness and outreach.

Exchange Program: IRIS conducts both study tour and internship exchange programs for professionals from many countries. Core staff members combine expertise in government, business, education, journalism, conflict management, and English language instruction. Programs in globalization are enhanced by staff members with international roots in Switzerland, Ukraine, Ecuador, and Korea. The IRIS Center offers highly customized programs in a home-like atmosphere for small groups or individuals.

Irish American Cultural Institute (IACI)

One Lackawanna Place
Morristown, NJ 07960

Tel.:   973/605-1991   **Fax:** 973/605-8875
Website: http://www.irishaci.org
E-mail: irishwaynj@aol.com

General Inquiries:
Receptionist, 973/605-1991
Industry Focus:
Arts/Humanities, Development

Mission Statement: The goal of the Irish American Cultural Institute (IACI) is to explore the heritage of Ireland, foster its growth, and increase awareness of its rich diversities.

Exchange Program: The Irish Artists in Residence Program is a one-year residence program in New York City for selected artists. The program is sponsored by the Arts Councils of Ireland and Northern Ireland.

The Japan Pacific Resource Network (JPRN)

310 Eighth Street, Suite 305-B
Oakland, CA 94607

Tel.:   510/891-9045   **Fax:** 510/891-9047
Website: http://www.jprn.org
E-mail: jprnusa@earthlink.net

General Inquiries:
jprn@igc.apc.org

Mission Statement: The Japan Pacific Resource Network is a public interest and educational organization that works toward a more just society, promoting civil rights, corporate social responsibility, and community empowerment in the context of U.S.-Japan relations. It carries out this mission through research/educational projects, bilingual technical assistance, and cross-cultural networking. Programs emphasize leadership development, volunteerism, internships, and coalition building.

Exchange Program: During the JPRN Summer Internship Program, participants are given opportunities to conduct research on specific topics in nonprofit organizations in the U.S. or to learn management techniques of U.S. nonprofits, including volunteer management, fundraising, programming, and strategic planning.

John Simon Guggenheim Memorial Foundation

90 Park Avenue
New York, NY 10016

Tel.:   212/687-4470   **Fax:** 212/697-3248
Website: http://www.gf.org
E-mail: fellowships@gf.org

General Inquiries:
Receptionist, 212/687-4470

Industry Focus:
Arts/Humanities, Science

Mission Statement: The John Simon Guggenheim Memorial Foundation offers fellowships to further the development of scholars and artists by supporting their research in any field of knowledge in any of the arts, under the freest possible conditions and irrespective of race, color, or creed.

Exchange Program: The Foundation provides fellowships for advanced professionals in all fields (natural sciences, social sciences, humanities, creative arts) with the exception of performing arts. Fellowships are awarded through two annual competitions: one open to citizens and permanent residents of the United States and Canada, and the other open to citizens of Latin America and the Caribbean.

Latin America Data Base (LADB)

801 Yale Northeast
University of Albuquerque
Albuquerque, NM 87131-1016

Tel.:   505/277-6839   **Fax:** 505/277-6837
Website: http://www.ladb.unm.edu
E-mail: info@ladb.unm.edu

General Inquiries:
Rebecca Reynolds Bannister,
Director, 505/277-6839

Mission Statement: The Latin America Data Base (LADB) is a news and information service on Latin America producing weekly on-line newsletters and a searchable on-line archive of articles on the region. The website also offers free lesson plans in English on Latin America aimed at secondary educators.

Exchange Research/Support Services: LADB produces three weekly electronic newsletters: SourceMax (economic and political affairs in Mexico); EcoCentral (sustainable development, politics, and economic affairs of Central America and the Caribbean); and NotiSur (political and economic affairs in South America). These are available by subscription, by e-mail, or through the LADB website. The website also offers a searchable on-line archive of 24,000 articles from newsletters dating back to 1986 on Latin America available by subscription and a searchable archive of Latin American economic journals in Spanish.

Latin American Studies Association (LASA)

949 William Pitt Union
University of Pittsburgh
Pittsburgh, PA 15260

Tel.:   412/648-7929   **Fax:** 412/624-7145
Website: http://lasa.international.pitt.edu
E-mail: lasa+@pitt.edu

General Inquiries:
Reid Reading,
Executive Director, 412/648-7929

Mission Statement: Latin American Studies Association (LASA) encourages effective training, teaching, and research in Latin American studies and provides a forum for dealing with matters of common interest to its members.

Exchange Research/Support Services: LASA hosts international congresses every 18 months where participants may present and discuss their research in a variety of disciplines. The Association provides travel funding for Latin Americans to attend these congresses. LASA Sections provide an opportunity for members to work in areas of common interest within Latin American studies.

Medical Eye and Dental International Care Organization (MEDICO)

2955 Dawn Street, Suite D
Georgetown, TX 78628

Tel.: 512/930-1893 **Fax:** 512/869-7500
Website: http://www.medico.org
E-mail: info@medico.org

General Inquiries:
Linda Peters,
Trip Coordinator, 512/930-1893

Industry Focus:
Science

Mission Statement: Since 1990, hundreds of volunteers from throughout North America have spent a week with Medical Eye and Dental International Care Organization (MEDICO), bringing basic health care to people in remote areas of Central America. MEDICO's mission is to provide free medical, dental, and optometric care and educational services to people in developing countries who have little or no access to basic medical care.

Exchange Programs: MEDICO leads week-long trips to Mexico, Nicaragua, Honduras, and Panama to provide health care. A typical team consists of 15-20 members and involves physicians, nurses, dentists, optometrists, pharmacists, medical students, and other volunteers. Program participants perform a variety of services which increase the general health of the individuals whom they serve.

Merce Cunningham Dance Studio, Inc.

55 Bethune Street
New York, NY 10014

Tel.: 212/691-9751 x30
Fax: 212/633-2453
Website: http://www.merce.org

General Inquiries:
Sonya Robbins,
Project Coordinator

Industry Focus:
Arts/Humanities

Mission Statement: The Merce Cunningham Dance Studio is committed to educating dancers at the professional level in Cunningham's technique and choreographic process. The Studio offers a continuous program of daily classes that emphasize strength, clarity of position, and precision in movement. A major strength of the Merce Cunningham Studio is its close association with Merce Cunningham Dance Company (MCDC). All of the dancers in MCDC come through the training program at the Studio.

Exchange Program: The Merce Cunningham Studio has had an exchange visitor program since 1979. A clear result of the touring activities of the Merce Cunningham Dance Company in Europe, Asia, and Latin America is the demand for professional dance training in the modern dance technique and choreography. International dance students take classes and interact with American dancers who share their goal of a professional career in dance. Faculty members of the Merce Cunningham Studio are frequently invited to teach workshops abroad and give performances of their own work, as well as teach the choreography and technique originated by Cunningham. This exchange is a result of contact with international dancers in the New York studio and the experiences of the faculty abroad.

Mid-America Arts Alliance (M-AAA)

912 Baltimore, Suite 700
Kansas City, MO 64105

Tel.:   816/421-1388   **Fax:** 816/421-3918
Website: http://www.maaa.org
E-mail: info@maaa.org

General Inquiries:
Bob Dustman,
Senior Coodinator, 816/421-1388
bob@maaa.org

Industry Focus:
Arts/Humanities

Mission Statement: Mid-America Arts Alliance (M-AAA) transforms and builds communities by uniting people with the power of art.

Exchange Program: M-AAA manages the U.S. Mexico/Arts Administrators Exchange Program, which is funded by the U.S. Department of State. This program provides opportunities for the interchange of ideas and methodology between a group of arts administrators from the United States and Mexico.

The Middle East Institute (MEI)

1761 N Street, NW
Washington, DC 20036-2882

Tel.:   202/785-1141   **Fax:** 202/331-8861
Website: http://www.mideasti.org
E-mail: mideasti@mideasti.org

General Inquiries:
Receptionist, 202/785-1141

Mission Statement: The Middle East Institute (MEI), founded in 1946, is dedicated to educating Americans about the Middle East, a complex and critically important region.

Exchange Research/Support Services: MEI offers cultural and political seminars, the quarterly *Middle East Journal*, Middle Eastern languages classes, an annual conference, the George Camp Keiser Library, educational outreach materials, and internships. MEI dedicates itself to the study of the following areas: Arab Africa, Turkey, Israel, Jordan, Lebanon, Syria, Iraq, Iran, Afghanistan, Pakistan, the Arabian Peninsula, the Caucasus, and Central Asia.

Middle East Studies Association, Inc. (MESA)

1643 East Helen Street
University of Arizona
Tucson, AZ 85721-0410

Tel.:   520/621-5850   **Fax:** 520/626-9095
Website: http://www.mesa.arizona.edu
E-mail: mesana@u.arizona.edu

General Inquiries:
Nancy Dishaw,
Membership Secretary, 520/621-5850

Mission Statement: The Middle East Studies Association of North America (MESA) is a private, nonprofit, non-political organization of scholars and other persons interested in the study of the Middle East, North Africa, and the Islamic world. MESA is dedicated to promoting high standards of scholarship and instruction, to facilitating communication among scholars through annual meetings and publications, and to promoting cooperation among those who study the Middle East.

Exchange Research/Support Services: MESA provides its members with an annual meeting, bringing together Middle East studies scholars from around the world for a three-day exchange of ideas and information. The formal sessions include over 100 panels and workshops, complemented by meetings of affiliated organizations, an extensive book exhibit, a three-day filmfest, and other informal events. MESA publishes the quarterly *MESA Newsletter* and *International Journal of Middle East Studies,* the biannual MESA bulletin, and the biennial Roster of Members. Through its affiliates, MESA is linked with organizations formed around specialized interests within the field.

The Mississippi Consortium for International Development (MCID)

1225 Robinson Street
Jackson, MI 39203

Tel.:   601/979-8648   **Fax:** 601/968-8657
Website: http://stallion.jsums.edu/~mcid
E-mail: mcid@stallion.jsums.edu

General Inquiries:
Adrienne Graham,
Assistant Director,
601/979-8652

Industry Focus:
Civil Society/Democracy, Business, Development

Mission Statement: The Mississippi Consortium for International Development's (MCID) mission is to provide technical training and assistance to developing countries, countries of the former Soviet Union and Central and Eastern Europe focusing on human resource development.

Exchange Program: MCID implements projects in the following areas: community and economic development; democratization and leadership development; English language training; higher education administration; judicial and legislative reform; journalism and media management, small business development and administration; women and leadership; civic education; development and management of nongovernmental organizations; and private and economic restructuring. In addition, the Consortium has developed international exchange programs that seek to develop the leadership potential of young adults. Educational exchange programs have been conducted for more than 250 high school students, teachers, and administrators in Mississippi, Russia, Kyrgystan, and Ukraine.

Modern Language Association of America (MLA)

26 Broadway, 3rd Floor
New York, NY 10004-1789

Tel.: 646/576-5000 **Fax:** 646/458-0030
Website: http://www.mla.org
E-mail: info@mla.org

General Inquiries:
Receptionist, 646/576-5000

Mission Statement: The Modern Language Association of America (MLA) is a nonprofit membership organization that promotes the study and teaching of language and literature. The MLA publishes books and journals; arranges an annual convention; assists job seekers and hiring departments; develops MLA style; and sponsors committees that oversee association activities.

Exchange Research/Support Services: The Advisory Committee on Foreign Languages initiates and advises on association activities and projects relating to foreign languages and literatures; works to open lines of communication among various levels and interest groups in the profession; and encourages the development of publications in the field.

National Academy of Sciences (NAS)

2101 Constitution Avenue, NW
Washington, DC 20418

Tel.: 202/334-2000 **Fax:** 202/334-2614
Website: http://www.nas.edu
E-mail: OCEE@nas.edu

General Inquiries:
Office for Central Europe and Eurasia,
202/334-3680

Industry Focus:
Science

Mission Statement: The Office of International Affairs (OIA) is concerned with the development of international and national policies and programs to promote more effective application of science and technology to pressing economic and social problems facing both industrialized and developing countries, and to promote U.S. economic and international security interests. OIA participates in international cooperative activities, conducts studies of international issues, engages in joint studies and projects with counterpart organizations, manages scientific exchange programs, and represents the National Academies at many national and international meetings directed toward facilitating international cooperation in science and engineering.

Exchange Program: With funding from the National Science Foundation, the NRC's Office for Central Europe and Eurasia offers grants to individual American specialists who plan to establish new research partnerships with their colleagues from Central/Eastern Europe (CEE), and the Newly Independent States (NIS). This grants program, entitled Collaboration in Basic Science and Engineering (COBASE), offers short-term project development grants which support American specialists who wish to host or visit their CEE or NIS colleagues for up to two weeks in order to prepare collaborative research proposals. Long-term grants support American specialists who wish to host or visit their CEE or NIS colleagues for collaborative research for periods of one to six months.

National Association of Schools of Public Affairs and Administration (NASPAA)

1120 G Street, NW, Suite 730
Washington, DC 20005

Tel.: 202/628-8965 **Fax:** 202/626-4978
Website: http://www.naspaa.org
E-mail: naspaa@naspaa.org

General Inquiries:
Jackie Lewis,
Office Manager, jlewis@naspaa.org

Mission Statement: The National Association of Schools of Public Affairs and Administration (NASPAA) is an international membership organization which exists to promote excellence in public service education. The membership includes 248 U.S. university programs in public affairs, public policy, public administration, and nonprofit management.

Exchange Research/Support Services: NASPAA sets program guidelines for member institutions. Although U.S. programs are its primary constituents, NASPAA also provides support for public affairs programs worldwide. It hosts an annual conference for academics and practitioners to share their public affairs knowledge and experiences.

National Center for State Courts (NCSC)

300 Newport Avenue
Williamsburg, VA 23815

Tel.: 757/253-2000 **Fax:** 757/220-0449
Website: http://www.ncsconline.org
E-mail: kheroy@ncsc.dni.us

General Inquiries:
Karen S. Heroy,
Director, Int'l. Visitor Training Program,
kheroy@ncsc.dni.us

Industry Focus:
Law

Mission Statement: The National Center for State Courts (NCSC) is a nonprofit organization serving the needs of courts, both nationally and internationally. NCSC's mission is to promote justice by providing assistance, leadership, and service to courts as they attempt to improve their ability to dispense justice fairly, quickly, and efficiently. NCSC provides technical assistance and education and training on a wide array of topics including case management, court technology, budgeting, judicial independence, and

court organization and administration. NSCS is the premier education and training organization in the United States on the rule of law and judicial administration topics. NCSC also serves as a clearinghouse for information and helps courts keep up with advances and improvements in court administration and with changes and innovations within the courts. NCSC's research and evaluation projects examine the most urgent issues facing courts and provide data essential for an accurate picture of the courts.

Exchange Program: The exchange of court administration ideas and methods between U.S. judicial personnel and judicial officials from other countries exposes both groups to new ideas and strengthens the rule of law worldwide. Through the International Visitors Training Program (IVTP), NCSC annually hosts study tours for hundreds of international judicial leaders. These study tours vary from a one-day overview of the court system to an in-depth study of all aspects of the United States' judicial system, taking a month or more. Over the past four years, the IVTP has provided programming for over 1,600 visitors from more than 135 countries.

National Conference of State Legislatures

444 North Capitol Street, N.W., Suite 515
Washington, D.C. 20001

Tel.:   202/624-5400   **Fax:** 202/737-1069
Website: http://www.ncsl.org
E-mail: info@ncsl.org

Industry Focus:
Civil Society/Democracy

Mission Statement: The mission of the National Conference of State Legislatures is to improve the quality and effectiveness of state legislatures; to foster interstate communication and cooperation and to ensure legislatures a strong, cohesive voice in the federal system.

Exchange Programs: The International Programs Department of the National Conference of State Legislatures brings U.S. state legislators and staff together with legislators, parliamentarians, and legislative staff from abroad to address issues of common concern and public policy. Because legislatures are the most representative institution of government, state legislators and staff are in a unique position to support emerging democracies and help them create independent, representative and well-informed legislative bodies. NCSL carries out several types of international exchanges with foreign counterparts around the globe, including technical assistance projects and legislative exchanges. NCSL also welcomes over one hundred international delegates at Annual Meetings.

National Council for the Social Studies (NCSS)

3501 Newark Street, NW
Washington, DC 20016

Tel.:   202/966-7840   **Fax:** 202/966-2061
Website: http://www.ncss.org
E-mail: information@ncss.org

General Inquiries:
Information Services, 202/966-7840 x106

Industry Focus:
Education

Mission Statement: The National Council for the Social Studies (NCSS) engages and supports educators in strengthening and advocating for social studies, where social studies is defined as the integrated study of the social sciences and humanities to promote civic competence. Social studies provides coordinated, systematic study drawing upon such disciplines as anthro-

pology, archeology, economics, geography, history, law, philosophy, political science, psychology, religion, and sociology, as well as appropriate content from the humanities, mathematics, and natural sciences.

Exchange Program: In cooperation with the Keizai Koho Center, NCSS offers 18 fellowships to visit Japan each summer. U.S. and Canadian educators involved in K-12 social studies education are eligible to apply. Fellowships cover round-trip transportation from the United States to Japan. The fifteen-day itinerary is designed with a particular focus on business and economics topics. Fellows are organized into three teams for the development of an economics source book for use with elementary, middle/junior, and senior high school students.

National Education Association (NEA)

1201 16th Street, NW
Washington, DC 20036

Tel.: 202/833-4000
202/822-7488 **Fax:** 202/822-7974
Website: http://www.nea.org
E-mail: oir@nea.org

General Inquiries:

Joanne Eide,
Director of International Relations,
202/822-7046

Mission Statement: The National Education Association (NEA) is the United States' largest professional employee organization with the mission to restore public confidence in education. It was founded in 1857 to "advance the interest of the profession of teaching and to promote the cause of education in the United States." The association seeks a quality education for each child in safe schools where children can learn basic skill, practice values and prepare for jobs.

Exchange Research/Support Services: The International Relations office of the NEA coordinates international work for the association by identifying valuable education models in use in other countries and supporting relations between the association and other education unions internationally. The office analyses international education experiences and incorporates relevant learnings to NEA's strategic priorities. NEA supports the international exchange of information and short term study missions that support the strategic priorities of the association. NEA's international work is conducted almost exclusively with Education International, the world's largest educators' federation representing 24 million members through its 305 member organizations.

National Foreign Language Center (NFLC)

1029 Vermont Avenue, NW, Suite 1000
Washington, DC 20005

Tel.: 202/637-8881 **Fax:** 202/637-9244
Website: http://www.nflc.org
E-mail: info@nflc.org

General Inquiries:

Receptionist, 202/637-8881

Mission Statement: The National Foreign Language Center (NFLC) is an independent policy and research institution. Its international mission is to contribute to the improvement of U.S. capacity for cross-cultural communication, particularly in languages other than English. The NFLC pursues its mission through research, policy analysis and development, collaborative projects, and a variety of programs designed to gather and disseminate language-related information.

Exchange Research/Support Services: The NFLC administers the Institute of Advanced Studies, a residential program funded by the Andrew W. Mellon Foundation and located at the NFLC. The IAS/Mellon Fellowship Program provides support to scholars from the United States and abroad for empirical research projects that have the potential for direct impact on the teaching and learning of foreign languages in the United States in a variety of educational settings. Fellowships are awarded to individual post-doctoral scholars and students who are at the dissertation phase or immediate post-doctoral phase and want to complete and/or continue their dissertation research; likewise, awards may be made to small teams of institutional-based researchers or faculty members.

National Humanities Center

7 Alexander Drive, Box 12256
Research Triangle Park, NC 27709-2256

Tel.:   919/549-0661   **Fax:** 919/990-8535
Website: http://www.nhc.rtp.nc.us:8080
E-mail: nhc@ga.unc.edu

General Inquiries:
Kent Mullikin,
Vice President and Deputy Director,
kent@ga.unc.edu

Mission Statement: The National Humanities Center, a privately incorporated, independent institute for advanced study in the humanities, exists to encourage excellent scholarship and to affirm the importance of the humanities in American society. The Center was founded in 1976 by leaders from higher education, the corporate world, and public life who shared a common conviction that we deepen our understanding of the human experience by the study of history, language and literature, philosophy, the arts, religion, law, and other fields traditionally associated with the humanities.

Exchange Research/Support Services: Each year, the Center awards up to 40 fellowships to leading scholars from across the United States and around the world. These scholars individually pursue their own research at the Center, and together they form a community in which the exchange of ideas enriches the work of all. Each resident scholar is provided with a stipend averaging $35,000, a private study, library and editorial services, e-mail and internet access, assistance with locating housing, a variety of meeting rooms, a daily lunch, and various administrative support for scholarship and intellectual exchange.

National League of Cities (NLC)

1301 Pennsylvania Avenue, NW
Washington, DC 20004-1763

Tel.:   202/626-3000   **Fax:** 202/626-3043
Website: http://www.nlc.org
E-mail: pa@nlc.org

General Inquiries:
James Brooks,
Manager, International Programs,
202/626-3163

Mission Statement: The mission of the National League of Cities (NLC) is to strengthen and promote cities as centers of opportunity, leadership, and governance. NLC was established in 1924 by and for reform-minded state municipal leagues. NLC now represents 49 leagues, approximately 1,800 member cities, and through the membership of the state municipal leagues, NLC represents more than 18,000 cities and towns of all sizes in total.

Exchange Research/Support Services: The Global Connections Partnership (GLOBECON) is a resource and information sharing network for local economic decision makers from the public, private, and community-based sectors. GLOBECON is a service program designed to help counties, cities, and towns position themselves to compete in the global economy. Members are part of a network of people in communities who have responsibilities for international economic development–trade promotion, tourism, investment, business creation, overseas contacts, and strategic planning. Individuals who participate are elected and appointed officials in counties, cities and towns, executives and staff in chambers of commerce and world trade associations, coordinators of sister city programs and international visitor bureaus, administrators of foreign trade zones, and specialists in community development corporations.

North American Institute

708 Paseo de Peralta
Santa Fe, NM 97501

Tel.:   505/982-3657   **Fax:** 505/983-5840

Website:
http://www.northamericaninstitute.org
E-mail: nami@northamericaninstitute.org

General Inquires:
Ian Burnes,
Administrative Officer

Mission Statement: The North American
Institute (NAMI) was founded in 1988 to deep-
en understanding and promote new approaches
to North American issues. NAMI's mission is to
examine all aspects of North American regional
relationship, recognizing the challenges facing
the governments, peoples and cultures of North
America, and to develop better approaches to
this changing relationship. NAMI reaches out
across all sectors of society as a catalyst and
convener, in an effort to create networks and
real changes in the fabric of the North
American community.

Exchange Activities: The North American
Community Service Project is designed to provide volunteer service opportunities for young
people from the United States, Canada, and
Mexico in projects involving cultural and historic preservation, environmental conservation
and community development. NAMI, in its
capacity as a tri-national convening organization
that fosters transborder dialog, is sponsoring a
series of conferences in the southern part of
New Mexico to promote discussion on the Santa
Teresa development.

Organization of American Historians

112 North Bryan Avenue
Bloomington, IN 47408-4199

Tel.:   812/855-7311   **Fax:** 812/855-0696
Website: http://www.oah.org
E-mail: oah@oah.org

General Inquiries:
John R. Dichtl,
Deputy Executive Director, 812/855-7345

Mission Statement: Founded in 1907, the
Organization of American Historians (OAH) is
the largest professional society for the investigation, study, and teaching of American history.
Its 11,000 members include college and university professors; archivists; curators and other
public historians; teachers and students; and
institutional subscribers such as libraries, museums, and history-related organizations.

Exchange Research/Support Services: OAH
sponsors prizes for the best book and best article
on American history published in a foreign language, offers three short-term residences at
Japanese universities for OAH historian members,
co-sponsors with New York University fellowships for scholars wishing to attend a series of
annual conferences in Florence, Italy on internationalizing the study of American history, and
publishes an international announcements
newsletter called *Connections*. The newsletter
provides a concise digest of information for students, scholars, and professionals who wish to
develop international contacts with others interested in the transnational study of American history and culture. The OAH publishes the *Journal
of American History*, *OAH Newsletter*, an Annual
Meeting Program, and the *OAH Magazine of
History*, a publication for teachers of history. The
Journal has a board of more than 80 international
contributing editors from outside the United
States who help bring international scholarship
on America to its readers. The organization's
newsletter and its annual meeting each spring
both frequently include international material.

Open Society Institute (OSI)

**400 West 59th Street
New York, NY 10019**

Tel.: 212/548-0600   **Fax:** 212/548-4679
Website: http://www.soros.org/osi
E-mail: osnews@sorosny.org

General Inquiries:
Sarah Margon,
Communications Associate,
smargon@sorosnyc.org

Mission Statement: The Open Society Institute (OSI) is a private operating and grantmaking foundation that seeks to promote the development and maintenance of open societies around the world by supporting a range of programs in the areas of educational, social, and legal reform, and by encouraging alternative approaches to complex and often controversial issues. Established in 1993 and based in New York City, OSI is part of the Soros Foundations Network, an informal network of organizations created by George Soros operating in over 30 countries around the world, principally in Central and Eastern Europe and the former Soviet Union.

Exchange Research/Support Services: The Open Society Institute's Network Scholarship Programs fund the participation of students, scholars, and professionals from Eastern and Central Europe, the former Soviet Union, Mongolia, and Burma in rigorous, competitive academic programs outside of their home countries. The goals of these programs are: to revitalize and reform the teaching of the social sciences and humanities at higher education institutions; to provide professional training in fields unavailable or underrepresented at institutions in the countries served; and to assist outstanding students from a range of backgrounds in pursuing their studies in alternative academic and cultural environments.

Public Administration Service (PAS)

**7927 Jones Branch Drive, Suite 100 South
McLean, VA 22102-3322**

Tel.: 703/734-8970   **Fax:** 703/734-4965
E-mail: postmaster@pashq.org
Website: www.pashq.org

General Inquiries:
Theodore Sitkoff,
President, 703/734-8970, x3018

Mission Statement: Public Administration Service (PAS), established in 1933 by a number of organizations and public officials, is a private, self-supporting, nonprofit institution dedicated to improving the quality and effectiveness of governmental and public service agencies, capitalized institutions, and state-owned enterprises.

Exchange Research/Support Services: PAS has conducted more than 2,800 consulting and technical assistance projects spanning almost every governmental field. In the past 50 years, PAS has provided assistance to countries overseas to government organizations, corporations, and quasi-public institutions in more than 100 different countries through diverse sponsorship and financial support from organizations such as the World Bank, specialized agencies of the United Nations, the Asian Development Bank, the Inter-American Development Bank, the Agency for International Development, and the International Fund for Agricultural Development.

Rotaplast International Inc.

55 New Montgomery Street, Suite 713
San Francisco, CA 94105

Tel.:   415/538-8120   **Fax:** 415/777-3335
Website: http://www.rotaplast.org
E-mail: info@rotaplast.org

General Inquiries:
Anita Strangl,
Executive Director, 415/538-8120

Industry Focus:
Science

Mission Statement: Rotaplast seeks to eliminate the incidence of untreated cleft lip and palate anomalies in children by the year 2025. To accomplish this goal, Rotaplast will partner with Rotary Clubs throughout the world and foster international goodwill and fellowship among medical professionals, Rotarians, and other volunteers. The mission of Rotaplast International is to provide free reconstructive surgery to indigent children worldwide, together with education and prevention of birth defects.

Exchange Programs: Rotaplast facilitates medical missions to provide surgical intervention for children who are not able to receive treatment or who are in need of more complicated medical procedures than can be provided by local physicians. Volunteer teams are sent throughout South America on 12-day trips. Rotaplast recruits medical volunteers such as plastic surgeons, operating room nurses, anesthesiologists, recovery room nurses, pediatricians, orthodontists, dentists, speech pathologists, as well as many other non-medical volunteers.

Sabre Foundation, Inc.

872 Massachusetts Avenue, Suite 2-1
Cambridge, MA 02139

Tel.:   617/868-3510   **Fax:** 617/868-7916
Website: http://www.sabre.org
E-mail: sabre@sabre.org

General Inquiries:
Tania Vitvitsky,
Executive Director, 617/868-3510

Mission Statement: Sabre Foundation, Inc., founded in 1969, works to build free institutions and to examine the ideals that sustain them. Sabre's Book Donation Program distributes new donated books, CD-ROMS, videos, and other educational materials through partner organizations overseas. In keeping with the mission to meet the information needs of individuals in developing countries, Sabre also provides training in Internet and related information technologies to individuals at its headquarters in Cambridge, MA, and as funding permits, at sites overseas.

Exchange Research/Support Services: Sabre welcomes participants to its Information Technology Workshops program from countries around the world and other training and visitor programs in the United States. Participants apply directly from their home country institution, through other organizations, or while engaged in other research or study activities while in the United States. In each case, the trainees participate in a program that combines classroom training at Sabre and site visits with counterpart professionals in the area. Sabre's customized, hands-on workshops are designed for beginner and advanced computer users. Sabre supports the work of other training and exchange organizations by providing its expertise and other resources as requested. Sabre is also an active member of WorldBoston, the Boston area's official coordinator for U.S. government sponsored visits by foreign visitors.

Salzburg Seminar

The Marble Works, P.O. Box 886
Middlebury, VT 05753

Tel.: 802/388-0007 **Fax:** 802/388-1030
Website: http://www.salzburgseminar.org
E-mail: info@salzburgseminar.org

General Inquiries:
Cathy Walsh,
Program Officer, 802/388-0007
cwalsh@salzburgseminar.org

Industry Focus:
Education

Mission Statement: Since its founding in 1947, the Salzburg Seminar has emerged as one of the world's foremost educational centers committed to the development of leaders with global perspective. With the principles of reconciliation and intellectual inquiry central to its activities, the Seminar is dedicated to promoting the free exchange of ideas, opinions, and experience. As the Seminar continues to become more global in its reach, it remains committed to the idea that individuals throughout the world can make a difference in their institutions, communities, and societies. The Salzburg Seminar believes that intensive interaction among peers from diverse backgrounds in a neutral forum will broaden perspectives, facilitate the establishment of worldwide professional networks, and bring about enlightened change in the future.

Exchange Program: Each year, approximately 1,000 professionals of exceptional promise from more than 100 countries gather at Schloß Leopoldskron in Salzburg, Austria, to discuss issues of far-reaching importance in a multi-disciplinary, cross-cultural environment. The Salzburg Seminar promotes global dialogue through its multi-faceted academic program: core sessions form the basis of the program; special sessions convene senior level professionals; the universities project higher education reform; the American Studies Center provides a venue for the teaching of American Studies; and Schloß Leopoldskron Conference Center offers conference services for programs consonant with the goals of the Seminar.

Social Science Research Council (SSRC)

810 Seventh Avenue, 31st floor
New York, NY 10019

Tel.: 212/377-2700 **Fax:** 212/377-2727
Website: http://www.ssrc.org

General Inquiries:
Mary Byrne McDonnell,
Executive Director-SSRC, 212/377-2700 x420
exec@ssrc.org

Mission Statement: The Social Science Research Council (SSRC) is an independent, nonprofit organization composed of social and behavioral scientists and humanists from all over the world. Founded in 1923, the SSRC throughout its history has established intellectual bridges among the academy, foundations, the disciplines, government, and the public. The SSRC encourages scholars in different disciplines to work together on topical, conceptual and methodological issues that can benefit from interdisciplinary and international collaboration. The Council also links researchers, practitioners and policymakers in exploring new intellectual paths and testing theories and methods against challenges of national and international concern. Its work is carried out through workshops and conferences, research consortia, scholarly exchanges, summer training institutes, fellowships and grants, and publications.

Exchange Research/Support Services: A central task of SSRC is to serve as a resource for international scholarship. The SSRC is currently building a program for scholars throughout the world—scholars who want to strengthen the social sciences in their respective regions but to do so in a manner that links them with international research colleagues around the world. This program includes collaborative research networks which are reshaping the study of pressing theoretical and substantive issues by linking scholars separated by region, discipline, and methodological tradition; the Human Capital Committee, which evaluates issues associated with training, retention and utilization of scholars and researchers globally; and seven regional advisory panels, which identify how global issues impact and are influenced by the history, culture and politics of their world regions.

Solomon R. Guggenheim Museum

1071 Fifth Avenue
New York, NY 10128-0173

Tel.: 212/423-3500 **Fax:** 212/423-3650
Website: http://www.guggenheim.org
E-mail: education@guggenheim.org

General Inquiries:
Education Department, 212/423-3781
education@guggenheim.org

Industry Focus:
Arts/Humanities

Mission Statement: The Solomon R. Guggenheim Museum provides an opportunity for students from different cultures to gain some practical experience of museology through the Peggy Guggenheim Studentship Program located in Venice, Italy. Through the program, students gain close familiarity with an important collection of modern art in a creative international atmosphere while acquainting themselves with the life and culture of Venice.

Exchange Program: The Peggy Guggenheim Studentship Program is available to university students worldwide. The studentship program involves study of the operation of the museum, preparation and staffing of the galleries, as well as periodic exhibition installation. Twice weekly seminars are held to discuss aspects of museology and of modern art with special reference to the works in the Peggy Guggenheim collection. Students will have the opportunity to carry out independent study programs. Visits may be organized to other museums and exhibitions in Venice. Internships are also available at the New York location. Both United States citizens and foreign nationals are encouraged to apply for fall and spring (part-time) and summer (full-time) positions.

Soros Foundation Network

400 West 59th Street
New York, NY 10019

Tel.: 212/548-0600 **Fax:** 212/548-4000
Website: http://www.soros.org
E-mail: osnews@sorosny.org

General Inquiries:
Department of Communications, 212/548-0668

Mission Statement: The various independent foundations, programs, and institutions established and supported by philanthropist George Soros share a common goal: to foster the development of open societies around the world, particularly in the previously communist countries of Central and Eastern Europe and the former Soviet Union. These organizations seek to help build the infrastructure and institutions necessary for open societies by supporting a broad array of programs in education, media, and communications, human rights and humanitarian aid, science and medicine, arts and culture, economic restructuring, and legal reform.

Exchange Research/Support Services: The network of foundations established by philanthropist George Soros supports a wide variety of research and educational exchange programs.

Tahoe-Baikal Institute (TBI)

P.O. Box 13587
South Lake Tahoe CA 96151-3587

Tel.:   530/542-5599   **Fax:** 530/542-5567
Website: http://tahoe.ceres.ca.gov/tbi
E-mail: tbi@etahoe.com

General Inquiries:
Silke Rover,
Program Coordinator, 530/542-5599
tbi@etahoe.com

Industry Focus:
Education, Environment

Mission Statement: The mission of the Tahoe-Baikal Institute (TBI) is to further environmental protection and resource management efforts at Lake Tahoe, California, and Lake Baikal, Siberia, and other significant natural areas around the world. The Institute sponsors programs to foster the long-term engagement and participation of young adults in environmental issues, together with international exchanges of students, scholars, government officials, and other experts.

Exchange Program: Every summer, TBI holds an environmental exchange, to take place in Lake Tahoe and Lake Baikal. The ten-week program brings together an interesting national team of university-level students and young professionals to focus on the threatened environment of two of the world's unique lakes, and provides a cultural and scientific forum where future environmental leaders can gain insight into regional and global ecological problems.

Teachers of English to Speakers of Other Languages, Inc. (TESOL)

700 South Washington Street, Suite 200
Alexandria, VA 22314

Tel.:   703/836-0774   **Fax:** 703/836-7864
Website: http://www.tesol.edu
E-mail: info@tesol.edu

General Inquiries:
Receptionist, 703/836-0774

Mission Statement: The Teachers of English to Speakers of Other Languages' (TESOL) mission is to develop the expertise of its members and others involved in teaching English to speakers of other languages to help them foster effective communication in diverse settings while respecting individuals' language rights. TESOL articulates and advances standards for professional preparation, continuing education, and student programs; links groups worldwide to enhance communication among language specialists; produces high quality programs, services, and products; and promotes advocacy to further the profession.

TESOL encourages access to and standards for English language instruction, professional preparation, and employment to its worldwide members. TESOL has 46 autonomous affiliates outside the United States and cooperates with various international language or English teaching organizations.

Exchange Research/Support Services: TESOL offers self-study guidelines provided for program regulation; an employment clearinghouse on-site at the Annual Convention; placement services and career information; and workshop materials for in-service teacher training.
TESOL publishes *TESOL Quarterly*, the *TESOL Journal*, and *TESOL Matters*.

The Tibet Fund

241 East 32nd Street
New York, NY 10016

Tel.: 212/213-5011 **Fax:** 212/213-1219
Website: http://www.tibetfund.org
E-mail: caroline@tibetfund.org

General Inquiries:
Tenzing Chhodak,
Director, Treasurer, 212/213-5011

Industry Focus:
Arts/Humanities, Education

Mission Statement: The Tibet Fund's primary mission is the preservation of the distinct culture, religion, and national identity of the Tibetan people. The Fund is a private, nonprofit organization which administers grants and support projects and advances its mission by: supporting and strengthening the Tibetan

Refugee community in India, Nepal, and elsewhere; providing educational and informational materials and events about Tibet and Tibetan culture, religion, history, and arts; offering scholarships and cultural exchange programs; and coordinating international humanitarian and educational assistance efforts.

Exchange Program: Under an exchange and cooperative agreement with the Fulbright program of the U.S. Department of State, the Tibet Fund administers a scholarship program for Tibetan refugees from India, Nepal, and elsewhere. Each year, the Tibet Fund brings approximately 13 Tibetan scholars and students to the United States.

United Negro College Fund (UNCF)

8260 Willow Oaks Corporate Drive
Fairfax, VA 22301

Tel.: 703/205-3400 **Fax:** 703/205-3446
Website: http://www.uncf.org
E-mail: webmaster@uncf.org

General Inquiries:
Veda Lamar,
Chief Information Officer, 703/205-3440

Mission Statement: United Negro College Fund (UNCF), founded in 1944, has grown to become the nation's oldest and most successful African American higher education assistance organization. Its mission is to enhance the quality of education by raising operating funds for member colleges and universities, providing financial assistance to deserving students, and supplying technical assistance to member institutions.

Exchange Research/Support Services: UNCF's international programs and services include foreign language studies, work experience, faculty exchange, and an educational institute to prepare under-represented minorities for careers in international affairs.

U.S. Association of Former Members of Congress (USAFMC)

223 Pennsylvania Avenue, S.E., Suite 200
Washington, DC 20003

Tel.:   202/543-8676   **Fax:** 202/543-7145
Website: http://www.usafmc.org
E-mail: usafmc1@mindspring.com

General Inquiries:
Linda A. Reed,
Executive Director, 202/543-8676

Industry Focus:
Civil Society/Democracy, Education, Government

Mission Statement: The nonpartisan United States Association of Former Members of Congress (USAFMC) was founded in 1970 as a nonprofit, educational, research, and social organization. Chartered by the United States Congress, it has approximately 600 members who have represented American citizens in both the U.S. Senate and House of Representatives. The Association promotes improved public understanding of the role of Congress as a unique institution as well as the crucial importance of representative democracy as a system of government, both domestically and internationally. The Association brings together decision makers from the United States and other countries so that they will learn, among other things, what impact their laws will have on each other.

Exchange Program: The Congressional Study Group on Germany is an unofficial and informal organization open to all Members of Congress that facilitates better understanding and greater cooperation between members of Congress and their counterparts in the German Bundestag. The Group conducts a Distinguished Visitors Program at the U.S. Capitol for guests from Germany; sponsors annual seminars involving Members of the U.S. Congress and the German Bundestag; encourages Members of Congress to become involved with participants in the Congress-Bundestag Youth Exchange Program; and arranges for Members of the Bundestag to visit Congressional Districts with Members of Congress. The objectives of the Japan Study Group are to develop a Congressional forum for the sustained study and analysis of policy options on major issues in U.S.-Japan relations and to increase opportunities for Members of Congress to meet with their counterparts in the Japanese Diet for frank discussions of those key issues. Ongoing activities include: monthly roundtable discussion meetings that are held throughout the year with invited U.S. and Japanese government officials and nongovernmental experts; and hosting visiting delegations from the Diet to discuss economic, security, trade and other policies. The Association is in the process of initiating similar parliamentary exchange programs with Mexico and the People's Republic of China.

United States Conference of Mayors

1620 Eye Street, NW
Washington, DC 20006

Tel.:   202/293-7330   **Fax:** 202/293-2352
Website: http://www.usmayors.org/uscm
E-mail: info@usmayors.org

General Inquiries:
Jim Welfley,
Office of Information Systems, 202/293-7330
jwelfley@usmayors.org

Industry Focus:
Civil Society/Democracy, Government

Mission Statement: The United States Conference of Mayors is the official nonpartisan organization of cities with populations of 30,000 or more. There are about 1,100 such cities in the country today. Each city is represented in the Conference by its chief elected official, the mayor. Today, the principal roles of the Conference

of Mayors are to aid the development of effective national urban policy, strengthen federal-city relationships, ensure that federal policy meets urban needs, and provide mayors with leadership and management tools of value in their cities.

Exchange Program: The Conference has a variety of international activities, including providing training for mayors in other countries, assisting mayors of other countries in establishing associations similar to the Conference of Mayors, briefing visiting mayors from other countries about the activities of the Conference, working with various international organizations, and taking policy stands on various international issues. The John J. McCloy Urban Fellows Program promotes international cultural exchange between German and American city government staff. The Conference of Mayors has collaborated with the American Council on Germany and the Congress of German Cities since 1980 in the selection of Fellows and in development of their itinerary. Fellows are mid-level city government staff who have chosen public service as their profession.

United States-Japan Foundation

145 East 32nd Street
New York, NY 10016

Tel.:   212/481-8753   **Fax:** 212/481-8762
Website: http://www.us-jf.org
E-mail: info@us-jf.org

General Inquiries:
James Schoff,
Program Officer,
jschoff@us-jf.org

Mission Statement: The United States-Japan Foundation is committed to promoting stronger ties between Americans and Japanese by supporting projects that foster mutual knowledge and education, deepen understanding, create effective channels of communication, and address common concerns in an increasingly interdependent world.

Exchange Program: The U.S.-Japan Leadership Program aims to create closer ties of communication and understanding among a new generation of young Japanese and American leaders. As the world's two most powerful economies and leading democracies, Japan and the United States will play critical roles in shaping the world of the 21st Century. This program works to create an informed body of leading citizens on each side who will have a trusted network of friends in the other country.

University of the Middle East Project (UME)

1318 Beacon Street
Suite 9
Brookline, MA 02446

Tel.:   617/232-6331   **Fax:** 801/365-4214
Website: http://www.ume.org
E-mail: ume@ume.org

General Inquiries:
Ana Maria Angel,
Office Manager, 617/232-6331 ext.3

Chief Executive Officer:
Dr. Ron Rubin,
Executive Director

Mission Statement: The mission of the University of the Middle East Project is to create in the Middle East and North America a new system of interconnected academic centers promoting academic excellence, regional cooperation, development, the values of equal human dignity and open inquiry, and peace.

Exchange Research/Support Services:
Providing a tertiary education training of the highest academic level for students dedicated to become primary and secondary teachers in the Middle East is an important academic priority of the University of the Middle East.

William Joiner Center for the Study of War and Social Consequences

University of Massachusetts Boston
100 Morrissey Boulevard
Boston, MA 02125-3393

Tel.: 617/287-5850 **Fax:** 617/287-5855
Website: http://omega.cc.umb.edu/~joiner
E-mail: kevin.bowen@umb.edu

General Inquiries:
Kevin Bowen,
Director, 617/287-5850
kevin.bowen@umb.edu

Industry Focus:
Arts/Humanities, Education

Mission Statement: Established in response to the needs of Vietnam veterans, the William Joiner Center for the Study of War and Social Consequences explores the consequences and lingering effects of war through research on issues such as post-traumatic stress disorder, veterans advocacy, education, and the promotion and support of artistic expression.

Exchange Program: The William Joiner Center conducts educational, literary, and cultural exchange in its effort to educate about war and to diminish its effects. The Center also sends English language instructors at the university level to Vietnam and sponsors artists and musicians in exhibits and performances in the United States.

Winrock International

38 Winrock Drive
Morrilton, AR 72110

Tel.: 501/727-5435 **Fax:** 501/727-5417
Website: http://www.winrock.org
E-mail: communications@winrock.org

General Inquiries:
Pamela E. Woodard,
Manager, Scholarship Management and
Training Unit, 501/727-5435 x284

Industry Focus:
Agriculture

Mission Statement: Winrock International is a private, nonprofit organization that works with people to build a better world by increasing agricultural productivity and rural employment while protecting the environment. Winrock International programs make the greatest difference for people worldwide by strengthening education and training, developing and extending technology, and improving public policies.

Exchange Program: The Scholarship Management and Training Unit (SMTU) of Winrock International provides project management and scholar support services to a number of international development projects worldwide. For the past four decades, Winrock International has been a leader in programs that identify and develop young men and women professionals capable of leadership in agricultural and natural resource research, education, and extension. Scholar support services include recruitment; selection; placement or program design; facilitation of travel; administration of the J-1 Exchange Visitor Program; orientation; payment of fees and allowances; international scholar advising; program monitoring and reporting; and re-entry services.

World Council of Credit Unions, Inc.

5710 Mineral Point Road
P.O. Box 2982
Madison, WI 53705

Tel.:   608/231-7130   **Fax:** 608/238-8020
Website: http://www.woccu.org
E-mail: mail@woccu.org

General Inquiries:
Kicia Doyle,
Marketing Manager, 608/231-7110

Industry Focus:
Business/Commerce, Development

Mission Statement: The World Council of
Credit Unions is the international organization
of credit unions and similar cooperative financial institutions. Its mission is to assist members to organize, expand, improve and to inte-
grate credit unions and related institutions as
effective instruments for the economic and
social development of people.

Exchange Program: The People-to-People
Program brings individuals from different
credit union movements together through
partnerships, volunteer assignments, and
internships. Staff and leaders from developing
credit union movements receive training in
U.S. credit unions, while U.S. credit union
professionals work in developing movements
as volunteers who provide technical assistance
and training. Leagues of credit unions in the
U.S. partner with developing national movements or overseas credit union leagues in an
effort to ensure consistency in the training
and technical assistance efforts.

Section III
International Organizations

This section includes basic information on organizations located throughout the world that are involved in the field of international exchange. Programs range from international exchanges at the high school and university levels, conferences and seminars, English language and au pair programs, scholarships for international study and research, and the promotion of cooperation among institutions and between nations in support of international exchange.

Each entry contains general information about the organization, as well as information on specific programs and services. For complete information on an organization's programs and services, refer to its website or contact the organization directly.

Academic Cooperation Association (ACA)

15, rue d'Egmontstraat
Brussels B-1000
Belgium

Tel.: 32 0 2 513 22 41 **Fax:** 32 0 2 513 17 76
Website: http://www.aca-secretariat.be
E-mail: info@aca-secretariat.be

Chief Executive Officer:
Bernd Wächter, Director

Mission: The Academic Cooperation Association (ACA) is a European organization dedicated to the promotion of higher education cooperation in Europe and beyond. The ACA members are major independent organizations at the national level who have been entrusted by their governments and other parties with the management of international academic cooperation and exchange. ACA was founded in 1993 at the initiative of the *British Council, the Netherlands Organization for International Cooperation in Higher Education* and the *German Academic Exchange Service*. Today, the association has 17 member organizations in Europe, and associate members in three additional continents.

Exchange Activities: ACA undertakes a wide variety of activities, which can be broadly grouped into the following categories: management of programs and projects; research and evaluation of international higher education cooperation; advocacy in the field of European and international education cooperation, strengthening of cooperation between member organizations. ACA enjoys close relations with national governments, international governmental organizations, such as the European Union, the Council of Europe, UNESCO, and OECD, and with major non-governmental associations in the field of higher education.

Alternative Academic Educational Network (AAEN)

Masarikova 5/XVI
Belgrade 11000
Yugoslavia

Tel.: 381 11 3061 509 **Fax:** 381 11 688 123
Website: www.aaen.edu.yu
E-mail: aaen@aaen.edu.yu

Chief Executive Officer:
Dr. Srbijanka Turajlic, Chair of the Board

Mission Statement: The Alternative Academic Educational Network (AAEN) operates on several levels. Through AAEN, a number of guest lecturers from abroad take an active part in educational programs and visits organized by individual contacts of the Network's lecturers. Vital to the operation of the Network is support from the Association of European Universities (CRE) and the Council of Europe. This support translates to opportunities for Network representatives to participate in a number of conferences, seminars and workshops concerning higher education issues.

Exchange Activity: AAEN offers a Higher Education Support Program and an Academic Mobility Grant.

American International Education (AIE)

Bor Fontesta, 14 6° 4 ª
Barcelona 08021
Spain

Tel.:   34 93 200 5143   **Fax:** 34 93 200 3985
E-mail: aie@aieducation.es

Chief Executive Officer:
Katie McArthur, Head Program Coordinator

Mission Statement: American International Education promotes inter-cultural exchange and understanding through semester and academic-year high school programs abroad. Students attend public or private high schools and live with local host families or in the boarding facilities of the school.

Exchange programs and activities: Exchange programs and activities include high school academic-year and semester long exchange programs for Spanish students in the United States, Canada, Ireland, Great Britain, and other countries. AIE also offers public high school, private and boarding school placement options.

Centre for International Mobility (CIMO)

Hakaniemenkatu 2
Helsinki 00531
Finland

Tel.:   358 9 7747 7033 **Fax:** 358 9 7747 7064
Website: http://www.cimo.fi
E-mail: cimoinfo@cimo.fi

Mission Statement: The Centre for International Mobility (CIMO), an organization operating under the Finnish Ministry of Education, offers services and expertise to encourage cross-cultural communication.

Exchange Activities: CIMO administers scholarship and exchange programs and is responsible for implementing nearly all European Union education, training and youth programs at the national level. To support internationalization of educational and training institutions in Finland, CIMO offers training, information, advisory services and publications. CIMO also promotes and organizes international trainee exchanges. In addition, CIMO advances teaching of Finnish language and culture in universities abroad and arranges summer courses in Finnish language and culture for international students.

The Chase Foundation – Argentina (CF—Ar)

A. Schweitzer 1717
Villa Carlos Paz
X-5152-JVA Cordoba
Argentina

c.c. 147
Villa Carlos Paz
X-5152-JVA Cordoba
Argentina

Tel.:   54 3541 584 000
Website: www.chase.org.ar
E-mail: chase@onenet.com.ar

Chief Executive Officer:
Duncan B.C. Chase, CEO and President

Mission Statement: The objective of the Foundation is to promote, organize and facilitate by means of agreements made with other international organizations with similar aims, the exchange of students. The Foundation seeks to provide the opportunity to South American to students to access academic courses from the secondary school level to the post-graduate level, thus allowing students to acquire knowledge that would normally not be available to them in their country of origin. It is also the objective of the Foundation to inform and educate foreign students visiting Argentina about aspects of the Argentine way of life by providing selected local host families to receive them in their homes and provide the means of insertion in a family and educational environment.

Exchange Activities: The Chase Foundation provides scholarships and/or economic support to qualified students for whom participation in international academic programs will allow them to progress and provide a successful future in Argentina.

Club de Relaciones Culturales Internacionales – Language Connection

Ferraz 82
Madrid 28008
Spain

Fax: 34 91 5 59 11 81
E-mail: spain@clubrci.es

Chief Executive Officer:
Paloma Sierra Mendez, President

Mission Statement: The Club provides opportunities to live with Spanish families as Au Pairs and Language Assistants.

Exchange Programs and Activities: The Club sends Spanish students to the United States for language and Au Pair programs in partnership with the American Institute for Foreign Study. It also send students to summer camps in conjunction with InterExchange during summer months. The Club places American students in Spain as Au Pairs and language assistants and some of them attend Spanish universities in Alcala de Henares for further study in the Spanish language and culture.

Denmark's International Study Program (DIS)

Vestergade 7
DU-1456 Copenhagen K
Denmark

Tel.:   45 33 11 01 44   **Fax:** 45 33 93 26 24
Website: http://www.disp.dk
E-mail: dis@disp.dk

Chief Executive Officer:
Anders Uhrskov, Director

Mission Statement: Denmark's International Study Program (DIS) founded in 1959 and affiliated with the University of Copenhagen, is a nonprofit university institution recognized, supported and supervised by the Danish Ministry of Education. The DIS Board of Directors is appointed by the Ministry of Education, the Rector of the University of Copenhagen, the Rector of Copenhagen Business School, the Rector of the Royal Academy of Fine Arts, School of Architecture, the DIS faculty, the DIS staff, and the National Danish Student Union.

Exchange Programs and Activities: DIS provides programs in architecture and pre-architecture, interior design, business, marine and environmental biology and arctic geology, environmental studies, pre-medicine and public health, multi-cultural and special education, and in the humanities and social sciences, including specialty tracks in international relations, political science, environmental politics, modern European studies, psychology, and ethnic studies, the European arts, history and sociology. Field study and European, Eastern European, and Russian study tours are part of the DIS programs.

Deutscher Akademischer Austausch Dienst/ German Academic Exchange Service (DAAD)

Kennedyallee 50
Bonn 53175
Germany

Tel.:   49 228 882 0   **Fax:** 49 228 882 444
Website: http://www.daad.de
E-mail: postmaster@daad.de

Chief Executive Officer:
Dr. Christian Bode, Chief Executive Officer

U.S. OFFICES (DAAD)
German Academic Exchange Service
950 Third Avenue, New York, NY 10022

Tel.:   (212) 758-3223   **Fax:** (212) 755-5780
Website: http://www.daad.org
E-mail: daadny@daad.org

Director:
Britta Baron

Mission Statement: The German Academic Exchange Service (DAAD) is a joint organization of the German institutions of higher education. The purpose of the DAAD is to promote relations between these German institutions and higher education institutions abroad, primarily through the exchange of students and academics. The DAAD's priority goals include that of encouraging members of the international, young, up-and-coming academic elite to come to Germany for a study or research stay and, as far as possible, of keeping in contact with these people as life-long partners, as well as the goal of qualifying young German research scientists at the very best locations around the world in a spirit of tolerance and liberal-minded, cosmopolitan attitudes, of assisting the developing countries of the South as well as the reforming states of the East establish efficient higher education structures and, finally, the goal of maintaining or establishing German studies and the German language, literature and area studies at important foreign universities and colleges around the world at a level worthy of and appropriate for a great cultural nation.

Exchange Programs and Activities: The DAAD runs more than 200 programs, ranging from short-term exchanges for research or teaching purposes through to several year long doctorate scholarships for graduates from developing countries, from information visits by delegations of foreign university vice-chancellors through to the long-term regional programmers conceived to establish efficient higher education systems in the Third World. DAAD grants are available to faculty and students in Canada and the United States to participate in a wide variety of academic activities. Descriptions of these programs, application deadlines, and guidelines are available on the website (http://www.daad.org).

Did Deutsch-Institut (Did)

Hauptstr. 26
Stockstadt/Main
Bavaria 63811
Germany

Tel.: 49 0 6027 41 77 0
Fax: 49 0 6027 41 77 41
Website: www.did.de
E-mail: office@did.de

Chief Executive Officer:
Madeleine Kotter, Managing Director

Mission Statement: Did Deutsch-Institut has been devoted for 31 years to the imparting of German language and culture as well as offering insights into education and work in Germany. Did's aim has been to contribute to a widening of cultures and personal knowledge:

students coming from various countries in order to learn about Germany's language and culture learn at the same time to reflect upon their own cultural background as well as other cultures.

Exchange Programs and Activities: Did offers, in addition to short and long term language courses, special programs such as language courses with internship, academic year (guest at a German school and guest at a German university) and Au Pair/Demi Pair. Did works in worldwide cooperation with schools and universities as well as agents. Did administers a special program in conjunction with the University of Nebraska consisting of a 12 week language course for which students receive academic credit plus a 12 week internship.

Don Quijote-in-country Spanish Language Courses

Plaza San marcos 7
Apartado de Correos 333
Salamanca 37002
Spain

Tel.: 34 923 26 88 74 **Fax:** 34 923 26 06 74
Website: www.donquijote.org
E-mail: usa@donquijote.org

Chief Executive Officer:
Carmen Cantariño, dQ USA Director

Mission Statement: Don Quijote is the leading organization for Spanish language courses in Spain. With 15 years of experience, it runs year-round schools in Spain, including Barcelona, Granada, Madrid, Salamanca, Puerto la Cruz (Tenerife), Sevilla, Valencia and in Cuzco in Peru.

Exchange Programs and Activities: Don Quijote's intensive four hours per day course is available at all don Quijote schools, offering courses for beginners to advanced students. Students in the United States may earn college credit for Spanish through don Quijote. Don Quijote guarantees small groups (a maximum of eight per classroom), qualified, native-speakers as teachers, and multimedia classrooms. Students may live with Spanish host families, or in student flats. It offers supplementary extracurricular courses to encourage students to explore different aspects of Spanish culture and society. Don Quijote also offers additional formal courses related to business, the travel industry and other professional areas of interest.

Educational Exchange International e.V. (EEI)

Sedanstr. 31 - 33
Köln 50668
Germany

Tel.: 49 2217391958 68 **Fax:** 49 221 7391919
Website: http://www.eei.de
E-mail: nfo@eei.de

Chief Executive Officer:
Lilo Vey, Managing Director

Mission Statement: As a nonprofit organization, Educational Exchange International (EEI) aims to promote peace and understanding and reduce prejudice, distrust, and misunderstanding between young people from different cultures. EEI program participants have the unique opportunity to participate in the social life of another country. They share daily life, school and free time with their foreign hosts, an experience that fosters tolerance, openness, and personal growth. EEI allows only a small group of students to participate in its programs to guarantee intensive and personal care before, during, and after the stay.

Exchange Programs and Activities: The USA -

Long Term Program places 15 to 18 year-old German high school students in a local community in the U.S. The students live with a host family and study at a local high school for one academic year or one semester.

The USA - Easter Program is designed for students aged 15 to 17 who are interested in spending their Easter Vacation as a member of an American host family. They regularly attend local high schools for a three-week period. The students are organized in small groups and accompanied by a chaperone, who will also arrange group activities. Return visits from American student groups usually take place during the weeks preceding the German summer vacation.

The New Zealand and Australia programs allow 15 to 18 year-old German high school students to attend a high school in New Zealand or Australia for an academic year, semester or term while living with a local host family. The students participate in local, family, and school activities. The New Zealand program allows students to choose the region and school they would like to attend.

European Association for International Education (EAIE)

PO Box 11189
Amsterdam
1001 GD
The Netherlands

Tel.: 31 20 525 4999 **Fax:** 31 20 525 4998
Website: http://www.eaie.nl
E-mail: eaie@eaie.nl

Chief Executive Officer:
Alex Olde Kalter, Director

Mission Statement: The European Association for International Education (EAIE) is a nonprofit organization whose main aim is the stimulation and facilitation of the internationalisation of higher education in Europe and around the world, and to meet the professional needs of individuals active in international education. The Association seeks to enhance and defend the quality of international education by sup-

porting the professional activities of its members. It has a unique role within Europe in bringing together fellow-professionals in all aspects of the international relations of education, throughout the continent and beyond.

Exchange Activities: The EAIE promotes international education through: conferences and seminars; training courses; development of a coordinated training program; and research, consultancy and project management within the field. It also collects and disseminates information essential to members, such as publications; electronic networks, and enhancing competence in their use; and responds, reviews and makes recommendations on policies, programs and systems within the field of international education.

Experimento de Convivencia Internacional, A.C.

Varsovia 44-602, Col. Juarez,
Deleg. Cuauhtemoc 06600
Mexico

Tel.:   55 25 7373   **Fax:** 52-08-6332
Website: www.experimento.org.mx
E-mail: experime@mail.internet.com.mx

Mission Statement: The Experiment in International Living, since its inception almost 68 years ago, has been a catalyst for creative personal growth in people of all ages, cultures, and races. Its position as an international institution dedicated to intercultural understanding makes its positive contributions felt in individuals' lives, families, schools, communities, organizations, governments, and board rooms around the world. Its founder, Donald B. Watt, believed young people from different countries could learn from each other by sharing daily life experiences, speaking one another's languages, and enhancing their individual perceptions of the world through international exchange visits. He saw the home as a learning laboratory for collaboration and understanding.

Exchange Programs and Activities: Exchange programs include the Intensive Spanish Language Courses; High School Program (academic year or semester in a Mexican high school; each student lives with a family); Senior Citizen Programs (special interest group – history, arts, birds, etc.); Group Homestay; and Voluntary Social Work.

Fee – Sprachreisen Gmbh

Leibnizstr. 3
Stuttgart 70193
Germany

Tel.:   49 711 638048   **Fax:** 49 711 6366 597
Website: www.fee-sprachreisen.de
E-mail: info@fee-sprachreisen.de

Chief Executive Officer:
Brigitte Grimm, Chief Executive Officer

Mission Statement: Fee – Sprachreisen's mission is to promote the learning of languages and intercultural understanding.

Exchange Programs and Activities: Fee – Sprachreisen offers a high school year program for public and private schools; a college study program; short term individual/group programs; and homestays.

Gemeinnuetzige Gesellschaft fuer internationale Sprachstudien und Kulturaustausch (GGS)

Hoelderlinstr. 55
Stuttgart 70193
Germany

Tel.:   49 711 632125   **Fax:** 49 711 632125

Chief Executive Officer:
Dr. H. Kraemer, Chief Executive Officer

Mission Statement: GGS's mission is to promote the learning of languages and intercultural understanding and to support talented students by providing scholarships.

Exchange Programs and Activities: GGS offers a public high school year program.

Gesellschaft fur Internationale Jugendkontakte (GIJK)

Baunscheidtstr. 11
Bonn 53113
Germany

Tel.:   49 228 95 73 00
Fax: 49 228 95 73 018
Website: www.gijk.de
E-mail: info@gijk.de

Mission Statement: GIJK aims to provide the highest quality educational and cultural exchange programs to enrich the lives of people throughout the world.

Exchange programs and activities: GIJK recruits approximately 2,500 young Germans each year to participate in the following programs: Camp America; Resort America; Academic Year in America; and Au pair in America.

House of English Sprachreisen Gmbh

Hoelderlin Platz 2A
Stuttgart 70193
Germany

Tel.: 49 711 631089 **Fax:** 49 711 63 14 37

Chief Executive Officer:
Brigitte Grimm, Chief Executive Officer

Mission Statement: House of English Sprachreisen Gmbh promotes language learning and intercultural understanding

Exchange Programs and Activities: House of English Sprachreisen offers the following programs: public/private high school year program and college study programs.

Institute for American Universities (IAU)

27, Place de l'Universite
Aix-en-Provence 13100
France

Tel.: 4 42 23 39 35
Website: www.iau-univ.org
E-mail: iauadm@univ-aix.fr

U.S. Offices: IAU United States
P.O. Box 592
Evanston, IL 60204

Chief Executive Officer:
David Wilsford, President

Mission Statement: The Institute for American Universities (IAU) was founded in 1957 under the auspices of l'Universite d'Aix-Marseille. The IAU serves as a center for education abroad in the south of France for more than 700 North American colleges and universities and more than 12,000 American undergraduate students.

Exchange Programs and Activities: IAU is involved in the following exchange areas: Arts/Cultural, Language Study. It administers exchange programs for the following academic levels: Undergraduate Students. Exchange related services include courses for credit.

InterHispania

Zaragoza, 36 P 2
Barcelona 08006
Spain

Tel.: 34 93 416 18 66 **Fax:** 34 93 415 48 14
Website: www.interhispania.com
E-mail: info@interhispania.com

Chief Executive Officer:
Juan Rafols Raventos, Director

Mission Statement: InterHispania is an inbound company whose goal is to help foreign high school students who would like to spend a month, semester or a complete academic year in a host family and attend a local high school. InterHispania also can place students for a summer sports camp, language tours and language programs for adults.

Exchange Programs and Activities: InterHispania is involved in the following exchange activities: Homestay; Language Study; Short-Term Visitors; Sports; Student/Educators.

International Workshop of Ceramic Art in Tokoname (IWCAT)

c/o Tokoname Chamber of Commerce
and Industry
2:5-58 Shinkai-cho
Tokoname
Aichi 479-0837
Japan

Tel.: 05693 34 3200 **Fax:** 05693 34 3223
Website: http://www.japan-net.ne.jp/~iwat
E-mail: iwcat@japan-net.ne.jp

Chief Executive Officer:
Mr. Masaru Ichihara, Chairman

Mission Statement: The IWACT is a nonprofit volunteer group of Tokoname citizens founded in 1985. The purpose of the organization is to share the city's heritage, exchange ideas and work together to improve techniques while participating in various forms of the ceramic arts. The annual workshop is a valuable opportunity to experience daily life with a Japanese family for the period of the workshop.

Exchange Programs and Activities: Every summer, a ceramic workshop is offered for overseas participants at Tokoname, one of the six ancient kilns of Japan. Participants enjoy studio work including glazing, loading, firing, and unloading kilns during the one-month program. They stay in the homes of volunteer Japanese families.

Juventud Y Cultura (JYC)

c/Alcala, 42
Madrid 28014
Spain

Tel.:   91 5312886   **Fax:** 91 5327971
Website: www.juvycult.es
E-mail: juvycult@juvycult.es

Chief Executive Officer:
Mª Carmen Ferreiro, Secretario General

Mission Statement: Established in Madrid in 1977, Juventud Y Cultura is an organization dedicated primarily to youth. It firmly believes that traveling around the world with wise supervision is greatly enriching.

Exchange Programs and Activities: JYC offers the following programs: academic year; summer program; family life programs; and au pair.

Lotty Agency Educational and Work Exchange Programs

Mlynske Nivy 31
Bratislava 82109
Slovak Republic

Tel.:   421 2 5556 3939 **Fax:** 421 2 5556 5873
Website: www.lotty.sk
E-mail: lotty@nextra.sk

Chief Executive Officer:
Sarlota Elkova, Director

Mission Statement: Lotty´s mission is to facilitate international cooperation and understanding by providing Slovak youth with various educational and work exchange programs in 10 countries.

Exchange Programs and Activities: In the United States, Lotty works with Work&Travel, Camp Counselor, Au-Pair, and Language programs. In so doing, the Lotty contributes to a valuable exchange of international experiences, ideas, cultures, skills, and knowledge between U.S. citizens and Slovak youth.

Open Society Institute (OSI)

H-1397 Budapest, P.O. Box 519
Budapest 1051
Hungary

Tel.:   212 548 0175   **Fax:** 212 548 4652
Website: www.osi.hu/NSP
E-mail: scholar@osi.hu

U.S. Offices: Open Society Institute
Network Scholarship Programs
400 West 59th Street, New York, NY 10019
USA

Chief Executive Officer:
Martha Loerke, Director
Network Scholarship Programs

Mission Statement: The Open Society Institute – Budapest was established in 1993 to develop and implement programs in the areas of educational, social and legal reform. OSI-Budapest is part of the Soros foundations network, a group of autonomous organizations created and supported by George Soros and operating in nearly 60 countries around the world, principally in Central and Eastern Europe and the former Soviet Union, but also in Guatemala, Haiti, Mongolia, West and Southern Africa and the United States. The Network Scholarship Programs (NSP) fund students, scholars and professionals from Central and Eastern Europe, the former Soviet Union, Mongolia and Burma to participate in rigorous and competitive academic programs outside their home countries. NSP supports post-secondary studies and faculty development in the social sciences and humanities, professional degree programs in targeted fields, and supplemental grants to students. All network scholarships are granted via open, merit-based competitions with multi-tiered, impartial selection procedure. Students should review the website for further information on the awards available in their home country.

Exchange Programs and Activities: The following programs are administered by the NSP/Budapest office:
- OSI Chevening Awards: up to 50 one-year sponsored research grants, and 60 MA degree awards for study in the United Kingdom.
- DAAD-OSI Awards: up to 100 grants over two years for study in Germany. Awards are offered in the Caucasus and Central Asia to follow postgraduate studies.
- OSI/CNOUS Awards: (Uzbekistan only) up to 10 awards to study at the Masters and Doctorate levels
- American University in Bulgaria
- Soros Supplementary Grants Program: up to 20 awards to students from Central and Eastern Europe, former Soviet Union and Mongolia who are studying within the region but outside of their home countries.

Southern Cross Cultural Exchange (SCCE)

14 Ranelagh Drive
MT Eliza Vic. 3930
Australia

Tel.:   61 3 9775 4711   **Fax:** 61 3 9775 4971
Website: www.scce.com.au
E-mail: scceaust@scce.com.au

Chief Executive Officer:
Betty Lane, National Director

Mission Statement: The mission statement of Southern Cross Cultural Exchange is to further tolerance; to challenge youth towards international understanding and further learning; to provide self-knowledge and awareness.

The Swedish Institute

P O Box 7434
Stockholm SE-113 24
Sweden

Tel.:   46 8 789 2000   **Fax:** 46 8 204872
Website: www.si.se
E-mail: si@si.se

Chief Executive Officer:
Mr. Erland Ringborg, Director General

Mission Statement: The Swedish Institute is a public agency entrusted with disseminating knowledge abroad about Sweden and organizing exchanges with other countries in the spheres of culture, education, research and public life in general. The institute is also charged by the Ministry of Education with responsibility for spreading information about the Swedish higher education system.

Exchange Programs and Activities: The Swedish Institute administers the Guest Scholarship Program which is open to U.S. citizens. In addition, the Swedish Institute disseminates information about studying in Sweden and about Sweden in general. For more information on the Guest Scholarship Program, including application deadlines and scholarship criteria, please contact the Swedish Institute.

Section IV
Foreign Affairs Agencies

Federal foreign affairs agencies are responsible for much federally-sponsored international exchange activity, including the facilitation and administration of U.S.-sponsored exchange programs. Through formal and public diplomacy, foreign affairs agencies aim to create a more secure, prosperous, and democratic world for the American people. To that end, foreign affairs agencies explain and execute official U.S. foreign policy and national security interests, provide support services to Americans abroad, and promote mutual understanding between the U.S. and other countries through a wide range of diplomatic, cultural, educational, and information programs. Additionally, these agencies support the people of developing and transitional countries in their efforts to achieve economic and social progress and to participate more fully in resolving the problems of their countries and the world. This section also profiles relevant branches of the Immigration and Naturalization Service, an agency which facilitates the entry of exchange visitors to the United States.

While the information provided is correct at the time of publication, offices and personnel are subject to change.

AGENCY FOR INTERNATIONAL DEVELOPMENT
Ronald Reagan Federal Building
1300 Pennsylvania Avenue, NW
Washington, DC 20523-3901
202/712-0000
www.info.usaid.gov

All telephone numbers are in area code 202 unless specified otherwise.

Office of the Administrator
Administrator
    Andrew S. Natsios,
    Room 6.09-010......................................712-4040
Chief of Staff
    Douglas J. Aller, Room 6.08-025.............712-5090
Deputy Administrator
    Janet Ballantyne (Acting),
    Room 6.09-025......................................712-4070
Counselor
    Janet Ballantyne, Room 6.08-029............712-0089

Office of the General Counsel
General Counsel
    John Gardner,
    Room 6.06-125......................................712-4476
Deputy General Counsel
    Patricia Ramsey, Room 6.06-123.............712-1903
Deputy General Counsel
    Drew W. Luten, Room 6.06-127 712-4698
Assistant General Counsel for Africa
    Mary Alice Kleinjan, Room 6.06-093 712-4700
Assistant General Counsel for Asia and Near East
    Michael Williams, Room 6.06-013..........712-4266
Assistant General Counsel for Europe/Newly
    Independent States
    Margaret Alexander, Room 6.06-095 712-4700
Assistant General Counsel for Food and
    Humanitarian Response
    Gary Winter, Room 6.06-015.................712-0900
Assistant General Counsel for Global
    Michael Kitay, Room 6.06-096...............712-5019
Assistant General Counsel for
    Latin America and Carribean
    Belinda Barrington, Room 6.06-0291......712-0170
Assistant General Counsel for Legislation and Policy
    Robert M. Lester, Room 6.06-070...........712-4984

Bureau for Policy and Program Coordination
Assistant Administrator
    Patrick M. Cronin, Room 6.08-113.........712-1430
Office of Development Partners
Director
    Norman K. Nicholson,
    Room 6.08-075....................................712-04233
Office of Program Coordination
Director
    Skip Waskin, Room 6.07-014..................712-4976
Center for Development Information and Evaluation
Director
    Gerald Britan, Room 6.07-154................712-1158
    Development Information and Outreach Division
    Chief
        Lee White, Room 6.07-105.............712-4627
    Performance Measurement and Evaluation Division
    Chief
        Dan Blumhagen, Room 6.07-131...712-5816
    Program and Operations Assessment Division
    Chief
        Jean DuRette, Room 6.07-153 712-4276

Bureau for Global Programs, Field Support and Research
Assistant Administrator
    Barbara Turner (Acting),
    Room 3.08-008....................................712-1190
Center for Democracy and Governance
Deputy Assistant Administrator
    James Vermillion (Acting),
    Room 3.10-008....................................712-1892
Center for Economic Growth and Agricultural Development
Deputy Assistant Administrator
    Jonathan Conly (Acting),
    Room 2.10-085....................................712-1140

Center for Human Capacity Development

Deputy Assistant Administrator
Donald "Buff" Mackenzie,
Room 3.09-036......................712-0236
Basic Education Team Leader
Gregory Loos, Room 3.09-079 712-4175
Higher Education Team Leader
Gary W. Bittner, Room 3.09-092 712-1556
Training Team Leader
David Songer, Room 3.09-101 712-4154
Information Technology Team Leader
Anthony Meyer, Room 3.10-014 712-4137

Bureau for Humanitarian Response

Assistant Administrator
Leonard M. Rogers (Acting),
Room 8.06-086....................................712-0100
Office of American Schools and Hospitals Abroad
Director
Mable Meares, Room 8.07-091 712-0510
Office of Food for Peace
Director
Tom Oliver, Room 7.06-157 712-5340
Office of Foreign Disaster Assistance
Director
Tamra Halmraft-Sanchez (Acting),
Room 8.06-017......................................712-0400
Office of Private and Voluntary Cooperation
Director
Judith W. Gilmore, Room 7.06-062........712-0840
Office of Program, Planning and Evaluation
Director
Lowell E. Lynch, Room 8.06-095...........712-4599
Advisory Committee on Voluntary Foreign Aid
Chairman
William Reese ....(410) 347-1500
Coordinator
Noreen O`Meara, Room 7.06-084..........712-5979

Bureau for Legislative and Public Affairs

Assistant Administrator
Edward Fox (Nominated),
Room 6.10-106.....................................712-4300
Deputy Assistant Administrator, Congressional Affairs
Robert Lester (Acting), Suite 6.10 712-4300
Deputy Assistant Administrator, Communications
Joanne Giordano, Suite 6.10 712-4300

Congressional Liaison Division

Deputy Assistant Administrator
Suzanne Smith Palmieri, David Liner
Room 6.10A 712-4028
Africa Legislative Program Specialist
Liz Baltimore,
Room 6.10A 712-0093
Asia & Near East, Global,
Peace Corps Legislative Program Specialist
Dorothy Rayburn, Room 6.10A 712-4416
Europe & New Independent States
Legislative Program Specialist
Todd Shelton, Room 6.10A....................712-4035
Joel Stark, Room 6.10A 712-5152
Public Liaison Division
Chief
Vacant, Room 6.10A..............................712-4427
Human Capacity Development Public Affairs Officer
(Vacant), Room 6.10A............................712-4018
Press Relations Division
Chief
Michelle King, Room 6.10 712-5139
....712-5152

Bureau for Sub-Saharan Africa

Assistant Administrator
Valerie Dickson-Horton (Acting),
Room 4.08-031 712-0500
Office of Development Planning
Director
James T. Smith Jr., Room 4.08-046.........712-0230
Office of Sustainable Development
Director
Thomas Park, Room 4.06-119.................712-1803
Office of Eastern Africa Affairs
Director
Pamela Callen, Room 4.07-014 712-0410
Office of Southern Africa Affairs
Director
Carole Palma, Room 4.07-004................712-4790
Office of West Africa Affairs
Director
Erna Kerst, Room 4.06-001....................712-0220

SECTION 4

Bureau for Asia and the Near East

Assistant Administrator
Lori A. Forman, Room 4.09-034 712-0200

Office of East and South Asian Affairs

Director
Peter Lapera, Room 4.10-007.................712-1990

Office of Middle East Affairs

Director
Kimberly Finan, Room 4.10-003.............712-0050

**Secretariat for U.S.-
Asia Environmental Partnership**

Director
Peter Kimm, Room 4.10-001..................712-0270

Bureau for Europe and Eurasia

Assistant Administrator
Linda E. Morse (Acting),
Room 5.06-193 712-0290

Office of Democracy and Governance

Director
Gerald Hymand, Room 5.07-118 712-1501

Office of Market Transition

Director
William Frej, Room 5.08-101..................712-1332

**Office of Environment, Energy
and Social Transition**

Director
Gene George, Room 5.10-053...........712-0070

Office of European Country Affairs

Director
Ron Ullrich, Room 5.06-015...................712-4115

Office of New Independent States Country Affairs

Director
Robin Phillips, Room 5.06-157...............712-1703

Office of Operations and Management

Director
Barry MacDonald, Room 5.06-151.........712-4894

Office of Program Coordination and Strategy

Director
Dianne Tsitsos, Room 5.06-055..............712-0367

**Office of Strategic Planning,
Ops and Tech Support**

Director
William Jeffers, Room 4.09-043 712-1843

Bureau for Latin America and the Carribean

Assistant Administrator
J. Michael Deal (Acting),
Room 5.09-12......................................712-4800

Office of Carribean Affairs

Director
John Cloutier, Room 5.08-032................712-5362

Office of Central American Affairs

Director
Peter Kranstover, Room 5.08-086...........712-0478

Office of South American and Mexican Affairs

Director
Oliver Carduner, Room 5.08-068 712-0478

Office of Regional Sustainable Development

Director
Letitia Butler, Room 5.09-055 712-1706

Strategy and Program Office

Director
Rosalie Fanale, Room 5.08-002 712-4768

SECTION

4

DEPARTMENT OF STATE

2201 C Street, NW
Washington, DC 20520
Tel.:   202/647-6575
       202/647-4000 (24-hour service)
Fax: 202/647-7120   **Website:** www.state.gov

All area codes are 202, unless otherwise listed.

Secretary
       Colin Powell, Room 7726 647-5291
Deputy Secretary
       Richard Armitage, Room 7220 647-9641
Under Secretary for Arms Control and
       International Security Affairs
       John Bolton, Room 7208 647-1049
Under Secretary for Economics, Business, and
       Agricultural Affairs
       Alan Larson, Room 7256......................647-7575
Under Secretary for Global Affairs
       Paula Dobriansky, Room 7250..............647-6240
Under Secretary for Management
       Grant Greene, Room 7207 647-1500
Under Secretary for Political Affairs
       Marc Grossman, Room 7240.................647-2471
Under Secretary for Public Diplomacy
       and Public Affairs
       Charlotte Beers 647-9199

BUREAU OF EDUCATIONAL AND CULTURAL AFFAIRS

U.S. Department of State
301 4th Street, SW, (State Annex 44)
Washington, DC 20547
Tel.: 203-5118 **Fax.:** 203-5115
Website: ....http://exchanges.state.gov

Bureau of Educational and Cultural Affairs

Assistant Secretary
  Patricia de Stacy Harrison, Room 800 ...203-5118
Secretary
  Ellen Ansah-Twum, Room 800 203-5118
Principal Deputy Assistant Secretary
  Vacant, Room 800 203-5118
Executive Assistant
  Vacant, Room 800 203-5111
Special Assistant
  Matt Hoyt, Room 800 203-5109
Special Assistant
  Mike Graham, Room 800 203-5108
Staff Assistant
  Mary Grant, Room 800 203-5106
Public Affairs Advisor
  Catherine Stearns, Room 800 203-5107

Office of the Executive Director

Executive Director
  David Whitten, Room 536.....................619-4949

Administrative Support Branch Chief
  Karen Starkey, Room 534 619-4948

Program Management Staff Chief
  Michael Weider, Room 534 619-4947

J. William Fulbright Foreign Scholarship Board
Staff Director
  Pat Kern Schaefer, Room 247 619-4290
Deputy Staff Director
  Lesley Moore Vossen, Room 247 619-4290

Deputy Assistant Secretary for Academic Programs

Acting Deputy Assistant Secretary
  Marianne Craven, Room 202.................619-6409
Managing Director
  Vacant, Room 202 619-6409

Office of Academic Exchange Programs
Office Director
  Barry Ballow, Room 234 619-4360
Senior Policy and Budget Officer
  Rosalind Swenson, Room 234................619-5384

Africa Programs Branch
Branch Chief
  Ellen Berelson, Room 232.....................619-5355
Senior Program Officer
  Ann Martin, Room 232 619-5355

East Asian Programs Branch
Branch Chief
  Patricia Garon, Room 208 619-5402
Senior Program Officer
  Tim Marshall, Room 208 619-5402

European Programs Branch
Branch Chief
  Jocelyn Greene, Room 246.....................619-4420
Senior Program Officer
  Nadine Asef-Sargent, Room 246 619-4420

Near Eastern/South Asian Programs Branch
Branch Chief
  John Sedlins, Room 212 619-5368
Senior Program Officer
  Anthony Kluttz, Room 212....................619-5368

Study of the United States
Branch Chief
  William Bate, Room 252 619-4557
Senior Program Officer
  Richard Taylor, Room 252.....................619-4557

Western Hemisphere Programs Branch
Branch Chief
  Cynthia Wolloch, Room 314..................619-5365
Senior Program Officer
  Debra Shetler, Room 314 619-5365

Office of Global Educational Programs
Division Chief
  Mary Ashley, Room 349........................619-5434

Educational Information and Resources Branch
Branch Chief
Beatrice Camp, Room 349.....................619-5434
Senior Program Officer
Catherine Friend, Room 349 619-5434

Humphrey Fellowships and Institutional Linkages Branch
Branch Chief
Paul Hiemstra, Room 349.....................619-5289
Senior Program Officer
Jonathan Cebra, Room 349 619-5289

Teacher Exchange Branch
Branch Chief
Jochen Hoffman, Room 349 619-4556
Senior Program Officer
Vacant, Room 349 619-4556

Office of English Language Programs
Office Director
Janet Wilgus, Room 304........................619-5887

Materials Development and Review Branch
William P. Ancker, Room 304................619-5892

Programs Branch
Kenneth Michael Jenson, Room 304......619-5886

Deputy Assistant Secretary for Professional and Cultural Exchanges
Deputy Assistant Secretary
Brian J. Sexton, Room 220 619-5348

Office of Citizen Exchanges
Office Director
Van S. Wunder III, Room 220................619-5348

Russia/Eurasia Division
Chief
Chris Miner 619-4572

European, Near East/South Asia/ Africa Division
Chief
Curtis Huff 619-5319

American Republics/East Asia Division
Chief
Raymond Harvey 619-5326

Cultural Programs Division
Chief
Mark McGrath, Room 568 619-4809

NIS Secondary School Initiative Division
Chief
Robert Persiko, Room 568 619-6299

Office of International Visitors
Acting Office Director
Kathleen Brion, Room 255 619-5217

Program Resources Branch
Branch Chief
Carmen Marrero, Room 266 619-5220

New York Reception Center
Director
Donna Shirrefs, Room 266.............212-399-5750

Voluntary Visitors Division
Division Chief
Deborah Underhill, Room 266 619-4582

Africa/Europe Branch
Branch Chief
Eileen Connolly, Room 266 619-4582

Western Hemisphere, East Asia/NearEast Asia Branch
Chief
Theresa Johnson, Room 266..................619-4582

Group Projects Division
Division Chief
Janet Beard, Room 255...........................619-6285

Grant Programs Division
Division Chief
Nan Bell, Room 271 619-5247

Africa Branch
Branch Chief
Mary H. Johnson, Room 268.................619-5243

East Asia Branch
Terry Blatt, Room 270...........................619-5241

Europe Branch
Branch Chief
Carol Grabauskas, Room 255 619-5247

Near East/ South Asia Branch
Branch Chief
>   Leslie McBee, Room 265........................619-5237

Western Hemisphere Branch
Branch Chief
>   Essie Wilkes-Scott, Room 267................619-5245

Office of Policy and Evaluation
Office Director
>   Robert E. McCarthy, Room 357.............619-5307

Exchange Visitor Program Services
Program Designation Branch
>   Chief Sally Lawrence, Room 734...........401-9810

Program Designation Officer
>   Dianne Culkin, Room 734.....................401-9810

Program Designation Officer
>   Vicki Rose, Room 734 401-9810

Program Designation Officer
>   Brenda Bragg, Room 734.....................401-9810

Program Designation Officer
>   Margaret Duell, Room 734....................401-9810

Program Designation Officer
>   Karen Hawkins, Room 734...................401-9810

Program Designation Officer
>   Gina Stephens, Room 734 401-9810

Waiver Review Branch Chief
>   Marcia Pryce, Room 734 401-9810

BUREAU OF CONSULAR AFFAIRS

U.S. Department of State
2201 C Street, NW
Washington, DC 20520
Tel.:   202/647-7948
           202/647-4000 (24-hour operator)
Fax: 202/647-7120
Website: www.state.gov

Overseas Citizen Services

American Citizen Services...........................647-5226
Director
     Patrick Hegarty, Room 4800..................647-9019

Passport Services

General Information and Inquiries
(\$.35/minute for recorded information and
\$1.05/minute for operator)..................900/225-5674

Deputy Assistant Secretary
     Georgia Rogers, Room 6811 ....

Visa Services

General information...................................663-1225
Deputy Assistant Secretary
     Vacant, Room 6811

Selected Country Offices

Afghanistan..647-9552
Albania (Tirana) 647-3747
Algeria (Algiers) 647-4680
Angola (Luanda)..647-9852
Argentina (Buenos Aires)...........................647-2296
Armenia (Yerevan) 647-6758
Australia (Canberra) 647-9690
Austria (Vienna) 647-2448
Azerbaijan (Baku)..647-6048
Bahrain (Manama) 647-6571
Bangladesh (Dhaka) 647-9552
Belarus (Minsk)...646-4443
Belgium (Brussels)......................................647-6592
Bhutan...647-2351
Bolivia (La Paz) 647-4193
Bosnia and Herzegovina (Sarajevo) 646-7024
Botswana (Gaborone) 647-8432
Brazil (Brasilia)...647-1926
Bulgaria (Sofia)...647-4850
Burkina Faso (Ouagadougou)......................647-0033

Burma (Rangoon) 647-0056
Burundi (Bujumbura) 647-3139
Cambodia (Phnom Penh)............................646-7056
Cameroon (Yaounde) 647-1707
Canada (Ottawa) 647-3135
Chad (N'Djamena) 647-1707
Chile (Santiago) 647-2296
China (Beijing) 647-6803
Colombia (Bogota) 647-4173
Costa Rica (San Jose) 647-3518
Cote d'Ivoire (Abidjan) 647-0033
Croatia (Zagreb) 647-2452
Cuba (Havana) 647-7479
Cyprus (Nicosia)..647-6948
Czech Republic (Prague)..............................647-1457
Denmark (Copenhagen) 647-8431
Dominican Republic (Santo Domingo) 647-4728
Ecuador (Quito)...647-4176
Egypt (Cairo) 647-4261
El Salvador (San Salvador)...........................647-3505
Eritrea (Asmara) 647-8852
Ethiopia (Addis Ababa)................................647-6485
Fiji (Suva)..647-3546
Finland (Helsinki) 647-5669
France (Paris) 647-4372
Gabon (Libreville) 647-3139
Gambia, The (Banjul) 647-0033
Georgia (Tbilisi) 647-6795
Germany (Bonn)..647-2622
Ghana (Accra) 647-2865
Greece (Athens) 647-6970
Guatemala (Guatemala City) 647-3559
Guinea (Conakry)...647-2865
Guyana (Georgetown) 647-4757
Haiti (Port-au-Prince)..................................646-4628
Honduras (Tegucigalpa)...............................647-0087
Hong Kong (Hong Kong)..............................647-8775
Hungary (Budapest) 647-3238
Iceland (Reykjavik)......................................647-8378
India (New Delhi) 647-2141
Indonesia (Jakarta) 647-3276
Iran...647-9449
Ireland (Dublin) 647-6587
Israel (Tel Aviv)...647-3672
Italy (Rome)..647-4395
Jamaica (Kingston) 647-4755
Japan (Tokyo)..647-2913
Jordan (Amman)..647-1022
Kazakstan (Almaty) 647-6859
Kenya (Nairobi)...647-8852
Korea, North...647-7717

SECTION 4

Korea, South (Seoul) 647-7717
Kuwait (Kuwait) 647-6571
Kyrgyzstan (Bishkek) 647-6740
Laos (Vientiane) 647-0036
Lebanon (Beirut) 647-1030
Liberia (Monrovia) 647-2865
Luxembourg (Luxembourg) 647-6557
Macedonia (Skopje) 647-2452
Malaysia (Kuala Lumpur) 647-2927
Mali (Bamako)....................................647-0033
Mexico (Mexico, D.F.) 647-9894
Micronesia, Federated States of (Kolonia) 646-4741
Moldova (Chisinau) 647-6733
Monaco..647-4361
Mongolia (Ulaanbaatar) 647-6782
Morocco (Rabat)..................................647-1724
Mozambique (Maputo) 647-8434
Namibia (Windhoek) 647-8432
Nepal (Kathmandu) 647-1450
Netherlands (The Hague) 647-6557
New Zealand (Wellington) 647-9690
Nicaragua (Managua) 647-4975
Niger (Niamey) 647-4567
Nigeria (Abuja)....................................647-4567
Norway (Oslo).....................................647-6582
Oman (Muscat) 647-6571
Pakistan (Islamabad) 647-9552
Panama (Panama City)..........................647-3519
Papua New Guinea (Port Moresby)..........647-9690
Paraguay (Asuncion) 647-2401
Peru (Lima) 647-4177
Philippines (Manila) 647-2301
Poland (Warsaw) 647-4139
Portugal (Lisbon) 647-2632
Romania (Bucharest) 647-4272
Russia (Moscow) 647-9806
Rwanda (Kigali)...................................647-3139
Saudi Arabia (Riyadh) 647-7550
Senegal (Dakar) 647-0033
Serbia (incl. Montenegro) 647-7479
Singapore (Singapore)..........................647-2927
Slovakia (Bratislava) 647-3191
Slovenia (Ljubljana).............................647-7152
Somalia 647-8852
South Africa (Pretoria).........................647-8432
Spain (Madrid) 647-1419
Sri Lanka (Colombo) 647-2351
Sudan (Khartoum) 647-8852
Sweden (Stockholm) 647-8178
Switzerland (Bern)...............................647-0425

Syria (Damascus).................................647-1131
Tajikistan (Dushanbe)..........................647-6757
Tanzania (Dar es Salaam)......................647-6473
Thailand (Bangkok) 647-2036
Togo (Lome) 647-0033
Trinidad and Tobago (Port-of-Spain)..........647-4757
Tunisia (Tunis)....................................647-4674
Turkey (Ankara) 647-5120
Turkmenistan (Ashgabat)......................647-6740
Uganda (Kampala)................................647-8852
Ukraine (Kiev) 647-9049
United Arab Emirates (Abu Dhabi) 647-6572
United Kingdom (London)......................647-6587
Uruguay (Montevideo)..........................647-2401
Uzbekistan (Tashkent) 647-6765
Venezuela (Caracas)..............................647-4216
Vietnam (Hanoi)..................................647-1699
Yemen (Sanaa) 647-6558
Zambia (Lusaka) 647-8432
Zimbabwe (Harare) 647-8432

FULBRIGHT BINATIONAL EDUCATIONAL FOUNDATIONS AND COMMISSIONS

In most countries of the world, the Fulbright program is administered by a binational Fulbright Commission. In countries without a Fulbright Commission, the program is administered by the Public Diplomacy Section of the U.S. Embassy.

Argentina

Dr. Norma Gonzalez, Executive Director
Commission for Educational Exchange Between the United States and the Argentine Republic
Viamonte 1653, Piso 2
1055 Buenos Aires, CF, Argentina

Tel: 54-11-4814-3561
Fax: 54-11-4814-1377
E-mail: ngonzalez@fulbright.com.ar
Website: http://www.fulbright.edu.ar/

Australia

Mr. Mark Darby, Executive Director
Australian Fulbright Commission
PO Box 9541 (1st Floor, 6 Napier Close)
Deakin ACT 2600, Australia

Tel: 02-6260-4460
Fax: 02-6260-4461
E-mail: fulbright@aaef.anu.edu.au
Website: http://www.fulbright.com.au

Austria

Dr. Lonnie Johnson,
Austrian-American Educational Commission
Schmidgasse 14
A1082 Vienna, Austria

Tel: 43-1-31339-732685
Fax: 43-1-4087-765
E-mail: lrj@usia.co.at
Website: http://www.oead.ac.at/Fulbright

Belgium and Luxembourg

Ms. Margaret Nicholson, Executive Director
Commission for Educational Exchange Between the United States of America, Belgium and Luxembourg
Royal Library Albert Ier
Boulevard de l'Empereur 4
B-1000 Brussels, Belgium

Tel: 32-2-519-57-70
Fax: 32-2-519-57-73
E-mail: fulbright@kbr.be
Website: http://www.kbr.be/fulbright

Brazil

Mr. Marco Antonio da Rocha, Executive Director
Fulbright Commission, Brazil
Ed. Casa Thomas Jefferson
SHIS QI 09 - Conj. 17 - Lote "L"
71625-170 - Brasília-DF, Brazil

Tel: 55-61-364-3824
Fax: 55-61-364-5292
E-mail: fulbright@brnet.com.br
Website: http://www.info.lncc.br/Fulbright

Bulgaria

Dr. Julia Stefanova, Executive Director
The Bulgarian-American Commission for Educational Exchange
Ministry of Culture
17 Alexander Stamboliiski Boulevard
1000 Sofia, Bulgaria

Tel: 359-2-981-85-67
Fax: 359-2-988-45-17
E-mail: jstefanova@fulbrsof.bol.bg
Website: http://www.fulbright-bg.org/

SECTION 4

Canada

Professor Michael Hawes, Acting Executive Director
Foundation for Educational Exchange Between
Canada and the United States of America
350 Albert Street, Suite 2015
Ottawa, Ontario K1R 1A4 Canada

Tel: 613-237-5366
Fax: 613-237-2029
E-mail: mhawes@fulbright.ca
Website:
http://www.usembassycanada.gov/content/content.asp
?section = fulbright&document = index

Chile

Dr. Denise Saint-Jean Matzen, Executive Director
Commission for Educational Exchange Between the
United States of America and Chile
Victoria Subercaseaux 41, Piso 4
Santiago (Casilla 2121), Chile

Tel: 562-633-0379
Fax: 562-638-0580
E-mail: dstjean@fulbrightchile.cl
Website: http://www.fulbrightchile.cl/

Colombia

Dr. Agustin Lombana, Executive Director
Commission for Educational Exchange Between the
United States of America and Colombia
Calle 38, #13-37, Piso 11
Bogota, Colombia

Tel: 571-287-7831
Fax: 571-287-3520
E-mail: alombana@fulbright.edu.co
Website:
http://usembassy.state.gov/posts/co1/wwwhfulb.html

Cyprus

Mr. Daniel Hadjittofi, Executive Director
Commission for Educational Exchange Between the
United States of America and Cyprus
2 Egypt Avenue
P.O. Box 24051
CY 1700 Nicosia, Cyprus

Tel: 357-2-663-605
Fax: 357-2-669-151
Email: cfc@fulbright.org.cy
Website: http://www.fulbright.org.cy/

Czech Republic

Dr. Hana Ripkova, Executive Director
J. William Fulbright Commission for Educational
Exchange in the Czech Republic
Taboritska 23
130 87 Praha 3, Czech Republic

Tel: 420-2-697-6526
Fax: 420-2-697-5600
E-mail: fulbright@fulbright.cz
ripkova@fulbright.cz
Website: http://fulbright.cz/

Denmark

Ms. Marie Monsted, Executive Director
Denmark-America Foundation/Danish American
Fulbright Commission
Fiolstraede 24, 3 sal
DK-1171 Copenhagen, Denmark

Tel: 45-33-12-82-23
Fax: 45-33-32-53-23
E-mail: daf-fulb@daf-fulb.dk
Website: http://www.daf-fulb.dk/Home_English.html

Ecuador

Ms. Susana Cabeza de Vaca, Executive Director
Commission for Educational Exchange Between the
United States of America and Ecuador
Av. Diego de Almagro 961 y Av. Colon
Quito (PO Box 17-079081), Ecuador

Tel: 593-2-222-103
Fax: 593-2-508-149
E-mail: scdevaca@fulbright.org.ec
Website:
http://www.usis.org.ec/Spanish/fulbright/indexful.htm

Egypt

Dr. Ann Bos Radwan, Executive Director
Commission for Educational and Cultural Exchange
between the United States of America and the Arab
Republic of Egypt
20 Gamal El Din Abou El Mahasin Street
Garden City, Cairo, Egypt

Tel: 20-2-354-8679
Fax: 20-2-355-7893
E-mail: bfceexec@frcu.eun.eg
Website: http://www.frcu.eun.eg/www/organiza-
tions/fulbrightegypt/linkpage.htm

Finland

Ms. Leila Mustanoja, Executive Director
Fulbright Center
Kaisaniemenkatu 3 (Fifth floor)
00100 Helsinki, Finland

Tel: 358-9-5494-7400
Fax: 358-9-5494-7474
E-mail: office@fulbright.fi
Website:
http://www.fulbright.fi/uusi/englanti/index.html

France

Mr. Arnaud Roujou de Boubee, Executive Director
Franco-American Commission for Educational
Exchange
9, rue Chardin, 75016
Paris, France

Tel: 33-l-44-145-360
Fax: 33-1-42-880-479
E-mail: cfa@fulbright.worldnet.fr
Website:
http://www.fulbright-france.com/edefault.htm

Germany

Dr. Georg Schuette, Executive Director
Commission for Educational Exchange between the
United States of America and the Federal Republic of
Germany, Fulbright-Kommission
Oranienburger Str. 13/14
D-10178 Berlin, Germany

Tel: 49-30-284443-0
Fax: 49-30-284443-42
E-mail: fulkom@fulbright.de
Website: http://www.fulbright.de

Greece

Ms. Artemis Zenetou, Executive Director
U.S. Educational Foundation in Greece
6 Vassilissis Sofias Avenue
106 74 Athens, Greece

Tel: 30-1-724-1811, 1812
Fax: 30-1-7226-510
E-mail: fbright@compulink.gr
Website: http://www.theasis.gr/fulbright

Hungary

Dr. Huba Bruckner, Executive Director
Hungarian-American Commission for
Educational Exchange
H-1146 Budapest
Ajtosi Durer Sor 19-21, Hungary

Tel: 36-1-462-8040
Fax: 36-1-252-0266
E-mail: hbruckner@fulbright.huninet.hu
Website: http://www.fulbright.hu

Iceland

Ms. Lara Jonsdottir, Executive Director
Iceland-United States Educational Commission
Laugavegur 59
101 Reykjavik, Iceland

Tel: 354-552-0830
Fax: 354-552-0886
E-mail: stella@fulbright.is
Website: http://www.fulbright.is

India

Prof. Jane E. Schukoske, Executive Director
United States Educational Foundation in India
"Fulbright House"
12 Hailey Road
New Delhi, 110001, India

Tel: 91-11-332-8944
Fax: 91-11-332-9718
E-mail: info@fulbright-india.org
Website: http://www.fulbright-india.org/

Indonesia

Dr. Sri Pamoedjo Rahardjo, Executive Director
American-Indonesian Exchange Foundation
Balai Pustaka Building, Sixth Floor
Jl. Gunung Sahari Raya No. 4
Jakarta 10720, Indonesia

Tel: 021-345-2016
Fax: 021-345-2050
E-mail: rahardjo@aminef.or.id
Website: http://www.usembassyjakarta.org/aminef/

SECTION 4

Ireland

Mr. Carmel Coyle, Executive Director
The Ireland-United States Commission for
Educational Exchange
79 St. Stephen's Green
Dublin 2, Ireland

Tel: 353-14-780-822
Fax: 353-14-082-611
E-mail: carmel.coyle@iveagh.irlgov.ie
Website: http://www.ucd.ie/~fulbright/

Israel

Dr. Neal Sherman, Executive Director
U.S.-Israel Educational Foundation (USIEF)
P.O.B. 26160
Tel Aviv 61261, Israel

Tel: 972-3-517-2392
Fax: 972-3-516-2016
E-mail: info@FULBRIGHT.ORG.IL
Website: http://www.fulbright.org.il/index1.html/

Italy

Ms. Laura Miele, Executive Director
Commission for Educational and Cultural Exchange
Between Italy and the United States of America
Via Castelfidardo 8
00185 Rome, Italy

Tel: 39-06-48-88-211
Fax: 39-06-48-15-680
E-mail: fulbright@fulbright.it
Website: http://www.fulbright.it/

Japan

Mr. Samuel M. Shepherd, Executive Director
Japan-United States Educational Commission
Sanno Grand Building 206
2-14-2 Nagata-cho, Chiyoda-ku
Tokyo 100-0014, Japan

Tel: 81-03-3580-3231
Fax: 81-03-3580-3231
E-mail: edo@jusec.org
Website: http://www.jusec.org/indexe.html/

Jordan

Mr. Alain McNamara, Executive Director
Jordanian-American Commission for
Educational Exchange (JACEE)
19, Mahdi Bin Barakah Street
P.O. Box 850215
Shmeisani, Amman 11185, Jordan

Tel: 962-6-568-4760
Fax: 962-6-568-4820
E-mail: fulbright@nets.com.jo
Website: http://www.fulbright-jordan.org/

Korea

Dr. Horace H. Underwood, Executive Director
Korean-American Educational Commission
Fulbright Building
168-15 Yomni-dong, Mapo-gu
Seoul 121-874 Korea

Tel: 82-2-3275-4000
Fax: 82-2-3275-4028
E-mail: admin@fulbright.or.kr
Website: http://www.fulbright.or.kr

Malaysia

Dr. Donald McCloud, Executive Director
Malaysian-American Commission on
Educational Exchange
Eighth Floor, Menara John Hancock
No. 6, Jalan Gelenggang
Damansara Heights
50490 Kuala Lumpur, Malaysia

Tel: 60-3-253-8107
Fax: 60-3-253-8423
E-mail: edmacee@pc.jaring.my
Website: http://www.macee.org.my

SECTION

4

Mexico

Vacant, Executive Director
Mexico - United States Commission for
Educational and Cultural Exchange
Benjamin Franklin Library
Londres 16, P.B. Colonia Juárez
C.P. 06600 Mexico, DF, Mexico
also: PO Box 3087
Laredo, TX 78044-3087

Tel: 525-592-2861
Fax: 525-208-8943
E-mail: becas@comexus.org.mx
Website: http://www.comexus.org.mx

Morocco

Mr. Daoud S. Casewit, Executive Secretary
Moroccan-American Commission for Educational
and Cultural Exchange
7 Rue d'Agadir
Rabat, Morocco

Tel: 212-7-760-468
Fax: 212-7-768-852
E-mail: macece@maghrebnet.net.ma
Website: http://www.alakhawayn.ma/macece/

Nepal

Mr. Michael Gill, Executive Director
Commission for Educational Exchange between
the United States and Nepal
P.O. Box 380, The American Center, Gyaneshwor
Kathmandu, Nepal

Tel: 977-1-415-845
Fax: 977-1-410-881
E-mail: mgill@fulbrightnepal.org.np
Website: http://www.fulbrightnepal.org.np/

Netherlands

Mr. Marcel M.M. Oomen, Executive Director
Netherlands America Commission for
Educational Exchange
Herengracht 430
1017 BZ Amsterdam, The Netherlands

Tel: 31-20-531-5930
Fax: 31-20-620-7269
E-mail: nacee@nacee.nl
Website: http://www.nacee.nl

New Zealand

Ms. Jenny Gill, Executive Director
Fulbright New Zealand
Physical Address:
Level Four, Norseman House
120 Featherston Street
Wellington, New Zealand
Postal Address: P.O. Box 3465
Wellington, New Zealand

Tel: 64-4-472-2065
Fax: 64-4-499-5364
E-mail: gen@fulbright.org.nz
Website: http://www.fulbright.org.nz/

Norway

Ms. Jean Nesland Olsen, Executive Director
U.S.-Norway Fulbright Foundation
for Educational Exchange
Arbinsgate 2
0253 Oslo, Norway

Tel: 47-22-01-40-10
Fax: 47-22-01-40-18
E-mail: fulbright@extern.uio.no
Website: http://www.fulbright.no

Pakistan

Dr. Nancy Ahson, Executive Secretary
United States Educational Foundation in Pakistan
P.O. Box 1128
Islamabad, Pakistan

Tel: 92-51-823-055
Fax: 92-51-271-563
E-mail: aHsonnm@aol.com

Peru

Vacanat, Executive Director
Commission for Educational Exchange
Between The United States and Peru
Juan Romero Hidalgo 438-444
San Borja, Lima 41, Peru

Tel: 511-475-3083
Fax: 511-475-3086
E-mail: commissi@fulbrt.org.pe
Website: http://www.fulbrightperu.org.pe/

The Philippines

Dr. Alexander Calata, Executive Director
Philippine-American Educational Foundation
10th Floor Ayala Life/FGU Center - Makati
6811 Ayala Avenue
Makati City 1200, Philippines

Tel: 632-895-29-93
Fax: 632-895-32-15
E-mail: fulbright@paef.org.ph
Website:
http://usembassy.state.gov/manila/wwwh2004.html

Poland

Mr. Andrzej Dakowski, Executive Director
Polish-U.S. Fulbright Commission
ul. Nowy Swiat 4, Room 113
00-497 Warsaw, Poland

Tel: 48-22-628-7950
Fax: 48-22-628-7943
E-mail: a.dakowski@fulbright.edu.pl
Website: http://www.fulbright.edu.pl

Portugal

Mr. Paulo Zagalo e Melo, Executive Director
Luso-American Educational Commission (LAEC)
Av. Elias Garcia, 59-5
1000-148 Lisboa, Portugal

Tel: 351-21-799-6390
Fax: 351-21-799-6391
E-mail: fulbright@ccla.pt
Website: http://www.ccla.pt/

Romania

Ioana Ieronim, Acting Executive Director
Romanian-U.S. Fulbright Commission
Str. Ing. Costinescu, nr. 2
Sector 1, Bucharest

Tel: 401-230-7719
Fax: 401-230-7738
E-mail: iieronim@fulbright.kappa.ro
Website: http://www.usembassy.ro/Fulbright.html

Slovak Republic

Ms. Nora Hlozekova, Executive Director
J. William Fulbright Commission for Educational
Exchange in the Slovak Republic
Levicka 3
821 08 Bratislava, Slovak Republic

Tel: 421-75542-5606
Fax: 421-75557-7491
E-mail: office@fulb.sanet.sk
Website: http://www.fulbright.sk

South Africa

Ms. Riana Coetsee, Executive Director
South Africa-United States Fulbright Commission
P O Box 28059
Sunnyside, Pretoria 0132, South Africa

Tel: 27-12-312-5104
Fax: 27-12-321-5186
E-mail: coetsee.R@doe.gov.za
Website: http://www.fulbright.org.za

Spain

Ms. Maria Jesus Pablos, Executive Director
Commission for Cultural, Educational and
Scientific Exchange Between the United States of
America and Spain
Paseo General Martinez Campos, 24
28010 Madrid, Spain

Tel: 34-91-702-7000
Fax: 34-91-702-7000
E-mail: postmaster@comision-fulbright.org
Website: http://www.fulbright.es/

Sri Lanka

Mr. Tissa Jayatilaka, Executive Director
United States - Sri Lanka Fulbright Commission
7 Flower Terrace
Colombo 5, Sri Lanka

Tel: 011-941-564-176
Fax: 011-941-564-153
E-mail: tissaj@sri.lanka.net
Website:
http://usembassy.state.gov/posts/ce1/wwwhful.html

SECTION

IV

Sweden

Ms. Jeannette Lindstrom, Executive Director
Commission for Educational Exchange between the
United States of America and Sweden
Vasagatan 15-17, 4th Floor
SE-111 20 Stockholm, Sweden

Tel: 46-8-24-85-81
Fax: 46-8-14-10-64
E-mail: ceeus@fulbright.se
Website: http://www.usemb.se/Fulbright/index.html

Taiwan

Dr. Wu Jing-jyi, Executive Director
Foundation for Scholarly Exchange
Second Floor, 1-A Chuan Chow Street
Taipei 100, Taiwan

Tel: 886-2-2332-8188
Fax: 886-2-2332-5445
E-mail: jjwu@saec.saec.edu.tw
Website: http://fulbright.saec.edu.tw/

Thailand

Dr. Pimon Ruetraku, Executive Director
Thailand-U.S. Educational Foundation
21/5 Thai Wah Tower I, Third Floor
South Sathorn Road
Bangkok 10120, Thailand

Tel: 662-285-0581-3
Fax: 662-285-0583
E-mail: TUSEF@fulbrightthai.org
Website: http://www.fulbrightthai.org

Turkey

Dr. Ersin Onulduran, Executive Director
Commission for Educational Exchange Between the
United States of America and Turkey
Sehit Ersan Caddesi 28/4 Cankaya 06680
Ankara, Turkey

Tel: 90-312-428-4824
Fax: 90-312-468-1560
E-mail: fulb-ank@tr.net
Website: http://www.fulbright.org.tr/

United Kingdom

Mr. James A.H. Moore, Executive Director
United States - United Kingdom
Educational Commission
Fulbright House
62 Doughty Street
London WC1N 2JZ, United Kingdom

Tel: 44-20-7404-6880
Fax: 44-20-7404-6834
E-mail: education@fulbright.co.uk
Website: http://www.ftclondon.co.uk/

Uruguay

Ms. Mercedes Jimenez de Arechaga,
Executive Director
Commission for Educational Exchange Between
Uruguay and the United States
Colonia 810
Piso 11
Montevideo 11100, Uruguay

Tel: 5982-901-4160
Fax: 5982-903-2031
E-mail: fulbrigh@chasque.apc.org
Website: http://www.embeeuu.gub.uy/fulbrigh.htm

IMMIGRATION AND NATURALIZATION SERVICE
425 I Street, NW
Washington, DC 20536
http//www.ins.usdoj.gov

Office of the Commissioner
Commissioner
James W. Ziglar, Rm. 7100 ....202/514-1900
Deputy Commissioner
(vacant), Rm. 7100.......................202/514-1900
Chief of Staff
Peter Becraft, Rm. 7100 ....202/514-1900
Congressional Relations Director
Geri Ratlifff (Acting), Rm. 7030......202/514-5231
Communications Director
Maria Teresa Cardona,
Rm. 7010......................................202/514-2648

Programs
Executive Associate Commissioner (Acting)
Michael D. Cronin, Rm. 7309 ....202/514-8223

Field Operations
International Affairs
111 Massachusetts Avenue, NW
Washington, DC 20001
Director
Jeffrey Weiss (Acting),
Third Floor 202/305-2769
Desk Unit Director
Marianne Kilgannoh-Martz,
Third Floor 202/305-2568
African Desk Officer
Randy Lefler, Third Floor 202/305-2658
Asian Desk Officer
Helen de Thomas, Third Floor 202/305-2658
European Desk Officer
Rodney Builford, Third Floor.........202/305-2658
Latin American Desk Officer
Andrew Lluberes, Third Floor 202/305-2658
Humanitarian Affairs Coordinator
Kenneth Leutbecker, First Floor.....202/305-2051

Student and Exchange Visitor Information System (SEVIS)
www.ins.usdoj.gov/graphics/services/CIPRIS/nafsa200.htm
Acting Assistant Commissioner,
Office of Adjudications
Thomas Cook, Rm. 3214................202/514-2685

Administrative Appeals Office
111 Massachusetts Avenue, NW
Washington, DC 20001
Director
Terrance O'Reilly, Third Floor 202/305-3217

INS Regional Offices

Central Operations
Regional Office
7701 North Stemmons Freeway
Dallas, TX 75247
Tel.: 214/767-7600
Fax: 214/767-7477

Eastern Operations
Regional Office
70 Kimball Avenue
South Burlington, VT 05403-6813
Tel.: 802/660-5000
Fax: 802/660-5114

Western Operations
Regional Office
24000 Avila Road
P.O. Box 30080
Laguna Niguel, CA 92607-0080
Tel.: 714/360-2995
Fax: 714/360-3081

INS Service Centers

California Service Center
U.S. INS Center
P.O. Box 30111
Laguna Niguel, CA 92607-0111
Tel.: 714/360-2769

Nebraska Service Center
U.S. INS Center
P.O. Box 82521
Lincoln, NE 68501-2521
Tel.: 402/437-5218

Texas Service Center
U.S. INS Center
P.O. Box 85185-1488
Mesquite, TX 75185-1488
Tel.: 214/381-1423

Vermont Service Center
U.S. INS Vermont
Service Center
75 Lower Welden Street
St. Albans, VT 05479-0001
Tel.: 802/527-3160

INS District Offices

Alaska
Anchorage District Office
620 East Tenth Avenue,
Suite 102
Anchorage, AK 99501-3701
Tel.: 907/271-3524
Fax: 907/271-3112

Arizona
Phoenix District Office
2035 North Central Avenue
Phoenix, AZ 85004
Tel.: 602/379-3114
Fax: 602/379-3880

Tucson Suboffice
6431 South Country Club Road
Tucson, AZ 85706-5907
Tel.: 520/670-4624

California
Fresno Suboffice
865 Fulton Mall
Fresno, CA 93721-2816
Tel.: 209/487-5091

Los Angeles District Office
300 North Los Angeles Street
Los Angeles, CA 90012
Tel.: 213/894-2780

Sacramento Suboffice
650 Capitol Mall
Sacramento, CA 95814
Tel.: 916/498-6480

San Diego District Office
880 Front Street, Suite 1234
San Diego, CA 92101-8834
Tel.: 619/557-6064
Fax: 619/557-5550

San Francisco District Office
630 Sansome Street
San Francisco, CA 94111-2280
Tel.: 415/705-4411

San Jose Suboffice
1887 Monterey Road
San Jose, CA 95113
Tel.: 408/918-4000

Colorado
Denver District Office
Albrook Center
4730 Paris Street
Denver, CO 80239-2804
Tel.: 303/371-3041

Connecticut
Hartford Suboffice
Ribicoff Federal Building
450 Main Street
Hartford, CT 06103-3060
Tel.: 860/240-3050

Florida
Jacksonville Suboffice
4121 Southpoint Boulevard
Jacksonville, FL 32216
Tel.: 904/232-2624

Miami District Office
7880 Biscayne Boulevard
Miami, FL 33138
Tel.: 305/530-7657
Fax: 305/530-7978

Orlando Suboffice
9403 Tradeport Drive
Orlando, FL 32827
Tel.: 407/826-5780

Tampa Suboffice
5524 West Cypress Street
Tampa, FL 33607-1708
Tel.: 813/228-1222

West Palm Beach Suboffice
301 Broadway
Riviera Beach, FL 33404
Tel.: 561/626-4119

SECTION 4

Georgia

Atlanta District Office
77 Forsyth Street, SW
Martin Luther King, Jr.
Federal Building
Atlanta, GA 30303-0253
Tel.: 404/331-0253
Fax: 404/331-7931

Guam

Agana Suboffice
Sirena Plaga
108 Hernan Cortez Avenue
Suite 801
Hagatna, GU 96910
Tel.: 671/472-738

Hawaii

Honolulu District Office
595 Ala Moana Boulevard
Honolulu, HI 96813
Tel.: 808/532-3748

Illinois

Chicago District Office
10 West Jackson Boulevard,
Suite 600
Chicago, IL 60604
Tel.: 312/353-7302
Fax: 312/886-8188

Kentucky

Louisville Suboffice
Gene Snyder U.S. Custom
House
601 West Broadway
Louisville, KY 40202
Tel.: 502/582-6953

Louisiana

New Orleans District Office
Postal Services Building
701 Loyola Avenue
Room T-8011
New Orleans, LA 70113
Tel.: 504/589-6521

Maine

Portland District Office
176 Gannett Drive
Portland, ME 04106
Tel.: 207/780-3399

Maryland

Baltimore District Office
George H. Fallon
Federal Building
31 Hopkins Plaza
Baltimore, MD 21201
Tel.: 410/962-2010
Fax: 410/962-7555

Massachusetts

Boston District Office
John F. Kennedy
Federal Building
Government Center, Room 1700
Boston, MA 02203
Tel.: 617/565-4214
Fax: 617/565-3097

Michigan

Detroit District Office
Federal Building
333 Mt. Elliott Street
Detroit, MI 48207-4381
Tel.: 313/568-6000
Fax: 313/568-6004

Minnesota

St. District Office
2901 Metro Drive, Suite 100
Bloomington, MN 55425
Tel.: 612/335-2211

Missouri

Kansas City District Office
9747 North Conant Avenue
Kansas City, MO 64153
Tel.: 816/891-0864

Montana

Helena District Office
2800 Skyway Drive
Helena, MT 59601
Tel.: 406/449-5220

Nebraska

Omaha District Office
3736 South 132nd Street
Omaha, NE 68144
Tel.: 402/697-9155

Nevada

Las Vegas Suboffice
3373 Pepper Lane
Las Vegas, NV 89120
Tel.: 702/451-3597

Reno Suboffice
1351 Corporate Boulevard
Reno, NV 89502-7102
Tel.: 702/784-5186

New Jersey

Newark District Office
Federal Building
970 Broad Street
Newark, NJ 07102
Tel.: 201/645-4421

New Mexico

Albuquerque Suboffice
1720 Randolph Road SE
Albuquerque, NM 87106
Tel.: 505/248-7356

New York

Albany Suboffice
1086 Troy-Schenectady Road
Latham, NY 12110
Tel.: 518/220-2100

Buffalo District Office
130 Delaware Avenue
Buffalo, NY 14202
Tel.: 716/551-4741
Fax: 716/551-3131

New York District Office
26 Federal Plaza
New York, NY 10278
Tel.: 212/264-3911
Fax: 212/264-5939

North Carolina

Charlotte Suboffice
210 E. Woodlawn Road
Suite 138, Building 6
Charlotte, NC 28217
Tel.: 704/523-1704

Ohio

Cleveland District Office
Anthony J. Celebreeze
Federal Building
1240 East Ninth Street,
Room 1917
Cleveland, OH 44199
Tel.: 216/522-4766
Fax: 216/522-7039

Oklahoma

Oklahoma Suboffice
4149 Highline Boulevard,
Suite 300
Oklahoma City, OK 73108-2081
Tel.: 405/231-5928

Oregon

Portland District Office
Federal Office Building
511 NW Broadway
Portland, OR 97209
Tel.: 503/326-7184
Fax: 503/326-7182

Pennsylvania

Philadelphia District Office
1600 Callowhill Street
Philadelphia, PA 19130
Tel.: 215/656-7150

Pittsburgh Suboffice
INS/Department of Justice
Federal Building, Room 2130
1000 Liberty Avenue
Pittsburgh, PA 15222

Puerto Rico

San Juan District Office
7 Tabonuco Street, Suite 100
Guaynabo, PR 00968
Tel.: 718/766-5329

Rhode Island

Providence Suboffice
200 Dyre Street
Providence, RI 02903
Tel.: 401/528-5528

Tennessee

Memphis Suboffice
1341 Sycamore View, Suite 100
Memphis, TN 38134
Tel.: 901/544-0256
Fax: 901/544-0281

Texas

El Paso District Office
1545 Hawkins Boulevard,
Suite 167
El Paso, TX 79925
Tel.: 915/540-1763
Fax: 915/540-1709

Dallas District Office
8101 North Stemmons Freeway
Dallas, TX 75247
Tel.: 214/905-5886 (recording)

Harlingen District Office
2102 Teege Road
Harlingen, TX 78550
Tel.: 210/427-8592

Houston District Office
126 North Point
Houston, TX 77060
Tel.: 281/847-7979

San Antonio District Office
U.S. Federal Building
8940 Four Winds Drive
San Antonio, TX 78239
Tel.: 210/967-7000

Vermont

St. Albans Suboffice
Federal Building
64 Gricebrook Road
St. Albans, VT 05478
Tel.: 802/524-6743

Virginia

Norfolk Suboffice
Norfolk Commerce Park
5280 Henneman Drive
Norfolk, VA. 23513
Tel.: 757/858-7519

Virgin Islands

San Juan Suboffice
Nisky Center
Suite 1A First Floor South
P.O. Box 610
Charlotte Amalie
St. Thomas, VI 00802
Tel.: 809/774-1390

Washington, DC:

Washington District Office
4420 North Fairfax Drive
Arlington, VA 22203
Tel.: 202/307-1640

Washington State:

Seattle District Office
815 Airport Way, South
Seattle, WA 98134
Tel.: 206/553-0936

Spokane Suboffice
United States Courthouse
920 W. Riverside, Room, 691
Spokane, WA 99201
Tel.: 509/353-2758

Section V
Federal Government Exchanges

This section contains a compilation of exchange and training programs administered by the federal government. Over 40 federal agencies and departments report exchange activities, encompassing more than 175 programs and over 165,000 participants. Programs are designed to train leaders, specialists, fellows, scholars, and officials working in foreign governments or other key sectors of society. Programs also offer qualified U.S. federal government employees and the public the opportunity to gain training through short-term assignment in foreign institutions or international organizations. These exchanges strengthen our nation's binational relationships through the provision of information, development of skills, and the transfer of techniques related to specific professional landscapes.

For a comprehensive inventory of federal government exchange and training programs, refer to the Interagency Working Group on U.S. Government-Sponsored International Exchanges and Trainings. The FY 2000 inventory of Programs is available at http://www.iawg.gov/info/reports/ fy2000inventory.pdf

DEPARTMENT OF AGRICULTURE

1400 Independence Avenue, SW
Washington, DC 20250
Website: www.usda.gov

COOPERATIVE STATE RESEARCH, EDUCATION, AND EXTENSION SERVICE (CSREES)

International Programs

The International Programs Office of the CSREES (CSREES-IP), USDA, provides national leadership for the international activities of CSREES and U.S. cooperating universities. The office also serves as a clearinghouse for information about international programs, upcoming overseas assignments and projects, training opportunities, scientific and technical exchanges, development education and technical assistance issues for CSREES and cooperating universities.

> **USDA/CSREES/SERD/IP**
> **1400 and Independence Avenue, SW**
> **Stop 2203**
> **Washington, DC 20250-2203**
> **Tel.:** 202/720-3801   **Fax:** 202/690-2355
> **Website:** www.reeusda.gov/serd/ip

FOREIGN AGRICULTURE SERVICE

Cochran Middle Income Fellowship Program (CFP)

Targeting middle-income countries, emerging markets, and emphasizing market development, this program is very selective. The CFP provides exposure to U.S. economic policies, agricultural business practices and products, the benefits of the U.S. market oriented system, and serves as an entree to U.S. agribusiness and public sector agencies.

Professional Development Program (PDP)

The program focuses on arranging and implementing both short and long-term training and/or technical assistance related to food industries/agribusiness either in a direct technical sense (e.g. micro-enterprise development, business planning) or the provision of training that supports private sector/agribusiness development (e.g. rural credit, capital mobilization).

Trade and Investment Program (TIP)

This transaction orientated program focuses on linkages between U.S. agribusiness and their counterparts in developing and middle income countries and emerging markets to promote mutually beneficial commercial relationships and economic development. Major activities include short-term seminars and workshops on specific marketing issues, participation in trade shows, market assessments and agribusiness opportunity missions.

> **Foreign Agriculture Service,**
> **Food Industry Division**
> **1400 Independence Avenue, SW**
> **Room 3243 South Building, Mail Stop 1085**
> **USDA/FAS/ICD/FID**
> **Washington, DC 20025-1085**
> **Tel.:** 202/690-1339   **Fax:** 202/690-3982
> **Website:** www.fas.usda.gov/icd/
> food-industries/index.html

Food and Agriculture Organization Fellowship Training Program (FAO)

This program arranges academic and technical training programs for FAO participants in a wide range of agricultural subjects including crop production, forestry and natural resources, biotechnology, animal health, water management, aquaculture nutrition, food safety, agricultural policy, management, and agribusiness development.

> **Foreign Agriculture Service,**
> **Food Industry Division**
> **1400 Independence Avenue, SW**
> **South Building, Stop 1085**
> **Washington, DC 20250-1091**
> **Tel.:** 202/690-1141   **Fax:** 202/690-3952

Scientific Cooperation and Research Program (SCRP)

Providing financial support for international cooperation in research efforts that benefit U.S. agriculture and forestry, this program funds scientific exchanges and longer-term collaborative research between U.S. and foreign scientists.

Foreign Agriculture Service,
Food Industry Division
South Building, Stop 1091, Room 3230
1400 Independence Avenue, SW
Washington, DC 20250-1091
Tel.: 202/720-0618 **Fax:** 202/690-1955
Website: www.fas.usda.gov/icd/grants/scrp.htm

U.S.-Japan Cooperative Program in Natural Resources

A 37-year old collaboration between U.S. and Japanese counterparts to protect marine and terrestrial life through cooperation in applied science and technology includes programs on aquaculture and forestry.

Foreign Agriculture Service
International Cooperation and Development
1400 Independence Avenue, SW
Washington, DC 20250
Tel.: 202/690-4872 **Fax:** 202/690-0892
Website: www.lib.noaa.gov/japan/ujnr/ujnr.html

DEPARTMENT OF COMMERCE

Herbert Clark Hoover Building
14th Street and Constitution Avenue, NW
Washington, DC 20230
Website: www.doc.gov

BUREAU OF ECONOMIC ANALYSIS (BEA)

National Economic Accounting And Training Program For Foreign Nationals

Foreign nationals are trained through regular visits, targeted workshops, and a formal seminar program in the areas of national accounts and related statistics.

Foreign Training Program
BEA-30
1441 L Street, NW
Room 2022
Washington, DC 20230
Tel.: 202/606-9728 **Fax:** 202/606-5324
Website: www.bea.doc.gov

BUREAU OF EXPORT ADMINISTRATION (BXA)

Non-proliferation and Export Control Cooperation (NEC) Program

Focusing on proactive initiatives with the Newly Independent States (NIS), Baltic Republics, and Central Europe, this program includes technical exchanges in the export control functional areas of legislative and regulatory framework, licensing procedures, preventive enforcement mechanisms, industry-government relations, and automation support.

Non-proliferation and Export Control Cooperation (NEC) Program
14th Street & Constitution Avenue, NW
Room 4511
Washington, DC 20230
Tel.: 202/482-1455 **Fax:** 202/581-8224
Website: www.bxa.doc.gov/

INTERNATIONAL TRADE ADMINISTRATION

American Management and Business Internship Training Program (AMBIT)

The initiative provides managers and technicians from Northern Ireland and the border counties of Ireland with two weeks to six months of training with U.S. host companies. AMBIT provides participating U.S. companies with an opportunity to develop lasting relationships with key buyers and decision-makers on the island of Ireland and gain insight into the business climate there and in the rest of Europe, enhancing their prospects for trade.

U.S. Department of Commerce
14th Street & Constitution Avenue, NW
Room 3319
Washington, DC 20230
Tel: 202/482-2076   **Fax:** 202/482-2443
Website: www.mac.doc.gov/ambit/home.html

Special American Business Internship Training Program (SABIT)

Focusing on proactive initiatives with the Newly Independent States (NIS), Baltic Republics, and Central Europe, SABIT includes technical exchanges in the export control functional areas of legislative and regulatory framework, licensing procedures, preventive enforcement mechanisms, industry-government relations, and automation support. This program exposes executives from the former Soviet Union to market-based management and scientific skills by placing them in U.S. companies for hands-on training for a period of two to six months.

U.S. Department of Commerce
14th Street & Constitution Avenue, NW
Room 3319
Washington, DC 20230
Tel.: 202/482-0073   **Fax:** 202/482-2443
Website: www.mac.doc.gov/sabit/sabit.html

NATIONAL INSTITUTE OF STANDARDS AND TECHNOLOGY (NIST)

The NIST provides several services for visiting scholars and researchers, including exchange visitors. The Office of International & Academic Affairs coordinates the following programs.

Office of International &
Academic Affairs
100 Bureau Drive, Stop 1090
Administration Building, Room A505
Gaithersburg, MD 20899-1090
Tel: 301/975-2386   **Fax:** 301/975-3530
Website: www.nist.gov/oiaa/intlaffr.htm

Exchange Visitor Program

The NIST brings scientists from institutions of many countries to the U.S. as exchange visitors to conduct research, usually at the Ph.D. level, in the areas of chemistry, physics, and engineering measurement sciences.

Foreign Guest Researcher Program

The Foreign Guest Researcher Program offers scientists from around the world the opportunity to work collaboratively with NIST scientists. Foreign guest researchers at NIST fall into three categories: those supported by their home institutions; researchers supported through bilateral programs or international organizations; and direct scientist-to-scientist collaboration or support.

Russian Academy of Sciences Exchange Program

The NIST and the Russian Academy of Sciences provide for the exchange of scientists, scientific and technical information and documentation, joint meetings, and seminars and joint projects. OIAA coordinates and provides support for the exchange of scientists on a receiving-side-pays basis. The total length of stay is limited to 6 person-months. Scientific exchanges are carried out under the principle of mutual benefit and equality.

SECTION
5

Standards in Trade Program

To assist U.S. companies in overcoming standards-related barriers in foreign markets, NIST cooperates with the Department of Commerce's U.S. and Foreign Commercial Service to place standards experts in U.S. Embassies in key markets - in Brussels, Belgium (to interface with the European Commission), Mexico and Brazil - and to support these experts once in place. All standards experts work with U.S. business, other U.S. government agencies, and foreign counterpart organizations to identify and remove technical barriers to trade.

National Institute of Standards and Technology
100 Bureau Drive, Stop 2100
Gaithersburg, MD 20899-2100
Tel: 301-975-3089 **Fax:** 301-975-4715
Website: http://ts.nist.gov/ts/htdocs/210/216/
sitdescr.htm

NATIONAL OCEANIC AND ATMOS-PHERIC ADMINISTRATION (NOAA)
SSMC-3
1315 East-West Highway
Silver Spring, MD 20910

Cooperative Institute for Research in the Atmosphere (CIRA) Activities

The institute trains foreign scientists on site at Regional Meteorological Training Centers in Costa Rica and Barbados. Covering virtually all physical, economic and societal aspects of weather and climate, CIRA's principal interests include: applications of meteorological satellite imagery, air quality, visibility, mesoscale studies, forecasting, agricultural meteorology, cloud physics, and atmospheric model evaluation.

Website: www.cira.colostate.edu

International Turtle Excluder Device Technology Transfer Program

The NOAA exchanges information on these turtle saving devices used on intake/outtake information.

National Environmental Satellite, Data, and Information Services (NESDIS) International Activities

NESDIS acquires, manages, and provides access to the Nation's operational environmental satellites, provides data and information services, and conducts related research.

Website: www.nesdis.noaa.gov/

National Sea Grant College Program

This network of 29 university-based programs located in several coastal and Great Lakes states involves more than 300 institutions nationwide in research, education, and outreach concerning coastal, marine and aquatic issues. There have been several exchanges with East Asian and Pacific Island countries.

Tel.: 301/713-2451 **Fax:** 301/713-0799
Website: www.nsgo.seagrant.org

Office of Oceanic and Atmospheric Research International Activities

The International Activities Office administratively supports international environmental research programs for Sea Grant, the National Undersea Research Program and NOAA Research Labs by administering bilateral ocean research agreements with counterparts in Japan, China, and France. Program includes assistance with Country Clearance Cables, Memoranda of Understanding and Agreements, visas for foreign scientists visiting NOAA Research (IAP-66), international travel information, and international operational issues.

1315 East West Highway
SSMC-3, Room 11424
Silver Spring, Maryland 20910
Tel: 301/713-2469 **Fax:** 301/713-1459
Website: www.oarhq.noaa.gov/ia/ia_home.htm

U.S.-Peoples' Republic of China Protocol on Atmospheric Sciences and Technology

Developed in 1979 between the NOAA and the China Meteorological Administration, program areas include climate/monsoon studies, mesoscale meteorology, satellite meteorology, atmospheric chemistry, meteorological modernization, and training/participation.

Website: http://www.nws.noaa.gov/ia/china.htm

U.S.-China Marine and Fisheries Science and Technology Protocol

This bilateral agreement, developed in 1979 between the NOAA and the Chinese State Oceanic Administration, facilitates data and information exchange, resource leveraging, scientific collaboration, and the optimalization of national capabilities in marine and fisheries science and technology.

Website: ww.nmfs.noaa.gov/sfa/international/
2001int'lagrmts_up.htm

U.S.-France Cooperation in Oceanography

Cooperative activities with France in oceanography occur primarily on a scientist-to scientist level and have included joint experiments and studies, symposia, exchanges of scientists and information, and joint planning of future activities.

Tel.: 301/713-2465 **Fax:** 301/713-0158
Website: www.nmfs.noaa.gov/sfa/
international/2001int'lagrmts_up.htm

U.S.-Japan Cooperative Program (Marine Exchange)

The principal aims of this 1964 bilateral agreement is to develop and conserve natural resources, share information and the results of research activities, and provide a continuing forum for applied science and technology cooperation.

Office of Oceanic And Atmospheric Research
1315 East-West Highway
Silver Spring, MD 20910
Tel.: 301/713-2469 **Fax:** 301/713-1459
Website: www.lib.noaa.gov/japan/ujnr/ujnr.html

U.S.-Russia Cooperation in Meteorological and Climate Data Exchange

Carried out though a U.S.-Russia bilateral agreement, this program includes exchanging data, preparing computer software to quality control data, and researching observation practices to adjust data and making resulting data sets available for research.

NATIONAL WEATHER SERVICE

International Activities Office

This office coordinates all international activities of the National Weather Service, a U.S. federal agency that falls under the NOAA. Training is offered in tropical meteorology, operational hydrology, computer assisted learning, and the use of the Internet.

National Weather Service
International Activities Office
1325 East-West Highway
Silver Spring, MD 20910
Tel.: 301/713-1784 **Fax:** 301/587-4524
Website: www.nws.noaa.gov/ia/home.htm

Voluntary Cooperation Program

A component of the World Meteorological Organization (WMO), this program provides training and equipment to help developing countries participate in WMO programs, particularly in the World Weather Watch that gives the U.S. and other nations the basic information needed to make meteorological and hydrological forecasts and warnings.

SSMC-3
1315 East-West Highway
Silver Spring, MD 20910
Tel.: 301/713-2451 **Fax:** 301/713-0799
Website: www.nws.noaa.gov/ia/home.htm

NATIONAL TELECOMMUNICATION AND INFORMATION ADMINISTRATION (NTIA)

Office of International Affairs
National Telecommunications &
Information Administration
Room 4701
U.S. Department of Commerce
1401 Constitution Avenue, NW
Washington, DC 20230
Tel: 202/482-1866 **Fax:** 202/482-1865
Website: www.ntia.doc.gov/oiahome/
oiahome.html

Office of Spectrum Management

This office conducts training in radio frequencies for citizens of developing countries. Most participants are employed by their government's regulators and are technical specialists in radio frequency management; others are employed by telecommunications carriers or private industry.

Office of Spectrum Management
1401 Constitution Avenue, NW
Room 4099
Washington, DC 20230
Tel.: 202/482-1850 **Fax:** 202/482-4396
Website: www.ntia.doc.gov/
osmhome/osmhome.html

U.S. CENSUS BUREAU

International Programs Center (IPC)

The IPC provides technical assistance and training in all phases of survey and census design, data collection, processing, analysis. Since 1947, the IPC has offered training and workshops to statisticians from developing countries.

Washington Plaza 2
Room 309
4700 Silver Hill Road, Stop 8860
Washington, DC 20233-8860
Tel.: 301/457-1444 **Fax:** 301/457-3033
Website: www.census.gov/ipc/www/index.html

U.S. PATENT & TRADEMARK OFFICE (PTO)

Visiting Scholars Program

By training visitors from developing countries and countries with emerging market economies on intellectual property rights protection and intellectual protection enforcement, the PTO assists countries in reducing losses resulting from piracy of U.S. intellectual property.

Office of Legislative and International Affairs
Box 4
Washington, DC 20231
Tel.: 703/305-9300 **Fax:** 703/305-8885
Website: www.uspto.gov/web/offices/dcom/olia/

DEPARTMENT OF DEFENSE
The Pentagon
Washington, DC 20301
Tel.: 703/697-5737
Website: www.defenselink.mil

DEFENSE SECURITY COOPERATION AGENCY

Foreign Military Sales Program/Foreign Military Financing Program (FMS/FMF)
This is a non-appropriated program through which eligible foreign governments can purchase training from the U.S. Government.

International Military Education And Training (IMET) Program
Foreign students are exposed to the professional military establishment and the American way of life, including regard for democratic values, respect for human rights, and belief in the rule of law.

> **International Military Education And Training Program**
> **1111 Jefferson Davis Highway**
> **Arlington, VA 22202**
> **Tel.:** 703/604-6617 **Fax:** 703/604-6542

Professional Military Education (PME) Exchanges
This program sends officers and academics to full-year training in military staff schools abroad.

DEFENSE THREAT REDUCTION AGENCY

Moscow State University (MSU) Immersion Training
A two-week comprehensive program of study through the On-site Europe Division (DTRA-OSE) at Moscow University that combines theoretical and practical Russian Language studies, valuable practical courses related to extralinguistics (i.e. Russian cultural and political history, social customs and habits, situational behavior, etc.), and lectures by MSU instructors. All students must have an in-country clearance from the U.S. Embassy at Moscow before attending this two-week course.

> **Website:** www-perscom.army.mil/select/
> dtra-ose.htm

National Security Education Program (NSEP)
This program provides scholarships to U.S. undergraduate and graduate students to promote understanding of foreign cultures; strengthening of U.S. economic competitiveness; and enhancement of international cooperation and security. Recipients of NSEP scholarships and fellowships incur an obligation to work either for an office or agency of the Federal Government involved in national security affairs (broadly defined) or in higher education.

> **National Security Education Program**
> **1101 Wilson Boulevard**
> **Suite 1210**
> **PO Box 20010**
> **Arlington, VA 22209-2248**
> **Tel.:** 703/696-1991 **Fax:** 703/696-5667

OFFICE OF THE JOINT CHIEFS OF STAFF

Asia-Pacific Center for Security Studies
Located in Honolulu, Hawaii, this center serves as a central location for national officials, decision makers, and policy makers to gather to exchange ideas, explore issues, and achieve a greater understanding of Asia-Pacific regional challenges.

> **Asia-Pacific Center for Security Studies**
> **2058 Maluhia Road**
> **Honolulu, HI 96815**
> **Tel:** 808/971-8900 **Fax:** 808/971-8999
> **Website:** www.apcss.org

SECTION

5

The Center for Hemispheric Defense Studies

Through graduate-level programs in defense planning and management, executive leadership, civil-military relations, and interagency operations, the center develops civilian specialists in defense and military matters.

> **Center for Hemispheric Defense Studies**
> **National Defense University**
> **Coast Guard Headquarters Building**
> **2100 2nd Street, SW – 4th Floor**
> **Washington, DC 20593-0001**
> **Tel:** 202/685-4670   **Fax:** 202/685-4674
> **Website:** www3.ndu.edu/chds/

George C. Marshall European Center for Security Studies

The Center is a bi-lateral institution of higher security and defense learning for foreign and security policy officials. The Center coordinates programs in post-graduate level studies, foreign area officer training, foreign language training, conferences, and research. Participants include Americans who have traveled abroad or are foreign nationals who have traveled to the U.S.

> **George C. Marshall Center**
> **Gernackerstrasse 2**
> **82467 Garmisch-Partenkirchen**
> **Germany**
> **Website:** www.marshallcenter.org

Olmstead Scholar Program

This program immerses military officers and their families in a foreign culture of choice while the officer studies a foreign language in a field of his/her choosing.

> **Olmstead Scholar Program**
> **George and Carol Olmstead Foundation**
> **1515 North Courthouse Road, Suite 305**
> **Arlington, VA 22201**
> **Tel:** 703/527-9070
> **Website:** www.mscn.org/scholarships/
> Scholarship56.html

State Partnership Program (NATIONAL GUARD BUREAU)

By aligning U.S. State National Guard Commands with Partnership for Peace Members from the Newly Independent States (NIS), the program provides contacts with "citizen soldiers" to foster democratic control of the military as well as focusing on those missions performed by the National Guard.

> **Website:** www.ang.af.mil/ngbia/

OFFICE OF THE UNDERSECRETARY OF DEFENSE FOR PERSONNEL AND READINESS

Reserve Officer Foreign Exchange Program

Over 20 reservists from all services are sent to the United Kingdom or Germany on this historic officer exchange program. Rank requirements vary.

Service Academy Foreign Student Program

The U.S. annually invites selected countries worldwide to nominate candidates to compete for admission at each of the four U.S. service academies. These include the U.S. Military Academy (USMA) in West Point, NY; the US Air Force Academy (USAFA) in Colorado Springs, CO; the US Naval Academy (USNA) in Annapolis, MD; and the US Coast Guard Academy (USCGA) in New London, CT. The Military, Air Force, and Naval Academies normally will not review more than six candidates from a single country. The Coast Guard Academy does not limit the amount of candidates a country can nominate. Applicants must request information from the U.S. Embassy in their home country. For more information regarding each institution, please contact:

> **HQ USAFA/RRS**
> **2304 Cadet Dr, Ste 200**
> **U.S. Air Force Academy, CO 80840**
> **Tel:** 800/443-9266   **Fax:** 719/333-3647
> **Website:** www.usafa.af.mil/rr/intstu.htm

> **Director of Admissions**
> **U.S. Coast Guard Academy**
> **31 Mohegan Avenue**
> **New London, CT 06320-8103**
> **Tel:** 860/444-8500   **Fax:** 860/701-6700
> **Website:** www.cga.edu/default.htm

> **U.S. Military Academy**
> **Building 606**
> **West Point, NY 10996**
> **Tel:** 845/938-4041
> **Website:** www.usma.edu/admissions/
> more_international.asp

> **Candidate Guidance Office**
> **U.S. Naval Academy**
> **117 Decatur Road**
> **Annapolis, MD 21402-5018**
> **Tel:** 410/293-4361
> **Website:** www.usna.edu/Admissions/intlapl.htm

OFFICE OF THE UNDERSECRETARY OF DEFENSE FOR POLICY

Defense Personnel Exchange Program

These military and civilian exchange programs are designed to foster mutual understanding and cooperation between governments by familiarizing exchange program participants with the organization, administration and operations of the other party.

DEPARTMENT OF EDUCATION
600 Independence Avenue, SW
Washington, DC 20202
Website: www.ed.gov

OFFICE OF EDUCATIONAL RESEARCH AND IMPROVEMENT

Economic Education Program

Educators from eligible countries are assisted in reforming their educational systems and educating their citizens in market economy transition.

> **Office of Educational Research And Improvement**
> **555 New Jersey Avenue, NW**
> **Washington, DC 20208**
> **Tel.:** 202/219-1496   **Fax:** 202/219-2135

Civics and Government Education Program

To support international education exchange activities between the United States and eligible countries in civics and government education and economic education.

OFFICE OF POST SECONDARY EDUCATION

The following International Education and Graduate programs can be contacted at this address, unless otherwise listed:

> **International Education and**
> **Graduate Programs Service**
> **400 Maryland Avenue, SW**
> **Portals Building, Suite 600**
> **Washington, DC 20202-5332**
> **Tel.:** 202/401-9785   **Fax:** 202/205-9485

American Overseas Research Centers (AORC) Program

AORC provides grants to a consortium of U.S. higher education institutions. These grants provide support to establish or operate overseas research centers that promote post-graduate research, exchanges and area studies.

> **Website:** www.ed.gov/offices/OPE/HEP/
> iegps/aorc.html

Fulbright-Hays Doctoral Dissertation Research Abroad (DDRA) Program

Conducted through U.S. institutions of higher education, this program provides fellowships to doctoral candidates to conduct full-time dissertation research abroad in the field of modern languages and area studies.

> **Tel.:** 202/401-9774   **Fax:** 202/205-9489
> **Website:** www.ed.gov/offices/OPE/HEP/iegps/
> ddrap.html

Fulbright-Hays Faculty Research Abroad (FRA) Program

Conducted through U.S. institutions of higher education, this program provides fellowships to faculty members to enable them to conduct full-time research abroad in the filed of modern foreign languages and area studies.

> **Tel.:** 202/401-9777   **Fax:** 202/205-9489
> **Website:** www.ed.gov/offices/OPE/HEP/
> iegps/fra.html

Fulbright-Hays Group Projects Abroad (GPA) Program

Designed to improve and develop the field of modern foreign language and area studies throughout the educational structure of the United States, teachers, students, and faculty at higher education institutions are provided educational opportunities overseas.

Tel.: 202/401-9798 **Fax:** 202/205-9489
Website: www.ed.gov/offices/OPE/HEP/
iegps/gpa.html

Fulbright-Hays Seminars Abroad (SA) Program

This program provides opportunities for qualified U.S.-educators to participate in short-term seminars abroad on topics in the social sciences and the humanities, or on the languages of participating countries.

Tel.: 202/401-9798 **Fax:** 202/205-9489
Website: www.ed.gov/offices/OPE/HEP/iegps/
sap.html

FUND FOR THE IMPROVEMENT OF POSTSECONDARY EDUCATION (FIPSE)

International Programs
Fund for the Improvement of
Postsecondary Education (FIPSE)
1990 K Street, NW, 8th Floor
Washington DC, 20006-8544
Tel: 202/502-7500 **Fax:** 202/502-7877

European Community-USA Joint Consortia for Cooperation in Higher Education and Vocational Education Program

The US-EC program is a grant competition run cooperatively by FIPSE and the European Commission's Directorate General for Education and Culture. The purpose of this competition is to promote a student-centered, transatlantic dimension to higher education and training in a wide range of academic and professional disciplines. The US-EC Program fosters student exchange within the context of multilateral curricular development. Students benefit from having an added "international" curriculum and cultural dimension to their studies through a combination of curricular innovation and study abroad.

Office of Post Secondary Education
400 Maryland Avenue, SW
ROB-3 Room 3100
Washington, DC 20202
Tel.: 202/708-5750 **Fax:** 202/708-6118
Website: www.ed.gov/offices/OPE/FIPSE/EC/

Program for North American Mobility in Higher Education

Promoting cooperative student-centered higher education and training activities between the US, Canada, and Mexico, the program fosters student exchange within the context of multilateral curricular development. Students benefit from having an added "North American" curriculum and cultural dimension to their studies through combination of trilateral curricular innovation and study abroad.

Website: www.ed.gov/offices/OPE/
FIPSE/northam

US-Brazil Higher Education Consortia Program

The US-Brazil Program fosters university partnerships through the exchange of undergraduate and graduate students, faculty, and staff within the context of bilateral curricular development.

Website: ww.ed.gov/offices/OPE/FIPSE/Brazil/
index.html

DEPARTMENT OF ENERGY

1000 Independence Ave, SW
Washington, DC 20585
Website: www.doe.gov

OFFICE OF ENERGY EFFICIENCY AND RENEWABLE ENERGY (EERE)

Energy Efficiency and Renewable Energy NETWORK (EREN) Programs

EERE develops and deploys efficient and clean energy technologies that meet national energy needs, enhance the environment, and strengthen competitiveness. EERE is strengthening its partnerships with other government entities and the private sector to better leverage the Federal investment in research, development and deployment (RD&D) of new technologies.

> **Website:** www.eren.doe.gov/ee.html

OFFICE OF ENVIRONMENT, SAFETY AND HEALTH (ES&H)

ES&H is the Departmental advocate for excellence in programs to protect the environment, as well as the health and safety of workers at Department of Energy facilities and the public.

> **1000 Independence Ave, SW**
> **Washington, DC 20585-0119**
> **Fax:** 202/586-0956
> **Website:** http://tis.eh.doe.gov/portal/home.htm

OFFICE OF THE ASSISTANT SECRETARY FOR FOSSIL ENERGY

Fossil Energy Programs

The office is responsible for research, development, and other duties, including managing the Strategic Petroleum Reserve to reduce vulnerability to economic, national security, and foreign policy consequences of supply interruptions. Several exchange opportunities available.

> **Office of Fossil Energy (FE)**
> **U.S. Department of Energy**
> **1000 Independence Avenue, SW**
> **Washington, DC 20585**
> **Tel:** 202/586-6503   **Fax:** 202/586-5146
> **Website:** www.fe.doe.gov/

ENERGY INFORMATION ADMINISTRATION (EIA)

Energy Information Administration Programs

EIA provides policy-independent data, forecasts, and analyses to promote sound policy making, efficient markets, and public understanding regarding energy and its interaction with the economy and the environment.

> **Energy Information Administration**
> **1000 Independence Avenue**
> **Washington, DC 20585**
> **Tel:** 202/586-8800
> **Website:** www.eia.doe.gov/

OFFICE OF NUCLEAR ENERGY, SCIENCE, AND TECHNOLOGY

Nuclear Energy, Science, and Technology

The Nuclear Energy Program represents the core of the nation's expertise, and the office actively seeks international public participation in the areas of nuclear power research and development, space power systems, isotope production and distribution, facilities management, and science education.

> **Website:** www.ne.doe.gov/

NATIONAL NUCLEAR SECURITY ADMINISTRATION (NNSA)

Office of Fissile Materials Disposition Programs

The Office of Defense Nuclear Nonproliferation (NN) in NNSA is at the forefront of efforts to address proliferation dangers in partnership with governments and organizations worldwide.

Congress, Federal, state, and local governments, Tribal officials, non-government organizations, and the public have all contributed to shaping this program.

> **Website:** www.doe-md.com/

SECTION

5

Defense Programs

Defense Programs within the NNSA, among other duties, manage the Stockpile Stewardship Program, which encompasses operations associated with manufacturing, maintaining, refurbishing, surveilling, and dismantling the nuclear weapons stockpile; activities associated with the research, design, development, simulation, modeling, and non-nuclear testing of nuclear weapons; and the planning, assessment and certification of safety and reliability. Defense Programs develops and maintains partnerships with other NNSA, DOE, and DoD entities, as well as with external scientific, research, and development agencies; industry; and academia.

Website: www.dp.doe.gov/dp_web/

NATIONAL SECURITY AND ENVIORN-MENTAL MANAGEMENT PROGRAMS

Office of the Assistant Secretary for Environmental Management (EM) Programs

Provides program policy development and guidance for the assessment and cleanup of inactive waste sites and facilities, and waste management operations; develops and implements an aggressive applied waste research and development program to provide innovative environmental technologies to yield permanent disposal solutions at reduced costs; and oversees the transition of contaminated facilities from various Departmental programs to environmental restoration once they are determined to be surplus to their original mission

Office of the Assistant Secretary for Environmental Management
Washington, DC 20585-0113
Fax: 202/586-7757
Website: www.em.doe.gov/

Office of Radioactive Waste Management (OCRWM) Programs

To assure an exchange of information on nuclear waste management, cooperative programs have evolved among countries and various international agencies. The Department of Energy (DOE) has bilateral agreements with several western European countries and Canada. The U.S., as a member of the International Atomic Energy Agency (IAEA) and the Nuclear Energy Agency of the Organization for Economic Cooperation and Development (NEA/OECD), cooperates with the Commission of the European Communities. Through such cooperation, nations share the cost of nuclear waste disposal testing programs; exchange information, technology, and experience; and develop a consensus to improve confidence in the safety of each nation's disposal system.

Office of Civilian Radioactive Waste Management
U.S. Department of Energy
Forrestal Building
1000 Independence Avenue, SW
Washington DC 20585-0453
Website: www.rw.doe.gov/program/int/int.htm

SECTION 5

DEPARTMENT OF HEALTH AND HUMAN SERVICES

200 Independence Avenue, SW
Washington, DC 20201
Website: www.os.dhhs.gov

CENTERS FOR DISEASE CONTROL AND PREVENTION

Exchange Visitor Program

To prevent and control both infectious and non-communicable causes of disease and death, this program promotes and supports medical and scientific research and related capacity building.

> **Office of Global Health**
> **4770 Buford Highway**
> **Mailstop K-01**
> **Atlanta, GA 30341-3724**
> **Tel.:** 770/488-1218   **Fax:** 770/488-1003
> **Website:** www.cdc.gov/hrmo/INTSHPS2.htm

HEALTH RESOURCES AND SERVICES ADMINISTRATION (HRSA)

International Health Affairs

This office coordinates, develops and oversees the agency's efforts to improve health beyond the U.S. border. HRSA focuses on the following activities: (1) collaboration between the U.S. government and international partners to improve and enhance foreign nation's capacity to provide basic health care services to under-served populations; (2) provide consultation to HRSA's international and domestic partners, as well as, to foreign governments; and (3) support international training opportunities for U.S. and foreign citizens.

> **International Health Affairs**
> **Office of the Administrator**
> **Health and Resources and**
> **Services Administration**
> **5600 Fishers Lane, Room 14-14**
> **Rockville, MD 20857**
> **Tel.:** 301/443-6152   **Fax:** 301/443-7834
> **Website:** www.hrsa.gov

NATIONAL CANCER INSTITUTE (NCI)

The Oncology Research Faculty Development Program

This program offers post-doctoral cancer researchers from developing countries the opportunity to work with NCI intramural scientists or extramural scientists for up to three years.

> **Office of International Affairs**
> **National Cancer Institute**
> **Executive Plaza North, Suite 100**
> **6130 Executive Boulevard MSC 7301**
> **Bethesda, MD 20892-7301**
> **Tel.:** 301/496-4761   **Fax:** 301/496-3954
> **Website:** http://cancernet.nci.nih.gov

The Short-Term Scientists Exchange Program

This program promotes one-week collaborations in cancer research between post-doctoral foreign scientists and NCI intramural scientists or extramural scientists.

NATIONAL INSTITUTE OF HEALTH (NIH)

> **Fogarty International Center**
> **National Institutes of Health**
> **Building 31, Room B2C39**
> **31 Center Drive MSC 2220**
> **Bethesda, MD 20892-2220**
> **Tel.:** 301/496-1653   **Fax:** 301/402-0779
> **Website:** www.nih.gov/fic

AIDS International Training and Research Program (AITRP)

Offering a variety of training options, the program seeks to increase the proficiency of scientists from developing countries to undertake biomedical and behavioral research related to AIDS and to develop and use these acquired skills in clinical trails and prevention and related research.

Fogarty International Research Collaboration Award (FIRCA)

This award facilitates collaborative research between U.S. biomedical scientists supported by the NIH and investigators in the developing world as well as in Central and Eastern Europe, and countries of the former Soviet Union.

International Research Fellowship Program

This program provides opportunities for post-doctoral biomedical or behavioral scientists that are in the formative stage of their career to extend their research in a laboratory in the U.S.

Tel.: 301/496-7613   **Fax:** 301/402-0779

International Training and Research Program in Environmental and Occupational Health

This program has been developed to train foreign health scientists, clinicians, epidemiologists, toxicologists, engineers, industrial hygienists, chemists, and allied health workers from developing countries and emerging democracies in both general environmental and occupational health.

International Training and Research Program in Population and Health

Supporting international population priorities, this program enables NIH grant recipients to extend the geographic base of their research and training efforts to developing nations.

**National Institute on Drug Abuse Program/
International Visiting Scientists and Technical
Exchange Program
Building 31
Room 1B59
9000 Rockville Pike
Bethesda, MD 20892
Tel.:** 301/594-1928   **Fax:** 301/402-5654

NIH Guest Researchers/Special Volunteers

Guest Researchers use NIEHS facilities to further their own research or training by using equipment and resources that are not otherwise available to them for up to two years. Volunteers provide services without direct compensation from NIH and may receive funding from outside sources.

Website: www.niehs.nih.gov/omhrmb/
procedur/guessre.htm

NIH Visiting Program

This program provides opportunities for foreign scientists to train and conduct collaborative research at the National Institutes of Health.

**International Service Branch
Fogarty International Center
National Institutes of Health
Building 16A, Room 101
16A Center Drive MSC 6710
Bethesda, MD 20892-6710
Tel.:** 301/496-6166   **Fax:** 301/496-0897
Website: www.nih.gov/fic/services/visiting.html

National Research Service Award (NRSA)

Available to international visitors, various grants provide funding for training in several medical fields for up to two years.

Website: http://grants.nih.gov/training/
careerdev/pbopporte.html

Senior International Fellowships

This program provides opportunities for mid and senior-career level U.S. scientists to conduct biomedical research studies at foreign institutions.

Website: http://grants.nih.gov/training/careerdev/
fogarty.html#fsenior

NATIONAL INSTITUTE OF NEUROLOGICAL DISORDERS AND STROKE

International Neurological Science Fellowship Program

This program provides opportunities for junior to mid-career health professionals and scientists in the neurological sciences to enhance their basic or clinical science research skills in a research setting in the United States.

**National Institute of Neurological
Disorders and Stroke
Building 31, Room 8A03
31 Center Drive MSC 2540
Bethesda, MD 20892
Tel.:** 301/496-9271   **Fax:** 301/402-2186
Website: www.nih.gov/fic/programs/grants.html

A pre-application to the World Health Organization is required. For pre-application materials, contact:

Unit on Neuroscience
Division of Mental Health and
Prevention of Substance Abuse
World Health Organization
CH-1211 Geneva 27
SWITZERLAND
Tel.: 41-22-791-21-11 **Fax:** 41-22-791-07-46

DEPARTMENT OF HOUSING AND URBAN DEVELOPMENT
451 Seventh Street, SW
Washington, DC 20410
Website: www.hud.gov

OFFICE OF POLICY DEVELOPMENT AND RESEARCH

HUD International Visitors Program

PD&R is responsible for maintaining current information on housing needs, market conditions, and existing programs, as well as conducting research on priority housing and community development issues. The International Affairs office coordinates international visitors and university partnerships.

International Affairs
451 Seventh Street, SW
Room 8118
Washington, DC 20410
Tel.: 202/708-0770 **Fax:** 202/708-5536

DEPARTMENT OF INTERIOR

1849 C Street, NW
Washington, DC 20240
Tel.: 202/208-3100
Website: www.doi.gov

BUREAU OF RECLAMATION

International Visitors Program
The IV program is one of several international activities of the Bureau of Reclamation that involves exchange, training, and technical assistance.
    Website: www.usbr.gov/international

NATIONAL PARK SERVICE

International Volunteers in Park (IVIP) Program
The IVIP program provides opportunities to work or study at a national park of your choice. Applicants must contact the Volunteer Coordinator in the park of their choice. For a complete information packet to begin your IVIP program contact the Office of International Affairs at:

    NPS / OIA
    International Volunteer Coordinator
    800 N. Capital St. NW, Suite. 330
    P.O. Box 37127
    Washington, D.C. 20013-7127
    Tel.: 202/343-7063

OFFICE OF INTERNATIONAL AFFAIRS

Office of International Affairs Programs
DOI international activities, including several program listings, include arranging appointments and coordinating visits for foreign governments officials and non-governmental professionals with staff from Interior bureaus and services.

    Office of International Affairs
    1849 C Street, NW
    Room 4429 MIB
    Washington, DC 20240
    Tel.: 202/219-0537   **Fax:** 202/501-6381
    Website: www.doi.gov/intl

DEPARTMENT OF JUSTICE
Tenth Street and Constitution Avenue, NW
Washington, DC 20530
Website: www.usdoj.gov

CRIMINAL DIVISION

International Criminal Investigative Training Assistance Program (ICITAP)

Supporting U.S. foreign policy, this program provides developmental assistance to foreign criminal justice systems, particularly to developing police forces for participation in peacekeeping operations and in emerging democracies.

> **1331 F Street, NW, Suite 500**
> **Washington, DC 20004**
> **Tel.:** 202/514-1323   **Fax:** 202/514-1792
> **Website:** www.usdoj.gov/criminal/icitap.html

Overseas Prosecutorial Development, Assistance, and Training Program (OPDAT)/International Visitors Program

This program has been a key component of U.S. efforts to strengthen democratic governments by helping to build justice systems that promote the rule of law and serve the public interest. Specifically, OPDAT manages the training of judges and prosecutors abroad in coordination with various government agencies and U.S. embassies.

> **1331 F Street, NW, Suite 500**
> **Washington, DC 20004**
> **Tel.:** 202/514-1323   **Fax:** 202/616-8429
> **Website:** www.usdoj.gov/criminal/opdat.html

DRUG ENFORCEMENT ADMINISTRATION (DEA)

International Narcotics Control Training Section

The DEA's new Justice Training Center offers state-of-the-art training for visiting international law enforcement officers. In addition, the international training section of the DEA offers counter-narcotics training at three International Law Enforcement Academies: one in Budapest, Hungary; a second, operated by the DEA in cooperation with the Royal Thai Police in Bangkok, Thailand; and a third, dedicated to counter-narcotics training, in Latin America.

> **Office of Training**
> **FBI Academy**
> **P.O. Box 1475**
> **Attn: Camp Upshur – International Training**
> **Quantico, VA 22134**
> **Tel.:** 703/640-1100   **Fax:** 703/640-7477
> **Website:** www.dea.gov/programs/training.htm

FEDERAL BUREAU OF INVESTIGATION (FBI)

> **J. Edgar Hoover Building**
> **935 Pennsylvania Avenue, NW**
> **Washington, D.C. 20535-0001**
> **Tel.:** 202/324-3000

International Cooperation Unit (ICU)

The ICU staff works in conjunction with foreign law enforcement professionals to complete a specific investigation or to combine expertise in tracking down a bilateral threat.

> **935 Pennsylvania Avenue, NW**
> **Washington, DC 20535**
> **Tel.:** 202/324-4682   **Fax:** 202/324-9265
> **Website:** http://newyork.fbi.gov/contact/fo/nyfo/ert/ert.htm

International Training Program (ITP)

The FBI offers international training through the FBI Academy in Quantico, Virginia. Coordinating with the State Department and other agencies, activities cover various elements such as the Mexican/American Law Enforcement Training (MALET) initiative and the Pacific Rim Initiative, including in-country training.

Website: www.fbi.gov/hq/td/academy/itp/itp.htm

OFFICE OF JUSTICE PROGRAMS

National Institute of Justice (NIJ)
International Activities

In 1997, NIJ created the International Center in response to growing globalization of crime. The center operates several programs ranging from international visitors, exchanges, research grants, partnership opportunities, and programs with the United Nations.

National Institute of Justice
810 Seventh Street, NW
Washington, DC 20531
Website: www.ojp.usdoj.gov/nij/international/
programs.html

Office for Victims of Crime International Activities

For American citizens victimized abroad and foreign nationals victimized in the U.S., the office provides assistance through a variety of program areas ranging from human trafficking and terrorism, and includes the international visitors program.

U.S. Department of Justice
Office for Victims of Crime
810 7th Street NW
Washington, DC 20531
Website: www.ojp.usdoj.gov/ovc/welcome.html

SECTION

DEPARTMENT OF LABOR
200 Constitution Avenue, NW
Washington, DC 20210
Website: www.dol.gov

BUREAU OF INTERNATIONAL LABOR AFFAIRS (ILAB)

International Child Labor Program
Various programs include teacher training, development of curriculum and traditional and transitional educational systems are available, including grants. The program works closely with the International Labor Organization's International Program on the Elimination of Child Labor (IPEC).

> **International Child Labor Program**
> **U.S. Department of Labor**
> **200 Constitution Avenue, NW**
> **Room N2431**
> **Washington, DC 20210**
> **Tel.:** 202/693-4843 **Fax:** 202/693-4830
> **Website:** www.dol.gov/dol/ilab/public/programs/iclp/welcome.html

Office of Foreign Relations (OFR)
International Technical Assistance Programs
With the majority of programs supporting labor market transitions in Central and Eastern Europe, these programs develop and strengthen host country's institutionalized capacity in order to create and implement democratic and market-oriented labor and social sector programs. OFR offers study tours and foreign visitor programs.

> **Office of Foreign Affairs**
> **ILAB**
> **Room S-5325**
> **U.S. Department of Labor**
> **Washington, DC 20210**
> **Website:** www.dol.gov/dol/ilab/public/programs/ofr/main.htm

National Administrative Office (NAO) Programs
The NAO focuses on labor law issues between the U.S., Canada, and Mexico, as established by the North American Agreement on Labor Cooperation (NAALC), as a side agreement to the North American Free Trade Agreement (NAFTA). NAO offers technical training, exchange of best practices and information on several subject areas.

> **U.S. National Administrative Office**
> **U.S. Department of Labor**
> **200 Constitution Avenue, NW**
> **Room C-4327**
> **Washington, DC 20210**
> **Tel.:** 202/501-6653 **Fax:** 202/501-6615
> **Website:** www.dol.gov/dol/ilab/public/programs/nao/main.htm

BUREAU OF LABOR STATISTICS

International Labor Statistics Center
Through International Technical Cooperation programs the Bureau offers many opportunities for international participation, including the International Labor Statistics Center, which organizes visits for about 300 international visitors each year in addition to annual international seminars. The majority of visitors are economists, statisticians, researchers, analysts, and managers working with labor statistics in their own national governments.

> **International Labor Statistics Center**
> **Bureau of Labor Statistics**
> **U.S. Department of Labor**
> **Two Massachusetts Avenue, NE**
> **Room 2190**
> **Washington, DC 20212-0001**
> **Tel.:** 202/606-5666 **Fax:** 202/606-7900
> **Website:** www.bls.gov/intvisit.htm

SECTION

5

DEPARTMENT OF STATE
2201 C Street, NW
Washington, DC 20520
Website: www.state.gov

BUREAU OF DIPLOMATIC SECURITY

Antiterrorism Assistance Program
While promoting democratic and human rights values essential for free and stable societies, the antiterrorism assistance program is designed to improve the capabilities of foreign countries to prevent and combat terrorist threats by training foreign civilian security personnel.

> **Office of Antiterrorism Assistance Program**
> **2121 Virginia Avenue, NW**
> **Third Floor**
> **Washington, DC 20520**
> **Tel.:** 202/663-2554   **Fax:** 202/663-0653
> **Website:** www.ds.state.gov/ata.htm

BUREAU OF INTELLIGENCE AND RESEARCH

Research and Training Program on Eastern Europe and the Independent Sates of the Former Soviet Union
This program supports advanced research data, methods, and findings; and contact and collaboration among government and private specialists.

> **Advisory Committee for**
> **Studies of Eastern Europe and the**
> **NIS of the Former Soviet Union**
> **INR/RES, Room 6841**
> **U.S. Department of State**
> **2201 C Street, NW**
> **Washington, DC 20520-6510**
> **Tel.:** 202/736-4572

BUREAU OF INTERNATIONAL NARCOTICS LAW ENFORCEMENT (INL)

International Demand Reduction Training and Technical Assistance
INL programs include in-country training centers for law enforcement and cooperative agreements with several foreign governments.

> **Website:** www.state.gov/g/inl/

FOREIGN SERVICE INSTITUTE

Micronesian Diplomat Training Program (MDTP)
This program provides training for foreign diplomats from Micronesia.

> **4000 Arlington Boulevard**
> **Arlington, VA 22204-1500**
> **Tel.:** 703/302-7184   **Fax:** 703/302-6949

OFFICE OF INTERNATIONAL INFORMATION PROGRAMS (IIP)

U.S. Speakers, Specialists, and the Professionals-in-Residence Programs
> **Website:** http://usinfo.state.gov/

SECTION 5

DEPARTMENT OF TRANSPORTATION

Nassif Building
400 Seventh Street, SW
Washington, DC 20590
Tel.: 202/366-5580
Website: www.dot.gov

FEDERAL AVIATION ADMINISTRATION

800 Independence Ave, SW
Washington, DC 20591

Exchange Visitor Program

By arranging visas for specialists of foreign aviation departments to enter the U.S. for periods of up to three years, this program allows specialists to conduct studies, exchange information and expertise, and/or participate in cooperative research projects.
Website: www.intl.faa.gov/

International Visitors Program

Designed to facilitate cooperation and exchange in the filed of aviation, most international visitors are air traffic controllers.
Website: www.intl.faa.gov/

Office of International Aviation
International Training Program

Training is provided to foreign aviation officials under government-to-government agreements.

> **Office of International Aviation**
> **800 Independence Avenue, SW**
> **Washington, DC 20591**
> **Tel.:** 202/267-8157 **Fax:** 202/267-5036
> **Website:** www.academy.jccbi.gov

FEDERAL HIGHWAY ADMINISTRATION (FHA)

Office of International Programs

The FHA office works to improve the technological and institutional base of highway transportation system performance and program delivery in the U.S. and abroad.

> **Website:** http://international.fhwa.dot.gov/
> index.html

Border Technology Exchange Programs (BTEP)

This program was created to improve transportation along the U.S./Mexico/Canada border region in support of the North American Free Trade Agreement (NAFTA) through technical training, strengthening relationships/communication, harmonizing institutional developments, and coordinating operational efficiencies.

> **Website:** http://international.fhwa.dot.gov/
> tmpl.cfm?title=BrdrTech

International Technology Scanning Program

Serving as a means for identifying, assessing, and importing foreign highway technologies and practices that can be cost-effectively adapted to U.S. federal, state, and local highway programs.

> **Office of International Programs**
> **400 Seventh Street, SW, Room 3325**
> **Washington, DC 20590**
> **Tel.:** 202/366-0111 **Fax:** 202/366-3644
> **Website:** http://international.fhwa.dot.gov/
> tmpl.cfm?title=Scanning

National Highway Institute
International Training Program

This team is dedicated to providing expertise worldwide and increasing the transfer of highway technology to the international transportation community. This office assists the Office of International Programs in establishing and maintaining partnerships for transportation technology sharing.

> **National Highway Institute**
> **4600 N. Fairfax Drive, Suite 800**
> **Arlington, VA 22203**
> **Tel.:** 877/558-6873
> **Website:** www.nhi.fhwa.dot.gov/inter.html

SECTION 5

FEDERAL RAILROAD ADMINISTRATION

International Visitors Program

This program provides liaison and technical assistance between foreign government-owned and operated railway systems and the U.S. rail industry.

1120 Vermont Avenue, N.W.
Washington, D.C. 20590
Website: www.fra.dot.gov/site/index.htm

MARITIME ADMINISTRATION

United States Merchant Marine Academy Programs

The academy educates professional officers and leaders dedicated to serving the economic and national defense interests of the U.S. International students who are interested in applying to the U.S. Merchant Marine Academy must contact the Academy and request an International Application Package.

Admissions Office
Attention: International Applications
U.S. Merchant Marine Academy
300 Steamboat Road, Wiley Hall
Kings Point, NY 11024-1699
Website: www.usmma.edu /
admissions/intstud.htm

OFFICE OF INTERNATIONAL TRANSPORTATION AND TRADE

TRANSPORT Project

The objective of this project is to provide training in support of Saudi Arabia's transportation program and to foster technology exchange between Saudi Arabia and the United States.

400 Seventh Street, SW
Room 9215A
Washington, DC 20590
Tel.: 202/366-9540   **Fax:** 202/366-7483
Website: http://ostpxweb.dot.gov/aviation/
x20/x23.htm

U.S. COAST GUARD

International Affairs Commandant (G-CI)
U.S. Coast Guard
2100 Second Street, SW
Washington, DC 20593-0001
Tel.: 202/267-2280   **Fax:** 202/267-4588
Website: www.uscg.mil/hq/g-ci/intl.htm

International Personnel Exchange Program

The Coast Guard participates with the United Kingdom, Canada, and Australia's armed services in personnel exchanges with pilots from the Royal Air Force, the Royal Navy, and the Canadian Forces, and a reciprocal exchange with the Australian Navy.

International Training

Programs for officer, enlisted, and civilian personnel from foreign military and civilian agencies vary among the U.S. Coast Guard Academy, International Cadet Program, leadership, management, and technical training at schools and operational units in the U.S. and Mobile Training Teams (MTTs) in host countries.

International Visitors Program

The International Affairs office arranges official visits ranging from courtesy calls to meetings related to policy or operations at U.S. Coast Guard field units.

DEPARTMENT OF TREASURY
1500 Pennsylvania Avenue, NW
Washington, DC 20220
Website: www.ustreas.gov

BUREAU OF ALCOHOL, TOBACCO, AND FIREARMS (ATF)

Explosives Detection Canine Training
The ATF, in conjunction with the Connecticut State Police, and State Department Office of Antiterrorism Assistance provide trained explosives detection canine teams to selected foreign countries to assist them in their efforts to combat terrorism.

> **Bureau of Alcohol, Tobacco and Firearms Canine Operations Branch**
> **650 Massachusetts Avenue, NW**
> **Room 7100**
> **Washington, DC 20226**
> **Tel.:** 202/927-8680
> **Website:** www.atf.treas.gov/explarson/ canine.htm

International Training Program
Training programs are provided abroad and in the U.S. in law enforcement, firearms and explosives identification, firearms trafficking, and K-9 explosives detection.

> **Office of Training and Professional Development**
> **650 Massachusetts Avenue, NW**
> **Room 8300**
> **Washington, DC 20226**
> **Tel.:** 202/927-9380   **Fax:** 202/927-0752
> **Website:** www.atf.treas.gov

FEDERAL LAW ENFORCEMENT TRAINING CENTER (FLETC)

Computer Investigations and Security Training Program (CISTP)
CISTP is a popular program of the Financial Fraud Institute (FFI) that has recently been presented in Khabarovsk, Voronezh, and on three iterations to Tashkent, Uzbekhstan.

> **Website:** http://63.117.243.216/ffi/internat.htm

International Banking And Money Laundering Training Program
This program is designed for criminal investigations and law enforcement intelligence analysts involved in financial investigations.

International Law Enforcement Academy - Bangkok
ILEA-Bangkok works closely with local and federal U.S. law enforcement on illicit drug trafficking, money laundering, white collar and organized crime, among others.

> **International Law Enforcement Academy**
> **47/101 Building 3, Floor 4, Suite 3404**
> **Tiwanont Road**
> **Muang Nontaburi, Nontaburi 11000**
> **THAILAND**
> **Tel.:** 662/527-7500   **Fax:** 662/527-7506
> **Website:** http://www.ileabangkok.com/

International Law Enforcement Academy - Budapest
Located in Budapest, Hungary, the academy provides training on law enforcement issues during an eight-week personal and professional development program, conducted for 50 students, in five sessions per year.

> **International Law Enforcement Academy**
> **650 Massachusetts Avenue, NW**
> **Room 8300**
> **Washington, DC 20226**
> **Tel.:** 202/927-9380   **Fax:** 202/927-0752
> **Website:** www.treas.gov/enforcement/ enforc01.html

International Marine Law Enforcement Training Program (MLETP)
This program provides basic training for employees of those agencies and organizations involved in specialized areas of marine regulation and law enforcement. The program is intended for Federal law enforcement officers, though State and Local officials may attend as space permits.

> **Website:** http://63.117.243.216/dmd/ mtbprogs.htm

SECTION **5**

International Small Craft Enforcement Training Program (SCETP)

The SCETP provides instruction on the operation and navigation of highly specialized enforcement watercraft and is designed to meet the needs of officers assigned to inland marine law enforcement. Intended for Federal full-time officers, Non-Partner Organization personnel and state or local law enforcement officers may attend on a space-available basis. Applicants must be recommended by their supervisors or other agency officials and currently be assigned to inland marine law enforcement duties.

> **Website:** http://63.117.243.216/dmd/
> mtbprogs.htm

INTERNAL REVENUE SERVICE (IRS)

Tax Administration Advisory Services (TAAS) Division Programs

Tax Administration Advisory Services (TAAS) Division provides IRS Tax Advisors to work overseas for the purpose of providing technical assistance, training, and management programs to foreign governments or U.S. territories in the tax administration. The office also provides International Tax (INTAX) worldwide management seminars and hosts international visitors.

> **1111 Constitution Avenue, NW**
> **Washington, DC 20224**
> **Tel.:** 202/622-7263   **Fax:** 202/622-6513
> **Website:** www.irs.ustreas.gov/prod/tax_edu/taas/
> index.html

OFFICE OF THE COMPTROLLER OF THE CURRENCY (OCC)

Foreign Technical Assistance Program

Promoting a safe and sound international banking system, this program maintains the OCC's relationship with the international financial community and providing technical advice and assistance to foreign bank supervisory authorities.

OFFICE OF THRIFT SUPERVISION (OTS)

Foreign Visitors Program

The OTS meets with members of foreign governments to share ideas and experiences on banking systems.

> **1700 G Street, NW**
> **Washington, DC 20552**
> **Tel.:** 202/906-5900   **Fax:** 202/906-7477

U.S. CUSTOMS SERVICE

International Training and Assistance Programs

This program develops and coordinates short-term training and long-term advisory programs for foreign customs officials. Primary areas of focus are international narcotics control, export control/non-proliferation, commercial operations, Industry Partnerships Program.

> **International Assistance Division**
> **Office of International Affairs**
> **1300 Pennsylvania Avenue, NW**
> **Washington, DC 20004**
> **Tel.:** 202/927-1490   **Fax:** 202/927-0460
> **Website:** www.customs.gov/about/intl/
> training.htm

UNITED STATES SECRET SERVICE

The Combating Counterfeiting and Economic Fraud Course

This course introduces participants to current international trends in financial systems fraud specific to financial institutions, credit cards and money laundering.

The Forensic Applications and Combating Counterfeiting and Economic Fraud Course

This course introduces participants to current forensic applications employed in financial crime investigations.

> **Office of Training**
> **1800 G Street, NW**
> **Washington, DC 20223**
> **Tel.:** 202/435-7180
> **Website:** www.treas.gov/usss

BROADCASTING BOARD OF GOVERNORS (BBG)
330 Independence Avenue
Washington, DC 20237
Tel.: 202/619-2538   **Fax:** 202/619-1241
Website: http://www.ibb.gov/bbg/

International Media Training Program
An independent, autonomous Federal entity responsible for all U.S. government and government sponsored international broadcasting, BBG organizations include Voice of America, Radio Free Europe/Radio Liberty, Radio Free Asia, Office of Cuba Broadcasting, and WorldNet.

ENVIRONMENTAL PROTECTION AGENCY (EPA)
Waterside Mall
401 M Street, SW
Washington, DC 20460
Website: www.epa.gov/oia

Environmental Protection Agency Programs
In order to facilitate multilateral cooperation in achieving the EPA's environmental goals, foreign visitors are invited to observe U.S. environmental protection facilities and procedures. The Office of International Activities hosts 2,000-3,000 visitors annually. EPA also works collaboratively with Mexico, Canada, and other countries, and provides international technical assistance.

> **Office of International Activities**
> **Ronald Reagan Building**
> **1300 Pennsylvania Avenue, NW**
> **Washington, DC 20004**
> **Tel.:** 202/564-6600   **Fax:** 202/565-2407

FEDERAL COMMUNICATIONS COMMISSION (FCC)

445 12th Street, SW
Washington, DC 20554
Tel.: 888/225-5322 **Fax:** 202/418-0232
Website: www.fcc.gov

International Visitors Program

The IV program is part of the Telecommunications Division of the International Bureau, which handles all international telecommunications and satellite programs and policies. Foreign delegations interact in informal discussions with FCC personnel who provide legal, technical, and economic perspectives on a wide range of communications issues involving broadcasting, cablecasting, and telecommunications.

    International Visitors Program
    Federal Communications Commission
    445 12th Street, SW, Room 6-C825
    Washington, DC 20554
    Tel.: 202/418-1483 **Fax:** 202/418-2824
    Website: www.fcc.gov/ib/ivp/

FEDERAL DEPOSIT INSURANCE CORPORATION (FDIC)

550 17th Street, NW
Washington, DC 20429
Website: www.fdic.gov

Overseas Technical Assistance And Visitors

This program provides technical training assistance on banking-related deposit insurance issues. The FDIC also schedules visits, briefings, and technical discussions with foreign officials seeking information on its activities.

    550 17th Street, NW
    Washington, DC 20429
    Tel.: 202/898-3681 **Fax:** 202/898-3778

FEDERAL EMERGENCY MANAGEMENT AGENCY (FEMA)

500 C Street, SW
Washington, DC 20472
Website: www.fema.gov

Emergency Management Institute (EMI) Programs

This institute enhances U.S. emergency managements practices and enrolls foreign participants.

> **Emergency Management Institute**
> **16825 South Seton Avenue**
> **Emmitsburg, MD 21727**
> **Website:** www.fema.gov/emi

Emergency Preparedness and Disaster Management Visitors Program

This program hosts the emergency preparedness and disaster management officials from foreign government who are seeking information on disaster preparedness, response, recovery and mitigation policies, programs, methods, and techniques.

> **500 C Street, SW**
> **Washington, DC 20472**
> **Tel.:** 202/646-3051   **Fax:** 202/646-3397

National Fire Academy Foreign Seminars Program

This program conducts overseas training seminars in a wide variety of emergency management topics.

> **U.S. Fire Administration**
> **16825 South Seton Avenue**
> **Emmitsburg, MD 21727**
> **Website:** www.usfa.fema.gov/nfa

U.S.-Japan Earthquake Policy Cooperation Forum

In response to devastating earthquakes over the past century, the United States and Japan have developed broad programs of research, engineering and emergency management to mitigate the damage and disruption from seismic hazards.

> **Website:** www.fema.gov/mit/usjapan.htm

U.S.-Russian Federation Cooperation on Natural and Technological Disaster Prevention and Response

Increasing cooperation in the areas of mitigation, emergency preparedness, response, and recovery with Russia are the primary focuses of this FEMA program.

> **Website:** www.fema.gov/library/us_russ.htm

SECTION 5

FEDERAL ENERGY REGULATORY COMMISSION

888 First Street, NE
Washington, DC 20426
Tel.: 202/208-0200
Website: www.ferc.gov

International Visitor Program

This program shares its regulatory approach and lessons learned with professional counterparts from around the world.

GENERAL SERVICES ADMINISTRATION

1800 F Street, NW
Washington, DC 20405
Website: ww.gsa.gov

Office of Intergovernmental Solutions (OIS)

OIS provides assistance for information and communications technology and public administration.

1800 F Street, NW
Room 5224
Washington, DC 20405
Tel.: 202/501-0291
Website: www.gsa.gov/intergov

JAPAN-UNITED STATES FRIENDSHIP COMMISSION

1110 Vermont Avenue, NW, Suite 800
Washington, DC 20005
Website: www.jusfc.gov/commissn/commissn.html
Tel: 202/418-9800   **Fax:** 202/418-9802

Education and Training Programs

The Committee supports education and training for both scholarly and non-academic professions in such areas as broadcast media, language teaching, CD-ROM development and faculty exchanges for the purpose of curriculum development. It also sponsors individual research on issues of critical importance to U.S.-Japan relations and provides support to cultural institutions for collaborative production and individual artist exchanges.

Policy-Oriented Research Programs

The Commission supports team or individual projects that are germane to long-range relationship of the two countries, especially those that seek to explain fundamental issues of change in the structure of the economy, the nature of political leadership, Japan's international role, the dynamics of change in Japanese culture and society, and other contemporary issues.

Website: www.jusfc.gov/commissn/
Brochure2001.htm#por

The US/Japan Creative Artists' Program

Each year five mid-career leading contemporary and traditional artists from the United States spend six months in Japan on this highly selective program.
Website: www.jusfc.gov/commissn/guide.html

LIBRARY OF CONGRESS
10 First Street, SE
Washington, DC 20540
Website: www.loc.gov

Hispanic Division Internship Program
Two internships programs are offered for 1) college juniors or seniors, recent graduates, and graduate students for a paid summer internship and 2) the general public (post high school) for a year long internship for credit.

> **101 Independence Avenue, SW**
> **Washington, DC 20540-4850**
> **Tel.:** 202/707-5400   **Fax:** 202/707-2005

National Digital Library Visitors Center
> **Tel.:** 202/707-978   **Fax:** 202/707-0190

Scholarly Programs/Exchange Visitors Program
> **101 Independence Avenue, SW**
> **Washington, DC 20540-4860**
> **Tel.:** 202/707-1673   **Fax:** 202/707-3595

Visitors Services Office/
International Visitors Program
> **Tel.:** 202/707-9781   **Fax:** 202/707-0190
> **Website:** www.loc.gov/loc/visit/

International Copyright Institute
> **United States Copyrights Office**
> **Office of the Registrar, LLM-403**
> **101 Independence Avenue, SW**
> **Washington, DC 20559-6000**
> **Tel.:** 202/707-3000   **Fax:** 202/707-8366
> **Website:** www.loc.gov/copyright/

Global Legal Information Network (GLIN)
GLIN maintains and provides a database of laws, regulations, and other complementary legal sources that government organizations and agencies exchange over the Internet.

> **Tel.:** 202/707-9836   **Fax:** 202/707-1820
> **Website:** http://lcweb2.loc.gov/law/GLINv1/
> GLIN.html

Conservation Division Intern Training Program
101 Independence Avenue, SW
LLMG-38
Washington, DC 20540
Tel.: 202/707-1036   **Fax:** 202/707-1525

NATIONAL AERONAUTICS AND SPACE ADMINISTRATION (NASA)

Two Independence Square
300 E Street, SW
Washington, DC 20546
Website: www.hq.nasa.gov

National Exchange Visitor Program

The Office of External Relations, Assessments and Technology Division, administers the NASA foreign visits program, the NASA International Exchange Visitor Program (J-1 visa), and the Agency-wide coordination of international travel of NASA personnel.

> **Website:** http://www.hq.nasa.gov/office/codei/codeid.html

Resident Research Associateship (RRA) Program

The National Research Council, through its Associateship Programs offices, conducts a national competition to recommend and make awards to outstanding scientists and engineers at recent postdoctoral and experienced senior levels for tenure as guest researchers at participating laboratories.

Associateship Programs - TJ 2114
National Research Council
2101 Constitution Avenue NW
Washington, DC 20418
Tel.: 202/334-2760   **Fax:** 202/334-2759
Website: www.national-academies.org/rap

NATIONAL ARCHIVES AND RECORD ADMINISTRATION (NARA)

700 Pennsylvania Avenue, NW
Washington, DC 20408
Website: www.nara.gov

International Visitors Program

The focus of the IVP is to host foreign nationals from around the world and allow NARA staff to attend meetings of the International Council on Archives

> **Website:** www.ica.org

SECTION
5

NATIONAL ENDOWMENT FOR THE ARTS (NEA)
1100 Pennsylvania Avenue, NW
Washington, DC 20506
Website: www.arts.endow.gov

ArtsLink
ArtsLink, administered by CEC International Partners, encourages artistic exchange between the U.S. and Central and Eastern Europe, Newly Independent States, and the Baltic states.

CEC International Partners
12 West 31st Street
New York, NY 10001-4415
Tel.: 212/643-1985   **Fax:** 212/643-1996
Website: www.cecip.org/artslink/index.html

Fund For U.S. Artists at
International Festivals And Exhibitions
Through "The Fund", $1.1 million is available annually to support performing artists who have been invited to attend international festivals and to support U.S. representation at major contemporary visual arts exhibitions.

Administered by Arts International
251 Park Avenue South, 5th Floor
New York, NY 10010
Tel.: 212/674-9744   **Fax:** 212/674-9092
Website: http://www.artsinternational.org/

International Partnerships Office
This office brings the benefits of international exchange to arts organizations, artists and audiences, nationwide through its collaborative initiatives with other funders.

Tel.: 202/682-5429   **Fax:** 202/682-5602
Website: www.arts.endow.gov/partner/
International.html

U.S.-Ireland-Northern Ireland
Community Residences Exchange

NATIONAL ENDOWMENT FOR DEMOCRACY
1101 15th Street, NW
Washington, DC 20005
Website: www.ned.org

Visiting Fellows Program
Enabling journalists, scholars, and practitioners of democracy from around the world to spend three to ten months in residence at the Washington, DC, offices of the International Forum for Democratic Studies, the program focuses on exploring the theory and practice of democracy.

International Forum for Democratic Studies
National Endowment for Democracy
1101 15th Street, NW, Washington, DC 20005
Tel.: 202/293-0300   **Fax:** 202/293-0258
Website: www.ned.org/forum/
visiting_fellows.html

SECTION

5

NATIONAL ENDOWMENT FOR THE HUMANITIES
1100 Pennsylvania Avenue, NW
Washington, DC 20506
Website: www.neh.fed.us

Fellowship Programs at
Independent Research Institutions
Funds are awarded to humanities scholars conducting research in archives, museums, and archeological sites in countries throughout the world.

Division of Research And Education Programs
1100 Pennsylvania Avenue, NW, Room 3018
Washington, DC 20506
Tel.: 202/606-8200   **Fax:** 202/606-8394
Website: www.neh.gov/grants/onebook/
fpiri.html

NATIONAL SCIENCE FOUNDATION (NSF)
4201 Wilson Boulevard
Arlington, VA 22230
Tel.: 703/292-5111
Website: www.nsf.gov

Division of International Programs (INT) Programs
Supporting an array of targeted programs covering all regions of the world, these programs aim to promote new partnerships between U.S. scientists and engineers and their foreign colleagues.

Website: www.nsf.gov/home/int

OFFICE OF PERSONNEL MANAGEMENT
Theodore Roosevelt Federal Building
1900 E Street, NW
Washington, DC 20415
Website: www.leadership.opm.gov

Federal Executive Institute (FEI)

Leadership for a Democratic Society
This four-week program brings together managers and executives from 25 to 30 domestic and defense agencies for a unique, residential learning experience.

> **Federal Executive Institute**
> **1301 Emmet Street**
> **Charlottesville, VA 22903**
> **Tel.:** 804/980-6200   **Fax:** 804/979-1030
> **Wesite:** www.leadership.opm.gov/lds/index.html

PEACE CORPS
Headquarters
1111 20th Street NW
Washington, DC 20526
Tel.: 800/424-8580
Website: www.peacecorps.gov

Peace Corps Volunteer Service Programs
The Peace Corps was created in 1961 to promote international peace and friendship through the service abroad of American volunteers. It has since evolved as a model of citizen service on an international scale and of practical assistance to people in developing countries.

SECURITIES AND EXCHANGE COMMISSION

450 Fifth Street, NW
Washington, DC 20549
Website: www.sec.gov

International Training Programs

SOCIAL SECURITY ADMINISTRATION (SSA)

6401 Security Boulevard
Baltimore, MD 21235-6401
Website: www.ssa.gov

International Visitors Program
The SSA provides foreign social security officials and experts in related fields an opportunity to consult with U.S. staff experts on a wide variety of issues.
    Tel.: 410/965-3554   **Fax:** 410/966-7025

TENNESSEE VALLEY AUTHORITY (TVA)

400 West Summit Hill Drive
Knoxville, TN 37902
Website: www.tva.gov

International Visitors Program

This program receives visitors for general and technical purposes from all over the world in three general categories: Business Development, TVA International Visitors' Showcase Tours, Courtesy Visits.

Website: www.tva.gov/foia/readroom/policy/
prinprac/bun16.htm

TRADE AND DEVELOPMENT AGENCY
Orientation Visits
U.S. INSTITUTE FOR PEACE
1200 17th Street, NW
Suite 200
Washington, DC 20036-3011
Tel.: 202/457-1700   **Fax:** 202/429-6063
Website: www.usip.org

Balkans Initiative

Formerly the "Bosnia in the Balkans Initiative", this expanded program, which now includes education and training among tasks that strengthen partnerships to promote peace and reconciliation in the region, and promote greater awareness and understanding in the U.S., through partnerships such as workshops, conferences, and education and training programs.
> **Website:** www.usip.org/balkans/balkans.html

Education Program

The Education Program provides scholarships, intensive teaching seminars, research resources and curriculum materials. In addition, the Institute provides grants for educational projects and fellowships open to educators and scholars.
> **Website:** www.usip.org/ed.html

The Grant Program

Through this program the Institute offers financial support for research, education and training, and the dissemination of information on international peace and conflict resolution.
> **Website:** www.usip.org/grants.html

International Conflict Resolution Skills Training

These seminars are intended to increase the store of knowledge and practical skills available to political, military, and humanitarian professionals for preventing, managing, and working toward the resolution of violent international conflict.

Jennings Randolph Program
for International Peace

This program focuses on fulfilling the Institute's mandate of building a worldwide network of international affairs experts who can contribute to resolving the daunting problems of the post-Cold War world.
> **Website:** www.usip.org/fellows.html

The Research Studies Program

This program designs, directs and supervises the implementation of research projects on a broad range of current issues affecting international peace. It also strives to bridge the all-too-frequent gap between academia and government by convening meetings of academics and foreign officials with current policy-makers.
> **Website:** www.usip.org/research.html

Training Program

The program develops and presents programs that help government officials, military and police personnel, international organization representatives, and employees of non-governmental organizations-both American and international- improve their conflict management skills. Training in these skills is highly interactive, and draws heavily on the professional experiences of the participants themselves.
> **Website:** www.usip.org/tr.html

Virtual Diplomacy Initiative

The initiative is fostering cooperation among crisis management groups, including civilian and military organizations, using information and communications technologies; encouraging partnerships and resource sharing; and attracting support for collaborative enterprises from business, industry, and philanthropic circles.
> **Website:** www.usip.org/oc/virtual_dipl.html

SECTION 5

U.S. POSTAL SERVICE
475 L'Enfant Plaza West, SW
Washington, DC 20260
Website: www.usps.gov

Training Program

Visitors Program

WOODROW WILSON INTERNATIONAL CENTER FOR SCHOLARS
One Woodrow Wilson Plaza
1300 Pennsylvania Avenue, NW
Washington, DC 20004-3027
Website: www.wilsoncenter.org

Woodrow Wilson International Center for Scholars (WWICS) Programs
The center sponsors research, meetings, and publications in virtually all academic disciplines, with an emphasis on the social sciences and humanities. It also has several programs of international exchange, all of which are aimed at post-graduate scholars.

> **One Woodrow Wilson Plaza**
> **1300 Pennsylvania Avenue, NW**
> **Washington, DC 20523**
> **Tel.:** 202/691-4000   **Fax:** 202/691-4001

Section VI
U.S. Congress

This section contains information on congressional committees that play an important role in setting public policy governing international exchanges. Congressional committees make policy and funding decisions for a wide array of international activities including international exchange, Department of Education Title VI programs, Agency for International Development education and training programs, and immigration issues. The resources in this section will allow you to follow legislative developments and to contact Members of Congress.

Each Congressional entry includes a brief description of jurisdiction the committee has over exchange policy, and relevant subcommittee addresses for the majority and minority offices. The web addresses listed will allow you to quickly determine the membership of key congressional committees. Because all Members of Congress can affect exchange issues, you may wish to use these sites to determine how to contact the offices of individual Members of the House and Senate. You can get the address and phone number of any Member of Congress by calling the Capitol Switchboard at 202/224-3121.

U.S. SENATE

Website: http://www.senate.gov
>Link to Senator, committee, leadership offices, the annual and weekly Senate schedule, and other Senate organizations, task forces, and commissions. A section at the bottom of the website allows a search of current Senate bills and resolutions.

U.S. HOUSE OF REPRESENTATIVES

Website: http://www.house.gov
>Link to Member, committee, leadership offices, the annual and weekly congressional schedule, and other House organizations, task forces, and commissions.

Website: http://www.house.gov/writerep/
>Identify and contact your elected Member to the U.S. House of Representatives by entering your state and zip code.

Website: http://www.house.gov/house/Legproc.html
>Find information on bills and resolutions being considered in the Congress.

Website: http://clerkweb.house.gov/floor/current.htm
>Follow debate in minute-by-minute floor debate proceedings.

MISCELLANEOUS CONGRESSIONAL RESOURCES

Website: http://thomas.loc.gov/home/thomas.html
>Thomas, a service of the Library of Congress, is the most comprehensive source of information relating to current and past Congresses. The website includes searchable databases of the text of bills and resolutions since 1989, and bill summaries since 1973. The database contains Congressional Records, including roll call votes, speeches, and floor debate, since 1989.

Useful telephone numbers:

To register your opinion or comment on an issue (House or Senate)........................202/456-1111
To learn if a bill is signed into law or vetoed (House or Senate)...............................202/456-2226

Senate Switchboard (to be connected to a Member's office) 202/224-3121
Senate Document Room (to order single, free copies of legislation) 202/224-7860
Senate Republican Cloakroom (to hear a tape of current floor proceedings) 202/224-8601

House Switchboard (to be connected to a Member's office)....................................202/224-3121
House Document Room (to order single, free copies of legislation).........................202/225-1772
House Republican Cloakroom (to hear a tape of current floor proceedings).............202/225-2020

Various congressional committees wield broad oversight over international exchange policy in creating immigration policy, funding exchange programs, setting international affairs spending caps, authorizing international education policy, and other areas. The zip code for all Senate offices is 20510, and 20515 for all House offices. The area code for telephone numbers listed below is 202.

SENATE COMMITTEE INFORMATION

Senate Appropriations Committee
Website: http://appropriations.senate.gov/

The Appropriations Committee allocates funding for international education and training activities of the federal government. Activities and programs include the Fulbright and International Visitors programs, overseas educational advising, and other educational and cultural exchange programs. The Committee funds Agency for International Development education and training programs, as well as Title VI and Fulbright foreign language and international studies programs of the Department of Education.

Majority Office: S-128 Capitol
Tel.: 224-3471

Minority Office: S-146A Capitol
Tel.: 224-7363

Subcommittee on Commerce, Justice, State, the Judiciary, and Related Agencies
Website: http://www.senate.gov/~appropriations/commerce/index.htm

The Commerce, Justice, and State Subcommittee is responsible for funding State Department educational and cultural exchange programs.

Majority Office: S-206 Capitol
Tel.: 224-7277

Minority Office: S-125 Capitol
Tel.: 224-7271

Subcommittee on Defense
Website: http://www.senate.gov/~appropriations/defense/index.htm

The Defense Subcommittee funds Defense Department and selected national security exchange programs.

Majority Office: 119 Dirksen
Tel.: 224-7255

Minority Office: 119 Dirksen
Tel.: 224-7255

Subcommittee on Foreign Operations
Website: http://www.senate.gov/~appropriations/fops/index.htm

The Foreign Operations Subcommittee is responsible for funding Agency for International Development education and training programs.

Majority Office: 125 Dirksen
Tel.: 224-8202

Minority Office: 123 Hart
Tel.: 224-5095

Subcommittee on Labor, Health and Human Services, Education, and Related Agencies
Website: http://www.senate.gov/~appropriations/labor/index.htm

The Labor, Health and Human Services, and Education Subcommittee is responsible for funding decisions for the Department of Education's Title VI and Fulbright foreign language and international studies programs.

Majority Office: 125 Dirksen
Tel.: 224-8202

Minority Office: 123 Hart
Tel.: 224-5095

SECTION 6

Senate Budget Committee

Website: http://budget.senate.gov/

The Budget Committee is responsible for determining the amount of funding available for each broad area of federal activity, including international affairs, and sets spending caps for State Department and U.S. Agency for International Development international programs, and international education programs through the Department of Education. The Budget Committee has no subcommittees.

Majority Office: 621 Dirksen	**Minority Office:** 634 Dirksen
Tel.: 224-0642	**Tel.:** 224-0642
Fax: 224-4835	**Fax:** 224-4835

Senate Foreign Relations Committee

Website: http://foreign.senate.gov/menu.html

The Foreign Relations Committee has authorizing jurisdiction over all aspects of international affairs, including State Department international education and exchange programs such as Fulbright and International Visitors, and education and training programs of the U.S. Agency for International Development.

Majority Office: 446 Dirksen	**Minority Office:** 450 Dirksen
Tel.: 224-4651	**Tel.:** 224-6797

Subcommittee on African Affairs

Website: http://foreign.senate.gov/committee/sub_mbr.html#african_affairs
The African Affairs Subcommittee has jurisdiction over United States foreign policy relating to nations in Africa.

Subcommittee on East Asian and Pacific Affairs

Website: http://foreign.senate.gov/committee/sub_mbr.html#east_asian_affairs

The East Asian and Pacific Affairs Subcommittee has jurisdiction over United States foreign policy relating to nations in East Asia and the Pacific region.

Subcommittee on European Affairs

Website: http://foreign.senate.gov/committee/sub_mbr.html#european_affairs

The European Affairs Subcommittee has jurisdiction over United States foreign policy relating to nations in Europe.

Subcommittee on International Economic Policy, Export, and Trade Promotion

Website: http://foreign.senate.gov/committee/sub_mbr.html#economic_policy

The International Economic Policy, Export, and Trade Promotion Subcommittee has jurisdiction over international financial institutions.

Subcommittee on International Operations and Terrorism

Website: http://foreign.senate.gov/committee/sub_mbr.html#international_operations

The International Operations Subcommittee has broad jurisdiction over international exchange policy, general matters of international law and illegal activities, and oversight responsibilities for the Department of State and the U.S. Agency for International Development.

Subcommittee on Near Eastern and South Asian Affairs
Website: http://foreign.senate.gov/committee/sub_mbr.html#near_eastern_affairs

The Near Eastern and South Asian Affairs Subcommittee has jurisdiction over United States foreign policy relating to nations in the Near East and South Asia.

Subcommittee on Western Hemisphere, Peace Corps, and Narcotics Affairs
Website: http://foreign.senate.gov/committee/sub_mbr.html#western_hemisphere

The Western Hemisphere, Peace Corps, and Narcotics Affairs Subcommittee has jurisdiction over the United States foreign policy relating to nations in the Western Hemisphere and general oversight responsibilities for the Peace Corps.

Senate Health, Education, Labor and Pensions Committee
Website: http://labor.senate.gov/

The Committee has jurisdiction over Department of Education policy, including matters relating to the Department's Title VI and Fulbright-Hays 102(b)(6) international programs and authorization of the Higher Education Act.

Majority Office: 644 Dirksen
Tel.: 224-3961

Minority Office: 835 Hart
Tel.: 224-6770

Senate Judiciary Committee
Website: http://judiciary.senate.gov/

The Judiciary Committee has jurisdiction over immigration policy relating to international exchange participants, including F, J, H, and M non-immigrant visa classes, and oversees the operations of the Immigration and Naturalization Service.

Majority Office: 224 Dirksen
Tel.: 224-7703

Minority Office: 148 Dirksen
Tel.: 224-5225

Subcommittee on Immigration
Website: http://judiciary.senate.gov/subcom107a.htm

The Immigration and Claims Subcommittee has jurisdiction over all matters relating to immigration policy, including policy issues affecting exchange participants in F, H, J, M, and other visa categories. The Subcommittee exercises Congressional oversight of the Immigration and Naturalization Service and claims against the United States.

Majority Office: 520 Dirksen
Tel.: 224-7878

Minority Office: 323 Dirksen
Tel.: 224-9494

HOUSE COMMITTEE INFORMATION

House Appropriations Committee
Website: http://www.house.gov/appropriations/

The Appropriations Committee allocates funding for international education and training activities of the federal government. Activities and programs include the Fulbright and International Visitors programs, overseas educational advising, and other educational and cultural exchange programs. The Committee funds Agency for International Development education and training programs, as well as Title VI and Fulbright foreign language and international studies programs of the Department of Education.

> **Majority Office:** H-218 Capitol
> **Tel.:** 225-2771

> **Minority Office:** 1016 Longworth
> **Tel.:** 225-9476

Subcommittee on Commerce, Justice, State, the Judiciary, and Related Agencies
Web link through main Appropriations Committee page

The Commerce, Justice, and State Subcommittee is responsible for funding State Department educational and cultural exchange programs.

> **Majority Office:** H-309 Capitol
> **Tel.:** 225-3351

> **Minority Office:** 1016 Longworth
> **Tel.:** 225-3481

Subcommittee on Defense
Web link through main Appropriations Committee page

The Defense Subcommittee funds the Defense Department and selected national security exchange programs.

> **Majority Office:** H-149 Capitol
> Tel: 225-2847

> **Minority Office:** 1016 Longworth
> **Tel.:** 225-3481

Subcommittee on Foreign Operations, Export Financing, and Related Agencies
Web link through main Appropriations Committee page

The Foreign Operations Subcommittee is responsible for funding Agency for International Development education and training programs.

> **Majority Office:** H-150 Capitol
> **Tel.:** 225-2041

> **Minority Office:** 1016 Longworth
> **Tel.:** 225-3481

Subcommittee on Labor, Health and Human Services, Education, and Related Agencies
Web link through main Appropriations Committee page

The Labor, Health and Human Services, and Education (LHHS) Subcommittee is responsible for funding decisions for the Department of Education's Title VI and Fulbright foreign language and international studies programs.

> **Majority Office:** 2358 Rayburn
> **Tel.:** 225-3508

> **Minority Office:** 1016 Longworth
> **Tel.:** 225-3481

House Budget Committee

Website: http://www.house.gov/budget/

The Budget Committee is responsible for determining the amount of funding available for each broad area of federal activity, including international affairs, and sets spending caps for State Department and Agency for International Development international programs, and international education programs through the Department of Education.

Majority Office: 309 Cannon	**Minority Office:** 214 O'Neill
Tel.: 226-7270	**Tel.:** 226-7200

House Education and the Workforce Committee

Website: http://edworkforce.house.gov/

The Committee has jurisdiction over Department of Education policy, including matters relating to the Department's Title VI and Fulbright-Hays 102(b)(6) international programs and authorization of the Higher Education Act.

Majority Office: 2181 Rayburn	**Minority Office:** 2101 Rayburn
Tel.: 225-4527	**Tel.:** 225-3725

Subcommittee on Select Education

Website: http://edworkforce.house.gov/members/mem-sed.htm
The Select Education Subcommittee has jurisdiction over all programs administered by the Department of Education that concern education beyond the secondary level, including the Department's Title VI and Fulbright- Hays 102(b)(6) international education programs.

Majority Office: 2181 Rayburn	**Minority Office:** 1040 Longworth
Tel.: 225-4527	**Tel.:** 225-7116

Subcommittee on Education Reform

Website: http://edworkforce.house.gov/members/mem-edr.htm
The Subcommittee on Education Reform has jurisdiction over all programs administered by the Department of Education that concern education at the elementary, secondary, overseas dependent schools, and vocational levels.

Majority Office: 2181 Rayburn	**Minority Office:** 1107 Longworth
Tel.: 225-4527	**Tel.:** 226-2068

House International Relations Committee

Website: http://www.house.gov/international_relations/

The International Relations Committee has authorizing jurisdiction over all aspects of international affairs, including State Department international education and exchange programs such as Fulbright and International Visitors, and education and training programs of the U.S. Agency for International Development.

Majority Office: 2170 Rayburn	**Minority Office:** B-360 Rayburn
Tel.: 225-5021	**Tel:** 225-6735

Subcommittee on Africa

Website: http://www.house.gov/international_relations/sub107.htm

The Africa Subcommittee has jurisdiction over United States foreign policy relating to the nations of Africa.

Majority Office: 255 Ford	**Minority Office:** 2209 Rayburn
Tel.: 226-7812	**Tel.:** 226-4524

Subcommittee on East Asia and the Pacific

Website: http://www.house.gov/international_relations/sub107.htm

The East Asia and the Pacific Subcommittee has jurisdiction over United States foreign policy relating to the nations of Asia and the Pacific region.

Majority Office: B-359 Rayburn
Tel.: 226-7825

Minority Office: 2217 Rayburn
Tel.: 225-3531

Subcommittee on Europe

Website: http://www.house.gov/international_relations/sub107.htm

The Europe Subcommittee has jurisdiction over United States foreign policy relating to the nations in Europe.

Majority Office: 2401A Rayburn
Tel.: 226-7820

Minority Office: 2401A Rayburn
Tel.: 225-7820

Subcommittee on International Operations and Human Rights

Website: http://www.house.gov/international_relations/sub107.htm

The International Operations and Human Rights Subcommittee has broad jurisdiction over the international exchange policy, general matters of international law and illegal activities, and oversight responsibility for the Department of State and the Agency for International Development.

Majority Office: 257 Ford
Tel.: 225-3345

Minority Office: B-358 Rayburn
Tel.: 225-1139

Subcommittee on Middle East and South Asia

Website: http://www.house.gov/international_relations/sub107.htm

The Middle East and South Asia Subcommittee has jurisdiction over United States foreign policy relating to nations in the Middle East and South Asia.

Majority Office: 259 Ford
Tel.: 226-9970

Minority Office: 259 Ford
Tel.: 226-9980

Subcommittee on Western Hemisphere

Website: http://www.house.gov/international_relations/sub107.htm

The Western Hemisphere Subcommittee has jurisdiction over United States foreign policy relating to nations in the Western Hemisphere.

Majority Office: 259 Ford
Tel.: 226-9970

Minority Office: 259 Ford
Tel.: 226-9980

House Judiciary Committee

Website: http://www.house.gov/judiciary/

The Judiciary Committee has jurisdiction over immigration policy relating to international exchange participants, including F, J, H, and M non-immigrant visa classes, and oversees the operations of the Immigration and Naturalization Service.

Majority Office: 2138 Rayburn
Tel.: 225-3951

Minority Office: B-351C Rayburn
Tel.: 225-6906

Subcommittee on Immigration and Claims

Website: http://www.house.gov/judiciary/submembers.htm

The Immigration and Claims Subcommittee has jurisdiction over all matters relating to immigration policy, including policy issues affecting exchange participants in F, H, J, M, and other visa categories. The Subcommittee exercises Congressional oversight of the Immigration and Naturalization Service and claims against the United States.

Majority Office: B-370B Rayburn
Tel.: 225-5727

Minority Office: B-336 Rayburn
Tel.: 225-2022

Academic Levels

Academic Levels

Organization Name	K - 12	UNDERGRADUATE STUDENTS	GRADUATE STUDENTS	TEACHERS	FACULTY
AACSB International	●	●		●	
Academic Adventures in America	●			●	
Academy for Educational Development		●	●	●	●
Accent on Understanding	●			●	
Adventures in Real Communication Year Program	●	●			
Africa-America Institute		●	●	●	●
AFS-USA, Inc.	●	●	●		
AHA International	●	●		●	
AIESEC United States, Inc.		●	●		
Alliances Abroad	●	●			
America-Mideast Educational and Training Services		●	●		●
American Academic and Cultural Exchange	●	●		●	
American Association of Community Colleges		●			
American Council of Learned Societies			●	●	●
American Councils for International Education: ACTR/ACCELS	●	●	●	●	●
American Cultural Exchange	●	●		●	
American Institute for Foreign Study	●	●		●	
American Institute for Foreign Study Foundation	●	●			
American Intercultural Student Exchange, Inc.	●				
American International Youth Student Exchange Program	●				
American Secondary Schools for International Students and Teachers	●				
Amity Institute		●	●	●	●
ASA International	●				
Asian Cultural Council			●		
ASPECT Foundation	●	●			
ASSE International Student Exchange Programs	●	●			
Association for International Practical Training (AIPT)		●	●		
Association of International Education Administrators		●	●		●
Association of Professional Schools of International Affairs (APSIA)			●		●
AYUSA International	●			●	
Better Exchange for Student Teenagers (BEST)	●				
BUNAC		●	●		
Center for Cultural Interchange	●	●			
Center for Global Partnership	●	●		●	
Children's International Summer Villages, Inc.	●				
College Consortium for International Studies		●			●
Concordia Language Villages	●				
Cooperative Extension 4-H Youth Development	●				
Cordell Hull Foundation for International Education	●				
Council for Educational Travel USA	●	●			●
Council of American Overseas Research Centers					●
Council on International Programs, USA			●		

Academic Levels

Organization Name	K - 12	UNDERGRADUATE STUDENTS	GRADUATE STUDENTS	TEACHERS	FACULTY
Council on International Educational Exchanges, Inc.	●	●	●	●	●
Cross-Cultural Solutions		●	●	●	
Cultural Academic Student Exchange	●				
Cultural Homestay International	●	●		●	
DM Discoveries	●				
Educational Resource Development Trust	●	●	●		
Educational Testing Service					●
Education Travel and Culture Exchange	●				
EF Foundation for Foreign Study	●				
Eurocentres	●	●	●	●	●
Exchange: Japan	●	●	●	●	●
Face the World Foundation	●				
Foreign Study Language	●	●	●		
Foundation for Worldwide International Student Exchange	●	●	●	●	
Friendship Force, Inc.	●	●			
GeoVisions		●			
German American Partnership Program, Inc.	●				
Homestay Educational and Cultural Foundation	●				
Institute for American Universities		●			
Institute for the International Education of Students		●			
Institute of International Education		●	●	●	●
Institute of Public Administration			●		
Intercultural Dimensions	●	●	●	●	●
International Cultural Exchange Services	●				
International Education	●				
International Internship Programs		●	●		●
International Research and Exchanges Board			●		●
International Student Exchange	●				
International Student Exchange Program		●	●		●
Intrax	●	●			
Japan-America Student Conference		●	●		
Japan Foundation			●		●
Japan Foundation Center for Global Partnership	●	●			●
Japan Society				●	
Kosciuszko Foundation		●	●	●	●
LASPAU: Academic and Professional Programs for the Americas		●	●		●
Laurasian Institution	●				
LEXIA International		●	●		
Lisle Fellowship, Inc.		●	●	●	●
Nacel Open Door	●				
National Association of State Universities and Land-Grant Colleges		●	●		
National Committee on United States-China Relations	●				

Academic Levels

Organization Name	K-12	UNDERGRADUATE STUDENTS	GRADUATE STUDENTS	TEACHERS	FACULTY
National Council for Eurasian and East European Research					●
National FFA	●	●			
North Carolina Center for International Understanding	●			●	
North-South Center			●		●
Northwest International Study Exchange, Inc.	●			●	
Ohio International Agricultural and Horticultural Interns Program		●	●		●
Organization for Cultural Exchange Among Nations	●				●
Pacific Intercultural Exchange	●				
Partners of the Americas	●	●	●	●	●
People Link	●				
People to People International	●	●	●		
Presidential Classroom	●				
Proamerican Educational and Cultural Exchange	●	●			
Program of Academic Exchange	●				
Project Harmony	●	●	●	●	●
Resource Euro-Asian American Cultural Homestay, Inc.	●				
Rotary International		●	●		●
Scandinavian Seminar, Inc.	●	●			
School Year Abroad	●				
STS Foundation	●				
United Studies Student Exchange	●				
University and College Intensive English Program		●	●		
USDA Graduate School International Institute				●	●
Wo International Center	●				
World Education Services Foundation	●				
World Experience Teenage Student Exchange	●				
World Families	●				
World Learning, Inc.	●	●	●	●	●
WorldTeach	●	●	●	●	●
Youth for Understanding	●	●			

Exchange Areas

Exchange Areas

Organization Name	ARTS/CULTURAL	COMMUNITY/CITIZEN	HOMESTAY	LANGUAGE STUDY	PERSONS WITH DISABILITIES	PROFESSIONAL/BUSINESS	SENIOR CITIZENS	SHORT-TERM VISITORS	SPORTS	STUDENTS/EDUCATORS	TRAINING	WORK EXCHANGES
Academic Adventures in America	●	●	●	●				●		●		
Academic and Cultural Exchange			●					●		●		
Academy for Educational Development	●	●				●		●		●	●	
Accent on Understanding		●	●							●	●	
Adventures in Real Communication Year Program	●	●	●	●				●		●		
Africa-America Institute	●	●	●			●		●		●		
AFS-USA, Inc.			●	●						●		
AHA International			●					●		●		
AIESEC United States, Inc.											●	
Alliances Abroad	●	●	●	●		●					●	
America-Mideast Educational and Training Services			●	●		●		●		●	●	
American Academic and Cultural Exchange			●	●				●		●		
American Association of Community Colleges						●		●				
American Association of Intensive English Programs				●		●				●		
American Council of Learned Societies										●		
American Council of Young Political Leaders								●				
American Councils for International Education: ACTR/ACCELS			●	●		●				●	●	
American Cultural Exchange			●	●		●		●		●	●	
American Institute for Foreign Study			●									●
American Institute for Foreign Study Foundation			●							●		
American Intercultural Student Exchange, Inc.			●						●	●		
American International Youth Student Exchange Program	●	●	●	●								
American Youth Work Center								●			●	
American-Scandinavian Foundation	●										●	
Amity Institute	●		●	●						●	●	●
Amizade, Ltd.		●	●					●		●		
ASA International			●					●		●		
Asia Foundation						●					●	
Asian Cultural Council	●											
ASPECT Foundation			●							●		
ASSE International Student Exchange Programs			●	●						●		

Exchange Areas

Organization Name	ARTS/CULTURAL	COMMUNITY/CITIZEN	HOMESTAY	LANGUAGE STUDY	PERSONS WITH DISABILITIES	PROFESSIONAL/BUSINESS	SENIOR CITIZENS	SHORT-TERM VISITORS	SPORTS	STUDENTS/EDUCATORS	TRAINING	WORK EXCHANGES
Association for International Practical Training (AIPT)						●		●		●	●	●
Association of International Education Administrators										●		
Association of Professional Schools of International Affairs (APSIA)										●		
AuPairCare												●
AYUSA International			●	●						●		
Better Exchange for Student Teenagers (BEST)		●		●						●		
BUNAC											●	●
Camp Counselors, USA						●				●	●	●
CDS International				●							●	●
CEC International Partners	●					●		●				
Center for Citizen Initiatives		●				●		●			●	
Center for Cultural Interchange		●	●	●	●			●				●
Center for Global Partnership		●								●	●	
Children's International Summer Villages, Inc.		●	●					●		●		
College Consortium for International Studies			●	●		●				●		
Communicating for Agriculture											●	
Concordia Language Villages	●	●		●						●		
Connect/US-Russia		●				●					●	
Cooperative Extension 4-H Youth Development		●								●	●	
Cordell Hull Foundation for International Education	●			●				●		●	●	●
Council for Educational Travel USA			●	●				●		●		
Council of American Overseas Research Centers	●			●								
Council of Chief State School Officers	●					●		●		●	●	
Council on International Programs, USA					●	●				●	●	
Council on International Educational Exchanges, Inc.			●	●						●		●
Cross-Cultural Solutions	●	●					●			●	●	
Cultural Academic Student Exchange			●	●						●		
Cultural Homestay International			●	●				●	●	●		●
Culturelink										●	●	
DM Discoveries		●	●					●				
East-West Center	●					●				●	●	

Exchange Areas

Organization Name	ARTS/CULTURAL	COMMUNITY/CITIZEN	HOMESTAY	LANGUAGE STUDY	PERSONS WITH DISABILITIES	PROFESSIONAL/BUSINESS	SENIOR CITIZENS	SHORT-TERM VISITORS	SPORTS	STUDENTS/EDUCATORS	TRAINING	WORK EXCHANGES
Educational Resource Development Trust			●	●				●		●		
Education Travel and Culture Exchange			●									
EF Foundation for Foreign Study										●		
Eisenhower Exchange Fellowships						●						
EurAupair Intercultural Childcare Programs												●
Eurocentres			●	●				●		●		
Exchange: Japan				●						●		
Experience International						●				●		
Face the World Foundation			●					●		●		
Foreign Study Language			●	●						●		
Foundation for International Cooperation	●	●	●			●	●	●				
Foundation for Worldwide International Student Exchange	●		●			●		●		●	●	●
Freedom House						●		●		●		
French-American Chamber of Commerce											●	
Friendship Ambassadors Foundation	●		●							●		
Friendship Force, Inc.	●	●				●		●		●		
GeoVisions						●	●				●	●
German American Partnership Program, Inc.		●	●	●						●		
German Marshall Fund of the United States						●		●				
Girl Scouts of the U.S.A.			●					●				
Global Outreach, Inc.			●								●	
Homestay Educational and Cultural Foundation			●	●								
Institute for American Universities	●		●	●	●	●				●		
Institute for the International Education of Students	●		●	●	●	●				●		
Institute of International Education	●	●				●		●		●	●	
Institute of Public Administration		●				●		●		●	●	
Intercambio Internacional de Estudiantes	●							●				
Intercultural Dimensions	●		●	●						●		
InterExchange											●	●
International Agricultural Exchange Association											●	●
International Cultural Exchange Services			●									

Exchange Areas

Organization Name	ARTS/CULTURAL	COMMUNITY/CITIZEN	HOMESTAY	LANGUAGE STUDY	PERSONS WITH DISABILITIES	PROFESSIONAL/BUSINESS	SENIOR CITIZENS	SHORT-TERM VISITORS	SPORTS	STUDENTS/EDUCATORS	TRAINING	WORK EXCHANGES
International Education										•		
International Internship Programs	•		•			•				•		•
International Research and Exchanges Board	•	•		•		•		•		•	•	
International Student Exchange			•					•				
International Student Exchange Program										•		
Intrax			•	•								•
Japan-America Student Conference										•		
Japan Foundation	•							•		•	•	
Japan Foundation Center for Global Partnership		•								•		
Japan Society	•	•		•		•				•	•	
Japan-U.S. Community Education and Exchange		•						•		•		
Kosciuszko Foundation	•			•		•				•		
LASPAU: Academic and Professional Programs for the Americas	•			•		•		•		•	•	
Laurasian Institution			•	•								
LEXIA International	•			•						•	•	
Lisle Fellowship, Inc.	•	•	•					•		•		•
Mansfield Center for Pacific Affairs						•					•	•
Meridian International Center	•		•			•		•		•	•	
Metro International Program Services of New York, Inc.	•	•	•			•		•		•		
Minnesota Agricultural Student Trainee Program											•	
Mobility International USA/National Clearinghouse on Disability and Exchange		•			•					•	•	
Multinl Exchange Sustainable Ag (MESA)											•	
Nacel Open Door			•	•						•		
National Committee on United States-China Relations		•				•						
National Council for Eurasian and East European Research	•									•	•	
National Council for International Visitors	•	•	•					•			•	
National FFA								•		•	•	
North Carolina Center for International Understanding		•	•							•		
North-South Center						•				•		
Northwest International Study Exchange, Inc.			•	•					•	•		
Ohio International Agricultural and Horticultural Interns Program											•	

Exchange Areas

Organization Name	ARTS/CULTURAL	COMMUNITY/CITIZEN	HOMESTAY	LANGUAGE STUDY	PERSONS WITH DISABILITIES	PROFESSIONAL/BUSINESS	SENIOR CITIZENS	SHORT-TERM VISITORS	SPORTS	STUDENTS/EDUCATORS	TRAINING	WORK EXCHANGES
Organization for Cultural Exchange Among Nations	●		●	●				●		●		
Pacific Intercultural Exchange	●	●	●	●				●		●		
Partners of the Americas	●	●	●	●	●	●	●	●	●	●	●	
People Link	●	●	●	●				●		●		
People to People International	●	●	●			●		●		●		
Phelps-Stokes Fund						●		●		●		
Presidential Classroom								●		●		
Proamerican Educational and Cultural Exchange			●	●								
Program of Academic Exchange			●							●		
Project Harmony	●	●	●	●		●					●	
Resource Euro-Asian American Cultural Homestay, Inc.			●									
Rotary International				●		●		●		●		
School Year Abroad			●	●						●		
Sister Cities International	●	●			●	●				●	●	
STS Foundation										●		
United States Servas, Inc.	●	●	●		●		●	●				
United Studies Student Exchange			●		●					●		
University and College Intensive English Program					●			●		●		
USDA Graduate School International Institute						●		●		●	●	
Wo International Center										●		
World Education Services Foundation			●							●		
World Education Services, Inc.						●				●		
World Exchange	●		●	●				●	●			
World Experience Teenage Student Exchange			●					●				
World Families	●		●	●		●		●	●			
World Learning, Inc.	●	●	●	●		●					●	
WorldTeach										●		
YMCA International Program Services								●			●	●
Youth Exchange Service, Inc.	●	●	●	●		●		●				
Youth for Understanding	●		●		●					●	●	

Geographic Focus by Region

Geographic Focus by Region

Organization Name	AFRICA	ASIA	CARIBBEAN	CENTRAL AMERICA	EASTERN EUROPE	MIDDLE EAST	NEWLY INDEPENDENT STATES	NORTH AMERICA	OCEANIA	SOUTH AMERICA	WESTERN EUROPE
AACSB International	●	●	●	●	●	●	●	●	●	●	●
Academic Adventures in America		●						●	●	●	●
Academic and Cultural Exchange		●			●			●		●	●
Academy for Educational Development	●	●	●	●	●	●	●	●	●	●	●
Accent on Understanding						●					
Adventures in Real Communication Year Program		●		●		●	●			●	●
Africa-America Institute	●		●								
AFS-USA, Inc.	●	●	●	●	●	●	●	●	●	●	●
AHA International		●									●
AIESEC United States, Inc.	●	●	●	●	●	●	●	●	●	●	●
Alliances Abroad	●	●		●				●		●	●
America-Mideast Educational and Training Services	●					●					
American Academic and Cultural Exchange	●	●	●	●	●	●	●	●	●	●	●
American Association of Collegiate Registrars and Admission Officers (AACRAO)	●	●	●	●	●	●	●	●	●	●	●
American Association of Community Colleges	●	●	●	●	●	●	●	●	●	●	●
American Association of Intensive English Programs	●	●	●	●	●	●	●	●	●	●	●
American Association of Teachers of German											●
American Council of Learned Societies		●			●						
American Council of Young Political Leaders	●	●	●	●	●	●	●	●	●	●	●
American Council on Education	●	●	●	●	●	●	●	●	●	●	●
American Councils for International Education: ACTR/ACCELS					●		●				
American Cultural Exchange	●	●	●	●	●	●	●	●	●	●	●
American Institute for Foreign Study	●	●	●	●	●	●	●	●	●	●	●
American Institute for Foreign Study Foundation	●	●	●	●	●	●	●	●	●	●	●
American Intercultural Student Exchange, Inc.	●	●	●	●	●	●	●	●	●	●	●
American International Youth Student Exchange Program	●	●	●	●	●	●	●	●	●	●	●
American Secondary Schools for International Students and Teachers		●			●				●		●
American Youth Work Center			●								●
American-Scandinavian Foundation											●
Amity Institute	●		●	●			●			●	●
Amizade, Ltd.		●							●	●	
ASA International	●	●	●	●	●	●	●	●	●	●	●
Asia Foundation		●									

Geographic Focus by Region

Organization Name	AFRICA	ASIA	CARIBBEAN	CENTRAL AMERICA	EASTERN EUROPE	MIDDLE EAST	NEWLY INDEPENDENT STATES	NORTH AMERICA	OCEANIA	SOUTH AMERICA	WESTERN EUROPE
Asian Cultural Council		•									
ASPECT Foundation		•			•			•		•	•
ASSE International Student Exchange Programs	•	•			•		•	•	•		•
Association for International Practical Training (AIPT)	•	•	•	•	•	•	•	•	•	•	•
Association of International Education Administrators	•	•	•	•	•	•	•	•	•	•	•
Association of Jesuit Colleges and Universities	•	•	•	•	•	•	•	•	•	•	•
Association of Professional Schools of International Affairs (APSIA)	•	•	•	•	•	•	•	•	•	•	•
AuPairCare	•	•	•	•	•	•	•	•	•	•	•
AYUSA International	•	•	•	•	•	•	•	•	•	•	•
Better Exchange for Student Teenagers (BEST)		•			•			•		•	•
BUNAC	•							•	•		•
Camp Counselors, USA	•		•		•		•	•	•	•	•
CDS International		•						•		•	•
CEC International Partners		•			•		•				
Center for Citizen Initiatives							•				
Center for Cultural Interchange		•			•		•	•		•	•
Center for Global Partnership		•						•			
Children's International Summer Villages, Inc.	•	•	•	•	•	•	•	•	•	•	•
College Board-International Education	•	•	•	•	•	•	•	•	•	•	•
College Consortium for International Studies	•	•	•	•	•	•	•	•	•	•	•
Communicating for Agriculture	•	•	•	•	•	•	•	•	•	•	•
Concordia Language Villages	•	•	•	•	•	•	•	•	•	•	•
Connect/US-Russia							•				
Cooperative Extension 4-H Youth Development		•						•			
Cordell Hull Foundation for International Education	•	•		•			•	•	•	•	•
Council for Educational Travel USA	•	•	•	•	•	•	•	•	•	•	•
Council of American Overseas Research Centers	•	•				•					•
Council of Chief State School Officers	•	•	•	•	•	•	•	•	•	•	•
Council of Graduate Schools	•							•			
Council on International Programs, USA	•	•	•	•	•	•	•	•	•	•	•
Council on International Educational Exchanges, Inc.	•	•	•	•	•	•	•	•	•	•	•
Council on Standards for International Educational Travel	•	•	•	•	•	•	•	•	•	•	•
Cross-Cultural Solutions	•	•	•				•			•	
Cultural Academic Student Exchange	•	•	•	•	•	•	•	•	•	•	•

Geographic Focus by Region

Organization Name	AFRICA	ASIA	CARIBBEAN	CENTRAL AMERICA	EASTERN EUROPE	MIDDLE EAST	NEWLY INDEPENDENT STATES	NORTH AMERICA	OCEANIA	SOUTH AMERICA	WESTERN EUROPE
Cultural Homestay International	●	●	●	●	●	●	●	●	●	●	●
Culturelink	●	●	●	●	●	●	●	●	●	●	●
DM Discoveries	●	●		●						●	●
East-West Center		●							●		
Educational Resource Development Trust	●	●	●	●	●	●	●	●	●	●	●
Educational Testing Service	●	●	●	●	●	●	●	●	●	●	●
Education Travel and Culture Exchange	●	●	●	●	●	●	●	●	●	●	●
EF Foundation for Foreign Study	●	●	●	●	●	●	●	●	●	●	●
Eisenhower Exchange Fellowships	●	●	●	●	●	●	●	●	●	●	●
EurAupair Intercultural Childcare Programs	●	●	●	●	●	●	●	●	●	●	●
Eurocentres		●					●				●
Exchange: Japan		●	●								
Experience International	●	●	●	●	●	●	●	●	●	●	●
Face the World Foundation									●		
Foreign Study Language	●	●	●	●	●	●	●	●	●	●	●
Foundation for International Cooperation	●	●	●	●	●	●	●	●	●	●	●
Foundation for Worldwide International Student Exchange		●								●	●
Freedom House	●	●	●	●	●	●	●	●	●	●	●
French-American Chamber of Commerce	●	●	●	●	●	●	●	●	●	●	●
Friendship Ambassadors Foundation	●	●	●	●	●	●	●	●	●	●	●
Friendship Force, Inc.	●	●	●	●	●	●	●	●	●	●	●
Fulbright Association	●	●	●	●	●	●	●	●	●	●	●
GeoVisions		●		●					●	●	
German American Partnership Program, Inc.											●
German Marshall Fund of the United States					●			●			●
Girl Scouts of the U.S.A.	●	●	●	●	●	●	●	●	●	●	●
Global Outreach, Inc.				●	●				●	●	
Homestay Educational and Cultural Foundation		●									●
Institute for the International Education of Students		●							●	●	●
Institute of International Education	●	●	●	●	●	●	●	●	●	●	●
Institute of Public Administration	●	●	●	●	●	●	●	●	●	●	●
Intercambio Internacional de Estudiantes				●					●		
Intercultural Dimensions	●										
InterExchange	●	●	●	●	●	●	●	●	●	●	●

Geographic Focus by Region

Organization Name	AFRICA	ASIA	CARIBBEAN	CENTRAL AMERICA	EASTERN EUROPE	MIDDLE EAST	NEWLY INDEPENDENT STATES	NORTH AMERICA	OCEANIA	SOUTH AMERICA	WESTERN EUROPE
International Agricultural Exchange Association		●							●		●
International Cultural Exchange Services		●					●	●	●	●	●
International Education										●	●
International Internship Programs	●	●	●	●	●	●	●	●	●	●	●
International Research and Exchanges Board		●			●	●	●				
International Student Exchange		●			●	●		●		●	●
International Student Exchange Program	●	●		●	●		●	●	●	●	●
Intrax	●	●	●	●	●	●	●	●	●	●	●
Japan-America Student Conference		●									
Japan Foundation		●									
Japan Foundation Center for Global Partnership		●						●			
Japan Society		●									
Japan-U.S. Community Education and Exchange		●									
Kosciuszko Foundation					●			●			
LASPAU: Academic and Professional Programs for the Americas			●	●				●		●	
Laurasian Institution		●			●			●			●
LEXIA International	●	●	●		●					●	●
Lisle Fellowship, Inc.	●	●	●	●	●	●	●	●	●	●	●
Mansfield Center for Pacific Affairs		●									
Meridian International Center	●	●	●	●	●	●	●	●	●	●	●
Metro International Program Services of New York, Inc.	●	●	●	●	●	●	●	●	●	●	●
Minnesota Agricultural Student Trainee Program	●	●	●	●	●	●	●	●	●	●	●
Mobility International USA/ National Clearinghouse on Disability and Exchange	●	●	●	●	●	●	●	●	●	●	●
Mounbatten Internship Programme								●	●		●
Multinl Exchange Sustainable Ag (MESA)	●	●	●	●	●	●	●	●	●	●	●
Nacel Open Door	●	●		●	●	●	●	●		●	●
NAFSA: Association of International Educators	●	●	●	●	●	●	●	●	●	●	●
National Association of State Universities and Land-Grant Colleges	●	●	●	●	●	●	●	●	●	●	●
National Committee on United States-China Relations		●						●			
National Council for Eurasian and East European Research					●		●				
National Council for International Visitors	●	●	●	●	●	●	●	●	●	●	●
National FFA	●	●	●	●	●	●	●	●	●	●	●
North Carolina Center for International Understanding	●	●	●	●	●	●	●	●	●	●	●

Geographic Focus by Region

Organization Name	AFRICA	ASIA	CARIBBEAN	CENTRAL AMERICA	EASTERN EUROPE	MIDDLE EAST	NEWLY INDEPENDENT STATES	NORTH AMERICA	OCEANIA	SOUTH AMERICA	WESTERN EUROPE
Northwest International Study Exchange, Inc.		•		•	•		•			•	•
Ohio International Agricultural and Horticultural Interns Program					•						•
Open Society Institute		•			•		•				
Organization for Cultural Exchange Among Nations		•			•				•	•	•
Pacific Intercultural Exchange	•	•	•	•	•	•	•	•	•	•	•
Partners of the Americas			•	•				•		•	
People Link	•	•	•	•	•	•	•	•	•	•	•
People to People International	•	•			•		•	•	•		•
Phelps-Stokes Fund	•										
Presidential Classroom	•	•	•	•	•	•	•	•	•	•	•
Proamerican Educational and Cultural Exchange					•			•		•	
Program of Academic Exchange	•	•	•	•	•	•	•	•	•	•	•
Project Harmony							•				•
Resource Euro-Asian American Cultural Homestay, Inc.		•								•	•
Rotary International	•	•	•	•	•	•	•	•	•	•	•
Scandinavian Seminar, Inc.					•						•
School Year Abroad		•									•
Sister Cities International	•	•	•	•	•	•	•	•	•	•	•
STS Foundation	•				•				•	•	•
United States Servas, Inc.	•	•	•	•	•	•	•	•	•	•	•
United Studies Student Exchange		•			•			•		•	•
University and College Intensive English Program	•	•	•	•	•	•	•	•	•	•	•
USDA Graduate School International Institute	•	•	•	•	•	•	•	•	•	•	•
Wo International Center		•							•		•
World Education Services Foundation	•	•		•	•					•	•
World Education Services, Inc.	•	•						•		•	•
World Exchange	•	•	•	•	•	•	•	•	•	•	•
World Experience Teenage Student Exchange		•			•	•	•	•	•	•	•
World Families		•							•		
World Learning, Inc.	•	•	•	•	•	•	•	•	•	•	•
WorldTeach	•	•		•					•	•	
YMCA International Program Services	•	•	•	•	•	•	•	•	•	•	•
Youth Exchange Service, Inc.	•	•	•	•	•	•	•	•	•	•	•
Youth for Understanding	•	•	•	•	•	•	•	•	•	•	•

U.S. Department of State Designations for the Exchange Visitor Program

U.S. Department of State Designations for the Exchange Visitor Program

Organization Name	AU PAIR	CAMP COUNSELOR	COLLEGE AND UNIVERSITY STUDENT	INTERN	GOVERNMENT VISITORS	INTERNATIONAL VISITOR	PHYSICIANS	PROFESSOR AND RESEARCH SCHOLAR	SECONDARY SCHOOL STUDENTS	SHORT-TERM SCHOLAR	SPECIALIST	SUMMER WORK/TRAVEL	TEACHER	TRAINEES
Academic and Cultural Exchange									●					
Academy for Educational Development			●											
Adventures in Real Communication Year Program									●					
Africa-America Institute			●			●								●
AFS-USA, Inc.									●					●
AIESEC United States, Inc.				●										●
America-Mideast Educational and Training Services			●							●				
American Academic and Cultural Exchange									●					
American Council of Learned Societies			●					●	●	●				
American Councils for International Education: ACTR/ACCELS	●		●	●	●									
American Institute for Foreign Study	●	●							●		●			
American Institute for Foreign Study Foundation			●						●	●				
American Intercultural Student Exchange, Inc.				●					●					
American International Youth Student Exchange Program									●					
American Secondary Schools for International Students and Teachers									●					
Amity Institute			●								●		●	
ASA International									●					
Asian Cultural Council								●		●				
ASPECT Foundation				●					●					
ASSE International Student Exchange Programs									●			●		
Association for International Practical Training (AIPT)														●
AYUSA International	●		●	●					●					●
Camp Counselors, USA		●	●									●		●
CDS International				●										●
CEC International Partners											●			
Cooperative Extension 4-H Youth Development			●						●					
Cordell Hull Foundation for International Education				●					●				●	●
Council on International Educational Exchanges, Inc.												●		●
Council on International Programs, USA														●
DM Discoveries									●					
Educational Resource Development Trust									●					

U.S. Department of State Designations for the Exchange Visitor Program

Organization Name	AU PAIR	CAMP COUNSELOR	COLLEGE AND UNIVERSITY STUDENT	INTERN	GOVERNMENT VISITORS	INTERNATIONAL VISITOR	PHYSICIANS	PROFESSOR AND RESEARCH SCHOLAR	SECONDARY SCHOOL STUDENTS	SHORT-TERM SCHOLAR	SPECIALIST	SUMMER WORK/TRAVEL	TEACHER	TRAINEES
Education Travel and Culture Exchange									●					
EF Foundation for Foreign Study	●													
Eisenhower Exchange Fellowships											●			
EurAupair Intercultural Childcare Programs	●													
Experience International				●										●
Face the World Foundation									●					
Foreign Study Language									●					
Foundation for Worldwide International Student Exchange			●	●					●				●	●
French-American Chamber of Commerce				●										●
GeoVisions				●								●	●	
German American Partnership Program, Inc.									●					
German Marshall Fund of the United States											●			
Global Outreach, Inc.														●
Homestay Educational and Cultural Foundation									●					
Institute of International Education			●					●		●	●		●	●
Intercultural Dimensions			●							●			●	
InterExchange	●	●										●		●
International Agricultural Exchange Association														●
International Cultural Exchange Services									●					
International Education									●					
International Internship Programs														●
International Research and Exchanges Board								●	●	●				
International Student Exchange									●					
LASPAU: Academic and Professional Programs for the Americas			●					●		●				
Meridian International Center						●								
Minnesota Agricultural Student Trainee Program														●
Multinl Exchange Sustainable Ag (MESA)														●
Nacel Open Door									●					
National Council for Eurasian and East European Research								●						
National FFA														●
North-South Center			●		●	●				●				
Ohio International Agricultural and Horticultural Interns Program														●
Organization for Cultural Exchange Among Nations									●					
Pacific Intercultural Exchange									●					
People Link									●					
Phelps-Stokes Fund				●		●								

U.S. Department of State Designations for the Exchange Visitor Program

Organization Name	AU PAIR	CAMP COUNSELOR	COLLEGE AND UNIVERSITY STUDENT	INTERN	GOVERNMENT VISITORS	INTERNATIONAL VISITOR	PHYSICIANS	PROFESSOR AND RESEARCH SCHOLAR	SECONDARY SCHOOL STUDENTS	SHORT-TERM SCHOLAR	SPECIALIST	SUMMER WORK/TRAVEL	TEACHER	TRAINEES
Proamerican Educational and Cultural Exchange									●					
Program of Academic Exchange									●					
Resource Euro-Asian American Cultural Homestay, Inc.									●					
Sister Cities International									●					
STS Foundation									●					
University and College Intensive English Program		●						●		●				
World Education Services Foundation									●					
World Experience Teenage Student Exchange									●					
World Heritage International Student Exchange									●					
World Learning, Inc.		●		●	●									●
YMCA International Program Services	●		●						●			●		●
Youth Exchange Service, Inc.									●					
Youth for Understanding									●					

Selected U.S. Offices by State

Selected U.S. Offices by State

Organization Name (columns):

1. AACSB International
2. Academic Adventures in America
3. Academic and Cultural Exchange
4. Academy for Educational Development
5. Accent on Understanding
6. Adventures in Real Communication Year Program
7. Africa-America Institute
8. AFS-USA, Inc.
9. AHA International
10. AIESEC United States, Inc.
11. Alliance for International Educational and Cultural Exchange
12. Alliances Abroad
13. America-Mideast Educational and Training Services
14. American Academic and Cultural Exchange
15. American Association of Collegiate Registrars and Admission Officers (AACRAO)
16. American Association of Community Colleges
17. American Association of Intensive English Programs
18. American Association of Teachers of German
19. American Council of Learned Societies

State	1	2	3	4	5	6	7	8	9	10	11	12	13	14	15	16	17	18	19
WEST VIRGINIA																			
WISCONSIN										●									
WASHINGTON					★					●									
VERMONT																			
VIRGINIA														★					
UTAH																			
TEXAS										●		★							
TENNESSEE				●															
SOUTH CAROLINA																			
RHODE ISLAND										●									
PENNSYLVANIA										●								★	
OREGON								●	★	●									
OKLAHOMA																			
OHIO						★				●									
NORTH DAKOTA																			
NORTH CAROLINA										●									
NEW YORK				●			★	★		★									★
NEW JERSEY	★									●									
NEW HAMPSHIRE																			
MONTANA																			
MISSISSIPPI																			
MISSOURI	★									●									
MINNESOTA								●		●									
MICHIGAN										●									
MAINE																			
MARYLAND								●											
MASSACHUSETTES																			
LOUISIANA																			
KENTUCKY																			
KANSAS										●									
INDIANA						●				●									
ILLINOIS										●									
IDAHO																			
HAWAII																			
GEORGIA										●									
FLORIDA										●									
DISTRICT OF COLUMBIA			★				●			●	★		●		★	★			
CONNECTICUT																			
COLORADO										●									
CALIFORNIA			★							●									
ARKANSAS																			
ARIZONA										●									
ALABAMA										●									

KEY: ★ organizational headquarters ● Office

Selected U.S. Offices by State

State	American Council of Young Political Leaders	American Council on Education	American Councils for International Education: ACTR/ACCELS	American Cultural Exchange	American Institute for Foreign Study	American Institute for Foreign Study Foundation	American Intercultural Student Exchange, Inc.	American International Youth Student Exchange Program	American Secondary Schools for International Students and Teachers	American Youth Work Center	American-Scandinavian Foundation	Amity Institute	Amizade, Ltd.	ASA International	Asia Foundation	Asian Cultural Council	ASPECT Foundation	ASSE International Student Exchange Programs	Association for International Practical Training (AIPT)
WEST VIRGINIA																			
WISCONSIN																			
WASHINGTON																		●	
VERMONT				★															
VIRGINIA																		●	
UTAH																			
TEXAS																			
TENNESSEE																			
SOUTH CAROLINA																			
RHODE ISLAND																			
PENNSYLVANIA			●										★	★					
OREGON				●															
OKLAHOMA																			
OHIO																			
NORTH DAKOTA																			
NORTH CAROLINA																			
NEW YORK											★					★			
NEW JERSEY																			
NEW HAMPSHIRE																			
MONTANA				●															
MISSISSIPPI																			
MISSOURI			●																
MINNESOTA																		●	
MICHIGAN																			
MAINE																			
MARYLAND																			★
MASSACHUSETTES																			
LOUISIANA																			
KENTUCKY																			
KANSAS																			
INDIANA																			
ILLINOIS				●															
IDAHO																			
HAWAII																			
GEORGIA																		●	
FLORIDA																			
DISTRICT OF COLUMBIA	★	★	★		★	★				★					●				
CONNECTICUT					★	●			★										
COLORADO																			
CALIFORNIA							★	★				★			★		★	★	
ARKANSAS																			
ARIZONA																			
ALABAMA																			

KEY: ★ organizational headquarters   ● Office

Selected U.S. Offices by State

Organization Name	Association of International Practical Training (AIPT)	Association of International Education Administrators	Association of Jesuit Colleges and Universities	Association of Professional Schools of International Affairs (APSIA)	AuPairCare	AYUSA International	Better Exchange for Student Teenagers (BEST)	BUNAC	Camp Counselors, USA	CDS International	CEC International Partners	Center for Citizen Initiatives	Center for Cultural Interchange	Center for Global Partnership	Children's International Summer Villages, Inc.	College Board-International Education	College Consortium for International Studies	Communicating for Agriculture
WEST VIRGINIA																		
WISCONSIN																		
WASHINGTON						●							●					
VERMONT																		
VIRGINIA																●		
UTAH													●					
TEXAS						●							●			●		
TENNESSEE																		
SOUTH CAROLINA																		
RHODE ISLAND																		
PENNSYLVANIA																●		
OREGON																		
OKLAHOMA													●					
OHIO														★				
NORTH DAKOTA																		
NORTH CAROLINA																		
NEW YORK	★			★						★	★			★		●		
NEW JERSEY																		
NEW HAMPSHIRE													●					
MONTANA																		
MISSISSIPPI													●					
MISSOURI						●												
MINNESOTA					●												★	
MICHIGAN					●													
MAINE																		
MARYLAND	★																	
MASSACHUSETTES																		
LOUISIANA																		
KENTUCKY						●												
KANSAS													●					
INDIANA						●												
ILLINOIS													★			●		
IDAHO																		
HAWAII																		
GEORGIA																●		
FLORIDA													●			●		
DISTRICT OF COLUMBIA			★													★	★	
CONNECTICUT								★										
COLORADO													●					
CALIFORNIA					★	★	★		★	●		★	●			●		
ARKANSAS																		
ARIZONA						●												
ALABAMA																		

KEY: ★ organizational headquarters   ● Office

Selected U.S. Offices by State

Organization Name →

State	Concordia Language Villages	Connect/US-Russia	Cooperative Extension 4-H Youth Development	Cordell Hull Foundation for International Education	Council for Educational Travel USA	Council of American Overseas Research Centers	Council of Chief State School Officers	Council of Graduate Schools	Council on International Programs, USA	Council on International Educational Exchanges, Inc.	Council on Standards for International Educational Travel	Cross-Cultural Solutions	Cultural Academic Student Exchange	Cultural Homestay International	Culturelink	DM Discoveries	East-West Center	Educational Resource Development Trust	Educational Testing Service
WEST VIRGINIA									●										
WISCONSIN																			
WASHINGTON			●		★														
VERMONT																			
VIRGINIA											★					★			
UTAH																			
TEXAS																			
TENNESSEE																			
SOUTH CAROLINA																			
RHODE ISLAND																			
PENNSYLVANIA									●							●			
OREGON																			
OKLAHOMA																●			
OHIO									★										
NORTH DAKOTA																			
NORTH CAROLINA																			
NEW YORK				★						★		★							
NEW JERSEY													★						★
NEW HAMPSHIRE																			
MONTANA																			
MISSISSIPPI																			
MISSOURI																		●	
MINNESOTA	★	★																	
MICHIGAN					●				●										
MAINE																			
MARYLAND																			
MASSACHUSETTES										●									
LOUISIANA				●												●			
KENTUCKY																			
KANSAS																			
INDIANA																			
ILLINOIS									●										
IDAHO																			
HAWAII																	★		
GEORGIA																			
FLORIDA															★				
DISTRICT OF COLUMBIA			★			★	★	★											●
CONNECTICUT																			
COLORADO									●										
CALIFORNIA					●				●					★				★	
ARKANSAS																			
ARIZONA																			
ALABAMA																			

KEY: ★ organizational headquarters ● Office

Selected U.S. Offices by State

State	Education Travel and Culture Exchange	EF Foundation for Foreign Study	Eisenhower Exchange Fellowships	EurAupair Intercultural Childcare Programs	Eurocentres	Exchange: Japan	Experience International	Face the World Foundation	Foreign Study Language	Foundation for International Cooperation	Foundation for Worldwide International Student Exchange	Freedom House	French-American Chamber of Commerce	Friendship Ambassadors Foundation	Friendship Force, Inc.	Fulbright Association	GeoVisions	German American Partnership Program, Inc.	German Marshall Fund of the United States	Girl Scouts of the U.S.A.
WEST VIRGINIA																				
WISCONSIN																				
WASHINGTON				●			★													
VERMONT																				
VIRGINIA				●	★															
UTAH																				
TEXAS										●										
TENNESSEE											★									
SOUTH CAROLINA																				
RHODE ISLAND																				
PENNSYLVANIA			★						★											
OREGON	★																			
OKLAHOMA																				
OHIO										●										
NORTH DAKOTA																				
NORTH CAROLINA																				
NEW YORK										●		●	★	★					★	★
NEW JERSEY																				
NEW HAMPSHIRE																	★			
MONTANA																				
MISSISSIPPI																				
MISSOURI																				
MINNESOTA				●						●										
MICHIGAN						★														
MAINE																				
MARYLAND																				
MASSACHUSETTES		★								●										
LOUISIANA																				
KENTUCKY										●										
KANSAS																				
INDIANA										●										
ILLINOIS										★										
IDAHO																				
HAWAII																				
GEORGIA				●							●				★					
FLORIDA										●										
DISTRICT OF COLUMBIA												★				★			★	
CONNECTICUT																				
COLORADO																				
CALIFORNIA		★						★		●	●						●			
ARKANSAS																				
ARIZONA										●										
ALABAMA										●										

KEY: ★ organizational headquarters   ● Office

Selected U.S. Offices by State

Organization Name

State	Global Outreach, Inc.	Homestay Educational and Cultural Foundation	Institute for the International Education of Students	Institute of International Education	Institute of Public Administration	Intercambio Internacional de Estudiantes	Intercultural Dimensions	InterExchange	International Agricultural Exchange Association	International Cultural Exchange Services	International Education	International Internship Programs	International Research and Exchanges Board	International Student Exchange	International Student Exchange Program	Intrax	Japan-America Student Conference	Japan Foundation	Japan Foundation Center for Global Partnership	Japan Society
WEST VIRGINIA																				
WISCONSIN																				
WASHINGTON														●		●				
VERMONT																				
VIRGINIA	★									●				●						
UTAH																				
TEXAS				●																
TENNESSEE																				
SOUTH CAROLINA														●						
RHODE ISLAND																				
PENNSYLVANIA																				
OREGON																●				
OKLAHOMA																				
OHIO																				
NORTH DAKOTA						★														
NORTH CAROLINA																				
NEW YORK				★	★			★						★		●		★	★	★
NEW JERSEY																				
NEW HAMPSHIRE																				
MONTANA									★											
MISSISSIPPI																				
MISSOURI														●						
MINNESOTA																				
MICHIGAN														●						
MAINE																				
MARYLAND																				
MASSACHUSETTES							★							●						
LOUISIANA																				
KENTUCKY																				
KANSAS																				
INDIANA																				
ILLINOIS		★	●							●				●		●				
IDAHO																				
HAWAII																				
GEORGIA																				
FLORIDA														●		●				
DISTRICT OF COLUMBIA				●								★	★	★			★			
CONNECTICUT																				
COLORADO				●																
CALIFORNIA	★			●						●	★			★		★		●		
ARKANSAS										★										
ARIZONA																				
ALABAMA																				

KEY: ★ organizational headquarters ● Office

Selected U.S. Offices by State

State	Japan-U.S. Community Education and Exchange	Kosciuszko Foundation	LASPAU: Academic and Professional Programs for the Americas	Laurasian Institution	LEXIA International	Lisle Fellowship, Inc.	Mansfield Center for Pacific Affairs	Meridian International Center	Metro International Program Services of New York, Inc.	Minnesota Agricultural Student Trainee Program	Mobility International USA/ National Clearinghouse on Disability and Exchange	Mounbatten Internship Programme	Multinl Exchange Sustainable Ag (MESA)	Nacel Open Door	NAFSA: Association of International Educators	National Association of State Universities and Land-Grant Colleges	National Committee on United States-China Relations	National Council for Eurasian and East European Research
WEST VIRGINIA																		
WISCONSIN																		
WASHINGTON				★														
VERMONT																		
VIRGINIA																		
UTAH																		
TEXAS						★												
TENNESSEE																		
SOUTH CAROLINA																		
RHODE ISLAND																		
PENNSYLVANIA																		
OREGON											★							
OKLAHOMA																		
OHIO																		
NORTH DAKOTA																		
NORTH CAROLINA																		
NEW YORK		★							★			★					★	
NEW JERSEY																		
NEW HAMPSHIRE					★													
MONTANA							●											
MISSISSIPPI																		
MISSOURI																		
MINNESOTA										★				★				
MICHIGAN																		
MAINE																		
MARYLAND																		
MASSACHUSETTES			★															
LOUISIANA																		
KENTUCKY																		
KANSAS																		
INDIANA																		
ILLINOIS																		
IDAHO																		
HAWAII																		
GEORGIA																		
FLORIDA																		
DISTRICT OF COLUMBIA							★	★							★	★		★
CONNECTICUT																		
COLORADO																		
CALIFORNIA	★			●									★					
ARKANSAS																		
ARIZONA																		
ALABAMA																		

KEY: ★ organizational headquarters ● Office

Selected U.S. Offices by State

KEY: ★ organizational headquarters   ● Office

State	National Council for International Visitors	National FFA	North Carolina Center for International Understanding	North-South Center	Northwest International Study Exchange, Inc.	Ohio International Agricultural and Horticultural Interns Program	Open Society Institute	Organization for Cultural Exchange Among Nations	Pacific Intercultural Exchange	Partners of the Americas	People Link	People to People International	Phelps-Stokes Fund	Presidential Classroom	Proamerican Educational and Cultural Exchange	Program of Academic Exchange	Project Harmony	Resource Euro-Asian American Cultural Homestay, Inc.	Rotary International
WEST VIRGINIA																			
WISCONSIN																			
WASHINGTON																			
VERMONT																	★		
VIRGINIA														★					
UTAH																			
TEXAS									●									★	
TENNESSEE																			
SOUTH CAROLINA																			
RHODE ISLAND																			
PENNSYLVANIA															★				
OREGON					★														
OKLAHOMA									●										
OHIO						★													
NORTH DAKOTA																			
NORTH CAROLINA			★																
NEW YORK							★		●				★						
NEW JERSEY																			
NEW HAMPSHIRE																			
MONTANA																			
MISSISSIPPI																			
MISSOURI												★							
MINNESOTA																	●		
MICHIGAN									●										
MAINE																			
MARYLAND																			
MASSACHUSETTES																	●		
LOUISIANA																			
KENTUCKY																			
KANSAS																			
INDIANA	★																		
ILLINOIS																			★
IDAHO									●										
HAWAII																			
GEORGIA																			
FLORIDA				★															
DISTRICT OF COLUMBIA	★								●	★									
CONNECTICUT																★			
COLORADO																			
CALIFORNIA									★		★								
ARKANSAS																			
ARIZONA								★											
ALABAMA																			

Organization Name

National Council for International Visitors
National FFA
North Carolina Center for International Understanding
North-South Center
Northwest International Study Exchange, Inc.
Ohio International Agricultural and Horticultural Interns Program
Open Society Institute
Organization for Cultural Exchange Among Nations
Pacific Intercultural Exchange
Partners of the Americas
People Link
People to People International
Phelps-Stokes Fund
Presidential Classroom
Proamerican Educational and Cultural Exchange
Program of Academic Exchange
Project Harmony
Resource Euro-Asian American Cultural Homestay, Inc.
Rotary International

Selected U.S. Offices by State

State	Scandinavian Seminar, Inc.	School Year Abroad	Sister Cities International	STS Foundation	United States Servas, Inc.	United Studies Student Exchange	University and College Intensive English Program	USDA Graduate School International Institute	Wo International Center	World Education Services Foundation	World Education Services, Inc.	World Exchange	World Experience Teenage Student Exchange	World Families	World Heritage	World Learning, Inc.	WorldTeach	YMCA International Program Services	Youth Exchange Service, Inc.	Youth for Understanding
WEST VIRGINIA																				
WISCONSIN																				
WASHINGTON														★						
VERMONT																★				
VIRGINIA				★			★													
UTAH																				
TEXAS								●												
TENNESSEE																				
SOUTH CAROLINA																				
RHODE ISLAND																				
PENNSYLVANIA								●												
OREGON																				
OKLAHOMA																				
OHIO																				
NORTH DAKOTA																				
NORTH CAROLINA																				
NEW YORK					★					★	★							★		
NEW JERSEY																				
NEW HAMPSHIRE																				
MONTANA																				
MISSISSIPPI																				
MISSOURI																				
MINNESOTA																				
MICHIGAN																				
MAINE													●							
MARYLAND																				
MASSACHUSETTS	★	★															★			
LOUISIANA																				
KENTUCKY																				
KANSAS																				
INDIANA																				
ILLINOIS								●			●									
IDAHO																				
HAWAII								●	★											
GEORGIA								●												
FLORIDA											●									
DISTRICT OF COLUMBIA			★					★			●					●				★
CONNECTICUT																				
COLORADO															★					
CALIFORNIA								●		★	●		★						★	
ARKANSAS						★														
ARIZONA																				
ALABAMA																				

KEY: ★ organizational headquarters ● Office

Selected Overseas Offices by Country

Organization Name	ALBANIA	ARGENTINA	ARMENIA	AUSTRALIA	AUSTRIA	AZERBAIJAN	BANGLADESH	BARBADOS	BELARUS	BELGIUM	BENIN	BOLIVIA	BOSNIA	BOTSWANA	BRAZIL	BULGARIA	BURKINA FASO	CAMBODIA	CANADA	CHILE	CHINA	COLUMBIA	CONGO	COSTA RICA	COTE D'IVOIR	CUBA	CROATIA	CYPRUS	CZECH REPUBLIC	DENMARK	DOMINICAN REPUBLIC	EAST TIMOR	ECUADOR	EGYPT	ESTONIA	ETHIOPIA	FINLAND	FRANCE	GEORGIA	GERMANY	GHANA	GREECE	GUATEMALA	GUINEA	GUINEA BISSAU	HAITI	HONDURAS	HONG KONG	HUNGARY	ICELAND	INDIA	INDONESIA	IRELAND	ISRAEL	ITALY	JAMAICA
Academic and Cultural Exchange															•						•	•																		•																
Academy for Educational Development			•		•	•						•	•													•					•			•	•			•		•							•	•			•					
Adventures in Real Commuication Year Program																								•																•																
Africa-America Institute											•			•			•						•		•																•			•	•											
AFS-USA, Inc.	•		•	•	•		•			•	•	•			•					•	•	•		•					•	•	•		•	•			•	•		•	•	•					•	•	•	•	•			•	•	•
AHA International		•		•																•																		•		•														•	
Alliances Abroad																								•																																
America-Mideast Educational and Training Services																																		•																						
American Council of Learned Societies																					•																																			
American Councils for International Education: ACTR/ACCELS			•			•			•																														•																	
American Cultural Exchange				•																																																				
American Secondary Schools for Internationa Students and Teachers				•																																				•																
Asia Foundation						•												•			•																															•				
Asian Cultural Council																					•																																			
ASPECT Foundation																					•									•										•																

JAPAN | JORDAN | KAZAKHSTAN | KENYA | KOREA | KUWAIT | KYRGYZSTAN | LATVIA | LEBANON | LITHUANIA | MADAGASCAR | MACEDONIA | MALI | MALAYSIA | MEXICO | MOLDOVA | MONGOLIA | MOROCCO | MOZAMBIQUE | NAMIBIA | NEPAL | NETHERLANDS | NEW ZEALAND | NICARAGUA | NIGERIA | NORWAY | PAKISTAN | PALESTINE | PANAMA | PARAGUAY | PERU | PHILIPPINES | POLAND | PORTUGAL | PUERTO RICO | ROMANIA | RUSSIA | SENEGAL | SERBIA | SIERRA LEONE | SLOVAK REPUBLIC | SLOVENIA | SOUTH AFRICA | SPAIN | SRI LANKA | SWEDEN | SWITZERLAND | SYRIA | TAJIKISTAN | TAIWAN | TANZANIA | THAILAND | TUNISIA | TURKEY | UGANDA | TURKMENISTAN | UKRAINE | UNITED KINGDOM | UZBEKISTAN | VENEZUELA | VIETNAM | YEMEN | YUGOSLAVIA | ZAMBIA | ZIMBABWE

Organization Name	ALBANIA	ARGENTINA	ARMENIA	AUSTRALIA	AUSTRIA	AZERBAIJAN	BANGLADESH	BARBADOS	BELARUS	BELGIUM	BENIN	BOLIVIA	BOSNIA	BOTSWANA	BRAZIL	BULGARIA	BURKINA FASO	CAMBODIA	CANADA	CHILE	CHINA	COLUMBIA	CONGO	COSTA RICA	COTE D'IVOIR	CUBA	CROATIA	CYPRUS	CZECH REPUBLIC	DENMARK	DOMINICAN REPUBLIC	EAST TIMOR	ECUADOR	EGYPT	ESTONIA	ETHIOPIA	FINLAND	FRANCE	GEORGIA	GERMANY	GHANA	GREECE	GUATEMALA	GUINEA	GUINEA BISSAU	HAITI	HONDURAS	HONG KONG	HUNGARY	ICELAND	INDIA	INDONESIA	IRELAND	ISRAEL	ITALY	JAMAICA
ASSE International Student Exchange Programs																			•																																					
AuPairCare																																								•									•							
AYUSA International																																								•									•							
Better Exchange for Student Teenagers (BEST)															•																						•			•																
BUNAC				•																																																				
Camp Counselors, USA		•		•					•						•					•								•												•													•			
CEC International Partners																																																								
Center for Citizen Initiatives																																																								
Center for Cultural Interchange																																																								
Center for Global Partnership																																																								
Children's International Summer Villages, Inc.																																																								
Cordell Hull Foundation for International Education																																										•														
Council for Educational Travel USA	•															•																								•																
Council of American Overseas Research Centers							•																					•						•							•										•				•	•
Council on International Programs, USA					•																							•									•	•		•	•										•				•	•

JAPAN | JORDAN | KAZAKHSTAN | KENYA | KOREA | KUWAIT | KYRGYZSTAN | LATVIA | LEBANON | LITHUANIA | MADAGASCAR | MACEDONIA | MALI | MALAYSIA | MEXICO | MOLDOVA | MONGOLIA | MOROCCO | MOZAMBIQUE | NAMIBIA | NEPAL | NETHERLANDS | NEW ZEALAND | NICARAGUA | NIGERIA | NORWAY | PAKISTAN | PALESTINE | PANAMA | PARAGUAY | PERU | PHILIPPINES | POLAND | PORTUGAL | PUERTO RICO | ROMANIA | RUSSIA | SENEGAL | SERBIA | SIERRA LEONE | SLOVAK REPUBLIC | SLOVENIA | SOUTH AFRICA | SPAIN | SRI LANKA | SWEDEN | SWITZERLAND | SYRIA | TAJIKISTAN | TAIWAN | TANZANIA | THAILAND | TUNISIA | TURKEY | UGANDA | TURKMENISTAN | UKRAINE | UNITED KINGDOM | UZBEKISTAN | VENEZUELA | VIETNAM | YEMEN | YUGOSLAVIA | ZAMBIA | ZIMBABWE

Organization Name	Albania	Argentina	Armenia	Australia	Austria	Azerbaijan	Bangladesh	Barbados	Belarus	Belgium	Benin	Bolivia	Bosnia	Botswana	Brazil	Bulgaria	Burkina Faso	Cambodia	Canada	Chile	China	Columbia	Congo	Costa Rica	Cote D'Ivoir	Cuba	Croatia	Cyprus	Czech Republic	Denmark	Dominican Republic	East Timor	Ecuador	Egypt	Estonia	Ethiopia	Finland	France	Georgia	Germany	Ghana	Greece	Guatemala	Guinea	Guinea Bissau	Haiti	Honduras	Hong Kong	Hungary	Iceland	India	Indonesia	Ireland	Israel	Italy	Jamaica
Council on Internationa Educational Exchanges, Inc.				•																	•																	•		•															•	
Cross-Cultural Solutions																					•					•															•										•					
Cultural Homestay International																			•																																					
Culturelink	•																			•													•																							
EF Foundation for Foreign Study				•	•										•				•	•	•	•								•			•				•	•													•				•	
EurAupair Intercultural Childcare Programs																			•										•	•			•				•	•		•															•	
Eurocentres																																						•		•															•	
Exchange: Japan																																																									
Freedom House													•																			•																•								
Friendship Ambassadors Foundation																																																	•								
Friendship Force, Inc.															•																									•																
German Marshall Fund of the United States																																						•																		
Institute for the International Education of Students	•		•	•															•	•																		•		•											•			•		
Institute of International Education																				•													•															•			•	•				
Intercambio Internacional de Estudiantes																																																									

JAPAN	JORDAN	KAZAKHSTAN	KENYA	KOREA	KUWAIT	KYRGYZSTAN	LATVIA	LEBANON	LITHUANIA	MADAGASCAR	MACEDONIA	MALI	MALAYSIA	MEXICO	MOLDOVA	MONGOLIA	MOROCCO	MOZAMBIQUE	NAMIBIA	NEPAL	NETHERLANDS	NEW ZEALAND	NICARAGUA	NIGERIA	NORWAY	PAKISTAN	PALESTINE	PANAMA	PARAGUAY	PERU	PHILIPPINES	POLAND	PORTUGAL	PUERTO RICO	ROMANIA	RUSSIA	SENEGAL	SERBIA	SIERRA LEONE	SLOVAK REPUBLIC	SLOVENIA	SOUTH AFRICA	SPAIN	SRI LANKA	SWEDEN	SWITZERLAND	SYRIA	TAJIKISTAN	TAIWAN	TANZANIA	THAILAND	TUNISIA	TURKEY	UGANDA	TURKMENISTAN	UKRAINE	UNITED KINGDOM	UZBEKISTAN	VENEZUELA	VIETNAM	YEMEN	YUGOSLAVIA	ZAMBIA	ZIMBABWE
•																																										•						•										•					
																															•					•																												
•			•																																					•																								
																																																											•					
•														•							•				•											•							•						•	•														
•																					•				•							•	•									•	•			•	•				•													
•																																				•						•					•										•								
•																																																																
																																•	•					•																			•							
																						•														•																												
																																								•																							
•																																																	•	•														
																•															•					•						•									•						•				•			
																•																																															

Organization Name	ALBANIA	ARGENTINA	ARMENIA	AUSTRALIA	AUSTRIA	AZERBAIJAN	BANGLADESH	BARBADOS	BELARUS	BELGIUM	BENIN	BOLIVIA	BOSNIA	BOTSWANA	BRAZIL	BULGARIA	BURKINA FASO	CAMBODIA	CANADA	CHILE	CHINA	COLUMBIA	CONGO	COSTA RICA	COTE D'IVOIR	CROATIA	CUBA	CYPRUS	CZECH REPUBLIC	DENMARK	DOMINICAN REPUBLIC	EAST TIMOR	ECUADOR	EGYPT	ESTONIA	ETHIOPIA	FINLAND	FRANCE	GEORGIA	GERMANY	GHANA	GREECE	GUATEMALA	GUINEA	GUINEA BISSAU	HAITI	HONDURAS	HONG KONG	HUNGARY	ICELAND	INDIA	INDONESIA	IRELAND	ISRAEL	ITALY	JAMAICA
International Agricultural Exchange Association				●															●											●																										
International Internship Programs																																																								
International Research and Exchanges Board	●		●						●																				●										●																	
Intrax																																								●								●								
Japan Foundation				●											●				●		●													●				●		●								●			●	●			●	
Japan Foundation Center for Global Partnership																																																								
Japan-America Student Conference																																																								
Japan-U.S. Community Education and Exchange																																																								
Kosciuszko Foundation																																																								
Laurasian Institution																																																								
LEXIA International		●																		●							●		●									●		●									●						●	
Mansfield Center for Pacific Affairs																																																								
Nacel Open Door															●				●		●																	●		●																
National Council for Eurasian and East European Research																																																								
Organization for Cultural Exchange Among Nations	●														●	●																								●																

JAPAN	JORDAN	KAZAKHSTAN	KENYA	KOREA	KUWAIT	KYRGYZSTAN	LATVIA	LEBANON	LITHUANIA	MADAGASCAR	MACEDONIA	MALI	MALAYSIA	MEXICO	MOLDOVA	MONGOLIA	MOROCCO	MOZAMBIQUE	NAMIBIA	NEPAL	NETHERLANDS	NEW ZEALAND	NICARAGUA	NIGERIA	NORWAY	PAKISTAN	PALESTINE	PANAMA	PARAGUAY	PERU	PHILIPPINES	POLAND	PORTUGAL	PUERTO RICO	ROMANIA	RUSSIA	SENEGAL	SERBIA	SIERRA LEONE	SLOVAK REPUBLIC	SLOVENIA	SOUTH AFRICA	SPAIN	SRI LANKA	SWEDEN	SWITZERLAND	SYRIA	TAJIKISTAN	TAIWAN	TANZANIA	THAILAND	TUNISIA	TURKEY	UGANDA	TURKMENISTAN	UKRAINE	UNITED KINGDOM	UZBEKISTAN	VENEZUELA	VIETNAM	YEMEN	YUGOSLAVIA	ZAMBIA	ZIMBABWE
																						•																																					•						
•																																																										•						
		•				•	•		•		•				•																						•	•		•												•					•							
•																																																															
•														•	•																•																					•						•						
•																																																															
•																																																															
•																																																															
																															•																																	
•																																•											•								•						•							
•				•											•																•												•														•							
																																				•																											
				•		•									•																																				•											•	

Organization Name	Albania	Argentina	Armenia	Australia	Austria	Azerbaijan	Bangladesh	Barbados	Belarus	Belgium	Benin	Bolivia	Bosnia	Botswana	Brazil	Bulgaria	Burkina Faso	Cambodia	Canada	Chile	China	Columbia	Congo	Costa Rica	Cote D'Ivoir	Cuba	Croatia	Cyprus	Czech Republic	Denmark	Dominican Republic	East Timor	Ecuador	Egypt	Estonia	Ethiopia	Finland	France	Georgia	Germany	Ghana	Greece	Guatemala	Guinea	Guinea Bissau	Haiti	Honduras	Hong Kong	Hungary	Iceland	India	Indonesia	Ireland	Israel	Italy	Jamaica
Pacific Intercultural Exchange		●		●																	●																																				
Partners of the Americas															●																																●									
People Link																			●																																					
Proamerican Educational and Cultural Exchange															●							●											●																								
Project Harmony																																																									
Rotary International		●		●											●																																				●					
Scandinavian Seminar, Inc.																														●							●																				
School Year Abroad																					●																	●																	●	
United States Servas, Inc.				●																																																				
World Education Services, Inc.																			●																																					
World Heritage International Student Exchange															●																							●		●																
WorldTeach																					●			●									●																							
Youth for Understanding		●		●											●																							●		●																

JAPAN · JORDAN · KAZAKHSTAN · KENYA · KOREA · KUWAIT · KYRGYZSTAN · LATVIA · LEBANON · LITHUANIA · MADAGASCAR · MACEDONIA · MALI · MALAYSIA · MEXICO · MOLDOVA · MONGOLIA · MOROCCO · MOZAMBIQUE · NAMIBIA · NEPAL · NETHERLANDS · NEW ZEALAND · NICARAGUA · NIGERIA · NORWAY · PAKISTAN · PALESTINE · PANAMA · PARAGUAY · PERU · PHILIPPINES · POLAND · PORTUGAL · PUERTO RICO · ROMANIA · RUSSIA · SENEGAL · SERBIA · SIERRA LEONE · SLOVAK REPUBLIC · SLOVENIA · SOUTH AFRICA · SPAIN · SRI LANKA · SWEDEN · SWITZERLAND · SYRIA · TAJIKISTAN · TAIWAN · TANZANIA · THAILAND · TUNISIA · TURKEY · UGANDA · TURKMENISTAN · UKRAINE · UNITED KINGDOM · UZBEKISTAN · VENEZUELA · VIETNAM · YEMEN · YUGOSLAVIA · ZAMBIA · ZIMBABWE

Name Index

Veit, Stephanie 152
Vera, Dean K. 204
Vermillion, James 252
Vespucci, Diane 80
Vey, Lilo 243
Villada, Martha 143
Vitvitsky, Tania 228
Vogt, Martin 44
Vossen, Lesley Moore 256
Vukoc, Elaine 115

W

Wächter, Bernd 238
Wagner, Carole D. 157
Walbroel, Werner 93
Waldman, Jacqueline D. 153
Walkinshaw, Charlie 82
Walsh, Cathy 229
Ward, David 22
Warren, Brenda 57
Waskin, Skip 252
Watson, Kevin 61
Watson, Terry 61
Wattenmaker, Beverly S. 7

Wechsler, Helen 175
Weider, Michael 256
Weiss, Jeffrey 268
Welch, Matthew 152
Welfley, Jim 233
Wetzel, Kim 103
Whatley, Jennifer 87
Whelpton, Shelley 44
Whisler, Ruth 51
White, Alisha 184
White, Greg C. 158
White, Lee 252
White, Sonia 158
Whiteley, Lora 151
Whitten, David 256
Wickliff, Jay 147
Wiebler, Peter 87
Wiitala, Bill 81
Wilgus, Janet 257
Wilkes-Scott. Essie 258
Wilhelm, John F. 43, 44, 111
Williams, Joy 95
Williams, Michael 252
Williams, Yvonne 5

Wilsford, David 246
Windsor, Jennifer 87
Winter, Gary 252
Woehl, Heidi 43
Wold, Denise Jones 130
Wolf, Kimberly 200
Wolloch, Cynthia 256
Wong, Harriet 169
Woodward, David 24
Workman, Willard 196
Wunderman, Gilda 97
Wunder III, Van S. 257

Y

Yff, Joost 175

Z

Zagalo e Melo, Paulo 266
Zenetow, Mrs. Artemis 263
Ziglar, James W. 268
Zimmer-Loew, Helene 19
Zipse, Dr. Philip 25

Comprehensive Index

Y